This book analyses the social, political and religious roles of confraternities – the lay groups through which Italians of the Renaissance expressed their individual and collective religious beliefs – in Bologna in the fifteenth and sixteenth centuries. Confraternities shaped the civic religious cult through charitable activities, public shrines and processions. This civic religious role expanded as they became politicized: patricians used the confraternities increasingly in order to control the civic religious cult, civic charity, and the city itself.

The book examines in detail how confraternities initially provided laypeople of the artisanal and merchant classes with a means of expressing a religious life separate from, but not in opposition to, the local parish or mendicant house. By the mid-sixteenth century, patricians dominated the traditional lay confraternities while artisans and merchants had few options beyond parochial confraternities which were controlled by parish priests.

CAMBRIDGE STUDIES IN ITALIAN HISTORY AND CULTURE

LAY CONFRATERNITIES AND CIVIC RELIGION
IN RENAISSANCE BOLOGNA

CAMBRIDGE STUDIES IN ITALIAN HISTORY AND CULTURE

Edited by GIORGIO CHITTOLINI, Università degli Studi, Milan
CESARE MOZZARELLI, Università Cattolica del Sacro Cuore, Milan
ROBERT ORESKO, Institute of Historical Research, University of London
and GEOFFREY SYMCOX, University of California, Los Angeles

This series comprises monographs and a variety of collaborative volumes, including translated works, which will concentrate on the period of Italian history from late medieval times up to the Risorgimento. The editors aim to stimulate scholarly debate over a range of issues which have not hitherto received, in English, the attention they deserve. As it develops, the series will emphasize the interest and vigor of current international debates on this central period of Italian history and the persistent influence of Italian culture on the rest of Europe.

Titles in the series

Family and public life in Brescia, 1580–1650
The foundations of power in the Venetian state
JOANNE M. FERRARO

Church and politics in Renaissance Italy
The life and career of Cardinal Francesco Soderini, 1453–1524
K. J. P. LOWE

Crime, disorder, and the Risorgimento
The politics of policing in Bologna
STEVEN C. HUGHES

Liturgy, sanctity and history in Tridentine Italy
Pietro Maria Campi and the preservation of the particular
SIMON DITCHFIELD

Lay confraternities and civic religion in Renaissance Bologna
NICHOLAS TERPSTRA

Other titles are in preparation

LAY CONFRATERNITIES AND CIVIC RELIGION IN RENAISSANCE BOLOGNA

NICHOLAS TERPSTRA

Luther College, University of Regina, Saskatchewan

CAMBRIDGE
UNIVERSITY PRESS

Published by the Press Syndicate of the University of Cambridge
The Pitt Building, Trumpington Street, Cambridge CB2 1RP
40 West 20th Street, New York, NY 10011–4211, USA
10 Stamford Road, Oakleigh, Melbourne 3166, Australia

First published 1995

Printed in Great Britain at the University Press, Cambridge

A catalogue record for this book is available from the British Library

Library of Congress cataloguing in publication data
Terpstra, Nicholas.
Lay confraternities and civic religion in Renaissance Bologna/Nicholas Terpstra.
p.   cm. – (Cambridge studies in Italian history and culture)
Includes bibliographical references.
ISBN 0 521 48092 2 (hardcover)
1. Confraternities – Italy – Bologna – History – 16th century.   2. Bologna (Italy) –
Church history – 16th century.   3. Italy – Church history – 16th century.
I. Title.   II. Series.
BX808.5.I8T47   1995
267'.1824541'09024 – dc20   94–37936   CIP

ISBN 0 521 48092 2 hardback

For Angela

CONTENTS

FIGURES

TABLES

ACKNOWLEDGMENTS

This study was made possible thanks to the contributions of others. Fellowships and research grants from the Social Sciences and Humanities Research Council of Canada funded archival work. Archivists in the Archivio di Stato di Bologna, the Biblioteca Communale dell'Archiginnasio, the Biblioteca del Centro di Documentazione dell'Istituto per le Scienze Religiose, and the Biblioteca Universitaria gave free access to records and generous help in sorting through them. Among these, Anna Maria Scardovi must be singled out for particular mention as the indefatigable ally of all those who enter the manuscript room at the Archiginnasio. Anyone remotely familiar with the subject of Bolognese confraternities will know how much this study is indebted to the work carried out by Mario Fanti for almost forty years.

Paul Grendler piloted an earlier version of this work through the shoals of dissertation writing. Jason Kelln has helped pilot this version through the only slightly less dangerous shoals of computerization, and Janet Hall through those of copy editing. Angela, Nigel, Christopher, and Alison have piloted me through shoals too numerous to mention. *Celebriamo il Signore.*

PREFACE

In 1960 scholars from across Italy gathered in Perugia to mark the seventh centenary of a devotional movement of 1260 which swept the Italian peninsula and led to the creation of flagellant confraternities in many cities and towns. Confraternities had been studied in Italy for years, both by local historians and antiquarians, and by those of a broader vision like G.M. Monti whose work *Le confraternite medievali dell'alta e media Italia* (1927) described developments across the peninsula. Yet the 1960 conference marked a departure. Historians intensified their research and brought new theoretical models to bear on their work. The conference papers were published under the title of *Il movimento dei Disciplinati nel Settimo Centenario dal suo inizio* (1962), and so stimulated research that a second conference was held in 1969. These papers too were published as *Risultati e Prospettive della Ricerca sul Movimento dei Disciplinati* (1972). Institutes devoted to confraternity studies have emerged in Perugia, Puglia, and elsewhere and the concentration of scholarly attention has generated a host of local studies and magisterial works like G.G. Meersseman's *Ordo Fraternitatis: Confraternite e Pietà dei laici nel medioevo* (1977), a study of Dominican confraternities from the thirteenth through the sixteenth centuries.

English-speaking scholars were less quick to recognize the significance of lay confraternities in Renaissance Italian society, due perhaps in part to a reluctance to deal with religion in a period which many still saw through Burckhardtian lenses. The greatest attention was given by those who quite self-consciously broke with conventional interpretations of Renaissance society, such as Brian Pullan in *Rich and Poor in Renaissance Venice: The Social Institutions of a Catholic State, to 1620* (1971), Richard Trexler in *Public Life in Renaissance Florence* (1980), and Edward Muir in *Civic Ritual in Renaissance Venice* (1981). After a slow start, English-language studies have grown rapidly, and have described the composition, character, and social role of Renaissance confraternities in diverse, albeit not mutually exclusive, ways. R.F.E. Weissman's pioneering study *Ritual Brotherhood in Renaissance Florence* (1982) set them in the context of the strained social relations of a society which was both highly competitive and yet closely inter-woven through professional and kin bonds. Focusing always on social networks, Weissman portrayed the confraternities as offering both psychological relief for the individual Florentine and socialization for both liminous adolescents and aging artisans. As the networks changed in the development from republican to grand ducal Florence, and as the Catholic Reformation altered priorities and pieties, new forms of ritual brotherhood emerged as well. Confraternities were "one of the principal forms of sociability available to males in pre-modern European society," and Weissman's rich and highly suggestive study set directions for research which are still being probed.

James Banker's investigation of the confraternities of the Tuscan town of San Sepolcro focused instead on what the development and use of the brotherhoods revealed about late medieval conceptions of death. His study, *Death in the Community: Memorialization and Confraternities in an Italian Commune in the Late Middle Ages* (1988), spans the mid-thirteenth through the mid-fifteenth centuries, and demonstrates that confraternities helped secure San Sepolcro's autonomy through a combination of civic religion and social welfare which put laymen rather than clergy at the intersection of temporal and eternal concerns. In a town with few clergy, they were the institutions which turned the secular city into a sacred community. Early praising confraternities brought a heterogeneous society together in bonds of brotherhood. Fourteenth-century flagellant confraternities fragmented this civic religious unity by recruiting more selectively from a middling artisanal group which in turn used its new sacral status to take political power from the nobility. Death "activated social mechanisms of great emotional intensity," and brought social power and wealth to confraternities which fulfilled testamentary obligations to the poor, the widowed, the sick, and the orphaned.

Weissman and Banker look closely at the meaning and social function of confraternities in particular Italian communities. By contrast, Christopher Black's *Italian Confraternities in Sixteenth Century Italy* (1989) examines the whole peninsula from roughly 1450 through 1650 in a synthetic study which describes institutional development, devotional life, and above all, charitable activity. Black draws skillfully on the extensive body of local studies which have emerged in the past three decades, and demonstrates that the lay brotherhoods are hardly less critical than the more frequently studied guilds as guides to under-

standing the institutions, roles, and relations which define Renaissance
society. The connection between confraternities and guilds has been
highlighted for Venice in R. Mackenney's *Tradesmen and Traders: The
World of the Guilds in Venice and Europe, c. 1250–c. 1650* (1987), while
connections to civic charity have been analyzed for Florence in J. Henderson's *Piety and Charity in Late Medieval Florence* (1994) and for Marseille in A. Barne's *The Social Dimension of Piety* (1994).

Black's work provides a useful introduction to the common characteristics of Renaissance Italian confraternities, and to the various approaches taken by scholars in recent years. Another recent work
demonstrates those approaches. *Crossing the Boundaries: Christian Piety
and the Arts in Italian Medieval and Renaissance Confraternities* (1991),
edited by Konrad Eisenbichler, is a collection of papers arising out of
the conference on "Ritual and Recreation in Renaissance Confraternities" held in Toronto in 1989. The interdisciplinary conference attracted scholars from the United States, Canada, England, and
Australia. Papers ranged from detailed analyses of confraternal literature, art, and music, in particular urban centers across Europe, to more
theoretical studies on the meaning of confraternal ritual and community. The community created in Toronto launched the international
Society for Confraternity Studies which is encouraging research and
publication on lay brotherhoods in Mediterranean and Northern
Europe, and in the Americas. In short, the Toronto conference did for
confraternity studies in English what the Perugian conference had
done for Italian research in 1960, gathering together scholars who had
been working individually on various aspects of the subject, and giving
an impetus to further collective work.

This study of lay confraternities adapts the sociological and anthro-
pological analyses of Weissman, Trexler, and Muir to the long-
neglected city of Bologna. It focuses on the fifteenth and early
sixteenth centuries, when the lay brotherhoods were undergoing their
greatest changes internally and in relation to the city as a whole. It
demonstrates how confraternities shape civic cults, charity, and politics,
and are in turn shaped by the social dynamic which they have set up.
The closing irony is that the ambitions of thirteenth-century idealists
who founded the earliest confraternities are realized only after the
brotherhoods lose the popolo character and lay autonomy characteristic of thirteenth-century *compagnie spirituali*.

On the surface, Bolognese confraternities were much like their
counterparts in other Italian cities. With no centralized ordinance, no
prescribed forms or national network, there nonetheless emerged a
common model defined by what canon law implicitly allowed and

what contemporary religious and secular corporations explicitly demonstrated. The model had a common vocabulary of rituals structured by a common grammar of conditions, expectations, and relations, but the language was always spoken in dialect. The confraternities were as thoroughly a part of the history of their own towns and cities as they were manifestations of peninsular and even European phenomena. This study attempts to cover the full range of Bolognese confraternities, recognizing general patterns and significant variations, and setting the whole in the context of contemporary devotional movements, the city's changing social and political structure, and the expansion of the civic-religious cult. A core of three analytic chapters (Two, Three, Four) deals with lay spirituality, membership composition and procedures, and finances, and demonstrates how ennobling and devotional changes work together to alter the character and social role of the groups. This is framed by two chapters (One and Five) which locate confraternities in civic politics as the shapers of the civic cult and civic charity through the fifteenth and early sixteenth centuries, and by a Prologue and Epilogue which trace roots into the thirteenth century and consequences into the early seventeenth. The Prologue sets the background by establishing the role of lay confraternities in civic politics from the time of factional disputes in the thirteenth-century commune through the struggles with Milan and the Papacy in the fourteenth century. Confraternities identified themselves as Spiritual Companies, to underline the self-conscious parallel to the Artisanal Companies (guilds) and Armed Companies (militias) which defined and upheld the popular commune. Their contribution to the civic cult at this early stage came through sponsoring public worship and public charity.

Chapter One covers the early fifteenth century, and demonstrates how confraternities and their role in the civic cult change under the influence of both the Observance movements and the development of the local oligarchy with the coming of the Bentivoglio. The former bring new forms of devotion which the latter help shape into a more definite local cult with local shrines, processions, and festivals.

Chapter Two demonstrates how confraternities embody but do not exhaust lay spirituality, and shows how individual laymen and -women could use confraternities to fashion a spiritual life distinct from the parish and religious orders. It examines how closely confraternities patterned their worship and community on the mendicant example, how different mendicant orders related to confraternities, and whether the close relationship makes confraternities deficient guides to lay piety. Their spirituality was expressed in collective rituals prescribed for the whole community (for example, divine office, flagellation, sacraments), and individual exercises prescribed for brothers in their personal devotions (for example, mental confession and prayer). This chapter brings the collective and individual dimensions together with the example of rituals surrounding death and dying.

Chapter Three demonstrates how one became a member, what duties this entailed, and how members were disciplined and expelled. Specific subjects dealt with here include the recruitment, retention, attendance, size, geographic concentration, and gender of members of the confraternities. Through the period of the study, the once heterogeneous groups become increasingly exclusive. Fifteenth-century devotional reforms intensified the inner devotional community, but also set in motion the process by which first women and later artisans found themselves eased out of the traditional *compagnie spirituali*.

Chapter Four demonstrates how the brotherhoods defined and defended their community. It shows how changing forms of administration (officials, voting procedures) reflected changing conceptions of community. Using three particular examples, it demonstrates how different confraternities finance themselves, and how some become quite wealthy over time through bequests and investments. Using two different groups, it shows how some financially underwrote the expansion of patrician holdings in the countryside around Bologna.

Chapter Five covers the later fifteenth and early sixteenth centuries, showing how confraternities take on major roles in the new shrines and processions of an expanding civic cult, and how they begin the rationalization and laicization of social welfare by consolidating and specializing their hostels. At an early stage in this expansion of their social role, these activities attract patrician interest and lead to increased ennobling of the long-established, wealthier and prominent confraternities. The ennobling in turn speeds up the process of expanding the civic cult and charity, in part because the patriciate realizes that this is one indirect avenue to increased power after the papacy recovers direct control of the city in 1506.

Finally, the Epilogue notes how the priorities of the ennobled confraternities fit in well with the priorities of Catholic Reform as promoted locally by Archbishop Gabriele Paleotti from 1566. Both exploit the traditional image of the brotherhoods (popolo character, lay autonomy) but ennobled groups push out the popolo while Paleotti takes autonomy away from the new parish confraternities which artisans have moved in to. While confraternities multiply, while they attract more members than ever, and while they take on larger roles in the civic cult and civic charity than ever before, they no longer have the popolo composition or lay autonomy which characterized the thirteenth-century *compagnie spirituali* that first framed those ideals.

This study draws on articles published previously, which are used here with permission of the publishers. Part of chapter two appeared as "Death and Dying in Renaissance Confraternities," in K. Eisenbichler (ed.), *Crossing the Boundaries: Christian Piety and the Arts in Italian Medieval and Renaissance Confraternities* (Kalamazoo: Medieval Institute Publications, 1991): 179–200. Part of chapter three appeared as "Women in the Brotherhood: Gender, Class, and Politics in Renaissance Bolognese Confraternities," *Renaissance and Reformation/Renaissance et Reforme*, 26/3 (1990): 193–212. Part of chapter five appeared as "Apprenticeship in Social Welfare: From Confraternal Charity to Municipal Poor Relief in Early Modern Italy," *Sixteenth Century Journal* 25/1 (1994): 101–20.

PROLOGUE

One crisp October day in 1260 the civic magistrates and bishop of Bologna stood at the Porta Maggiore looking eastward down the old Roman road which led to Imola and the Adriatic coast. Around them were hundreds and perhaps thousands of citizens. Behind them, within the recently completed walls of the city, the shops were shuttered, the market stalls closed, and the people were waiting. Down the road there appeared crosses and banners borne by priests and followed by marching ranks of Imolese men, women and children, wailing "peace and mercy, peace and mercy." The slash of whips punctuated their cries as some of the marching penitents beat themselves. As they reached the party waiting at the city gate their cry was taken up by the Bolognese, who moved down the Strada Maggiore into the heart of the city. For eight days normal urban life stopped as penitents of all ages and classes processed through the streets, squares, and churches of Bologna, flagellating, kneeling at altars, and crying out for "peace and mercy." On the ninth day they issued out of the westerly Porta San Felice and headed for Modena.[1]

The community which prostrated itself before God in this way was near the peak of its power and yet riven by tensions. The university gave it a continent-wide reputation, active bankers and merchants gave it wealth, and citizen armies gave it control over Romagna. The third ring of walls sheltered the population of what was then the fifth largest city in Europe. At Fossalta in 1249 the army had given Bologna control of the Romagna by defeating Modena and capturing King Enzo, son of the Holy Roman Emperor Frederick II; the Bolognese constructed the Palazzo Re Enzo in the central city square and held their trophy there until his death 22 years later. Yet the cry for "peace

---

[1] C. Ghirardacci, *Della historia di Bologna*, vol. 1 (Bologna: 1657), pp. 200–1; Varignana, [Cronaca B], in *Corpus Chronicorum Bononiensium*, ed. A. Sorbelli, *RIS* vol. 18, Pt. II, vol. iv, p. 158.

and mercy" was no formality, for both were in short supply in 1260. Bologna had become a self-governing commune under aristocratic dominance in 1123. As the merchants, bankers, and artisans organized into guilds (*Compagnie delle Arti*), they demanded a share of power and organized militias (*Compagnie delle Armi*) in order to defend themselves and assert their claims. The aristocratic commune banned both guilds and militias in 1219, but a military defeat by Modena in 1228 sparked a popular uprising which swept the aristocrats from office and installed a government made up of upper guildsmen and a few nobles. Bologna had then settled into its own variant of the divisions which split communes up and down the peninsula. The dispossessed aristocrats gathered in the Lambertazzi faction, while those who supported the popolo commune were known as the Geremei; the former were broadly Ghibelline while the latter were largely Guelph. The popolo ought to have felt confidence, yet they saw themselves as caught between the upper and nether millstones of the Lambertazzi, since the nobles of that faction were recruiting disaffected day labourers, unenfranchised minor guildsmen, and *sottoposti* in an effort to undermine the popolo regime. By the 1250s, the upper guildsmen broadened their power base within the Compagnie delle Arti by bringing members of the middle-ranked guilds into the ruling Council of the Anziani and giving the notaries a larger role in the Commune's administrative councils. The regime further boosted its defenses by bringing in an official, the Capitano del Popolo, to co-ordinate the city's twenty neighborhood Compagnie delle Armi. It also aimed to undermine the financial base of the Lambertazzi rural nobility by freeing the serfs in 1256–57; 5,855 serfs won their freedom from 379 proprietors, and their names were written into a communal register entitled the *Liber Paradisus*. The move was doubly self-serving, for the freed serfs now owed service and taxes to the Commune.[2]

So the popolo magistrates who stood at the Porta Maggiore in October 1260 to welcome the penitents from Imola did not see the call for "peace and mercy" in abstract terms. For them peace meant Lambertazzi capitulation and the consolidation of popolo institutions. They were not alone. Processions of flagellants had begun appearing in Perugia early in the year. By October they had gained numbers and spread to Rome, Bologna, Genoa, and other largely Guelph cities; Ghibelline Milan and Brescia turned them away. Yet it was not

[2] Ghirardacci, *Historia di Bologna*, I, pp. 200–1; Varignana, [Cronaca B], *RIS* vol. 18, Pt. II, vol. iv, p. 158. L. Martines, *Power and Imagination: City States in Renaissance Italy* (New York: 1979): 56–8. Ferri, A. and Roversi, G., eds., *Storia di Bologna*. Bologna: 1978, 157–9.

a papal initiative; chroniclers and commentators across Italy marvelled at the fact that the penitential movement of 1260 was so thoroughly lay in inspiration and organization. This helps explain its easy insertion into communal conflicts such as those between Bologna's popolo and magnate factions. Most urban Italians could agree on the goal of peace, but few of those fighting could see it on common terms. The procession allowed one side – in Bologna the popolo Guelphs – to make its case dramatically. But it was not enough to capture the procession. In many Italian communes penitents went on to form flagellant confraternities with the aim of perpetuating their dramatic devotional movement. Bologna was no exception, and while the confraternity which emerged from the 1260 movement was not the city's first, it soon became the most prominent.

Confraternities had begun appearing in Bologna in the decade or two before, usually in association with one of the mendicant houses. According to the Communal Statutes of 1259, the cavernous churches recently constructed by the Franciscans and Dominicans both sheltered lay groups dedicated to Mary, while two more confraternities met in a parish church. All of these were probably groups of *laudesi*, that is, confraternities whose worship centered on praise rather than penitence. Theirs was a spirituality of gratitude expressed through the celebration of both Mary and Christ in vernacular hymns, divine offices, and regular prayers. They were also known for acts of charity, chiefly the burial of the dead. Later laudesi groups were often quite large, attracting two to three hundred people to weekly or monthly services. Drawing on a wide social base, they included both men and women. They seldom built their own churches, but more often met in a parish or mendicant church. Confraternities were lay echoes of mendicant spirituality, and the friars typically played a large role in organizing and administering them. Laudesi confraternities offered them vehicles to advance their own programs for urban religious life, though as we will see below the degree of mendicant direction varied between different Orders and different cities.[3]

The confraternity which emerged from the penitential movement of 1260 identified more closely with the popolo regime than with any of the mendicant orders or parish churches. In place of a dedication to Mary or a saint, it was designated the *Congregatio devotorum civitatis bononie*, or the Congregation of the Devout of the Bolognese Commonwealth. While it met briefly in S. Giacomo da Savona,

---

[3] G.G. Meersseman, *Ordo fraternitatis: confraternite e pietà dei laici nel mondo medioevo*. 3 vols. Rome, 1977, p. 1008. C. Mesini, "La Compagnia di Santa Maria delle Laudi e di S. Francesco di Bologna," *Archivum Franciscanum Historicum* 52 (1959), p. 363.

one of the chief houses of the newly formed Augustinian hermits, this association entailed no mendicant administrative involvement and ceased after the Augustinians transferred to new quarters in 1267. Members modelled their administration on that of the guilds, with a Rector leading a Board of twelve self-perpetuating Guardians. Though ostensibly dedicated to peacemaking, this was not identified with neutrality, and members should not be in doubt as to where their real loyalties lay. If a call to arms was sounded in the city, members were not allowed to rush to the fortified towers or armed bands of the magnates. They were to gather instead with their Compagnia dell'Arte or their Compagnia delle Arme, and await instructions from the Capitano del Popolo. Those belonging to neither a guild nor a militia gathered instead at the quarters of the Congregatio Devotorum to pray for peace. Those who joined the magnates, and by implication those who stayed neutral, would be expelled from the confraternity without hope of readmission. It was not for nothing that from this time confraternities came to be known collectively as Compagnie Spirituali, for they functioned beside the Compagnie delle Arte and delle Arme as the third, spiritual pillar upholding the popolo commune.

The Congregatio Devotorum did not bring peace to Bologna. In 1271 and 1272, the Anziani introduced anti-magnate legislation, setting off a confrontation with the Lambertazzi Ghibellines. Over 2,000 citizens flocked to join a new, more overtly militaristic, spiritual company, the Compagnia della Croce, which defeated the Lambertazzi in a forty-day pitched battle in 1274. The Lambertazzi and their followers – 12,000 people in all – were expelled from the city of 50,000. Repeated anti-magnate legislation and the readmission and re-expulsion of the Lambertazzi in the last decades of the century demonstrated how tenuous the popolo's hold over the city was. That hold was further undermined in 1278 when Rudolph of Augsburg formally renounced the Romagna as an imperial possession, ceding it to the Papacy. Popolo guelphism had always been a strategic countervail to imperial authority, and cession to the papacy would repeatedly undermine Bolognese drives for autonomy in the centuries which followed.

While it may not have brought peace and security to the popolo commune, the Congregatio Devotorum brought concrete expression of that commune's fundamentally lay yet fundamentally religious character. Members first drew up statutes ca. 1262–63, and had doubled them with additional reform clauses by the time the Bolognese vicar-general approved them in 1286. The statutes demonstrate how members channelled the popular devotional movement into an organized society parallel to contemporary Compagnie delle Arti or Compagnie delle

Armi. The initial twenty clauses deal in turn with administrative structure, qualifications for membership, regulation of devotions, and the mutual obligations of members in sickness and at death. The following twenty-one reform clauses deal less systematically with some of the same issues, demonstrating the difficulties arising periodically in the first quarter century of what was still a new type of civic society.[4] Reformers were preoccupied with refining the administrative structure and circumscribing the devotional exercises of the new Compagnia Spirituale. The most dramatic devotional practice was flagellation. By beating themselves as Christ had been beaten, members of the Congregatio Devotorum reminded the Bolognese of their Saviour's sacrifice and expiated the sins of a divided city. Confraternal flagellation was not primarily a means for an individual to gain personal merit. The statutes brought it indoors and kept under group scrutiny; particular regulations banned its practice by solitary individuals, in the open air, or late at night. Similarly, processions were to become more orderly affairs, in which only songs ("*letanias et laudes*") approved by the Rector and the twelve adminstrative Guardians should be sung. The wails for mercy sounded in 1260 were replaced with dignified singing. Members adopted a prayer book specifying worship rituals and group prayers; this manual became the prototype which set liturgical practices adopted by other Bolognese confraternities.[5] Groups of flagellants were usually called *battuti* or *disciplinati* to distinguish them from psalm-singing laudesi, but clearly contemporaries did not see these exercises as mutually exclusive. Finally, members participating in religious services anywhere in the city were to wear the distinctive robes of the Congregatio Devotorum and make a public offering at the altar. These devotional regulations demonstrate concern for the public image of the new group. Members were not simply a new disorderly mob within the faction-ridden city, but a disciplined and devout group of honest and loyal citizens. This image was important to avoid public scandal, and to confirm the confraternity's loyalty to and spiritual service of the popolo regime.

The Bolognese did not see the Congregatio Devotorum's flagellants whipping themselves for the sins of their city. What they did see was confraternal brothers offering alms in the city's churches, and confraternal funeral processions bringing poor citizens to the grave. In 1289

---

[4] The statutes are reproduced in: M. Fanti, "Gli inizi del movimento dei disciplinati a Bologna e la confraternita di Santa Maria della Vita," *Bolletino della deputazione di storia patria per l'Umbria* vol. 66 (1969): 181–232, pp.186–191; and Angelozzi, *Confraternite laicali* pp. 85–97.

[5] Fanti, "S. Maria della Vita," p. 189.

they saw the brothers erect a hospital in the heart of the city to shelter pilgrims, derelicts, and the sick. Out of this charitable work there emerged a new name for the confraternity, that of S. Maria della Vita. Charity comprised the public face of a brotherhood whose private life was oriented to lauds, divine office, and flagellation. These were the two sides of the Compagnie Spirituali, which endured even as the political role of the Compagnie delle Arti eroded and the military effectiveness of the Compagnie delle Armi declined. As new confraternities arose in the changed political circumstances of the early fourteenth century, public charity was still seen as the natural work of any group which claimed to express the lay religious character of the popolo commune. Institutional charity was the characteristic mark of confraternal piety and of civic religion.

Like many faction-ridden popolo communes in Italy, Bologna began sliding towards signory in the late thirteenth century. By the early Trecento it was dominated by the Pepoli, a family of bankers whose head, Romeo, was one of the richest men in Italy. The Pepoli virtually ruled the city until a faction led by the rival Gozzadini expelled them in 1321. Romagnol dominance began to fade with a defeat by Modena in 1325 and, rather than see the return of the Pepoli, the Bolognese invited Cardinal Legate Bertrando del Poggetto to assume power. Bertrando ruled harshly from 1327 to 1334, suppressing traditional organs of communal government, imposing crushing taxes, and using Bolognese resources in a scheme to create a Papal state in the Po valley. With his ouster in 1334, there was a return to civic rule and civic factionalism between the Pepoli and the Gozzadini. The former regained power and in 1337 the Council of the Popolo and the Anziani proclaimed Romeo's son, Taddeo, *Governatore* of the commune. Two papal interdicts in 1338–40 could not unseat the new Pepoli signore. Instead, Taddeo Pepoli, a Doctor of Civil and Canon Law, proved a diplomatic moderate who worked through revived communal structures to give Bologna ten years of relatively peaceful government.

Throughout this period, Compagnie Spirituali were the only organized lay groups dedicated solely to expressing the Bolognese conviction that theirs was a holy city, loved and sometimes chastised by God. If anything, this conviction grew as real power slipped out of the popolo's grasp. Looking first at the laudesi confraternities, there was a remarkable flowering of companies in the first three decades of the century. Most initially took the generic name of S. Maria delle Laudi, and met in, and sometimes under the auspices of, the major mendicant churches of the quarters of Bologna. In the westerly quarter of Porta

Stiera, a large group began gathering for monthly devotions at the church of S. Francesco sometime shortly before 1317, the year members published a set of statutes and began a matriculation book.[6] In the northerly quarter of Porta Piera, a group began gathering monthly from 1298 at the Augustinian church of S. Giacomo.[7] In the easterly quarter of Porta Ravennate, the S. Maria dei Servi group served as the neighborhood laudesi confraternity, meeting in or close to the Servite church of S. Petronio Vecchio and, after the mendicants' move, in the new church of S. Maria dei Servi. Only one quarter and one mendicant congregation broke the emerging pattern. The Dominican monastery dominated the southerly quarter of Porta Procola, but no large neighborhood laudesi confraternity gathered there.[8] The congregation of lay devotees of Mary who met there monthly in the mid-Duecento was long since defunct and had no successor.[9] Possibly six smaller laudesi confraternities began in this period as well, and while most gathered outside the mendicant churches, none met in the Porta Procola quarter.[10]

Porta Procola nonetheless had many Compagnie Spirituale, for it was where almost all battuti confraternities originating in this period clustered. The geographical split reflects the different devotions of the two types of confraternities. In contrast to the large, laudesi confraternities which organized public worship services for a city quarter,

[6] The statutes refer to the company as a new foundation, indicating that the 1286 laudesi confraternity had likely folded. Mesini, "S. Maria delle Laudi," p. 363.

[7] This was the same mendicant congregation which had assisted the Congregatio Devotorum after 1260; according to a 1300 indulgence, confratelli and consorelle met on the second Sunday of every month. G. Guidicini, *Cose notabili della città di Bologna*. 5 vols. Bologna: Giacomo Monti, 1868–73 (Reprinted Bologna: Arnaldo Forni, 1982), II, p. 239. M. Fanti, "La confraternita di Santa Maria dei Guarini e l'ospedale di San Giobbe in Bologna," in G. Maioli and G. Roversi, eds., *Il Credito Romagnolo fra storia, arte e tradizione*, (Bologna: 1985), p. 350.

[8] The monastery had served as headquarters of the Dominican Inquisition since its inception in 1233, and the local friars' vigor in prosecuting heretics had stirred strong resentment and open animosity among the Bolognese. L. Paolini, *L'eresia a Bologna fra XIII e XIV secolo* vol. I: *L'eresia catara alla fine del duecento* (Rome: 1975), pp. 5; 78–9.

[9] Meersseman, *Ordo fraternitatis*, p. 1008.

[10] Three met in parish churches: S. Cristina di Pietralata (Porta Stiera); S. Maria della Mascarella (Porta Piera); S. Maria della Carità (also known as the Compagnia dei laudesi di Borgo S. Felice) (Porta Stiera): Fanti, "S. Maria dei Guarini," p. 350. The Compagnia dei Poveri met from ca. 1320 in an abandonned ospedale near S. Francesco in Porta Stiera: Guidicini, *Cose Notabili*, III, p. 363. The S. Maria delle Laudi in Borgo Galliera met from ca. 1324 next to the monastery of S. Benedetto in Porta Piera: Guidicini, *Cose Notabili*, II, p. 190. S. Maria della Consolazione met in the Augustinian church of S. Giacomo in Porta Piera: Guidicini, *Cose Notabili*, I, p. 174.

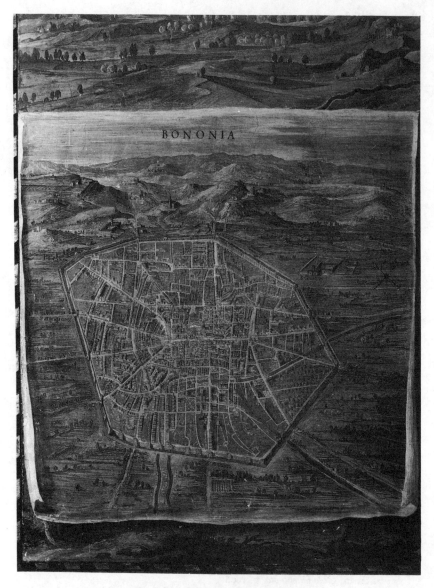

Fig. P.1   A detail of E. Datini's fresco, *Bononiensis ditio* (1580–81), in the Vatican library, showing the shrines of the Madonna del Monte (top center) and Madonna di San Luca (top right)

PROLOGUE   9

battuti groups in Bologna were smaller, secretive groups who sought
privacy for their liturgical worship. Porta Procola was suited to their
purpose since it was the largest but least populated of the four quarters.[11] Immediately outside its walls there rose the steep Apennine hills,
atop of one of which sat the shrine of the Madonna del Monte (Fig.
1.1). A number of the Bolognese battuti groups first established themselves outside of the city on the road leading to the shrine, and only
later moved within the city walls. For example, the Company of S.
Maria della Mezzaratta, began meeting ca. 1291 at the Madonna del
Monte shrine and moved into the Porta Procola quarter in 1352.[12] Yet
the most prominent of the new Trecento battuti confraternities originated in the very heart of the city and under circumstances much like
those of the Congregatio Devotorum in 1261. A little more than a
year after Papal Legate Bertrando del Poggetto was unceremoniously
chased out of the city, the commune was divided as magnate families
lined up behind the Pepoli (readmitted from exile in 1327) and the
Gozzadini. The popolo magistrates could no longer control events in
Bologna, and so in February 1335, they gladly opened the city gates to
a procession of laymen crying for "penitence, peace, and mercy." This
procession was led by a young Dominican friar, Venturino da
Bergamo.[13] Growing out of Venturino's preaching in Bergamo, the
procession was en route to Rome as the spearhead of a moral and penitential crusade which participants hoped would sweep Italy and carry
on to liberate the Holy Land. Its Roman destination was meant to encourage Benedict XII's return to the Holy City as leader of the
crusade, but all Venturino received for his troubles was a summons to
Avignon followed by "exile" to a French monastery. Venturino's
warm reception in Bologna was not due solely to his implicit criticism

[11] A.I. Pini, "Le ripartizioni territoriale urbane di Bologna medievale," *Quaderni culturali Bolognesi*, vol 1 (1977), p. 9.
[12] A 1291 fratellanze to the Dominicans refers to the company as a recent foundation.
Its 1338 oratory, richly decorated with frescoes by Vitale di Bologna which have
since been moved to the Pinacoteca Nazionale di Bologna, was located on the
road leading to the shrine. Compagnia del Buon Gesù, ASB Dem 3/7625 #1.
Fanti, "S. Maria della Vita," pp. 212–13. Ghirardacci, *Historia di Bologna*, II, p. 213.
A laudesi "Societa di S. Maria del Monte" with connections to the friars of S.
Francesco, may have started here in 1323. G.B. Melloni, *Atti o memorie degli uomini
illustri in santità, nati o morti in Bologna*, [Monumenta Italiae Ecclesiastica: Hagiogra-
phica #1], (Rome: 1971), p. 379.
[13] BBA Fondo Ospedale, Ms 40, p. 1. Fanti clears up many of the myths surrounding
this confraternity's origins, and vigorously defends the specific founding date of
July 13, 1335 in, "La Confraternita di Santa Maria della Morte e la Conforteria dei
condonnati in Bologna nei secoli XIV e XV," *Quaderni del centro di ricerca di studio
sul movimento dei disciplinati*, vol. 20 (1978), pp. 13–14.

of the papacy; the friar first gained a following during his tenure in the Dominican monastery of Bologna from 1331/2 to 1334, and his followers went on to form a confraternity in 1336. The new Compagnia di S. Maria della Morte immediately adopted flagellant exercises, but their rather odd name came from the charitable activity they undertook. Following the example set by Venturino when he had been a friar in the city, they undertook to comfort and bury criminals who were executed in Bologna. This was the first example in Italy of a *conforteria*, a lay confraternity dedicated to helping prisoners in general and condemned convicts in particular.

The focus of their charity was new, but the brothers of S. Maria della Morte were doing what was expected of Compagnie Spirituali. Following hard on the heels of the flowering of laudesi confraternities in the 1310s and 1320s came a flowering of *ospedali*. Between 1317 and 1327, five different confraternities opened six ospedali.[14] In almost all cases, these foundations were stipulated by legacies of a house, lands, or funds. Not all donors were confratelli, making the ospedali as much signs of general lay piety as indications of any peculiarly confraternal devotion; they also point to lay discontent with monastic ospedali. Their multiplication in such a short period reflects both the prosperity of Bologna, and the importance for pilgrims of its location at the head of the major pass through the Apennines; the ospedali of S. Maria dei Servi and S. Francesco were each sheltering up to 14,000 pilgrims annually by the mid-fifteenth century.[15] Flagellant confraternities were somewhat slower in this work. Their more introspective piety, smaller size, and less deliberately communal focus delayed the development of ospedali until after the famine of 1347 and the Black Death of 1348. Even then the battuti ospedali usually had a different focus than those of the laudesi, catering less to pilgrims than to the sick and dying of the city itself.

Taddeo Pepoli's relatively moderate rule did not lead to a signorial dynasty as he hoped. Two sons succeeded him in 1347, but they

---

[14] Ospedali for male pilgrims were founded by the laudesi of S. Giacomo (1317), S. Maria dei Servi and S. Francesco (1320), Borgo Galliera (ca. 1325), S. Maria della Carità (ca. 1327). S. Francesco opened an ospedale for female pilgrims in 1324. Fanti (ed.), *Gli archivi*, pp. 29; 32; 34. G. Gentili, "Ospedali non più esistenti in Bologna," in *Sette secoli di vita ospedaliera in Bologna*, (Bologna: 1960), pp. 33; 43–4.

[15] Fanti (ed.), *Gli archivi delle istituzioni di carità e assistenza attive in Bologna nel Medioevo e nell'Età moderna*. Bologna: 1984, p. 34. The ospedale of S. Francesco had 55 beds in 1329. The S. Giacomo laudesi ospedale (later known as S. Maria dei Guarini) noted 53 beds (45 male and 8 female) in inventories of 1359, 1361, and 1364, with a sudden doubling to 107 (90 male and 17 female) in 1368. G. Mira, "Prima Sondaggi," p. 244.

lacked his resources and skill. Unable to direct events in the wake of
the Black Death and unnerved by the revived factionalism stirred up
by Milanese, Florentine, and papal forces, they sold the signory to
Archbishop Giovanni Visconti, papal governor of Romagna. Visconti's
purchase brought occupation by Milanese troops and a levy of annual
payments to the papacy. Upon Giovanni's death five years later the
Bolognese elected his legate Giovanni da Oleggio as signore in the
hope of regaining their liberty. The new signore chose instead to sell
the signory once again, spurning the Visconti for a higher offer from
Pope Innocent VI. Bologna thereby passed under the direct rule of the
papacy once again. Renewed suppression of communal institutions
and the ruinous cost of the pope's anti-Viscontean policy led to a
general uprising in the winter of 1375–76. Moves toward a magnate
oligarchy were forestalled by the popolo's restoration of government
by the Anziani and the Council of the Popolo, directed by a citizen
vicar, Giovanni da Legnano, who was a Doctor of Canon Law at the
university. The civic pride and prosperity stimulated by the popolo
revival was reflected in the rewriting of communal and guild statutes,
and in a building boom which involved the clearing of the Piazza
Maggiore at the heart of the city. This was where the city's four quarters met, and to symbolize their emancipation – civic *and* religious –
from the papacy, the Bolognese cleared additional space and in 1390
began building San Petronio. This vast civic basilica, dedicated to the
city's fifth-century patron saint and planned by the Bolognese architect
Antonio di Vincenzo, joined the Communal, Notarial, and Podestà's
palaces as one of the chief public buildings framing the Piazza Maggiore. In keeping with local ambitions, the Bolognese would build the
biggest church in Christendom as a *civic* building at the very heart of
their city. Like the Venetians, they would leave the bishop's cathedral
church on a backstreet, very much overshadowed and in need of
repair. San Petronio served for over 150 years as a stage for the city's assertion of its autonomy against the Papacy.[16]

Construction of San Petronio marks the opening of a new stage in
the development of Bologna's civic religion. Before the late fourteenth
century, that civic religion was expressed through lay-organized
actions rather than through specific holy or symbolic places; apart from
the Madonna del Monte and the Bascilica di Santo Stefano, Bologna
hardly even had any holy shrines. From the time the popolo magistrates stood at the city gates in 1260, these actions meshed with the

---

[16] W. Lotz, "I simboli religiosi e del potere," in G. Roversi (ed.), *La Piazza Maggiore
di Bologna: storia, arte, costume.* (Bologna: 1984), pp. 123–42. N. Miller, *Renaissance
Bologna,* (New York: 1989), pp. 66–69.

political life of the commune and came to expression through the citizenry rather than the regular or secular clergy. Lay artisans organized into confraternities were responsible for much of the rich variety of public liturgical worship and organized charity found in the city; penitential confraternities flagellated to expiate the sins of the community while laudesi brotherhoods sang praises to Mary for the favor she showed her beloved Bologna. Brotherhoods buried the poor, tended the sick, sheltered the pilgrims, and comforted the dying; at the end of the century new brotherhoods arose to help Bolognese travelling to St. James in Galatia and to retrieve the bodies of those who had drowned in the city's canals. Their spirituality and organization reflected mendicant and guild influence and an intensely local, intensely autonomous spirit. The mendicant model suggested public charity as a natural expression of civic religion, but operating charitable institutions demanded a high degree of organization, which in turn led brotherhoods to rely heavily on guild administrative models. These were premised on protecting craft autonomy, and so encouraged Bolognese confraternities to maintain their autonomy from mendicant orders. As we will see below, Bolognese confraternities from the time of the Congregatio Devotorum civitatis bononie were unique in Italy for their degree of autonomy from mendicant supervision. This makes them particularly good guides to the changing expression of the city's civic religion, and to the way in which that civic religion becomes caught up in the devotional and political currents of the fifteenth and sixteenth centuries. As the walls of San Petronio rose, that civic religion gained new articulation. Thirteenth-century confraternities had expressed a civic religion of the Bolognese popolo in distinction from the Bolognese magnates; San Petronio expressed a civic religion of the Bolognese people in distinction from the Papacy. Though factionalism still incapacitated the city, the enemy outside the walls had achieved a size and threat sufficient to bring some degree of civic religious solidarity within the walls. San Petronio was a site, a shrine, a liturgical center; it was a civic project sponsored by the Communal governing bodies and underwritten by all the citizens. It did not supercede the lay confraternities as an expression of the civic religion, but marked a changing orientation which was picked up by the new and reformed Compagnie Spirituali of the fifteenth century. Public charity continued to be important, but it was supplemented with more public liturgical worship at local shrines and periodic processions commemorating communal events or connecting extra-mural shrines with San Petronio at the city's center. A rather vague civic religion metamorphosed into a more specific civic cult, and it did so under confraternal sponsorship.

San Petronio was never completed. By a Bull of 1561, Pius IV ordered construction of a palatial home for Bologna's famous university, but stipulated that it be located in a spot designated for San Petronio's unbuilt eastern transept. Bologna's Senate and the University's professors united to fight the plan, but Pius was determined that San Petronio never outshine St. Peter's in Rome. Faced with this conflict between the two key symbols of Bologna's autonomy and fame, local rulers decided that their civic religion could never realistically challenge the Church Universal, and acquiesced.[17] It was something their fourteenth- and fifteenth-century forebears would never have consented to. That they did, and that they even could, indicates the changes that had come over civic religion and civic government in the fifteenth and sixteenth centuries.

[17] Miller, *Renaissance Bologna*, pp. 124–5.

I

THE EARLY QUATTROCENTO:
CONFRATERNITIES, OBSERVANCE
MOVEMENTS AND THE CIVIC CULT

From 1385 northern Italy witnessed the relentless advance of Giangaleazzo Visconti. Having secured the territories of Milan by overturning
his uncle and father-in-law Bernabò, he proceeded through arms and
diplomacy to dominate and in places subject the communes of
Romagna, Tuscany, and Umbria. The hastily knit alliances of these
communes unravelled before him, and he in turn used their forces to
string a tighter noose around the prizes which eluded him. In July
1402, Bologna was the last major city to fall to Visconti. From there he
marched to what was to be the final triumph in the siege of Florence.
Plague claimed Giangaleazzo and Florence claimed the triumph; the
empire which Visconti had shaped over seventeen years quickly disin-
tegrated. Hans Baron noted the effect of Visconti's empire in shaping
Florentine republicanism, but there has been less attention paid to
those communes whose resistance failed. In the case of Bologna, the
Visconti threat was a catalyst which brought together religious and political movements and which turned confraternities more decidedly
towards the shaping of the civic cult that had begun with construction
of San Petronio.

Bologna's religious response to the Visconti threat focused around a
procession and a shrine: the 1399 processions of the Bianchi movement, and the 1401 creation of the shrine of S. Maria del Baraccano.
The movement of the Bianchi, taking their name from their white
robes, occured in 1399–1400, with ripples felt through succeeding
decades. The Visconti were only one of a series of factors creating the
atmosphere of crisis that gave it birth. End-of-century apocalyptic fears
and millenarian hopes were fed by recurring plagues, continuing
schism in the church, revived factionalism in Bologna itself, and hope
in the coming of a true pope and just emperor. All of Northern Italy
came under the Bianchi spell in the summer of 1399, as Visconti's diplomacy neutralized France and won over Sienna, Pisa, and Lucca. As

penitents like Francesco di Marco Datini, the merchant of Prato, marched in their tens of thousands through the quarters of Florence and by a circuitous nine-day route through the contado and home again, Modenese penitents brought the Bianchi cry of "Misericordia" to Bologna. The Modenese penitents had been preceded by ambassadors affirming the peaceful purpose of the procession and seeking permission for its passage through Bolognese territory. As in 1260, relations between the two communities were delicate, since Modena had followed other Romagnol and Tuscan cities in breaking with the League of Bologna, leaving only Florence and Bologna allied against Giangaleazzo Visconti. Despite its weakening political position, Bologna gave entry to the procession. A week later, on September 2, 1399, the Modenese arrived marching by parishes behind their standards and singing lauds. They were met outside the city by thousands of white-clad Bolognese – the estimates of contemporary chronicles range from 25,000 to an unlikely 50,000 – for an outdoor mass and sermon. As the bulk of the Modenese returned home, the devotional processions began in Bologna. All stores were closed and, under the stimulation of special indulgences and the direction of four communal officers, a nine-day devotional cycle began within the city. Processions of men and women dressed in white moved church by appointed church through the four quarters. On September 15, the Bolognese Bianchi issued out of the city by quarters, marching behind a troop of one hundred ambassadors on the route to Imola.[1]

Francesco di Marco Datini's account of the Florentine processions modifies the image of their pious intention and self-deprivation; many citizens were swept along in a movement which suited their liturgical expectations without seriously changing their lives. Yet there were others who, like their predecessors of 1260 and 1335, attempted to perpetuate some its devotional fervor by founding or renewing confraternities. In Budrio and S. Giovanni in Persiceto, two towns in the Bolognese contado, the Bianchi devotees created confraternities under the title of "Santa Maria della Misericordia," reminiscent both of the characteristic Bianchi cry of "Mercy" and of Mary's role in turning back disaster. In Cento an existing flagellant company was reinvigo-

---

[1] Hieronymo Bursellis, *Cronaca gestorum ac factorum memorabilium civitatis Bononie ab urbe condita ad anno 1497*, ed. A. Sorbelli, *RIS* vol. 23, Pt. II, p. 66 (22–30). Ghirardacci, *Historia di Bologna*, II, pp. 504–5. Guidicini, *Cose notabili*, II, p. 98. M. Fanti, "L'ospedale e la chiesa di S. Maria della Carità," in M. Fanti *et al.*, *S. Maria della Carità in Bologna* (Bologna: 1981), pp. 27–30. I. Origo, *The Merchant of Prato* (Harmondsworth: 1963), pp. 321–5. D. Bornstein, *The Bianchi of 1399: Popular Devotion in Late Medieval Italy* (Ithaca: 1993).

rated. In Bologna itself, the company of S. Maria delle Laudi del Borgo S. Felice embarked on a thorough internal renewal, assuming the new title of S. Maria della Misericordia, and adopting the white robes of the Bianchi. Members drew up new statutes and a new matriculation list, and employed the image of S. Maria della Misericordia characteristic of the Marian devotion of the Bianchi and later to be used by many observant reform confraternities in the city. The image derived from accounts of a French peasant's vision of Mary pleading with a vengeful Christ to be merciful and not bring the world to an immediate, apocalyptic judgment. Depicting Mary as Queen of Heaven standing with arms outstretched to shelter crowds of worshippers under her cloak, the symbol is most often encountered as a miniature heading revised statutes or matriculation lists. Some show white-robed Bianchi in the shelter of Mary; others show a diverse range of men and women, rich and poor, lay and clerical believers, gathering under the protective cloak. The image's longevity shows the continuing influence of the Bianchis' Marian devotion and penitential impetus long after the 1399 processions and their climax in the 1400 Jubilee in Rome.[2]

Mary's cloak did not shelter Bologna from Visconti troops and propaganda, nor from the factional rivalry which these two fostered within the city. Bologna had no civic humanists like Leonardo Bruni to construct a republican defense against Visconti; it had many patricians who thought a better defense lay in imitating Visconti's signorial power. Carlo Zambeccari had established a signory in all but name, and in 1399 Nanne Gozzadini, Giovanni Bentivoglio, and Giovanni da Barbiano joined forces unsuccessfully to take power from him; as the Bianchi were marching, Barbiano was captured and decapitated in the Piazza Maggiore. Zambeccari's death in October unleashed a year of bloodshed which had a brief pause in March 1401 when Giovanni Bentivoglio abandoned Gozzadini, allied with the Zambeccari, and seized the signory himself, chasing his enemies into the arms of the Duke of Milan and inaugurating an uneasy year of rule.

The Marian devotion triggered by the Bianchi had meanwhile found a more purely local focus in a shrine located on the southeast city wall. The area of the new shrine had long been frequented by un-

---

[2] The image of S. Maria della Misericordia predated and long outlived the Bianchi movement. Laudesi of S. Francesco had diverse men and women gathered under the Virgin's cloak in a miniature on their 1329 matriculation list (BBA Osp ms. 72, c.3r.), while the flagellants of S. Maria della Morte depicted only themselves, dressed in white robes, in a miniature heading their 1562 statutes (BBA Osp ms. 42, c.3r.).

desirables when, in the late fourteenth century, a man of the neighborhood seeking to improve its moral tone erected a small image of the Virgin sheltered under a lean-to shed or "baraccano." S. Maria del Baraccano attracted enough of a following to be perceived as a security problem by Giovanni Bentivoglio. Fearing that the wall shrine was too easy a conduit for civic malcontents and Visconti spies to exchange information on the city's defenses, he ordered it bricked up. In the legend of the shrine's first miracle, the first wall erected to seal it fell down immediately, as did a second larger wall which followed. Deciding it better to placate than fight forces beyond his control, Bentivoglio then ordered the cult expanded and promoted in a more secure church, under the watchful eye of a loyal confraternity. The change of heart did little to change Giovanni's fortunes. The new church was dedicated and placed under the direction of a well-bred confraternity, but only after the Bentivoglio signore had lost a battle to Visconti troops and his life to a Bolognese mob. Members of the confraternity, established a year after the dedication of the church in 1402, were appointed governors of the shrine and its alms, and were expected to pray continually in rotation for the peace of the *patria*.[3]

The Bianchi procession and Baraccano shrine illustrate tradition and innovation at work in fifteenth-century Bolognese confraternities. The procession follows the local tradition of artisanal confraternities blending the mendicant and guild ethos and emerging out of popular devotional movements which are themselves triggered by social and political upheavals. Whether flagellant battuti or praising laudesi, these confraternities functioned as the civic memory of the movement, perpetuating its robes, its images, and its language, and doing so through lay inspiration and organization. Mendicant preachers stimulated the devotion, and communal officials approved the procession, but no civic or ecclesiastical authority appointed S. Maria della Misericordia to its new task as the living memory of the events of 1399. Its mandate arose out of the rhetoric of the spiritual companies as the third pillar of popolo society, and out of the notion that civic religion centered around activities like processions and charity. Bolognese citizens remembered the vows they had made during the Bianchi processions every time the lay brothers of S. Maria della Misericordia marched in civic or confraternal processions. The Baraccano shrine and confraternity illustrate innovation in line with the construction of the civic

---

[3] P. Viziani, *Dieci libri della historia sua patria* (Bologna: 1602), pp. 272–3. G. Giovanantonij, *Historia della miracolosa imagine di Maria Vergine detta del baraccano...* (Bologna: 1674). Guidicini, *Miscellanea storico patria Bolognese.* Bologna: Giacomo Monti, 1872. Reprinted Bologna: Arnaldo Forni, 1980, p. 306.

basilica of San Petronio. Its fixed location and its deliberately created, largely functional, and politically safe confraternity demonstrate the more conscious construction of a locus for the civic cult. The shrine of S. Maria del Baraccano was the first major shrine developed within the city walls, and certainly the first to be developed with an eye to its potential as a pilgrimage site. The eponymous confraternity was one of the first to be established for a specific purpose and with a socially restricted membership. It therefore marks a step towards the fabrication of fixed religious symbols under elite proprietorship – a move consistent with the expectations on spiritual companies which nonetheless marked a step beyond the spontaneity, artisanal autonomy, and mendicant spirituality seen in S. Maria della Misericordia. It was as deliberate a creation as San Petronio, but its origins demonstrated that subtle changes had occured in the civic cult even since that basilica's cornerstone had been laid with great enthusiasm for the revival of the popular commune in 1390. In 1394, against the background of intense factional struggles and the ambitions of Giangaleazzo Visconti, and on the grounds of efficiency, the popolo Council of 4,000 had elected a seventeen-member executive and invested it with legislative power. Authorized to make and suspend laws, imprison or liberate citizens, and nominate the judiciary, the *Sedici Riformatori dello stato di libertà* was intended to reform and so preserve popolo government. In fact, this concentration of oligarchic power quickly overshadowed the existing executive colleges of the *Anziani*, the *Gonfalonieri*, and the *Artigiani*, and the Council of 4,000 itself, and prepared Bologna for signorial rule. Just as the Sedici Riformatori represented a political coup taken under cover of the rhetoric of popolo liberty, so the shrine and confraternity of S. Maria del Baraccano represented a move towards elite manipulation of civic religious symbols taken under cover of the rhetoric of confraternities as the third, spiritual pillar of the popolo commune.

This movement was as yet tentative, and would only become apparent after mid-century when the Bentivoglio returned, bringing a strengthened Sedici and relative stability in their tow. In the first decades of the Quattrocento, another force more in keeping with their traditions was shaping the spiritual companies. At bottom, confraternities were lay adaptations of mendicant communal life and spirituality. From the later fourteenth century the mendicant orders were shaken by the rise of Observance movements emphasizing the poverty and obedience of their founding *Regulae*, and a contemplative, penitential spirituality. While Giangaleazzo Visconti was the catalyst creating two companies early in the century, it was Observant spirituality and Observant clergy who truly shaped fifteenth-century confraternities, creating new groups and reforming existing ones. The Dominican Observant Manfredo da Vercelli established a group of lay flagellants in S. Domenico in 1418. Similarly, the Franciscan Observant S. Bernardino da Siena reinvigorated one Bolognese confraternity – which renamed itself "Buon Gesù" in recognition of Bernardino's devotional focus on the name and symbol of Christ – and inspired the erection of another.[4] Cardinal Bessarion, a member of the commission which recommended Bernardino's canonization, was a moving force behind the creation of a Compagnia di S. Bernardino soon after he arrived as Papal Legate in Bologna in 1450. Yet the most important cleric for Bolognese confraternal reform was Nicolò Albergati, Bishop of Bologna from 1417 to 1443, who can be credited with fostering at least four groups and reforming six others. Albergati's approach to reform brought mendicant spirituality together with the public symbols and shrines of a civic cult, and so at once furthered the confraternities' spiritual development while also preparing for their greater politicization in the latter half of the fifteenth century.

Born into a prominent Bolognese family in 1357, Nicolò Albergati joined the Carthusian order in 1394 and was serving as Prior of the Certosa outside Bologna when he was elected by the Cathedral Canons to be Bishop of Bologna in 1417. The election's questionable legality, coming after the deposition of Popes John XXIII and Boniface XIII and before the election of Martin V, initially gave him trouble with the restored papacy. These tensions notwithstanding, Pope Martin confirmed the episcopal election when he realized Albergati could be a loyal and indispensable diplomat assisting the papacy's post-schism restoration. Eugenius IV subsequently appointed him to the College of Cardinals. His work for the papacy would later put Albergati in bad odor with those Bolognese intent on ensuring that the revived Italian papacy did not jeopardize their autonomy. Despite these impediments to sustained pastoral work in the diocese, Albergati left a remarkable impact on the devotional patterns of fifteenth-century Bologna. Confraternal reform was only part of a program which included establishing new forms of Marian devotion, introdu-

[4] The Compagnia di S. Domenico may have assisted the Dominican inquisitor. ASB Dem, Compagnia di S. Domenico, busta 1/6415, filza #5/1; busta 7/6421, filza 3. G.G. Meersseman, *Ordo Fraternitatis*, pp. 611–12. The fratelli of S. Maria della Mezzaratta approached S. Bernardino after he preached in Bologna in 1430. Under his direction they took on the devotion to the Holy Name and adopted the new name: ASB Dem, Compagnia di Buon Gesù, busta 9/7631, filza 1. See also AAB, Ricuperi Beneficiari, fasc. 665 #4. The old name was not entirely abandoned; revised statutes of 1489 still refer to the "Compagnia di madona sancta Maria da la mezarata dal monte" (BBA Gozz 203 #7).

cing the Lateran Canons and the Gesuati into Bologna, and placing a greater emphasis on the training of both clergy and laity in the fundamentals of the Catholic faith. Albergati immediately conducted a series of pastoral visits around the diocese, arriving at churches on foot and without a retinue to hear confessions, celebrate mass with the priests, and examine closely the lives and livings of his clerics. His personal devotion was austere, moral, and learned in the manner of contemporary Christian humanism, drawing on both the penitential and educational aspects of the contemporary cult of St. Jerome and the *devotio moderna*, which he personally encountered on his many diplomatic legations to northern Europe; when Albergati was President of the Congress of Arras in 1435, Jan Van Eyck made a portrait of him as St. Jerome in his study. The author of many sermons, epistles, and theological treatises, he was also a patron of some of the leading humanists of the early Quattrocento, including Francesco Filelfo, Poggio Bracciolini, and the future popes Aeneas Silvius Piccolomini, and Tommaso Parentucelli. Albergati's program of devotional revival for Bologna focused around three symbols: Christ; the Eucharist; and the Madonna. Each was central to Observant spirituality, and Albergati believed that presenting each publicly in a dramatic fashion could foster a popular religious revival. Lay confraternities were the natural vehicle for a lay religious revival, and Albergati relied on them heavily as he worked to expand the local civic cult with more shrines, public plays and demonstrations, and regular processions.[5]

The Imitation of Christ was the main theme in the contemporary devotional revival, and served as the focus of the Compagnia dell'Ascensione di Nostro Signore, commonly called the "Trentatre" in honor of the years of Christ's life on earth. Albergati established the group to lead processions on the first Sunday of every month to a shrine of the Virgin Mary located on the Guardia hill immediately south of the city walls. The Madonna della Guardia shrine had originated in the late twelfth century, but was long overshadowed by the image of the Madonna del Monte on the Osservanza hill a short distance to the east. It played so small a role in the local cult that when a storm severely damaged it in 1395, the Bolognese simply left it in

[5] P. De Töth, *Il beato Nicolò Albergati e i suoi tempi (1375–1444)*, 2 vols. (Aquapendente: 1922, 1934). G. Fantuzzi, *Notizie degli scrittori bolognesi*, vol. 1 (Bologna: 1783, reprint 1965), pp. 99–133. Albergati conducted his pastoral visits in 1417–18; 1420; and 1425–26, using and annotating an extant 1408 list of all the diocesan churches: L. Novelli, "Manoscritto 2005 della Biblioteca Universitaria di Bologna, 'Liber Collecte imposte in clero bon.' con postille del card. Nicolò Albergati," *Ravennatensia* vol. 2 (1971), pp. 101–62. On Albergati as St. Jerome: E.R. Rice, *Saint Jerome in the Renaissance* (Baltimore: 1985), pp. 109–11.

ruins. Albergati ordered it repaired and worked to make it a focus of devotional life. To this end, the lay brothers of the "Trentatre" offered their monthly graphic demonstration of imitative piety as they led any who would follow up the steep hill, marching barefoot and bearing a cross and other symbols of Christ's passion. The procession culminated in a service at the shrine in honor of Mary.

Eucharistic piety lent itself less readily to graphic public demonstration, but its meaning could be conveyed through school lessons and in the context of *sacre rappresentazione*, the dramatic presentations mounted at festivals and markets. These became the chief functions of a second confraternity, the Compagnia di S. Girolamo, which had existed as a loosely organized worship group in the Porta Procola quarter since early in the century. This was one of the few youths' confraternities in Renaissance Bologna. By the time of Albergati's first contact with the company in 1417, its members were constructing an oratory and were engaged in a campaign to bring other young people away from taverns and gaming tables and instructing them in the Christian life. Albergati organized the group into a confraternity under the title of St. Jerome, and gave direction to its teaching activity by writing a catechism textbook; the frontispiece to the group's first statutes (ca. 1425–33) shows St. Jerome enthroned and the young lay brothers around his feet teaching little children.[6] Like the texts which would be used over a century later by Companies of Christian Doctrine, Albergati's catechism built on familiar texts like the Lord's Prayer, the Ten Commandments, and the Apostles' Creed in order to teach laypeople about faith's meaning, and it reviewed the Sacraments, the corporal and spiritual works of mercy, and the virtues and sins in order to teach faith's practice. And like Luther's early protestant Catechisms there was a condensed version for beginners and an expanded version for older youths and adults. Later in the century the lay brothers moved the classroom outdoors, teaching larger audiences through dramatic retellings of Bible stories and saints' lives presented

---

[6] There is no consensus on whether Albergati formed or simply organized the company. The case for a pre-existing core of lay devotees is made in two early histories: G.V. Vittorio, *Origine, fondatione e progressi della venerabile confraternita di S. Giralamo* (Bologna: 1698), pp. 8–9. A. Macchiavelli, *Origine, fondazione e progressi della veneranda compagnia laicale sotto l'invocazione de' gloriosi Santi Girolamo ed Anna posta nella via di Bagnomarino*, (Bologna: 1754), pp. 5–6. This position is affirmed by Guidicini, *Cose notabili*, III, pp. 245–6; and Fanti, *San Procolo: Una parrocchia di Bologna dal medioevo all'età contemporanea*, Bologna: 1983, pp. 139–40. The case for Albergati as founder is made by: De Töth, *Nicolò Albergati*, p. 247; and C. Mesini, "La catechesi a Bologna e la prima compagnia della dottrina cristiana fondata dal B. Nicolò Albergati (1375–1444)," *Apollinaris*, vol. 54 (1981), pp. 232–67.

before large crowds at public festivals. These were Tuscan in spirit and composition, but some were altered to give a deliberately Bolognese focus. In one, S. Dominic notes his crusading preaching in Spain, but begs God not to send him to the intractable Bolognese. Another, which the Angel Gabriel opens with "*Deh*, pay thoughtful attention, noble and worthy people of Bologna," elaborates the theme of S. Maria della Misericordia. Thoroughly fed up with a people who multiply their sins by the day, Christ is ready to rain down judgment on earth. Justice offers him three lances with which to plunge the disobedient into the Inferno. Mercy counters with a series of saints who intercede to plead the case of sinners; when this proves unsuccessful, she sends Gabriel to ask Mary to intervene. Mary calms Christ's rage and presents Saints Dominic and Francis to him; Christ commissions the former to head to Spain and preach against Pride, Luxury, and Avarice, and the latter to preach to the whole world of the Passion. The two saints embrace, and as Dominic leaves the stage Francis turns to preach to the crowd. A folio written in 1482 by Tommaso Leoni contains twenty-three *sacre rappresentazioni* which individually present the key events of Holy Week, Christ's Resurrection and Ascension, events from the lives of Mary and the saints and, most ambitiously, a history of the world covering the Old and New Testaments and the lives of leading popes, church fathers, martyrs, and saints. Requiring a cast of hundreds, this presentation ends with the Four Defenders, Saints Petronio, Ambrose, Francis, and Dominic, holding up a model of the city. The teenage confraternal brothers undoubtedly recruited some of the cast from among the young children they were teaching the catechism to, making this an early example of that durable staple of church instruction, the Sunday School Pageant. It is impossible to date these *sacre rappresentazioni* precisely or to determine when the Company of S. Girolamo began staging them; Leoni joined the Company of S. Girolamo before 1465, and his 1482 folio could represent either the beginning of the confraternity's dramatic program or simply the compilation of its various texts in one book.[7] With their local sponsors, cast, and references, the plays were an important vehicle for spreading the civic religion. Part hectoring, part congratulation, they put Bologna into the larger scheme of eternal history and European Christendom.

For his part, Nicolò Albergati characteristically reinforced S. Girola-

[7] V. De Bartholomaeis, *Le origini della poesia drammatica Italiana*, (Torino: 1952), pp. 427–33. A list of first lines and complete texts of two of the fifteenth-century S. Girolamo *sacre rappresentazioni* are reprinted in: G. Vecchi, "Le sacre rappresentazioni della compagnia dei battuti in Bologna nel secolo XV," *AMPR* n.s. vol. 4 (1951–53), pp. 281–324.

mo's educational work with public demonstrations of his patronage. On the opening of a new oratory in 1433, the bishop granted them new pink robes and caps, a sharp and fashionable contrast to the plain black or white robes favored by other local confraternities. Albergati then led them together with the Anziani in a procession from the Bishop's Palace to their new church. The symbols of Albergati's dignity as Cardinal of S. Croce had been raised above the main door of the church and woven into the tapestry before the altar. Lest future generations forget, the brothers had a large painting made of the procession and hung it in the sacristy.[8]

The third and greatest symbol which Albergati used to reinvigorate religious life in Bologna was the Virgin Mary. Although Bologna's patron saint was San Petronio, its local cult was decidedly Marian; Albergati encouraged this devotion to the Virgin and saw lay confraternities as ideal agencies for fostering it. Certainly Mary figured in the *sacre rappresentazione* of the Compagnia di S. Girolamo, but beyond this new processions and festivals underlined Mary's patronage of Bologna. The Compagnia di S. Maria degli Angeli organized popular devotions which had grown from ca. 1412 around an image of Mary located on the outer wall of an all-but-abandoned church in a shabby neighborhood on the south side of the city. The confraternity's name, "degli Angeli," was derived in part from the small angels flanking the image and supporting its protective roof. Albergati encouraged the company to capitalize on the connection in its public processions, and opened the way by granting it permission to participate in the annual display of the Veil of the Blessed Virgin at the nearby church of Santo Stefano. The basilica was a complex of buildings whose oldest parts date to the early Christian era. One part reproduced the Holy Sepulcher in medieval Jerusalem and held additional symbols of Christ's passion, from the bowl in which Pilate had washed his hands to the rooster whose call had signalled Peter's betrayal. These relics brought the immediacy of the Passion to Bologna, and led to the church being known as Holy Jerusalem; any connection with it brought great honor to a confraternity. The brothers of S. Maria degli Angeli made their procession more dramatic by dressing young children as angels to accompany them; in the flickering light cast by the lay brothers' lit torches, the children sang lauds praising Christ and Mary and calling the faithful to come and honor the Virgin's Veil.[9]

[8] Vittorio, *S. Girolamo*, pp. 14–15.
[9] G. Roversi, "La Compagnia e la chiesa di S. Maria degli Angeli nella via di 'Truffailmondo'," *Strenna storica Bolognese* vol. 12 (1962), p. 275. Ghirardacci, *Historia di Bologna* II, pp. 617–18. Guidicini, *Cose notabili* II, p. 618.

A more dramatic and politically more significant procession was already in the works, centered on the shrine of the Madonna della Guardia noted earlier. Three months of near-continuous rain in the summer of 1433 left the fields of the contado a sodden mess and raised real fears about the city's ability to feed itself. The College of the Anziani decreed a three-day procession of clerics, confraternities, and lay people through the city, but there was no change. It then decreed a five-day procession, and later an eight-day procession, but the rain kept pouring. As desperation grew, Graziolo Accarisi, a member of the Anziani, proposed that the Bolognese follow the example of the Florentines who, in times of crisis, appealed for the help of an image of the Virgin which they brought into the city from the suburban town of Impruneta. The Impruneta image had been at the center of a local cult since 1340, and was particularly associated with ending downpours and droughts.[10]

Aware of the miracles associated with the Madonna dell'Impruneta, Bishop Albergati and the Anziani agreed to Accarisi's proposal. The chief Marian shrine outside the city, that of the Madonna del Monte, had only frescoed images and so couldn't provide a portable painting for the procession. Attention fell instead on the Madonna della Guardia which had been gaining prominence through the monthly processions of the Trentatre confraternity. Albergati seized on the opportunity to increase the stature of the the shrine further. All that had to be decided was who would bring the image into the city. The canons and confraternity of the Impruneta church performed this honor in Florence, but the Guardia shrine had no clergy associated with it. The Trentatre confraternity would then have been the most likely candidate, but through either Albergati's desire to broaden the number of lay brotherhoods involved in the civic cult, or Accarisi's desire to bring increased honor to his own confraternity of S. Maria della Morte, the responsibility and the honor passed to the latter company instead. Using the Florentine rituals as their example, the brothers of S. Maria della Morte went in procession up the Guardia hill on the first Saturday in July. They lifted the image and by evening had carried it back down the hill to the small church of S. Mattia just outside the Saragozza gate. The following morning a formal procession of all spiritual and artisanal companies, together with magistrates and

[10] Varignana (Cronaca B), *RIS*, vol. 23, Pt. I, vol. iv, p. 63. M. Fanti, "La Madonna di S. Luca nella leggenda, nella storia e nella tradizione bolognese," *Il Carrobio*, 3 (1977), pp. 181–3. On the Florentine parallels: R. Trexler, "Florentine Religious Experience: The Sacred Image," *Studies in the Renaissance*, vol. 19 (1972), pp. 7–41. R. Trexler, *Public Life in Renaissance Florence*, (New York: 1980), pp. 63–4, 354–5.

people, gathered in the driving rain to carry the image into the city. As they entered the Saragozza gate, the rain stopped and the skies cleared. For three days the jubilant procession made its way through the city's streets and churches before arriving back at the Saragozza gate. Here the artisanal companies and the civic magistrates halted, while the spiritual companies continued up the Guardia hill, accompanied by thousands of Bolognese, returning the Madonna to her home. The Observant Franciscans joined this latter stage of the procession and sang a mass as the image was once again installed in the shrine.[11]

Albergati and the confratelli soon seized on the opportunity to turn the Madonna of the Guardia shrine into the center of an active local cult closely associated with the Company of S. Maria della Morte. The bishop ordered that the procession become an annual event, spanning three days during which the image would visit different churches in the city. The devotees' early debt to the Madonna dell'Impruneta is everywhere evident, from the stages of the procession, to its route through the different quarters, to its stay in the central civic space, the Piazza Maggiore in front of the Basilica of S. Petronio. Even the holy legend that the twelfth-century image was from the hand of St. Luke and had been brought from Constantinople by a devout pilgrim, may have been inspired by the Impruneta legend, though at the time all Italy seemed awash in icons credited to St. Luke.[12] Promoted in a small history written by Graziolo Accarisi around 1459 and 1460 when the image participated in visits by Pope Pius II, the legend took hold and the Madonna del Monte della Guardia soon became known as the Madonna di San Luca.[13]

For all their initial debt to Florentine and other contemporary models, the Bolognese soon devised new public rituals reflecting local priorities. Chief among these was the relatively greater role played by laymen. The prior of S. Maria della Morte continued organizing the procession, in which confratelli rather than clerics played the leading role. Since the original miracle had saved the crops in 1433, it became a Rogation procession taking place over the three days preceeding Ascension Day; this undoubtedly also allowed for participation by the

[11] Bursellis, *Cronaca gestorum*, *RIS*, vol. 23, Pt. II, p. 81 (ll. 19–22). Varignana (Cronaca B), *RIS*, vol. 23, Pt. I, vol. iv, p. 64. BBA ms. B502, p. 64. Fanti, "Madonna di San Luca," pp. 184–5.

[12] A. Cavallaro, "Antoniazzo Romano e le confraternite del Quattrocento a Roma," *RSRR*, 5 (1984), pp. 344–6. See also: Trexler, *Public Life*, pp. 63; 354–61.

[13] The attribution to St. Luke gained greater credibility and currency when perpetuated by the prominent sixteenth-century local historian Leandro Alberti in his *L'historia della Madonna di San Luca*, (Bologna: 1539).

Compagnia dell'Ascensione di Nostro Signore, though surviving records mention only S. Maria della Morte. On Saturday evening fratelli brought the Madonna to the church of S. Mattia, placing it on the altar. The next morning they began the series of processions, carrying the image through the city while preceded by the artisanal companies and Bologna's regular and secular clergy. Each night the Madonna rested in the chapel of the S. Maria della Morte ospedale, and each morning the fratelli once more took her in procession through the churches. The final circuit took place on Wednesday morning; the Madonna then rested briefly in the ospedale church before crossing to the Piazza Maggiore in the afternoon, and returning to S. Mattia in the evening. The next morning, Ascension Day, the fratelli climbed the steep Guardia Hill and brought the Madonna home. There they locked it behind an iron grate whose three keys were held by three chief agents of the civic-religious cult: the Convent of S. Maria del Monte representing religious orders, the Anziani representing the civic government, and S. Maria della Morte representing the Spiritual Companies of Bologna.[14]

The prominence given the confratelli of S. Maria della Morte and their church infuriated the cathedral canons of S. Pietro, who believed that they should organize and take pride of place in the procession, just as the high clergy did in Florence. Bishop Albergati consistently upheld the privileges of the confraternity, and when he died in May 1443 the confraternity turned to the papal governor for confirmation of the privilege; the canons repeated their challenges well into the sixteenth century, but never successfully.[15] Bologna's frequently tense relationship with the papacy may have been one reason why the annual procession remained so determinedly a lay affair. The priorship of S. Maria della Morte became one of the principal civic religious offices in the city, rotated annually among members of the patriciate. The company maintained custodial responsibility for the Guardia shrine and later rebuilt it. It also outfitted the image with an elaborate baldachino to shelter it during processions; a generous subsidy from the communal government subsidized costs of the annual procession. From 1436 the Madonna di S. Luca processions no longer followed a

---

[14] Varignana [Cronaca B], *RIS*, vol. 23, Pt. I, vol. iv , p. 64. Fanti, "Madonna di San Luca," p. 191. E. Gottarelli, *I Viaggi della Madonna di San Luca*, (Bologna: 1976), pp. 14; 19; Fanti, "Madonna di San Luca," p. 191.

[15] Popes Clement VII, Pius IV, Pius V, and Gregory XIII all confirmed the privileges of the Company of S. Maria della Morte. The cathedral canons' long fight won them an honorable position nonetheless, stationed immediately before and after the image in the annual procession. Gottarelli, *I Viaggi*, pp. 19–21.

circuit through the whole city, but visited the quarters of Porta Stiera, Procola, Ravennate, and Piera in a four-year rotation. And while the annual processions visited all the chief churches of a quarter, periodic crisis processions seeking the virgin's intercession in times of flood, drought, plague, or war, made a direct line for the civic basilica of S. Petronio where the image remained fixed for the full three-day cycle.[16] The strong civic connections were later exploited by Julius II, who ordered a procession commemorating his second victory over the Bentivoglio in 1512. The occasion was ostensibly an opportunity to show the image to the Imperial ambassador, but marked the first time the Madonna was moved from her shrine for reasons unrelated to civic crises. A few years later Leo X ordered a procession celebrating his elevation to the Papacy.[17] Both popes were seeking to bolster their seizure of power by appropriating the symbols of Bologna's civic cult; the existence of both the cult itself and its characteristic symbols owes much to Albergati's program of devotional reform channelled through lay confraternities.

S. Maria della Morte's hotly defended proprietorship over the Madonna di San Luca exemplifies one aspect of Quattrocento confraternal development, that of the accumulating processions and shrines which defined the local civic religious cult. This same confraternity also exemplified the tensions which could result when administering the public cult came in conflict with another aspect of confraternal development, that of devotional reform on the Observant model. Such tensions were ripe among the roughly twenty confraternities which could trace their roots to the thirteenth or fourteenth centuries. Some had developed significant institutional obligations over the years in the form of hostels or infirmaries which expressed the popolo consensus that spiritual companies must express their devotion through charitable service to the commune. To this could now be added the notion that spiritual companies must also play a significant role in the ceremonies and shrines of the civic religious cult. The press of administrative responsibilities could play havoc with any kind of devotional activity,

---

[16] Special processions were held on occasions of: flood (1454; 1474; 1477); drought (1434; 1540); plague (1438; 1444; 1449; 1459; 1576); war (1443; 1456; 1471; 1510; 1518); earthquakes (1457; 1466; 1505); famine (1504). Extraordinary processions generally declined over the decades: 1430s (4); 1440s (3); 1450s (5); 1460s (2); 1470s (3); 1480s (0); 1490s (0); 1500s (2); 1510s (4); 1520–90s (2). G.M. Moretti, "Raccolta di tutte le volte nelle quali la divota e miracolosissima Imagine della B.V. dipinta da S. Luca è stato portato in Bologna . . ." BBA Osp mss. #61; #62. BBA ms. B502, cc. 64ff.

[17] BBA Osp #61 c.101; 104; #62 c.1.

and particularly with the intense emphasis on daily offices, weekly mass, quarterly communion, and periodic flagellation that marked the more intense lay followers of Observant spirituality. As these two sides took shape in the early decades of the Quattrocento, some of the older confraternities seemed poised on the verge of breaking up.

S. Maria della Morte demonstrated both the problem and its solution. As seen earlier, from the time of its founding in 1336 members had fed and clothed the inmates of Bologna's prisons, and had comforted and buried those condemned to death. Its infirmary had become so busy that larger quarters were built in the city center in 1427. From 1433, it took over responsibility for the shrine and processions of the Madonna di San Luca. The pressure of increasing members, receipts, and administrative responsibilities added to the functional side of the company's activities and overwhelmed its devotional life. Some members were undisturbed by the imbalance, but others argued that spiritual exercises had to be at the core of a spiritual company's activities; this latter group had been bolstered by S. Maria della Morte's merger with the flagellant confraternity of S. Maria di Valverde in 1421. The only solution short of schism was some internal differentiation of functions. In 1436 the lay brothers separated the administrative from the devotional functions of the company; administration became the province of a group known as the Compagnia dell'Ospedale, or Compagnia Larga, while a stricter devotional regimen including flagellation was practiced by the Compagnia dell'Oratorio, or Compagnia Stretta. Both were equally part of the single Compagnia di S. Maria della Morte, and while members of the Stretta were free to take on administrative duties within the Larga, their own stricter devotional community was protected by provisions requiring members of the Larga to go through scrutiny and a novitiate before joining the Stretta. The solution, like the problem, was clearly patterned on the constitutional divisions between Conventuals and Observants within the mendicant orders. In its outworking over the succeeding decades, it provided a framework which allowed the lay brothers to work together far more amicably than their clerical mentors.

Albergati's part in negotiating this settlement is not clear. What is clear is his determination to introduce it to other Bolognese confraternities which were divided over the issue of charitable administration and devotional life. In 1439 he imposed it on the relatively new Company of S. Maria del Baraccano noted at the beginning of this chapter. The reform was carried in the face of considerable opposition from some of the high-born confratelli and included the charitable work of the confraternity as well. Like its counterpart in S. Maria della

Morte, the new flagellant cell called itself the Company or Congregation of the Oratory. The group's statutes put the distinction in terms drawn from contemporary humanism: "*la lore vita fondarono in essi da vita activa a pervenire a vita contemplativa.*"[18] Splitting the active life of administering a public shrine from the contemplative life of devotional exercises split the Trecento consensus that piety be expressed through charity and charity be expressed through institutions serving the urban community; only keeping both emphases under the umbrella of a single confraternity preserved this consensus. At the same time, the turn to the *vita contemplativa* was consistent with the more direct, interior, and meditative spirituality of the Observant reform, and stretta groups characteristically turned their charity inward, with individual acts of mercy towards brothers taking the place of institutional responses to social need. Institutions not only diverted groups from their devotion, but could also lead them into temptation. As stretta members of S. Maria del Baraccano abandoned the *vita activa* of the busy public shrine, their larga counterparts were being accused of mismanaging the shrine's oblations. Albergati ordered them to put the money to better use by opening a hostel for pilgrims, a reform they undertook with the advice of two leading hostel confraternities in Bologna, S. Francesco and S. Maria dei Servi.

In the space of little more than a decade, four other Bolognese confraternities experienced the movement to Observant or stretta devotional reform, including that of S. Francesco just noted. When a group of stretta established themselves within the Compagnia di S. Francesco in 1443, their statutes specifically noted both their determination to "separate ourselves from worldly things" ("*separarci da le cosse mondane*"), and the inspiration they had received from Bishop Albergati. One year later Dominican friars rewrote the statutes of the Compagnia di S. Domenico, hoping to infuse their lay brothers with some of the devotion they themselves had learned upon turning to stricter Observance in 1426. Finally in 1454, two major companies, S. Maria della Vita and S. Maria dei Guarini, joined the movement with quite similar sets of devotional exercises enshrined in new stretta statutes.[19] Almost seven decades passed before a new wave of stretta groups emerged in Bologna's confraternities. In general stretta companies were created by those who desired a communal setting for more inten-

---

[18] BBA Osp. ms. 83, c. 1r. De Töth, *Nicolò Albergati*, vol. 1, p. 283 n.1.

[19] S. Francesco: BBA B983, cc. 55r, 57v. S. Domenico: Meersseman, *Ordo Fraternitatis*, pp. 614–15; Meersseman reprints the reformed statutes on pp. 669–89. S. Maria della Vita: Angelozzi, *Confraternite laicali*, pp. 118–41. S. Maria dei Guarini: BBA Gozz 210 #11, cc. 169r–194v.

sely practiced spiritual exercises, more frequent worship and sacraments, and a more closely regulated moral life. This necessitated a second break with the Trecento consensus: the earlier praising confraternities had been inclusive, bringing men and women, adults and children into what were seen as the communal spiritual companies of artisanal society. The Observant stretta companies introduced an exclusivity policed through scrutinies and novitiates which would over the next century marginalize or exclude first women and children, and eventually artisanal men as well.

However in the short term this method of distinguishing stretta from larga groups effectively avoided schisms within the Bolognese confraternities. The one exception had little to do with devotional issues, and it affected the confraternity which had been most closely associated with Nicolò Albergati. Perhaps in part because of the success which the Compagnia di S. Girolamo enjoyed under Albergati's patronage, members of this youths' confraternity were unwilling to leave it at age 18 as the statutes required. As both groups considered themselves equally devout, Albergati in 1438 fashioned a generational split between *Minori* and *Maggiori*, retaining both under the umbrella of the single confraternity. Tensions continued, in part due to the Maggiori's determination to rule over the Minori, and their refusal to allow "graduating" members of the Minori to join their ranks automatically. A papal brief of April 1441, and an ecclesiastical commission in June of that year, upheld the rights of the Minori and established that their officials were to be appointed not by the Maggiori, but by a panel made up of Abbots of S. Procolo and S. Salvatore, the Prior of S. Domenico, and the Warden of the Observant Franciscans of the Monte dell'Osservanza. The Maggiori ignored both rulings. They justified their intransigence by citing an order of the Sedici Riformatori which prohibited Bolognese from obeying the rulings of Papal tribunals, and successfully appealed to the Sedici for confirmation of their stand. The case carried on regardless with the Minori pursuing it through ecclesiastical courts more sympathetic to their cause, and the Maggiori countering in the civic courts which, in the early 1440s, were set against any papal judicial interference in the city. A year after Albergati's death in 1443, the groups finally divided into two separate confraternities.[20] It was the only schism among Bolognese confraternities in the fifteenth century

---

[20] Summaries of the transactions are found in: BBA Fondo Malvezzi, Cartono 198, #5. ASB Dem, Compagnia di SS. Girolamo ed Anna, busta 1/6716 filza 1. See also A.A. Macchiavelli, *Origine, Fondazione, e progressi della veneranda Compagnia laicale sotto l'invocazione de gloriosi santi Girolamo ed Anna posta nella via di Bagnomarino di questa città di Bologna* (Bologna: 1754).

and the tensions reverberated for years. The youth group retained the original oratory, the confraternity's name, and the unofficial tag of "minori" or "giovani"; their elders went by the title of "I Maggiori di SS. Girolamo ed Anna," adding the title of the convent which the company had bought in 1438 and which had become the elders' home after the schism. At the same time, the two apparently cooperated in staging the *sacre rappresentazione* that explained the mysteries of the faith to Bolognese commoners. A reunion of the two groups was always in the air, and one was actually negotiated by the Vicar General in 1499, but ultimately it came to nothing.

Nicolò Albergati's reform program brought together in confraternities the two elements which we saw in Bologna's religious response to the threat posed by Giangaleazzo Visconti: the mendicant spirituality long common among confraternities and highlighted in penitential movements like the Bianchi, and the public symbols and shrines of a deliberately constructed civic cult which had been taking shape together with the bascilica of San Petronio from the 1390s. Both new and newly reformed confraternities shared these characteristics. It would be easy to exaggerate Albergati's impact on shaping Bologna's religious life in the early Quattrocento, or to reduce him to being a symbol of the age or an ideal type of its few reforming clerics. In fact he was frequently away from Bologna on legatine missions to France, Lombardy, and the Council of Basel; he died in Siena and was buried in Florence. More to the point, his episcopate spanned a period when Bologna's relations with the papacy were particularly strained. Both Martin V and Eugenius IV were determined to restore effective rule over the papacy's Italian territories, and while Bologna was equally determined to maintain its autonomy, patrician factionalism repeatedly delivered it into the hands of its enemies. Martin V granted local control over finances, judicial appointments, and the election of officials in 1419, but when the Bolognese pressed for more the following year, he used an interdict and force of arms to rescind the concessions and impose direct rule. Patricians at the time divided into the three factions of the Canetoli, Zambeccari, and Bentivoglio, and this facilitated papal rule until Legate Louis Aleman abandoned the practice of setting the factions against each other and tried instead to work with the Canetoli and Zambeccari, while keeping Antongaleazzo Bentivoglio occupied in papal service as the Count of Campania. In August 1428 the Canetoli launched a rebellion, seizing the Legate, sacking his palace, and reappointing the Sedici Riformatori; Nicolò Albergati was forced to flee the city disguised as a monk. While Martin V retaliated with an interdict and a seige, the new government adopted the signs and symbols of the popular commune. The brave face could not conceal the fact that Bologna's famous university had almost ceased to function, its water supply had ceased to flow, and its fields and hills had become locked behind beseiging troops who had overrun even the shrine of the Madonna della Monte. The recently enlarged Piazza del Commune was the scene not only of brave-face *palios*, but also of the beheading and hanging of traitors who had betrayed the shrine and were ready to open the city gates. After a year of rebellion, the city capitulated only to discover that it had lost the war and won the peace. Not wanting to incur again the ruinous cost of a seige, Martin V in August 1429 signed a treaty which left the rebels unpunished, the Sedici in office, the Bentivoglio in exile, and the Papal Legate in limbo. With victory over the papacy secure, the Bolognese fell once more into fighting among themselves. In February 1430 ten patrician exiles returned, but by April there were fears of a uprising in the works. Niccolò Ariosti rose in the Council of 600 to denounce Egano Lambertini, Nicolò Malvezzi, Bagarotto Bianchi, Filippo dalle Anelle, and Tommaso Montecalvi; over their protests of innocence, they were hustled from the chamber and immediately murdered. Fear once more gripped the city, muting all but a few objections; only Alberto Caccianemici, his brother Giacomo, and Antonio detto Negro protested the summary executions, and within a week they were beheaded on charges of treason. The Papal Legate fled the city and war resumed. Martin V's death in February 1431 provided a pretext for peace negotiations which culminated in a new treaty signed by Eugenius IV in April. Eugenius' confirmation of the powers of the Sedici in 1433 did not ease the tensions, and by the end of the year the Canetoli had once more launched a rebellion. Antongaleazzo Bentivoglio entered papal service and was rewarded with permission to return to the city after the rebellion sputtered out. His return in triumph on December 4, and the enthusiastic reception he received, made the Papal Governor Daniele Scotti distinctly uneasy; Antongaleazzo was dead before Christmas, beheaded by papal guards as he was leaving the Communal Palace where he had celebrated mass at Scotti's invitation. On the same day, Tommasso Zambeccari was seized and hanged from the windows of the Podestà's Palace.

The murder of two faction leaders set the Bolognese ever more firmly against Papal rule, and the itinerant Eugenius IV could remain there from April 1436 to January 1438 only by virtue of his armed guards. Upon his departure for the Council of Ferrara-Florence, the Bentivoglio faction negotiated with the Duke of Milan and then opened the city gates to his condottiere Niccolò Piccinino. This paved the way for the return of twenty-five year old Annibale Bentivoglio, Antongaleazzo's eldest son who had been fighting as a mercenary in Naples. Sensing their own security under Milan's protection of Annibale, the Bolognese began granting the young Bentivoglio tax concessions and membership in the city's chief magistracies and councils. He in turn betrothed Donnina Visconti, kinswoman of Milanese Duke Filippo Maria Visconti, and prepared to assume signory over the city. Peninsular politics had brought events to this pass, and now intervened to change the situation drastically. Visconti's protection of Bologna was strategic in light of his struggle against Venice, Florence, and the Papacy; with the Peace of Cavriana in December 1441, the Duke of Milan abandonned Bologna and pledged to help the Papacy recover the city. The condottiere Niccolò Piccinino had ambitions of his own, and in March 1442 he returned to the city to claim it for the papacy and, he hoped, for his own. Bologna's helplessness before these larger powers was underscored when Piccinino lured Annibale out of the city and imprisoned him in a Parmese castle. The arrival of Piccinino's son Francesco as signore stirred Galeazzo Marescotti and other members of the Bentivoglio faction to stage a daring jail break. Under cover of darkness on June 5, Annibale was pulled by ropes over the city wall at the shrine of S. Maria del Baraccano, ironically confirming his grandfather's fears that this was a strategic weak spot in the city's defenses. More to the point, it was a deliberate act calculated to invoke the protection of the Madonna del Baraccano, and to underscore the close identification of the shrine with the Bentivoglio which had grown since Giovanni I had turned from walling it up to expanding its quarters. Annibale's dramatic return was the signal for an uprising that threw out Piccinino. It also threw Bologna into war with both Milan and the Papacy. Annibale immediately set to work building bridges outside and inside the city, negotiating an alliance with Florence and Venice, and insisting that his old enemies the Canetoli be brought into government and that other exiles be allowed to return. A united commune defeated the armies of the Papacy and Milan in a bloody battle on August 14 before once again turning on itself. Annibale tried to bind the factions together through kinship ties, arranging his sister's marriage to Giacomo Canetoli and standing as godfather to the son of the prominent *Canetolisto* Francesco Ghisilieri. Returning with Ghisilieri from the baptism on June 24, 1445, Annibale was set upon by Baldassare Canetoli and murdered; the assassins also murdered three of the four Marescotti brothers, narrowly missing Galeazzo. The Anziani and Gonfaloniere di Giustizia initially fled before the well-organized conspiracy, but they and the *Bentivoleschi* were rallied by Galeazzo Marescotti to resist. A pitched battle raged through the city's streets, but by nightfall the Canetoli had fled. Forays by Milanese and Papal troops over the next two years were repulsed with the help of Florence and Venice, and in the absence of a local Bentivoglio willing to hazard the signory, the faction reached to Florence for Annibale's cousin, Sante. After some hesitation, the twenty-three year old Sante arrived in Bologna in November 1446; he would prove to be the only one of the five Bentivoglio who ruled the city in some form or other through the Quattrocento to die a natural death in his own bed in Bologna. Sante's relations with Cosimo de'Medici cemented the Florentine alliance. His good fortune in the election of Albergati's long-time secretary Tommaso Parentucelli as Pope Nicholas V secured a Concordat with the papacy in 1447. His marriage to Ginevra Sforza sealed the peace with Milan in 1454. The Canetoli, Ghisilieri, Pepoli, Fantuzzi, Zambeccari, and Vizzani were less easy to subdue. In 1448, Baldassare Canetoli was beheaded on the spot where he had assassinated Annibale, and three years later Francesco Ghisilieri was hanged in the ruins of his destroyed palace. His execution followed by a few days the defeat of the last major assault on the city by the anti-Bentivoglio factions. The Peace of Lodi in 1454 robbed these factions of their necessary outside support, and a relative calm settled over Bologna for the next three decades.

This brief account of Bologna's politics from the 1420s through the early 1450s underscores the difficulties facing Nicolò Albergati as he sought a hearing for his program of religious reform. Yet Albergati's twenty-year reign was a period of ecclesiastical stability in between periods when foreign and non-resident bishops served short episcopates. He pursued an active program of devotional reform which gained credibility from his undoubted personal piety. He heard appeals, like those of the Minori of S. Girolamo, even when papal business took him away from the city. And he was well served by his Vicars, particularly Tomasso Parentucelli, who was Albergati's secretary, confidant, and companion for the last twenty years of his life, and who succeeded him as Bishop of Bologna (1444–47). When Parentucelli was raised to the papacy he took the name Nicholas V in honor of his long-time patron and friend. The city's revolt against the papacy prevented Parentucelli from taking possession of the see in 1444, but his mentor had schooled him in Bolognese ambitions, sympathies, and factions, and it is a testament to the understanding he had gained that within six months of his election to the papacy in March 1447 he had negotiated the Concordat which fixed Bologna's constitutional relationship to the papacy on peaceful terms for the next five decades. The Concordat gave significant autonomy to the city, establishing the Sedici Riformatori and the Papal Legate as partners whose specific mandates were balanced with mutual consultation and oversight. Nicholas V subsequently appointed as Legate Cardinal Bessarion, a widely popular and influential governor who ruled more firmly than many of his successors, but who also acknowledged local sensitivies; significantly, Bessarion devoted special efforts to improving and decorating the shrines of Madonna del Monte and the Madonna di Guardia which had suffered damage during the seiges of the 1420s and 1430s and the battles of the 1440s.

The work of Albergati, mendicant preachers, and high clergy like Parentucelli and Bessarion indicates that clerics were playing a greater role in confraternal affairs than they had in the thirteenth and fourteenth centuries. Clergy were often the exemplars and sometimes the agents of reform. Yet, as later chapters will argue, this did not mean that lay people were passive receptors of clerical initiatives. There are ample signs that fifteenth-century confratelli could direct clerical help in ways which maintained their relative autonomy. Reforms were frequently consultative or self-generated efforts. Moreover, Albergati's influence over the confraternities derived not simply from his ecclesiastical dignity and strategic program. Before all else, he was a Bolognese citizen and a member of a family long prominent in the city. The clear parallel is to S. Antoninus (1389–1459), a Florentine of a generation younger than Albergati, who undoubtedly met the Cardinal when the two participated in the Council of Florence (1438–39). Antonio Pierozzi joined the Observant Dominicans in 1405, established the monastery of S. Marco under Cosimo de'Medici's patronage in 1436, and pursued a reform program similar to Albergati's when appointed Archbishop of Florence in 1446. Like Albergati, Antoninus emphasized visitations, preaching, and an interior piety expressed in charity and frequent sacramental observance, and like him he drew heavily on lay confraternities in order to advance his reform program. Moreover, Antoninus's pastoral work was interrupted by frequent absences on ambassadorial missions for the Florentine republic. Yet his influence among the common lay people of Florence was profound, earning him the affectionate diminutive "Antonino" and canonization in 1523. Albergati for his part became "il Beato Nicolò"; Bologna would not see another of its citizens pursuing so active a reform program from the episcopal throne until the coming of Gabriele Paleotti in 1565.

What clerics like Albergati and Antoninus provided was an expanded vocabulary of religious symbols and ceremonies through which the city could approach God and the saints to express penitence, plead for mercy, or celebrate victories. The symbols and ceremonies were not new, but their local expression was, and their concentration in the hands of lay confraternities was critical for the development and future politicization of the civic religious cult. There was some irony in the fact that Spiritual Companies could more dramatically express their traditional claim to be third pillars of popolo government against a background of patrician factional fighting and anti-papal uprisings that reduced the ideal of popolo government to pious rhetoric, and that they could do so thanks to the innovations of a patrician cleric closely identified with the papacy. This underscores the gap between the cherished ideal of popolo government supported by Artisanal, Militia, and Spiritual companies – what we could for lack of a better term describe as the "Myth of Bologna" similar to the "Myth of Venice" or the "Myth of Florence" – and the reality of an ungovernable city heading into authoritarianism. Such gaps are in the nature of civic religion, in the fifteenth as much as in the twentieth centuries, and underscore its critical legitimating role in political rhetoric. Two events in the crisis summer of 1443 illustrate how naturally the Bolognese integrated the new symbolic vocabulary of processions and ceremonies into their petitions and celebrations. Albergati died in May, Annibale Bentivoglio escaped prison and returned to Bologna in June, a league with Florence and Venice was crafted in July, and war broke out in August. As the prospect of war with the papacy loomed, the lay brothers of S. Maria della Morte headed up the Guardia hill to get the icon of the Madonna di San Luca and bring it in procession through the city and for a three-day stay in the civic basilica of S. Petronio. Extraordinary processions had been mounted in time of plague or drought, but this was the first time the Madonna's protection had been sought from acts of Man rather than acts of God. Since the man in this case was the pope, the procession demonstrated the degree to which the Bolognese now saw the shrine and its ceremonies as their own, and not simply as soon-to-be-forgotten rituals imposed by a deceased bishop whose service to the pope had occasioned some grumbling. The Madonna upheld Bologna's trust by granting a decisive victory on August 14, and the city responded in the terms of its new civic-religious vocabulary. The Anziani ordered a procession of all the rulers, guilds, confraternities, and clerics up to the shrine of the Madonna del Monte to offer thanks for Bologna's victory over the papacy; more significantly, they further ordered that this procession become an annual commemoration of the great victory granted by the Virgin to her favoured city of Bologna.[21] Insofar as the action was not taken at the prompting of some cleric, but occured at civic initiative at a time when there was no papal governor and for all intents and purposes no bishop, the Anziani decree is a clear lay appropriation of the civic-religious symbols and ceremonies initiated locally by Nicolò Albergati. Over the following decades, and into the sixteenth century, that civic-religious self-confidence would become the animating spirit behind an expansion of confraternities' social and political role, and the pretext for a progressive ennobling of their membership.

That slow development will be examined through the chapters that follow. On the surface and for the balance of the Quattrocento, confraternities' public role in the civic cult and their private devotions in their own oratories followed the lines established by the time of Albergati's death. The confraternal hostels of S. Francesco, S. Biagio, and S. Maria dei Guarini sheltered the lay pilgrims moving north and south through the Apennine passes. The infirmaries of S. Maria della Vita and S. Maria della Morte tended the sick of the city. The lay brothers of SS. Girolamo ed Anna instructed the public on feast days with *sacre rappresentazione* that put Bologna's sins before an angry Christ and recruited the saints as advocates of the penitent city. The Trentatre led the penitent in imitation of Christ bearing his cross up the Guardia hill; the Compagnia della Morte led them down again behind the image of the Virgin and Child. Confraternal processions frequently blocked the streets as spiritual companies celebrated their saints' days, buried their dead, summoned the Bolognese to shrines, or led them in repentance. Hundreds of men, women, and children still gathered regularly in the main mendicant churches where the sounds of their lauds would echo out onto the streets. Smaller numbers of flagellants would gather more frequently in their oratories to live out their goals of being an intense devout brotherhood like that of Christ's disciples or the early church. In short, confraternities wove their public and private devotions thoroughly into the fabric of Bologna's daily life, and were inevitably central players in the city's cultic life. Yet as the devotional reforms inspired by Albergati took firmer root and as the political potential of the civic cult became more apparent to the Bentivoglio and their successors, confraternal public life and private devotions changed. The final chapter of this study will return to confraternities' expanding role in civic-religious life and social welfare; it is time now to turn inside the Compagnie Spirituali in order to examine the evolution of their devotions, membership, administration, and finances.

[21] Bursellis, *Cronaca gestorum*, RIS, vol. 23, Pt. II, pp. 84 (28–42), 85 (4–6).

2

LAY SPIRITUALITY AND
CONFRATERNAL WORSHIP

Confratelli praying in their homes, flagellating in their oratories, and bearing a dead brother to the grave were living out a chosen rule for their individual and communal spiritual life. Their choice of confraternity would be dictated in part by the attraction of the rule and its exercises. Considering the number, variety, membership, and activities of lay confraternities, they are indispensable guides for investigating popular piety. In particular, confraternal religious life sheds light on Renaissance lay spirituality or popular piety, and on the question of whether lay religious beliefs and worship patterns are properly characterized as "lay" or "popular" when in many cases they are handed down from religious or secular authorities through sermons, books, and statutes. This chapter will first briefly review the administrative and spiritual relations between confraternities and mendicant orders to see how religious orders differed in their relations with confraternities, and what the consequences of this were for individual confratelli as they fashioned their religious life. This will set the context for examining two dimensions of confraternal spirituality: collective worship and private devotion. Lay confratelli collectively worshipped in their oratories, both with sacraments mediated by hired clergy, and with purely lay rituals. They also developed exercises leading them into the more intense and private spirituality of the regular clergy. Both the collective and individual dimensions of confraternal worship came together in what will be the fourth focus of this chapter, the rituals surrounding illness and death. These rituals will be examined in their application to an individual confratello, the notary Eliseo Mamelini, in order to illustrate first how they were set out abstractly in confraternal statutes, and second how they were integrated with the rituals and expectations of the networks of professional, guild, kinship, and mendicant connections which defined an individual's social life. The negotiation of confraternal with other networks confirms that the clerical models and lay character of confraternal spirituality were not in opposition or competition, but were equal and continuous parts of a single conception of the brotherhood of Christ's followers.

Eliseo Mamelini's example further demonstrates that while confraternities may be indispensable guides to lay piety, they do not in themselves exhaust it. He also demonstrates through his membership in at least six confraternities the paradox which lay at the core of fifteenth-century devotional reforms. Artisans willingly embraced the Observant message of spiritual equality and adopted flagellation, more frequent and more intense private and collective devotions, and the division of longstanding communal Compagnie Spirituali into stretta and larga cells. Yet in so doing, they abetted that politicization of the confraternities which would eventually see control of their brotherhoods shift into the hands of the patriciate. As later chapters will clarify, while devotional reforms were not an elite imposition, they indirectly led to elite control of the Compagnie Spirituali which had been symbols of popolo civic religion.

I. CONFRATERNAL AND MENDICANT BROTHERHOOD

The next two chapters will examine confraternal spiritual exercises and membership procedures in detail, but even the briefest review demonstrates how closely lay brotherhoods modelled themselves on the mendicant orders. Throughout our period, the confraternal spiritual ethos was one of regulated private and communal worship modelled closely on the mendicant example and oriented to countering the temptations of the world and structuring a life characterized by inward meditation and outward charity. Confraternal statutes laid out a rhythm of private prayer and mental confession aimed at sanctifying the day and protecting the confratello from evil; these were sometimes modified according to members' education, station, and literacy. In weekly services together, members heard divine office, and engaged in mutual confession of their violations of the brotherhood's statutes. On a monthly or quarterly basis, they made confession to the company priest and received communion from him. At key points in the liturgical calendar, they offered services in memory of dead brothers, and performed acts of charity in the broader community. As we have already seen, the liturgy which structured confraternal spirituality and the exercises that articulated it drew heavily from contemporary devotional movements. Across Europe, movements like the northern devotio moderna, the continental cult of St. Jerome, and the Observance movements shared common sources from the patristic and mendicant tradition, a common discontent with the state of the church, and a common desire to be near to God.

Coming nearer to God was work for which the soul must be trained. The deliberately fashioned courses of meditation and prayer calculated to bring about conversion to a life fully directed to the service of God, are usually identifed with Observance movements or with quasi-clerical groups like the northern Brethren of the Common Life. But such exercises were never limited to clergy. Exercises exemplifying vocal and mental prayer, self-control, and imitation of Christ figured strongly in mendicant preaching and contemporary spiritual literature, and appear with increasing frequency in lay confraternal statutes through the fifteenth and early sixteenth centuries. Any religious reform directed by and at the regular clergy inevitably touched the laity gathering in confraternities. The reform was a reaction against phenomena and events affecting clergy and laity alike. The Babylonian Captivity and Great Schism had undermined the institutional church; Christians looked for recovery of a simple relation of love to God and neighbor. And if clerical immorality, ignorance, and laxness were roundly condemned in the late fourteenth and early fifteenth centuries, laymen were also willing to blame the deplorable state of Christendom on their own sins and look for mercy through penitential exercises or in devotional processions like those of the Bianchi.

Beyond the exercises, confraternal membership procedures sought to incorporate the advantages of communal life for those who could not or would not take monastic vows. Mutual support and mutual discipline could be had without these vows, but only if members voluntarily policed themselves quite strictly. A later chapter will consider membership procedures in greater detail, but a brief review demonstrates how self-consciously they followed the mendicant example, particularly among penitential confraternities. Those seeking admission had to win nomination, pass an examination of their morals and spiritual condition, and gain the support of a majority of existing members. This allowed them to enter a novitiate in the confraternity lasting from six to twelve months, after which the whole procedure was repeated. The novitiate allowed both sides to test mutual compatibility, and was far from being a formality; in one fifteenth-century Bolognese confraternity fewer – often considerably fewer – than 50% of novices applied for full membership. Those who did and were accepted by the confraternity, swore an oath to obey the statutes and the *padre ordinario*, the chief elected official whom one historian has described as "a kind of

lay abbot ... [with] near-omnipotence in both administrative and spiritual matters."[1] Members who repeatedly ignored the statutes and officials were warned privately, then publicly, and, if obstinate, were
finally expelled from the brotherhood. As we will see later, extant Bolognese matriculation lists show expulsion rates of between 2.5% and
50% in the fifteenth century.

Given this close and deliberate modelling on mendicant spirituality
and communal life, any attempt to distinguish lay from clerical piety
qualitatively must assume a gap which fifteenth-century confratelli did
not recognize. Exercises regulating lay and clerical spirituality may
have varied, but all were expressions of a collective mentality, stages in
a continuum of exercises and rules which varied in intensity, but
which were all directed to the single religious end of salvation. Within
individual confraternities the literate and illiterate were prescribed different religious exercises according to their abilities. Exercises might
vary between confraternities depending on the guidance individual
groups took from different preachers, priests, or spiritual writings.
Further differences distinguished the exercises of the lay confraternities
from those of the religious orders on which they were modelled. All of
these differences reflected the accepted social, educational, and vocational distinctions within a single Christian tradition. Yet they were
differences of degree rather than kind. Contemporary religious
worship was expressed in rituals whose increasing repetition brought
increasing spiritual benefits; with some exceptions, lay rituals differed
only in number. The artisan *confratello* would have found incompre-
hensible the argument that he free himself from clerical or upper-class
models and worship according to his own cultural lights. He assumed
that however hierarchically mediated, neither *religio* nor *regula* was the
property of any segment of society; both were expressions of the
church to which all belonged regardless of condition. If he was de-
ceived in thinking this, it was a remarkably durable deception, extending to the early Christian era. This spiritual egalitarianism was the
meaning of the Pauline metaphor, repeated in many confraternal statutes, of the Church as a body of distinct but equal members united
under Christ's headship. It is also the message of the anti-hierarchical
popular devotional manuals such as *The Little Flowers of St. Francis*
found in many confraternal libraries; as J.J. Scarisbrick has noted, "The
saints inverted 'norms' as profoundly as did any charivari."[2] And it is
implicitly the message of confraternal reform. Flagellants explicitly

---

[1]   R. Hatfield, "The Compagnia de'Magi," *Journal of the Warburg and Courtauld Institutes*, vol. 33 (1970), p. 125.
[2]   J.J. Scarisbrick, *The Reformation and The English People*, (Oxford: 1984), p. 171.

adopted their head-to-toe robes in order to mask the social distinctions which clothes highlighted, and deliberately calculated their internal hierarchy by length of membership rather than social status. At the same time, however, fifteenth- and sixteenth-century reforms which increased the number and frequency of spiritual duties closely followed clerical example and often established *desideratae* which were beyond the means of poorer members. They were the work of clerics and lay committees of the more educated brothers and often reflected the fact that these members had more free time and discretionary income. While statistics on membership growth and retention show the reforms initially generated large numbers of new members from all classes, they also demonstrate increasing percentages of members from the upper guilds and the patriciate by the later fifteenth and sixteenth centuries.

The lay brothers' desire to imitate the spiritual exercises and disciplined community of the mendicants is at the heart of the dynamic between the two, and should cure us of any tendency to see confraternities as merely mutual aid societies offering death benefits to artisans. Yet, however strong the pull of mendicant spirituality, it was shaped by an opposite force. Confratelli did not want to become friars or even tertiaries: of the 416 children who became members of the company of S. Girolamo di Miramonte from the 1440s into the early sixteenth century, only 18 (or 4.3%) became friars.[3] For these laymen, the mendicant ethos was combined with a guild ethos which emphasized self-determination and civic solidarity. From the beginning, lay brothers seemed determined to regulate their own affairs, and apparently preferred to work with the mendicant orders which accommodated that. There was no single dynamic; different religious orders varied in their relations with confraternities, and different generations of confratelli varied in the closeness of their links to the mendicants. In general terms, the praising confraternities of laudesi were linked most closely to the Conventual mendicant houses while the flagellant battuti formed their ties with Observant groups. Beyond this, in Bologna the most amicable relations occurred with those orders which accommodated lay self-direction, and so reduced their expectations of what confraternities could do for the mendicant house. We can see this by briefly comparing the Dominicans, the Franciscans, and the Augustinians in their relations with confraternities. Of the three orders, the Dominicans typically maintained tighter control over their confrater-

---

[3] Of these, nine joined the Canons Regular of S. Salvatore, five the Dominicans, two the Franciscans, and one the Lateran Canons; one was unspecified. "Matricola di S. Girolamo di Miramonte," ASB Codici Miniati, ms. 65.

nities while the Augustinians and Franciscans more closely followed Nicolò Albergati's example and provided assistance and guidance without demanding obedience in return.

The Dominicans were the most active in establishing confraternities to serve particular ends. In 1451 they established the Compagnia della Croce, local lay auxilliaries to the Inquisition which they were then establishing across Italy.[4] The Crocesegnati were founded to meet the expenses of the Inquisitorial office which had previously been underwritten by the communal government. After four decades, this company attempted a union with the Compagnia di S. Domenico, a flagellant confraternity established by the Observant preacher Manfredo da Vercelli in 1418. The resulting fight demonstrates how firmly Bolognese confraternities wished to assert autonomy, and how firmly the Dominicans were determined to withhold it. The two companies had given considerable assistance to the Bolognese Dominicans at considerable expense to themselves, most notably in constructing two prisons (one for men and one for women) for the Inquisitor; they wished to unite in order to build new quarters that they could use at any time of day or night without disturbing the friars.[5] A preliminary agreement merging the two confraternities had been worked out by their members in 1485, and the confratelli demanded Dominican approval of the union as a condition for constructing an educational wing for the monastery. The wing was constructed between 1490 and 1493 and, believing they had kept their end of the bargain, the lay brothers proceeded with their union in 1494.[6] Both confraternities' statutes had emphasized obedience to the prior of San Domenico (in the case of the lay brothers of that name) or the Inquisitor (in the case of the Crocesegnati); the union document mentioned neither of these officials. The merger nonetheless had at least the tacit approval of the prior of the San Domenico friary and of the new Inquisitor Girolamo Borselli. Borselli was Bolognese, a celebrated preacher, a professor in the university, and a local chronicler. In 1493 he succeeded Vincenzo Bandelli, who the previous year had rewritten the Crocesegnati's statutes in order to emphasize their subordination to the friars. Yet for reasons that are unclear, he was replaced within the year. The lay

---

[4]   There is no archival evidence supporting L. Paolini's assertion that this is a continuation of a thirteenth-century confraternity. L. Paolini, "Le origini della 'Societas Crucis'," *Rivista di storia e letteratura religiosa*, vol. 15 (1979), pp. 179, 199–200.

[5]   ASB Dem, Compagnia di S. Domenico, busta 1/6415, filze 4, 6; busta 7/6421, filze 3, 5. Meersseman, *Ordo fraternitatis*, pp. 618–19.

[6]   The confratelli had already devised statutes for their company in 1492: ASB Dem, Compagnia dei Crocesegnati, busta 3/6669, filza 7.

brothers had seen three Inquisitors come and go since starting their merger talks ten years before, and so went ahead with the plan, hoping perhaps that the new Inquisitor might see things their way. Considering the work they had performed for the monastery, the frequent turnover of Inquisitors, and the replacement of the hostile Fra Vincenzo with the more sympathetic Fra Girolamo in 1493, the lay brothers very likely gambled that the Inquisitor would either capitulate, or be replaced with someone more sympathetic.[7] But there was to be no new Inquisitor for twenty years, and Borselli's successor Giovanni Cagnati was anything but sympathetic. The brunt of his disciplinary action fell on Andreas Allè, a longtime member of the Compagnia di S. Domenico who was promoted to Sindic when the two companies merged. While the confraternity ratified Allè's authority, the Inquisitor issued orders removing him from his post. When Allè refused the Inquisitor's demand that he resign, he was summoned before the curia in Rome; ignoring the summons earned him excommunication in November 1496. The curial court subsequently found in favor of the Inquisitor's assertion of authority and so cleared the way for reversing the merger in 1497.[8]

While this struggle was going on, the Dominicans were erecting another confraternity, this one dedicated to collecting alms for artisans and master craftsmen unaccustomed to begging (hence called "shameful poor"). Fra Antonio d'Olanda initiated the company in 1495, appointing its ten members, writing its statutes, and lodging it in rooms above the Compagnia della Croce's quarters within the monastery. In this case however, the highborn lay brothers soon escaped the authority of their mendicant overseers by moving into other quarters shared with another confraternity, and operating their charitable work as a loose extension of the civic government.[9] When the Dominicans next organized a confraternity, it was again the local manifestation of a devotion they were promoting across the peninsula; the Compagnia del Rosario arose before 1531 to promote use of the Rosary; the first reference to it is in the record of a Dominican, Fra Agostino, who had been elected confessor of another local confraternity and who at-

[7] "Catologus Inquisitorum Bononiensium ab anno 1273," BBA ms. B36 cc.166v–167r.

[8] The folio of records regarding the case is contained among the records of the company founded to succeed the Compagnia della Croce: ASB Dem, Compagnia dei Crocesegnati, busta 3/6669, filza H. See also: Meersseman, Ordo Fraternitatis, pp. 617–21.

[9] A review of the problems in dating both the group and its statutes is given in G. Ricci, "I primi statuti della compagnia bolognese dei poveri vergognosi," L'Archiginnasio, vol. 74 (1979), pp. 134–50.

tempted to have all its members join the new Compagnia del Rosario.[10]

The Augustinians and Franciscans had far more peaceful relations with their confraternities. The former gave shelter to two groups established in 1465 and 1495. The second of these was a large group formed in response to a series of Lenten sermons given at the Augustian church of S. Giacomo by the itinerant friar Martino Vercelle. The new company quickly enrolled 600 members, such an unusually high number for Bolognese confraternities that it came to be known as S. Maria dei Centurati. S. Giacomo was the church of the Bentivoglio, and Giovanni II and his wife Ginevra were the first members on the new company's matriculation list. Fashion and convention seem to have played a greater role than devotion in the Centurati's success, for in the cynical words of a contemporary Bentivoglio supporter, the charismatic Fra Martino "spoke and performed miracles, but yet he ate and drank like the others and was a great snare for cash." Apart from this, the Augustinians appear to have had very little to do with confraternities in the city.[11]

The Bolognese Franciscans adopted a position somewhere between the close supervison of the Dominicans and the laissez-faire of the Augustinians. Some independent confraternities preferred hiring a Franciscan when looking for a priest. This was the case with Buon Gesù which, after its reform by Bernardino da Siena, maintained friendly but informal relations with the Franciscans of L'Annunziata, the Observant house established outside the S. Mamolo gate in 1473. Both the laudesi and stretta Companies of S. Francesco had quarters in the Conventual church, though the latter went to the Observants when hiring a *Padre Spirituale*. This was not the only time local confratelli disregarded the strained relations between the two parties within the Franciscan order. When admirers of Bernardino da Siena wanted to erect a company dedicated to their late and recently canonized critic of Conventual laxness, they calmly met in the Conventual church where they planned and, in 1453, built a large chapel. They were aided by Cardinal Bessarion, papal legate in Bologna from 1450

---

[10] Fanti, "Santa Maria dei Guarini," pp. 338, 449 n.41.

[11] In 1465 the Augustinians conceded a former hospice to a confraternity which took the name of S. Maria Coronata; this confraternity soon moved into a separate oratory which it had built on land at the eastern city wall granted to it by the communal government. G. Guidicini, *Cose Notabili della città di Bologna*, (Bologna: 1868–73), vol. II, p. 235; III, p. 343; *Miscellanea*, pp. 363–4. Fra Martino, "... diceano e facea miracoli: ma pure manzava e beveva chome li altri e fu una gran trappola di denari." quoted in U. Santini, *Bologna sulla fine del Quattrocento*, (Bologna: 1901), p. 149.

to 1455, member of the 1450 papal commission which reviewed the Sienese preacher's eligibility for sainthood, and from 1458 Cardinal Protector of the Franciscan Order. Given the difficulties between Observant and Conventual Franciscans, it was likely through Bessarion's diplomacy that the Bolognese Conventuals formally accepted the Company of S. Bernardino under their protection in 1454; a year later Bessarion presided over the chapel's opening. The agreement with the Conventuals was necessary, but its implications were anything but clear. By the later sixteenth century the two parties were exchanging lawsuits over the confraternity's autonomy and its title to the chapel.[12] The closest the Franciscans came to the Dominican practice of establishing confraternities to fulfill particular aims came with the Monte di Pietà. Franciscan preachers had promoted these small pawnshops for the working poor across Italy, and local organization was often in the hands of a confraternity. Michele Carcano da Milano (1427–84) preached up the Monte in Bologna in 1473, but no confraternity was established and the Franciscans were shut out of administration until a reorganization in 1506 brought in both a confraternity and the Abbot of the Observant house of L'Annunziata as an ex-officio member.[13]

This is a summary treatment of a complex topic, but it demonstrates that the Dominicans, Augustinians, and Franciscans adopted quite different approaches in their relations with confraternities. At the risk of portraying these as ideal types, we can see them as stages on a continuum. From the mid-thirteenth century onwards, Bolognese Dominicans saw lay confraternities as extensions of the Inquisitorial, educational, and charitable work of the Order, and so viewed lay brothers as auxilliaries. As a result they were more prescriptive, intruded more into confraternal administration, and had less success gaining and retaining lay brothers. Contemporary Dominicans in Florence behaved in much the same way.[14] The Augustinians adopted a far more laissez-faire attitude, offering shelter and spiritual help when approached, but having little to do with confraternities on a continuing basis. The Franciscans fell in between; they were more active than the Augustinians in initiating confraternities, and seem to have provided priests more frequently. At the same time, they were

---

[12] "Informazione dell'Crezione dalla Compagnia di S. Bernardino," BBA Gozz., Ms. 404 #7/2.

[13] The Bolognese Monte was the first in Romagna, where it was followed by Cesena (1487), Parma (1488), Piacenza (1490), Ravenna (1492), and Reggio Emilia (1494). Maragi, I cinquecento anni del monte di Bologna. (Bologna: 1973), pp. 44–5.

[14] J. Henderson, "Confraternities and the Church in Late Medieval Florence," in W.J. Sheils and D. Wood, Voluntary Religion, (Oxford: 1986), pp. 75–6.

less prescriptive than the Dominicans. On the whole, both the Augustinians and Franciscans were less demanding and more successful in their relations with confraternities. They implicitly accepted confraternities as self-governing expressions of lay piety, and resisted turning them into lay auxilliaries of clerical projects. Certainly Bolognese laymen expected a significant degree of independence in running their confraternities; G.G. Meersseman notes that even the Dominicans had to give their lay brothers in Bologna more autonomy than was their practice elsewhere.[15] And Bolognese laymen willingly exploited the animosity between the two major orders in order to achieve their goal: in the sixteenth century the Compagnia di S. Maria della Morte opted to draw its hired priest from the Franciscans and Dominicans alternately, thereby remaining relatively free of both.[16] The communal government followed much the same strategy when choosing mendicant preachers for the civic basilica of S. Petronio, though it clearly favored the Franciscans.[17]

John Henderson has written of "a general tendency of the Church, and particularly the friars, to increase their control over confraternities in the fifteenth century"; yet significantly, the examples he cites in support of his case deal only with the Florentine Dominicans.[18] The Bolognese experience suggests that what is true for the Dominicans is not necessarily true for other religious orders. In this regard, perhaps the most significant thing about the fight between Andreas Allè and the Dominican Inquisitor is its atypicality; as the only open fight on record, it is the exception which proves how peaceful the dynamic usually was when the Orders accommodated themselves to confraternities which demanded a degree of autonomy. Deliberately modelling themselves on mendicant spirituality did not necessarily mean that confraternities were subject to mendicant friars or orders. Across Italy confraternities self-consciously modelled their spiritual exercises and communal life on the mendicant example, but the local confraternal–mendicant dynamic varied widely between cities, orders, and houses.

---

[15] Meersseman, *Ordo fraternitatis*, pp. 614, 620.
[16] "Nota de Reverendi Padri Spirituali dell'Oratoria della Compagnia, ora Arciconfraternita di Sa. Ma. della Morte," ASB Osp, Compagnia di S. Maria della Morte, busta 29/632, filza 5.
[17] The communal government appointed and paid the preachers for S. Petronio. From 1393 through 1500, the Franciscans provided 54 preachers, the Dominicans 25, the Augustinians 15, the Servites 10, the Lateran Canons 10, and the Carmelites 8: "Oratori sacri che hanno predicato in Bologna nella Perinsigne Basilica di S. Petronio," BBA ms. B504. See also *Diario Bolognese Ecclesiastico, e Civile per l'anno 1770 . . . in Bologna per Lelio dalla Volpe* (Bologna: n.d.), pp. 1–7.
[18] Henderson, "Confraternities and the Church," pp. 76–7.

This discussion has been restricted to confraternal relations with regular clergy for the simple reason that, the influence of a bishop like Nicolò Albergati notwithstanding, there was very little continuing relation to the secular clergy until the development of parish confraternities in the later sixteenth century. Scholars once pointed to confraternities as indicators that traditional Christian communities such as the parish were declining by the fourteenth century and that the Church as a "praying community of the faithful" was being replaced by more individualistic and extra-liturgical forms of worship.[19] This perhaps exaggerates the normativity of parochial organization in the fifteenth century. It also mistakenly pushes the confraternities to the ecclesiastical margins when, by their very ubiquity, they inevitably helped define the image of the Church for most lay people. Parishes and confraternities were both being promoted only from the thirteenth century, and the former were at best a feeble plant in North Italian cities.[20] While recent studies have emphasized the integration of confraternal devotion into the larger devotional life of urban communities, the fact remains that confraternities could function as an alternative to both the local parish and the monastic house.[21] Through them, the fratello obtained devotional community, sacraments, and mutual aid, with the added benefit of worshipping in the company of his own choosing, and of remaining in the lay state. Moreover, as we will see at the end of this chapter, he could fashion a very individual network of confraternal memberships and, if wealthy enough, supplement these with private chaplains or confessors. These realities of deliberate modelling on the mendicants, of the variety of mendicant models, of the possibility of duplicating, offsetting or supplementing

---

[19] M. Petrocchi, "Una 'Devotio Moderna' nel Quattrocento Italiano," *Storia della spiritualità Italiana*, vol. II (Roma: 1978), p. 128; F. Vandenbroucke, "New Milieux, New Problems: From the Twelfth to the Sixteenth Century," in J. Leclercq and L. Cognet (eds.), *The Spirituality of the Middle Ages* (London: 1968), pp. 353; 497–8; G. Alberigo, "Contributi alla storia delle confraternite dei disciplinati e della spiritualità laicale nei secc. XV e XVI," *Il movimento dei disciplinati nel settimo centenario dal suo inizio (Perugia, 1260)* (Perugia: 1962), pp. 180–1, T. Klauser, *A Short History of the Western Liturgy*, (Oxford: 1979), pp. 96–7.

[20] A. Vasina, "Pieve e parrocchie in Emilia-Romagna dal XIII al XV secolo," in *Pieve e parrocchie in Italia nel basso medioevo (sec XIII–XV): Atti del VI convegno di storia della chiesa in Italia (Firenze: 1981)*, (Rome: 1984), pp. 725–9. Henderson, "Confraternities and the Church," p. 69.

[21] Bossy, *Christianity in the West*, pp. 57–64. Scarisbrick, *Reformation and English People*, pp. 19–39. Henderson, "Confraternities and the Church," pp. 69–83. A.N. Galpern, *The Religions of the People in Sixteenth Century Champagne*, (Harvard: 1976), pp. 69–94. N. Terpstra, "Renaissance Congregationalism: Organizing Lay Piety in Renaissance Italy," *Fides et Historia*, vol. 20 (1988), pp. 31–40.

them by joining more than one confraternity or making private arrangements, to say nothing of the liturgical component in other Renaissance corporations like the guilds, undermine any effort to define lay piety in terms of any single institution. The Renaissance layman – and to a very lesser extent the laywoman – could exercise his or her religious life through a number of distinct, parallel, and sometimes competing institutions. This fact above all means that confraternities should not be taken in isolation as defining popular piety, but should be seen as agencies which allowed the layman to negotiate his liturgical life with considerable autonomy and creativity. Whatever the models he chose, he was not passive in receiving them, he seldom took them *in toto*, and he was not without options if the clerical hand became too heavy. The discussion that follows will attempt to sketch out the variety of options that confraternities could offer as laymen fashioned their worship life.

II. COLLECTIVE DEVOTIONS

The confraternity was fundamentally a self-governing congregation of lay Christians adapting and adjusting traditional clerical forms of group worship to their own situation and times. On one level, they offered members training in, and exercise of, the communal rituals of the Catholic faith. From the time of their novitiate, members recited the divine office, heard mass, confessed, and received communion. Confraternities structured the expression of a faith that was characteristically communal, but whose chief communal locus of the parish lay underdeveloped in the hands of an often ill-educated clergy and in the face of neighborhood indifference.[22] On another level, confraternities regulated an intensified spirituality of private devotions that took members beyond parish duties towards vocational worship, that is, towards the rule followed by those who had turned their lives into worship by vowing poverty, chastity, and obedience. Driven by the mendicant example, and at times by mendicant aid, confraternities reached beyond exercising merely the normal duties of the Catholic laity to adopt the regulated prayers, penitential and spiritual exercises, and communal obedience of mendicant piety. Lay piety was characteristically imitative and communal, concerned less with understanding or

---

[22] On his pastoral visits through the diocese, Nicolò Albergati found "crumbling buildings ... neglect of material resources ... and priests unable to identify the seven mortal sins or to read the breviary." He had to repeat an earlier bishop's warning that "no-one could celebrate mass who was not ordained as a priest." D. Hay, *The Church in Italy in the Fifteenth Century*, (Cambridge: 1977), p. 56.

verbalizing doctrines than with modelling Christian life. Spiritual exercises assisted the fratello in preparing for his own death and assisting his spiritual brothers and sisters to prepare for theirs. Confraternal care for the dying and dead can rightly be seen as the culmination of confraternal spirituality, but picturing the Compagnia Spirituale as little more than an early modern burial society undervalues the rich ongoing worship life of the community. The fratelli of S. Bernardino emphasized this by dividing their 1454 statutes into three parts, one dealing with the living, one with the dead, and one with the spiritual fruits of membership.[23]

Confraternal spirituality can be measured by sermon collections, inventories of devotional works, or samples of liturgical texts. Yet these rarely survived. The most numerous and accessible guides to confraternal spirituality are the statutes which each group drew up separately and revised periodically to regulate its administrative and spiritual life. They tell how laymen viewed their place within the *corpus christianum*. There are certainly limitations with these sources. Often formulaic and administrative, they may reveal little of the spiritual temper of a particular group of confratelli beyond the time of composition. More seriously, statutes prescribe ambitious *desideratae*; with confraternities regularly expelling large numbers of their negligent or disobedient recruits, there was obviously a gap between norm and practice. Yet expulsions also show that violations of the norms were not treated lightly by the community. Behind the repeated calls to order and obedience lies a concern that those criticisms of lassitude levelled so frequently against the clergy not be levelled against lay confraternities as well. Moreover, the very antiquity of the rule and the intensity of its exercises were symbols of vocational idealism which brought honor to the company as a whole and credit to even its negligent members. Much like modern Christian fundamentalists who trumpet a theoretical doctrine of inerrancy while quietly ignoring some of the Bible's less convenient demands, confratelli took their self-image from strict statutes even when in practice they bent the rules. They reaffirmed the rules as often as they reformed them. In 1465 the thirty brothers of S. Girolamo di Miramonte took the unusual step of individually signing a notarized repudiation of revisions to the statutes written some thirty years before by Fra Stefano Prendeparte of the Canons Regular of San Salvatore. For these brothers, only "*lj nostri viei et usati capitullj . . . habiano valore, autorità et efficatia.*" The awkward fact about the statutes was that they required members to leave the

---

[23] ASB Dem, Compagnia di S. Bernardino, busta 8/7639, filza 1.

confraternity at age eighteen, and some of those signing their solemn reconfirmations had been members for over twenty years. S. Girolamo did not write new statutes until prodded to do so by Archbishop Gabrielle Paleotti in 1579.[24] What makes these brothers' actions even more puzzling is the fact that they could have ratified a slightly older and even more prestigious set of statutes written specifically for the adult members. In 1425, Albergati or a deputy wrote a set of statutes for S. Girolamo and gained the approval of theologians from the Dominican, Augustinian, and Observant Franciscan houses in the city. The date corresponds with Albergati's third round of pastoral visits in the city, and approval by the bishop and friars suggests that Albergati intended it to be a widely adopted model for all confraternities in the city.[25] In the event, no other companies are known to have adopted the statutes in toto, and even the brothers of S. Girolamo adopted and later ratified another set of statutes which was less appropriate to their situation. Laymen were not necessarily overwhelmed by demonstrations of clerical authority. All of this suggests that statutes can legitimately be taken as a measure of lay piety even when they were not followed to the letter. Furthermore, as we will see later, departures from the rule did not necessarily represent backsliding or indifference.

Some statutes are written by the lay members, others by the group's Padre Spirituale, and yet others by the two acting together; most come from the pens of unknown authors. The S. Francesco stretta lay

---

24 Four of the 1465 signatories (Andrea de Zohane Lioni, Antonio da San Domengo, Christovallo di Jachomo Zanettini, and Baldisera di Ser Jacobi de Maltachidi) had joined S. Girolamo in the 1440s. "Matricola di S. Girolamo di Miramonte," ASB Codici Miniati, ms. 65, 2r., 3r, 6r. "Dichiarazione della Compagnia di S. Girolamo sopra li statuti della medesima," ASB Dem, S. Girolamo di Miramonte, busta 2/6719, filza 24. Fra Stefano da Prendaparte's statutes are undated, but order the brothers to offer prayers for Pope Eugenius IV (1431–47): BBA Gozz ms. 205 n. 5, cap. 18. They were most likely drawn up in conjuction with either the opening of the new confraternal oratory in 1433, or the splitting of the confraternity into "maggiori" and "minori" in 1438. The "new" statutes of 1579: "Statuti diversi," ASB Dem, S. Girolamo di Miramonte, busta 1/6718, filza 5, items c & d.

25 ASB Dem, Compagnia di S. Girolamo di Miramonte, busta 2/6719, filza 2, cap 11–12. Approval by the bishop, his vicar, or a friar was common enough; having representatives of the three major mendicant orders involved with confraternities sign the document indicates that Albergati had higher hopes for the rule. Given these aspirations, it is possible that the statutes were written by Albergati's secretary at the time, Tommaso Parentucelli. The friars who approved the rule were: Agnolo da Camorino, a Dominican Master in Sacred Theology; Agostino da Roma Bazaliero of the Augustinians in S. Giacomo; and Jacomo di Primadizi of the Franciscan Observant house, the Osservantia dal Monte. For more on Primadizi, see Melloni, Atti o memorie degli uomini illustri, pp. 255–68.

brothers wrote their own in 1443, but based them on "*certi statuti e ordine de altre compagnie spirituale*" and submitted them to their Padre Spirituale, Fra Silvestro da Forlì the Guardiano of the Observant Franciscan house, and to Bishop Albergati, asking these clerics for correction in case the laymen's statutes should be tainted "*per superbia o per ignorancia.*" At the opposite extreme, the four officials of S. Bartolomeo di Reno, a notary, a goldsmith, and two spinners, rewrote their confraternal statutes in 1471 and had them approved by a vote of 30 to 3 in a company "*parlamento*"; the statutes were never submitted to the bishop. Somewhere in between we have the case of Ugo di Antonio Ruggiero da Reggio, sometime cannonmaker and bombmaker to the Bentivoglio, but better known as one of the leading printers operating in the city in the late fifteenth century. Ruggieri published a wide range of texts, from the juridical treatise *Collectio florum in ius canonicum* (1496) of Lodovico Bolognini to Girolamo Manfredi's *Liber de homine* (1474) and Benedetto Morandi's *De laudibus Bononiae* (1481); he also published various religious texts including copies of the Office of the Blessed Virgin Mary. Ruggieri wanted to establish a confraternity and to locate it in a small chapel owned by the Celestines of S. Giovanni Battista. The Celestines were amenable, but drove a hard bargain, requiring Ruggiero to name his confraternity after the Celestine mother house of Santo Spirito, and to allow only Celestines to perform sacraments, act as Padri Spirituali, or take on any other paid tasks within the confraternity. Yet Ruggiero wrote the statutes for the Compagnia di Spirito Santo himself in 1496 and did not submit them to the Celestines or any other ecclesiastical authority for approval; the statutes were not revised until 1596. Finally, when in 1523 a group of Florentines established a confraternity under the banner of S. Giovanni Decollato, they trusted neither themselves nor a local cleric with writing statutes, but sent back to Florence for "*la regola et capitoli già antiquamente osservati in detta città.*"[26] These instances underscore the fact that there is no single pattern to authorship of confraternal statutes. What is consistent however is that all statutes and reforms, regardless of author, had to be approved by the membership; only the Dominicans departed from this practice. The bishop or his vicar had then to approve the result, but

---

[26] For S. Francesco: BBA ms. B983, cc. 79r–v. For S. Bartolomeo di Reno: ASB PIE, Compagnia di S. Bartolomeo di Reno, ms. I, c. 13r. For Ugo Ruggiero and the Compagnia di Spirito Santo: M. Fanti, *La chiesa di S. Maria dei Celestini e la Compagnia dello Spirito Santo* (Bologna: 1965), pp. 19–29. For S. Giovanni Decollato: G. Roversi, "La compagnia e l'oratorio dei Fiorentini in Bologna," in *San Giovanni Battista dei Celestini in Bologna*, (Bologna: 1970), p. 112. There is no record of which Florentine company provided the statutes.

this was a rule frequently ignored until the later sixteenth century.[27] The example of S. Girolamo shows that Quattrocento confratelli had few qualms about bypassing statutes written for them and sanctioned with high episcopal and mendicant authority; a century and a half later, Archbishop Gabrielle Paleotti would have greater success with a standardized rule issued in 1583.[28] Lay and clerical authors alike modelled confraternal statutes on mendicant examples, and while an Augustinian cleric might insert numerous quotations from the Bishop of Hippo, the resulting spiritual exercises do not differentiate neatly by vocation or class. No two are alike. Some were brief and to the point and others are discursive spiritual works in themselves; they draw on the Bible and the church fathers as they explain the meaning and importance of rules, offices, and rituals.[29] In many cases a succession of statutes plots the changing needs of the confraternity. The Compagnia dello SSmo. Crocifisso del Cestello emerged out of a devotional movement centered on miracles related to a crucifix on the Cestello bridge around 1514. Its first statutes written anonymously in that year are long on devotional practices and short on administrative details. A new set of statutes in 1538 is given over almost entirely to administration, as is a second revised set of 1570; a third set from 1549 lays out practices for a women's consorority under the men's direction. The later statutes, all of them written by committees of laymen, were supplements to those of 1514, which were never superceded as the core devotional guide for the confraternity.[30] Whatever their authorship, all statutes exude a very traditional piety. The authentic voice of the laity did not necessarily speak in tones contrary to the clergy, nor was harmony between the two the result of clerical imposition on the laity. We can legitimately speak of a common temperament or mentality

[27] J. Henderson notes few episcopal approvals in fourteenth-century Florence, but growing numbers after 1420 when more bishops were both resident and highly educated. Henderson, "Confraternities and the Church," pp. 78–82. Bologna's relations with its bishops were less consistent and less warm. Even Albergati was absent from Bologna much of the time, and after him few of Bologna's bishops were resident; none were Bolognese citizens until Achille Grassi (1511–23) whose residency, like Albergati's, depended on the city's relations with the papacy.

[28] G. Lercaro, "La riforma catechistica post-tridentina a Bologna," *Ravennatensia* vol. 2 (1971), p. 20.

[29] Discursive statutes include those of S. Geronimo (1433), S. Francesco stretta (1443), S. Maria della Vita stretta (1454), S. Maria della Mezzaratta del Monte (1484), Buon Gesù (1520), and S. Maria del Baraccano (1521). See note 31 for archival references.

[30] The four sets of statutes are: (1514) BBA Gozz 206 #1; (1538) BBA Gozz 206 #2; (1549) ASB Dem, Compagnia del SSmo. Crocifisso del Cestello, busta 1/6738, filza 10; (1570) BBA Gozz 206 #1b.

focused on the goal of salvation obtained through communal action consistent with Christian tradition. Given this mentality, neither the prescriptive idealism of confraternal statutes nor their collective authorship need make them deficient guides for understanding lay spirituality.

Turning then to the statutes themselves, the primary collective worship responsibilities of the confraternal congregation lay in educating members in Christian doctrine, and exercising the rituals which animated the doctrines and structured the community's life.[31] Three elements figure here: doctrine, liturgy, and the sacraments of confession and communion. Of these, doctrinal teaching, if practiced, began when the congregation accepted prospective members as novices and committed them to a lay master for training. This was not dogmatic theology, but tutoring in traditional statements of Catholic faith which would later become the core of many sixteenth-century catechisms: the Apostles' Creed, the Ten Commandments, and the seven sacraments. Novices also learned the guides to Christian life: the seven sins; the seven virtues; and the seven works of corporal and spiritual mercy Of these, only the Creed was recited in communal worship, but the

---

[31] What follows is based on the following sets of confraternal statutes (organized chronologically): Congregatio Devotorum (1261–83), in Angelozzi, *Confraternite laicali*, pp. 86–95; S. Francesco (1317), cap. 3–4, 7 in Mesini, "S. Maria delle Laudi," pp. 366–72; S. Maria della Misericordia (1399), ASB Dem busta 4/7673, filza 1, cc. 2r–v, 4r, 5r; S. Girolamo di Miramonte (1425), ASB Dem busta 2/6719, filza 2, cap. 2–5, 11–14; S. Geronimo (1433), BBA Gozz 206 #5, cap. 6–8, 17–19, 25, 28–29; S. Domenico stretta (1443), BBA Gozz 207 #2; S. Francesco stretta (1443), BBA B983, cap. 4–5, 25–29; S. Bernardino (1454), ASB Dem busta 8/7639 filza 1; S. Maria dei Guarini stretta (1454), BBA Gozz 210 #11, cap. 3–4, 8–9; S. Maria della Vita stretta (1454), BBA Osp #10, cap. 3–4, 8–9; S. Ambrogio (1456), ASB Codici Miniati #67, cap. 2–3, 7–9, 15; S. Bartolomeo di Reno (1471), ASB PIE ms. 1; S. Maria degli Angeli (1479), BBA Gozz 203 #7, cap. 2–4, 6–9; S. Maria degli Angeli stretta (1479) BBA Gozz 203 #7, cap. 3, 6–9; S. Maria della Mezzaratta del Monte (1484), BBA Gozz 203 #7; S. Francesco (1494), ASB Codici Miniati #61; Spirito Santo (1496), BBA B3180, cap. 2, 4–5, 11, 25–28; S. Maria della Pietà (1503), BBA Gozz 206 #7; S. Rocco (ca. 1511–23), ASB Dem busta 6/6589, filza 2, cap. 5, 8, 11; SSmo. Crocifisso del Cestello (1514), BBA Gozz 206 #1, cap. 1–7, 13; S. Maria Maddalena (1515), ASB PIE ms. 1, cap. 26, 29; S. Maria della Carità stretta (1518), BBA Gozz 210 #6, cap. 6–10; Buon Gesù (1521), ASB Dem busta 9/7631, filza 1, cap. 4–15, 20–22, 33; S. Maria del Baraccano (1521), BBA Gozz 213 #1, cap. 3–5, 11; S. Maria degli Angeli stretta (1522), BBA Gozz 203 #7, cap. 3–7; S. Maria dei Servi (1523), ASB Osp busta 2/307, cap. 24; SS. Sebastiano e Rocco, (1525), ASB Dem busta 16/6620, filza 1, cap. 9–15; SSmo. Crocifisso del Cestello (1538) BBA Gozz 206 #2 cap. 8; S. Maria della Pietà (1548), ASB Dem busta 10/7696 filza 3, cap. 4, 7; SSmo. Crocifisso del Cestello (1549), ASB Dem busta 1/6738 filza 10, cap. 4, 7; SSmo. Crocifisso del Cestello (1570) BBA Gozz 206 #1b.

others were frequently used as guides to confession in popular preaching and confessional manuals.

Doctrinal teaching, if carried out at all, was subordinate to the religious exercises which most clearly showed confraternities worshipping in the vocational model. "Seven times a day do I praise thee," said the prophet in Psalm 119: 164, and following him St. Benedict had prescribed prayers at matins, prime, terce, sext, nones, vespers, and completorium. Artisans, notaries, and merchants pleaded the press of the secular world in shying from so complete a regimen, but they demonstrated faith in its value when as confratelli they met for regular morning or evening prayer. As in other aspects of confraternal worship, fifteenth-century members differed from their predecessors primarily in the frequency of their observance. Thirteenth-century monthly gatherings of laudi singers became weekly Sunday morning recitations of the Divine Office in the Quattrocento. Most statutes routinely prescribed worship on feast days set by the church, and a number added days of specific meaning to the confraternity. The patron saint's day was adopted as a matter of course, singled out for special observances and celebrations. By all accounts, the Company del SSmo. Crocifisso del Cestello followed local custom when it appointed three or four members three months before their May 3 feast and charged them with decorating the oratory at whatever expense the occasion required; twelve masses were said to mark the day.[32] Reasons for observing other saints' days are less easy to determine unless, like St. Jerome, they were enjoying a general revival or, like Sts. Petronio, Proculo, Francis, and Dominic, they had particular civic significance. We should be cautious about putting too much weight on saintly patronage as a significant part of confraternal devotion. The invocations opening statutes had by the early sixteenth century replaced naming individual saints with the comparatively indiscriminate "all the celestial court" ("*tute la corte celestiale*"). In general, the sense of saintly patronage was not overly strong, with only S. Girolamo specifically charging members to say a daily Pater Noster and Ave Maria in its saint's honor so that he would intercede before God on the fratello's behalf. In fact, there were not many "saint's" companies in Bologna. "Ethnic" companies of Milanese, Florentines, and Genoese adopted their civic saint more out of nostalgic *campanilismo* than any sustained devotion. Surprisingly, there was never a Compagnia Spirituale dedicated to the city's patron, S. Petronio, though this may have represented the tacit recognition that the civic cult must remain focused around the civic basilica and not around any one of the many confraternities. The

[32] BBA Gozz 206 #2, ch. 2, 8.

singular exception was the Virgin Mary. Marian devotion overrode all others, even in confraternities formally dedicated to one or another saint. Companies erected around shrines maintained their saints in respectable style, but the Queen of Heaven still attracted more devotion than any canonized underling. What is significant here is that laymen reserved the right to mark or ignore their saint's day, or any other religious festival for that matter. The confraternity as a whole designated which feast days would be observed communally, while its serving lay head could prescribe observance of extraordinary feasts at his own discretion. In short, the confraternity established its own liturgical calendar within that of the church and diocese, and recognized a layman as its chief liturgist.

Until Archbishop Gabriele Paleotti brought in a standardized missal for confraternities in 1574, each company devised its own worship rituals surrounding the morning or evening Office.[33] The resulting mixture of particularity and tradition emerges by comparing two of the more detailed Matins liturgies, that of S. Ambrogio in the 1450s, and that of the stretta of Buon Gesù in the 1520s. The former came together as the *campana grossa*, the big bell of the cathedral church of St. Peter, was sounding. On entering they knelt before the altar, saluting Christ with a Pater Noster and an Ave Maria before rising to salute their brothers with a kiss of peace. Worship began by reciting the penitential psalms with their litanies and customary prayers in a low voice. The chief lay official then appointed two brothers to begin reciting the psalms and lessons according to company custom. A third reader then went to the lectern where, with covered head, he recited customary prayers before returning to his place and leading the brothers in singing the Credo. There followed the Magnificat, the hymn of St. Ambrose, and any special hymns or prayers for a special feast day. On completion of the Office, the Ebdomodario pronounced God's peace while the sacristan and a fratello gave the peace to the brothers, presumably by passing a "tavoleta" or prayer board which each member kissed in turn. Then the Ebdomodario gave the Holy Water, saying "Wash me God" and the customary prayer. After further prayers, the fratelli went to the altar by rank, beginning with the longest-serving members, and presented their offerings. Returning to their places, they listened as a chapter of the statutes was read and then were free to discuss any items pertaining to the company and its oratory. Those with pressing business could leave with the *Ordinario*'s permission.[34] On a Sunday

---

[33] G. Cherubino, *Libro delle compagnie spirituali* (Bologna: 1574).
[34] ASB Codici Miniati, ms. 67, cap. 2, 3.

morning almost seventy years later, the observant fratello of Buon Gesù would rise before the cathedral bell had sounded. Leaving the house, he made the sign of the cross, praying, "By the sign of the cross deliver us from our enemies, O God." He made his way to the confraternity's chapel reciting prayers and meditating on Christ's passion and Mary's sorrow. Arriving, he daubed himself with Holy Water and recited the prayer, "We enter your house and adore your holy house in fear of you." The fratello then went up the stairs to the private oratory and entered saying, "Peace on this house," before making his way to the altar where he knelt and thanked Christ for redemption. Going to his place, he passed the time in silent meditation, reading or prayer until the lay leader led the brothers in the morning office of the Blessed Virgin.[35] Silence reigned following the office as some remained in prayer at their places and others brought their offerings to the altar before leaving to begin their day's activity.[36]

Subtle differences between these two approaches to the rituals surrounding the office demonstrate distinct views of what confraternal worship meant. Communal worship was the focus of confraternal life for the brothers of S. Ambrogio, while it appears to be more of an aid to personal devotion for the silence-loving brothers of Buon Gesù. The former connected worship to the broader life of the congregation by concluding with reading a chapter from their own statutes and discussing confraternal business. The latter came in meditation and left in silence, "so as not to lose the devotion acquired" ["*finiti che sarano li offitij non se farano altri parlamenti per non perdere la devotione aquistata*"].[37] Of the two, Buon Gesù shows more consistently the interior piety of contemporary devotional movements but S. Ambrogio is more typical

[35] The meditative *fratello* could read from libraries stocked with traditional classics. The S. Francesco library included: *I fioretti di S. Francesco*; *La leggenda di S. Girolamo*; *La scuola celeste*; *Lo specchio della Croce*: Mesini, "S. Maria delle Laudi," p. 373. That of Buon Gesù included the *Fioretti* and *Specchio*, as well as *Omnis Mortalium Cura*; *La vita de Sancti Padri*; *Sancto Joanne Climacho*: ASB Dem Compagnia di Buon Gesù, busta 9/7631, filza 1, c.24r. A 1463 inventory of S. Girolamo notes: a two-volume *De vitis patrum*, *Lo transito de sam hieronymo*, *Lo spechio de la croce*, a book of *Prediche*, and various liturgical manuals. ASB Dem, S. Girolamo di Miramonte, busta 1/6718, filza 3a, c.2r. Most are included in A.J. Schutte's list of the top fifteen "bestsellers" of the late fifteenth century in Italy: A.J. Schutte, "Printing, Piety, and the People in Italy: The First Thirty Years," "*Printing, Piety and the People in Italy: The First Thirty Years.*" *Archiv Für Reformationsgeschichte* 71 (1980): 5–9, pp. 18–19.

[36] ASB Dem, Compagnia di Buon Gesù, busta 9/7631, filza 1, cap. 7.

[37] Buon Gesù deliberately moved administrative meeting times from immediately after morning prayers to late afternoon or evening for the same reason, noting that divisive and rancorous discussions spent the "beni spirituali" acquired during the office. ASB Dem, Compagnia di Buon Gesù, busta 9/7631, filza 1, cap. 23.

of other Bolognese confraternities. These are co-existing models of confraternal piety, not sequential developments. S. Ambrogio recommitted itself to its more communal piety by confirming the largely unchanged statutes in 1570, while the brothers of Buon Gesù did the same in 1604.

While the company priest conducted confraternal masses, the lay head, or Ordinario, ruled over recitation of the divine office. Latecomers kneeled for his sign of admission before going to their seats, and once worship had begun those with urgent business could not be dismissed without his leave. He appointed the readers and singers, chose the hymns and how they would be sung, and orchestrated worship by signaling celebrants.[38] The Ordinario guarded the tone of worship, disciplining those who treated their obligations and others' service lightly. If jesting, sour faces or rude noises greeted an off-pitch choir, the Ordinario fined or expelled the violators. He ruled out eating, drinking, sleeping, swearing, and gossiping, and with the aid of the sacristan made sure that everyone performed the requisite rituals. A lax Ordinario might let observance slip, while a zealot could wear his brothers out with extraordinary services. The wise officer, as the brothers of SSmo. Crocifisso del Cestello advised, was best governed by the company's customs and his own good sense: "Always have discretion not to fill up the time with tedious repetitions; search always the general good before your own preference and convenience."[39] Attention flagged during overlong services, and whispered gossip among the members must have been a frequent problem since numerous statutes prohibited discussing business or "worldly affairs" while in the oratory; as the brothers of S. Maria dei Guarini trenchantly observed in 1454, "the Oratory has the name of *orare* and not *parlare*."[40]

Reciting the office brought the brothers together at intervals whose regularity, if not frequency, was modelled on the mendicant rules.

[38] Numerous statutes leave the mode of singing to the Ordinario's discretion, S. Maria Maddalena allowing him to choose between "canto fermo" and "canto figurato," S. Maria Guerini advising singing "non troppo presto ne troppo adagio," and S. Domenico, "chiaramente e distinamente."

[39] "Avendo sempre discretione de non essere prolixo e lungo secundo l hora et comodita del tempo. Cercando sempre el bene universale prima chel proprio et comodita sua," BBA Gozz 203 #1, cap. 13. In 1443, S. Domenico pressed more specifically for a heartfelt devotion beyond extended ritual: "Do not go longer than an hour, for it is not our intention to base this company on many spoken prayers and offices, as much as love of God and neighbor, profound humility, continuous peace, and perfect patience of soul and life ("de fatti"), which things come from mental prayer." BBA Gozz 207 #2, cap. 7.

[40] Fanti, "S. Maria dei Guarini," p. 371.

From the beginning of the fifteenth century, increased use of confession and communion enhanced these meetings. The Sorbonne conciliarist theologian Jean Gerson (1366–1423) is credited with promoting monthly confession as a devotional aid for the laity, while eucharistic piety was a key element of the devotio moderna promoted in Italy by Pope Martin V among others; Bishop Nicolò Albergati saw both sacraments as indispensable tools for lay piety.[41] Neither sacrament figured prominently in confraternal practice of the preceding two centuries, or among larga confraternities of the fifteenth century. Annual Easter confession in the local parish was firmly associated with the mystery of communal integration into the Body of Christ. Frequent communion with the confratelli concentrated and recast the community experiencing this integration. It also underscored the confraternity's functioning on the vocational model as a communal aid to ĩndividual devotion. Yet judging by the frequent disciplinary strictures applied to those who absented themselves, sacramental piety was not readily accepted by all lay confratelli.

Along with the stick of discipline, company statutes taught the great value of confession and communion, drawing most frequently on medical analogies. These were at once immediately accessible and picked up on the double meaning of "*salute del anima*" as both the salvation and the health of the soul. The men of Buon Gesù put the issue in historical perspective, claiming that frequent confession and communion had been marks of the early church since lost in the "*malatia et negligentia et mancando fervor*" of later generations; annual confession was simply the church's response to human weakness. Frequent confession was good for the health of the soul because the more often one purged the soul of its bad humors of sin, the more often it rested clean and in the grace of God; if we are careful enough to wash our hands, we ought to be more careful in washing our consciences. Seventy years earlier, S. Maria della Vita likened the confessor to a doctor working for the health of the soul, noting that confessing one's sins was not shameful, but necessary "to wash and clean the soul of darkness."[42]

Almost all flagellant confraternities in the fifteenth and early sixteenth century prescribed monthly confession. Sacramental confession

---

[41] Bossy, *Christianity in the West*, p. 49; L. von Pastor, *History of the Popes*, I, p. 232; De Töth, *Nicolò Albergati*, p. 276. M. Rubin, *Corpus Christi: The Eucharist in Late Medieval Culture* (Cambridge: 1991), pp. 147–55, 232–43.

[42] Buon Gesù: ASB Dem, Compagnia di Buon Gesù, busta 9/7631, filza I, cap. 14. S. Maria della Vita: Angelozzi, *Le confraternite laicali*, p. 121. In 1514 SSmo. Crocifisso del Cestello spoke of confession as clearing the pollution (*imonditia*) of sin out of the soul: BBA Gozz 206 #1, cap. 1.

was private but not secret. In order to check attendance, some companies distributed tickets. S. Ambrogio's Ordinario gave each fratello a ticket, or *scrittarino*, at the first meeting of the month; this was passed to the Padre Spirituale during confession and returned by him to the Ordinario. S. Maria del Baraccano reversed the procedure. With this system fratelli could confess at their own convenience. Members who had missed confession were admonished and were either required to go twice the following month, or given a set term of two to eight days in which to correct their *negligentia*. Persistent violators were expelled. As Buon Gesù pointed out, it was not good if the sick man refused medicine, for he might infect other members.[43]

Apart from Easter communion in the local capella, most fifteenth-century companies required that members communicate three or four more times in the year in the company oratory, "and more times appropriate to your devotion." Few companies continued semi-annual communion on the old laudesi model. Eucharistic piety was Christocentric, judged by the fratelli of S. Maria Maddalena as the payment of a debt to the Redeemer. As such the sacrament was most often celebrated at Christmas and Pentecost. Mary continued to overshadow confraternal saints, for whereas almost all groups celebrated the August 15 feast of her Assumption by taking communion, only Ss. Sebastiano e Rocco so observed its saints' day. Only at the beginning of the sixteenth century did observance of the newer November 1 feast of All Saints begin gaining currency. As with confession, penalties up to expulsion were handed out to those who would not communicate with the prescribed regularity. But beyond such penalties, members were sometimes given exercises or duties encouraging eucharistic devotion by isolating or highlighting the rite. Buon Gesù cited Augustine in prohibiting sex for five days before and three days following communion and in requiring flagellation to bend minds and souls more firmly to devotion.[44] Buon Gesù's ever-idealistic requirements follow contemporary Observant norms, but here as elsewhere the gap between clerical and lay piety is evident. The laity could conceivably use the "mea culpa" of mental confession as an exercise for greater personal devotion, but without ordination they

---

[43] Buon Gesù set four steps of admonition, taking away the fratello's Oratory key after the second warning and expelling him after the fourth: ASB Dem, Compagnia di Buon Gesù, busta 9/7631, filza 1, cap. 3, 14–15. S. Maria del Baraccano stretta would not allow officeholding by anyone who had missed confession twice without making amends: BBA Gozz 213 #1, cap. 15.

[44] ASB Dem, Compagnia di Buon Gesù, busta 9/7631, filza 1, cap. 31.

could hardly practice the intense eucharistic piety which so animates a work like *The Imitation of Christ* and energizes the devotio moderna. The devotio moderna tended towards an individual identification with Christ, while confraternal piety emphasized collective identification with Christ's disciples, lay friends of the Signore. Hence the former employed frequent individual communion while the latter preferred such group exercises as flagellation. There was a limit to how far the layman could follow a cleric up the *scala perfectionis*. This must certainly be one reason why so many lay confratelli seem to have tried avoiding frequent communion while they adopted flagellation with enthusiasm.

Collective identification with the brotherhood of Christ's disciples emerged most clearly through the two rituals of foot washing and flagellation. Neither necessarily included the company's Padre Spirituale, for in these purely lay ceremonies the Ordinario represented Christ for the confraternal disciples. Each company devised its own liturgy, with foot washing an annual and flagellation a more frequent ritual. With regard to the former, Quattrocento fratelli in the Company of S. Girolamo gathered late in the evening on Holy Thursday. As members sang a setting of Christ's Passion, the Ordinario or one of the Rectors washed the feet of all the fratelli; following Christ, they then prepared and served a light meal for the disciples. The adult branch of the confraternity then retired to the Oratory to recite the office.[45] Rituals followed almost a century later by the men of Buon Gesù were largely similar. The brothers gathered in an antechamber before receiving the Ordinario's signal and moving to their places where, seated, they listened to a member read the chapter of the statutes describing the ceremony and its meaning. All then rose and went in procession to a set of benches facing the altar where they sat and heard the gospel passage describing the event. When the reader reached the passage describing how Christ took the water and began washing his disciples' feet, the Ordinario rose and began doing the same. He washed, dried, and kissed the feet of all the brothers, beginning with the least (i.e., the newest) member. If there were many brothers he was assisted by one or two deputies. Choral singing concluded the ceremony, after which the fratelli returned to their places and were exhorted by the Ordinario to remember and attend the sermons, offices, and flagellation marking Good Friday.[46] The Ordinario's actions in this early

---

[45] ASB Dem, Compagnia di S. Girolamo di Miramonte, busta 2/6719, filza 2, cap. 12. For 1433 statutes, BBA Gozz 206 #5, cap. 25.

[46] ASB Dem, Compagnia di Buon Gesù, busta 9/7631, filza 1, cap. 9.

sixteenth-century ritual – readopted in 1604 – are notable because some scholars have claimed that by this period confraternities were tending towards stylizations which removed the loss of honor threatened by such exercises of Christ-like humility. Ronald Weissman notes a Florentine confraternity which turned from washing the feet of fratelli to washing those of twelve men drawn from outside the brotherhood; another Bolognese confraternity had its Ordinario wash the feet of only one brother.[47] Here as elsewhere, arguing that these rituals fall into historical sequence may be less true to confraternal practice than recognizing a plurality of co-existing devotional models, differentiated by spiritual advisers, age, and a group's own tradition.

The second communal ritual of flagellation was one of the most characteristic marks of confraternal devotion as early as the thirteenth century. After allowing it to decline to a stylized rite through the fourteenth century, fifteenth-century fratelli once again picked up the cords of discipline under the encouragement of the Observants and, in Bologna, of Nicolò Albergati. It returned first in confraternities dominated by the well-born, but soon spread to a broad range of spiritual companies of all classes. Whether in new companies or stretta groups, flagellation became the devotional exercise most characteristic of fratelli's commitment to spiritual renewal. Indulgences encouraged a practice which fell well within the penitential tenor of the times, yet in its fifteenth-century revival, flagellation was less an act of individual expiation than a collective act of remembering Christ's passion.[48] Some companies flagellated only at certain times of the year; S. Ambrogio practiced it on every feast day falling between All Saints and Christmas, between Palm Sunday and Easter, and on designated days through the year. Other companies set aside a certain, regular time, with most flagellating every Sunday and feast day after fratelli had

---

[47] Weissman, *Ritual Brotherhood in Renaissance Florence* (New York: 1982), pp. 226–8.
[48] Flagellation had different dimensions. The Compagnia di S. Ambrogio looked on it as both praising and glorifying Christ, and easing the guilt of sin; S. Maria della Vita added to this the mortification of the flesh; Buon Gesù treated it more symbolically as a memorial of Christ's incarnation, passion, and sacrifice. To encourage members, S. Maria della Vita had a number of indulgences, one granting fratelli eighty years, four months, and twenty days for each time [*per ogni fiada*] they performed discipline, and another granting one year and two hundred and seventy five days to everyone who came for devotions when discipline was being performed: Angelozzi, *Confraternite laicali*, p. 120. On flagellation: J. Henderson, "The Flagellant Movement and Flagellant Confraternities in Central Italy, 1260–1400," *Studies in Church History*, vol. 15 (1978), p. 157.

recited the Divine Office. Time of day also varied, with some companies carrying it out at night and others, like S. Maria della Vita, following the psalmist's cry, "For all day long have I been beaten, and chastened every morning" (Ps. 73:14).

S. Girolamo's 1425 statutes contain a detailed liturgy for weekly flagellation, called the "Office of Darkness." As noted earlier, these were the statutes which Nicolò Albergati hoped would become a widely adopted model for Bolognese confraternities. On Saturday night the fratelli made their way to the company's oratory and meeting rooms. As each arrived, he first went into the oratory and said three Pater Nosters and three Ave Marias. He then went to where the others were gathered in the meeting rooms, exchanging with them the peace of Christ by words or a kiss. As they waited for their brothers, one of the members read some devotional work. When all were gathered, their lay head (the Massaro) led them back into the Oratory, reciting the "Misere mei" as they went. The massaro then led in the "Confiteor" and the fratelli responded with the seven penitential psalms and their prayers. Their prayers of preparation complete, the brotherhood returned to the meeting rooms reciting the "De Profundis" and the "Requiem eternam" for the souls of their dead brothers. The fratelli then bedded down for the night while the Massaro, like Christ in the Garden of Gethsemane, remained watching and praying. At the sound of the morning bell, all returned to the oratory singing a hymn as they processed and reciting the Matins office once in their places. After the office all the lamps but one small one were extinguished and flagellation began. The Office of Discipline had its own litanies: the "Misere mei," the "De profundis," the Requiem for fratelli of previous generations, the "Venite largite," and the "Salutis Amator." These prayers continued as discipline concluded and the lamps on the altar were lit; the fratelli then left their offerings at the altar. The "De profundis" was recited a third time as the Massaro returned to the meeting rooms and the fratelli were free to depart.

Albergati or his secretary had fashioned a liturgy which made few concessions to the lay state. Overnight preparation and temporary claustration (no one was allowed to leave until the end) were obviously greater problems for laymen than clerics, and were not adopted by the stretta companies arising in the decades following preparation of the 1425 S. Girolamo rule. At the same time, liturgies adopted by stretta fratelli of the Companies of S. Maria della Vita and S. Maria dei Guarini from 1454 follow the Jeromites in using the

Matins office, the same psalms and prayers, the same atmosphere of darkness, the Requiem drawing past fratelli into the discipleship of current brothers, and the concluding gift on the altar. Much of this is conventional and draws on the Mass, but there is good reason to believe that Albergati's specific Office of Discipline served as the model for other Bolognese confraternities. The two 1454 stretta statutes prefaced a description of the ritual with the note that it was "as is contained in our new book of the Office"; later confraternities simply referred to such a book without further description. Yet individual confraternities could still choose other models. The stretta of S. Maria degli Angeli in 1479 left the liturgy to the Ordinario's discretion while the men of Buon Gesù noted in 1520, "we use the office of the Friars minor as a brief and good form of psalms, prayers and discipline."[49]

In a more significant departure, the Compagnia di SS. Sebastiano e Rocco changed discipline in its 1525 stretta statutes from a conventional, collective ceremony into a stylized rite performed by the Ordinario on a single brother.[50] As early as 1454 in S. Maria della Vita, spiritual benefits had been offered to members who attended the Office of Discipline without joining the others in flagellation. This was different; although all present wore the flagellant's robes, the other fratelli participated only as respondents in the litanies. On one level this could be seen as a stylization of the rite reducing it to the refined sensibilities of an admittedly upper-class company. Yet there also appears to be a theological shift of sorts giving the act a more deliberately Christological focus. Discipline was preceeded by fratelli sharing the kiss of peace, and was followed by their recitation of the Nunc Dimittis. The Ordinario then led the brothers in litanies concentrating first on the Incarnation and working gradually into the sinner's need for grace. With such a cut-and-paste liturgy, this Office of Discipline seems more the result of theological experimentation in doctrinally fluid times than simply the loss of a taste for flagellation; S. Maria della Vita's example shows that wholesale transformation of the liturgy was not necessary when catering to the few who chose not to flagellate. In

---

[49] BBA Gozz 203 #7, c.142r. (S. Maria degli Angeli); ASB Dem, Compagnia di Buon Gesù, busta 9/7631, filza 1, cap. 8. Only minor differences separated the Franciscan from Albergati's model. For the Dominican model: ASB Dem, Compagnia di S. Domenico, busta 8/6422, cc. 22r–33v.

[50] ASB Dem, Compagnia di SS. Sebastiano e Rocco, busta 16/6620, filza 1, cap. 14. The stretta group originated in 1520 (ASB Dem Compagnia di SS. Sebastiano e Rocco, busta 1/6605, filza 30).

spite of its experimentation, SS. Sebastiano e Rocco remained firmly Catholic, and no others seem to have adopted its radically transformed liturgy.

"Orthodox" flagellant companies and stretta offshoots continued multiplying until at least the mid-sixteenth century, when the ritual began losing its earlier broad appeal.[51] While it was the most dramatic single sign that a confraternity had undergone devotional reform, the exercise set further changes in motion which few members could have foreseen. As we will see in the next chapter, the whips effectively drove women out of the confraternities and eventually drove artisanal men out as well.

III. PRIVATE DEVOTIONS

Divine Office, confession, communion, foot washing, and flagellation were all by necessity and confraternal fiat collective worship rituals. Yet personal devotion becomes an increasingly important part of confraternal membership from at least the early fifteenth century; it is the only exercise open to women in the sixteenth century.[52] The exercises most often took the form of prescribed prayers at waking, sleeping, and eating; mental confession; frequent attendance at mass; and weekly and lenten fasting. Among penitential confraternities they underscored the confraternity's identity as a brotherhood of Christ's disciples: S. Maria della Vita did not allow the eating of meat on Wednesdays since that was the day when the Signore's *carne* was sold by Judas. The personal spiritual exercises also gave devotional structure to more general rules about individual deportment, and accustomed the observant fratello to the rhythms of holiness prescribed by mendicant preachers like Manfredo da Vercelli, S. Bernardino da Siena, and Roberto Lecce. Through these exercises, confratelli and consorelle experienced the interiorized, affective spirituality of the mendicants. They also activated a

---

[51] Flagellation declined earlier elsewhere. By the early sixteenth century, members of the Venetian *Scuole Grandi* began paying paupers to flagellate for them. B. Pullan, *Rich and Poor in Renaissance Venice: The Social Institutions of a Catholic State* (Cambridge: 1971), p. 51. See also C. Black, *Italian Confraternities in the Sixteenth Century*, (Cambridge: 1989), pp. 100–3.

[52] As seen in the rules of two subordinate consororities in 1548 and 1549: ASB Dem, Compagnia di S. Maria della Pietà, busta 10/7696, filza 3. ASB Dem, Compagnia di SSmo. Crocifisso del Cestello, busta 1/6738, filza 10.

faith meant as much to protect the body from evil as to console and save the soul.[53]

The most common prayers required of fratelli and sorelle were the Pater Noster and Ave Maria; they followed one's steps and marked the passage of the day. Paters and Aves were called for at every public image of the Virgin, when passing a cemetery, or walking through a church. While Dominican advocates of the Rosary fought to bring uniformity to the recitation of these prayers, individual confraternities assigned them varying mnemonic, pedagogic, and incantory meanings. Three times in honor of the Trinity, five times in memory of the five wounds of Christ, his five holy tears, or his mother's five wounds; seven times marking the seven joys of the Blessed Virgin. Whatever their repetition, these prayers were seen by some in the early fifteenth century as a talisman; the fratello had to make sure that his mind was never empty and hence vulnerable to occupation by the devil. Prayers said immediately on waking and as the last act before sleeping, claimed day and night for God, barring the devil from entering into the thoughts of the fratello.[54]

---

[53] What follows is based on the following sets of confraternal statutes (organized chronologically): Congregatio Devotorum (1261–83) in Angelozzi, Confraternite laicali pp. 86–95; S. Francesco (1317), cap. 3 in Mesini, "S. Maria delle Laudi," pp. 366–72; S. Maria della Misericordia (1399), ASB Dem busta 4/7673, filza 1, cc.2v–r, 4r; S. Girolamo di Miramonte (1425), ASB Dem busta 2/6719 filza 2, cap. 1, 6; S. Geronimo (1433), BBA Gozz 206 #5, cap. 5, 9–17, 38; S. Domenico stretta (1443), BBA Gozz 207 #2; S. Francesco stretta (1443), BBA B983, cap. 1–3, 6–10; S. Bernardino (1454), ASB Dem busta 8/7639, filza 1; S. Maria dei Guarini stretta (1454), BBA Gozz 210 #11, cap. 21; S. Maria della Vita (1454), BBA Osp #10, cap. 21; S. Ambrogio (1456), ASB Codici Miniati #67, cap. 14; S. Bartolomeo di Reno (1471), ASB PIE ms. 1; S. Maria degli Angeli (1479), BBA Gozz 203 #7, cap. 7, 10, 12–13; S. Maria degli Angeli stretta (1479) BBA Gozz 203 #7, cap. 2, 4–5, 11; S. Maria della Mezzaratta del Monte (1484), BBA Gozz 203 #7; S. Francesco (1494), ASB Codici Miniati #61; Spirito Santo (1496), BBA B3180, cap. 3; S. Maria della Pietà (1503), BBA Gozz 206 #7; S. Rocco (ca. 1511–23), ASB Dem busta 6/6589, filza 2, cap. 2–3; SSmo. Crocifisso del Cestello (1514), BBA Gozz 206 #1, cap. 26; S. Maria Maddalena (1515), ASB PIE ms. 1; S. Maria della Carità stretta (1518), BBA Gozz 210 #6, cap. 9–10; Buon Gesù (1521), ASB Dem busta 9/7631 filza 1, cap. 3, 6, 31, 33; S. Maria del Baraccano (1521), BBA Gozz 213 #1, cap. 11; S. Maria degli Angeli stretta (1522), BBA Gozz 203 #7, cap. 1; S. Maria dei Servi (1523), ASB Osp busta 2/307; SS. Sebastiano e Rocco (1525), ASB Dem busta 16/6620 filza 1, cap. 1, 13; SSmo. Crocifisso del Cestello (1538) BBA Gozz 206 #2; S. Maria della Pietà (1548), ASB Dem busta 10/7696 filza 3, cap. 6, 8; SSmo. Crocifisso del Cestello (1549), ASB Dem busta 1/6738 filza 10, cap. 3; SSmo. Crocifisso del Cestello (1570) BBA Gozz 206 #1b.

[54] BBA Gozz 205 #5, cap. 9. This view of the efficacy of prayer held by the Compagnia di S. Girolamo in 1433 is shared by S. Ambrogio (1456, cap. 14); S. Girolamo di Miramonte (1425, cap. 5); and S. Maria della Vita (1454, cap. 27). In a similar vein, Buon Gesù advised bedtime washing of self and family with Holy Water as protection from evil spirits (1520, cap. 31).

After mid-century this incantory approach had faded from newer confraternal statutes to be replaced by emphases on prayer as praising God and feeding the soul.

But prayers were woven into a complete set of mental devotions which varied from company to company and, in some cases from member to member within a company. Members of S. Bernardino added seven Ave Marias at all the canonical hours to the daily regimen of morning and evening prayers, while those of S. Girolamo limited this observance to Saturdays, either reciting all the hours of the Office of our Lady or substituting the "Misere Mei." Buon Gesù was once again the most thorough in this respect, adapting the canonical hours not only to "*homeni mundani e simplici*," but also to the different abilities of members. Literate members recited the Office of Our Lady in the morning with the creed, antiphon, and prayers; the illiterate marked morning and evening with twelve Paters and Aves and all the seven intervening canonical hours with the Apostles' Creed and its prayer.[55] By the early sixteenth century prayers were being widely prescribed at mealtimes, on the principle, S. Maria degli Angeli claimed, of feeding the soul before the body; mealtime prayer is absent from most of the fifteenth-century confraternal rules.[56]

Beyond these prayers, some stretta confraternities prescribed two observances adapting the sacramental exercises of the modern devotion to a lay state: mental confession and attendance at mass. Mental confession was a private act between the believer and God, an evening review of the day in which the fratello examined what he had done poorly, where he could do better, and how he needed forgiveness. It did not replace sacramental confession, but nonetheless had some vague spiritual equivalency; statute prescriptions claimed that those who performed it would at least not be "without confession" should a fatal accident befall. Following procedures described in such popular confessional manuals as St. Antoninus' *Curam illius habe* (1465), mental confession was a systematic examination of conscience and not simply a repetition of conventional prayers. Meditative and free of formulas, it

---

[55] S. Bernardino: ASB Dem, Compagnia di S. Bernardino, busta 8/7639, filza 1, cap. 11–14. S. Geronimo: BBA Gozz 206 #5, cap. 8. Buon Gesù's regulations covered members who did not work through the day; illiterate laborers said seven Paters and Aves with the Creed on weekday mornings and evenings, adding the intervening canonical hours on feast days: ASB Dem, Compagnia di Buon Gesù, busta 9/7631, filza 1, cap. 4.

[56] BBA Gozz 203 #7, cap. 4. Other companies specifying mealtime prayer are S. Maria delle Laudi (1317), S. Maria della Misericordia (1399), S. Geronimo (1433), S. Domenico (1443), S. Francesco (1499), S. Maria della Pietà (1503), and Buon Gesù (1520).

reflected contemporary reformers' preference for mental over vocal prayers. Attending mass was more commonly given as a general obligation going far beyond simply attending those in the confraternity's oratory. Daily mass was a rule suggested for many confratelli though, as S. Domenico statutes noted, "this is a comfort, not a command" ("*Questo e conforto, non commandamento*"). If on workdays they could not stay for the whole mass, staying for the elevation of the host would do. No such toleration was granted on feast days. For procrastinators of a quantitative frame of mind, S. Maria della Vita noted that one mass heard during life was worth more to the soul than a hundred said after death.[57]

IV. DEATH AND DYING

Eliseo Mamelini was slipping fast. Struck by fever, and conscious of his approaching death, the sixty-nine year old notary called on family and friends for assistance. His sons knelt around the bedside to recite prayers and psalms and to receive a blessing "like that which Isaac had given to his children." Mamelini's brothers of the Confraternity of S. Croce trekked daily through the cold Bolognese winter to join in traditional confraternal prayers and help their *fratello* recite the Divine Office. They were joined by their sponsors, the friars of S. Domenico, and the notary's confessor for forty-eight years, Fra Giovanni da Bologna. For over a week these friends spent as much time raising his spirits as praying for his soul. After the Lateran Canons of S. Giovanni in Monte blessed the weakening man with holy oil, he spoke no more. Two friars of S. Domenico attended the sickbed through the nights and, at dawn on the eleventh day of his fever, Eliseo Mamelini died. The Dominicans recited the Office of the Dead and, after confratelli dressed their brother's body in the robes of the Confraternity of S. Croce, the house was opened to any wishing to pay respect to the dead man. Before the funeral procession, the confraternal robes were exchanged for those of the Dominican friars. Attended by crowds of family, neighbors, and friends, a rich procession made up of representatives of the Confraternity of S. Maria della Morte, the guild of Notaries, the Lateran Canons, and a dozen priests followed the Dominican friars to the family sepulcher at S. Domenico. Thereafter, all re-

---

[57] Not least because daily attendance averted venial sins; Angelozzi, *Confraternite Laicali*, pp. 135–41.

turned to the family's house where a Dominican friar preached a sermon of comfort.

This account of Eliseo Mamelini's death in 1531 was written by his son Andrea to conclude the notary's chronicle of his life and times in Bologna.[58] Andrea rounded out the portrait of a man who lived *"como buono et fedel christiano,"* daily attending mass and reciting the Divine Office, entertaining himself by listening to public sermons, and enrolling in more than five confraternities to channel his piety. The conventions of the *ars moriendi* shape and improve the image of a man whose own diary reveals vices mixed with virtues, but the account nonetheless gives us a good picture of the rituals which eased a Bolognese notary's passage to death. Family members, confraternal brothers, guild associates, friars, and priests all laid claim to Mamelini and shared in death-bed and funerary rites. This overlapping and co-operation among potentially competing social networks provides a good starting point from which to look at the significance of death and dying in Renaissance confraternities. Andrea Mamelini's account illustrates the rituals surrounding a confratello's mortal illness and death, and raises the question of what joining more than one confraternity might mean to an individual. Examining these aspects in the context of an individual confratello's life and death reduces the two temptations of looking at death and dying in isolation as a purely confraternal affair, and of seeing confraternities in strictly functional terms as mutual aid societies offering decent burial and requiem prayer. Beyond death, confraternities symbolized a life of charity and regulated worship directly patterned on and continuous with that of the mendicant friars. As voluntary lay communities of prayer, fellow-ship, and charity, they had a particular place and significance along-side other familial, professional, and ecclesiastical associations; from the late fifteenth century, changes in the intersection of politics and charity in the community of Bolognese confraternities deepened this symbolic value.

Confraternal rituals of death and dying reminded members individu-ally and collectively of their bonds of brotherhood and charity. Each member swearing the confraternal oath pledged to remember dead brothers in personal devotions, and with prayers, offices, and requiem masses said in the confraternal oratory. Membership benefits were as

---

[58] Three generations of Mamelini notaries contributed to the chronicle, which spans 1436–1580. A portion has been published as: V. Montanari (ed.), "Cronaca e storia bolognese del primo Cinquecento nel memoriale di ser Eliseo Mamelini," *Quaderni Culturali Bolognesi*, vol. 9 (1979), pp. 5–64. Eliseo Mamelini's death is re-counted on pp. 63–4.

much practical as spiritual, including financial assistance to the terminally ill, and subsidized funerals and burials for the poor.[59]

Care began with the sick. When a brother fell ill, family or confratelli brought his misfortune to the attention of the brotherhood's chief lay official, the Ordinario. The Ordinario then set about caring for the member's physical and spiritual needs, perhaps by visiting himself, but above all by calling on the collective resources of the brotherhood. He explained the sick man's needs at the next worship service, and encouraged all to add prayers for his recovery to their daily devotions. In close-knit flagellant companies, the Ordinario appointed some brothers as visitors, charged with visiting daily to determine the sick man's condition and keep him company should he wish it. Larger praising companies might authorize a single visit by the Ordinario. Visitors usually came in pairs, and in the case of a lengthy illness, were relieved in weekly rotation on a schedule drawn up by the Ordinario. Poor brothers received alms from the confraternal purse. Such acts of mercy had the potential of draining the purse of less-established brotherhoods, so a number of Quattrocento statutes required that the brothers hold special collections for this purpose, either from first need or when the

[59] Descriptions of care for the dying and dead are drawn from the following confraternal statute books (organized chronologically): Congregatio Devotorum (1261–83), cap. 15–19 in Angelozzi, Confraternite laicali, p. 95; S. Francesco (1317), cap. 5 & 6 in Mesini, "S. Maria delle Laudi," pp. 366–72; S. Girolamo di Miramonte (1425), ASB Dem busta 2/6719 fol. 2, cap. 15; S. Geronimo (1433), BBA Gozz 206 #5, cap. 13; S. Domenico stretta (1443), BBA Gozz 207 #2, cap. 14 & 15; S. Francesco stretta (1443), BBA B983, cap. 32; S. Bernardino (1454), ASB Dem busta 8/7639 fol. 1, pt. 2; S. Maria dei Guarini stretta (1454), BBA Gozz 210 #11, cap. 11; S. Maria della Vita (1454), BBA Osp #10, cap. 17; S. Ambrogio (1456), ASB Codici Miniati #67, cap. 17; S. Bartolomeo di Reno (1471), ASB PIE ms. 1, cap. 11; S. Maria degli Angeli (1479), BBA Gozz 203 #7, cap. 5, 14. S. Maria degli Angeli stretta (1479) BBA Gozz 203 #7, cap. 15–16. S. Maria della Mezzaratta del Monte (1484), BBA Gozz 203 #7; S. Francesco (1494), ASB Codici Miniati #61; Spirito Santo (1496), BBA B3180, cap. 13–14; S. Maria della Pietà (1503), BBA Gozz 206 #7, cap. 2; S. Rocco (ca. 1511–23), ASB Dem busta 6/6589 fol. 2, cap. 3; SSmo. Crocifisso del Cestello (1514), BBA Gozz 206 #1, cap. 17; S. Maria Maddalena (1515), ASB PIE ms. 1, cap. 27; S. Maria della Carità stretta (1518), BBA Gozz 210 #6, cap. 20; Buon Gesù (1521), ASB Dem busta 9/7631 fol. 1, cap. 11; S. Maria del Baraccano (1521), BBA Gozz 213 #1, cap. 17; S. Maria degli Angeli stretta (1522), BBA Gozz 203 #7; S. Maria dei Servi (1523), ASB Osp busta 2/307, cap. 19–20; SS. Sebastiano e Rocco, (1525), ASB Dem busta 16/6620 fol. 1, cap. 15; SSmo. Crocifisso del Cestello (1538) BBA Gozz 206 #2; S. Maria della Pietà (1548), ASB Dem busta 10/7696 fol. 3, cap. 8; SSmo. Crocifisso del Cestello (1549), ASB Dem busta 1/6738 fol. 10, cap. 5, 8; SSmo. Crocifisso del Cestello (1570) BBA Gozz 206 #1b. See also, J. Henderson, "Religious Confraternities and Death in Early Renaissance Florence," in P. Denley and C. Elam (eds.), Florence and Italy: Renaissance Studies in Honour of Nicolai Rubinstein (London: 1988), pp. 383–94.

brotherhood's resources had come to their limit. As the sixteenth-century demographic crisis squeezed all forms of voluntary charity, a few companies turned these sporadic alms donated out of brotherly charity into exclusive confraternal insurance plans with prescribed weekly premiums and predetermined scales of assistance regardless of need; this effectively pushed the truly needy out of the confraternity, since their inability to pay premiums robbed them of coverage.[60] Beyond attending to physical needs, the visitors assessed and reported on the spiritual health of the fratello, reading to him from the Bible and devotional works, encouraging him to set the affairs of his soul in order, and keeping the brotherhood informed of his progress. As death approached, the confraternity's hired priest arrived and, spiritually armed with the plenary indulgences every company collected, administered the last rites.

Upon death the confraternal kin mobilized to mourn and prepare the body for burial, activities that had traditionally been the preserve of natural kin. Practices varied from group to group on these points, with some companies limiting observance to a few private prayers while others turned burial into a major confraternal ritual; in general, these services became more elaborate and more public in the later Quattrocento and Cinquecento, particularly in flagellant companies. Bologna's earliest major confraternity, the Trecento Congregatio Devotorum, had brought its poorer members to the grave very simply on an unadorned bier and without great ceremony. Later confraternities continued underwriting the burial costs of poorer members, and the practice became so associated with serving the poor that by the early Quattrocento statutes for companies of high-born confratelli were silent on members' burial. By the mid-Quattrocento companies began restoring the practical services of a cooperative burial society, but on a more lavish scale which no doubt helped many members to overcome the traditional stigma of a pauper's burial and to rely on spiritual kin to conduct them to their grave. In flagellant companies, the Ordinario called all members to the Oratory and dispatched seven or eight of the better cantors to go the dead man's house ahead of the main procession. Armed with robes, candles, and psalters, on arrival they flanked the body, lit their candles and knelt to recite the penitential psalms. As the others arrived, this first group took up the body and with all

---

[60] ASB Dem, Compagnia di Buon Gesù, busta 9/7631, filza 1 (revision of May 2, 1588). The brotherhoods of S. Maria dei Guarini and S. Maria della Carità developed similar systems in this period. For similar developments in Florence see: R.F.E. Weissman, "Brothers and Strangers: Confraternal Charity in Renaissance Florence," *Historical Reflections/Réflexions Historiques*, vol. 15 (1988), p. 35.

members now bearing candles and singing psalms, the robed procession made its way behind the confraternal standard to the parish, mendicant, or confraternal church designated by the *defunto*. There was some exclusivity to the company's claim to the body; the brothers of S. Maria della Vita noted that they recited penitential psalms in procession because they were a devout form of grieving which could drown out the distracting racket made by female relations and professional mourners.[61] John Henderson has suggested that increasingly elaborate confraternal funeral processions in Florence may have been motivated by members' desire to circumvent sumptuary laws which from 1281 limited the number of candles, banners, and mourners who brought the defunto to his rest.[62] This may have been the case in Bologna as well, since funerary rites begin expanding at the time when civil and ecclesiastical authorities first began the attempt to limit funeral pomp. Papal Legate Francesco Gonzaga had some initial success with a decree of 1476, but the frequent renewal of sumptuary laws directed at funerals shows that in Bologna, as elsewhere, old habits died hard.[63] The sumptuary laws may be a negative factor behind expanding confraternal funerary rituals, but a parallel growth of requiems and prayers suggests that confratelli put spiritual intercession on a par with legal circumvention when increasing their collective role in the rituals of death.

Confraternal interest in the defunto did not end with his interment. As a rule, praising confraternities annually observed a single requiem mass for all those members who had "passed from this life to the other," but seldom marked the deaths of individual members. Flagellant confraternities had traditionally gone further, reflecting the greater personal ties formed between members of these small and intensely spiritual groups. Flagellant fratelli added prayers for particular dead brothers to their personal devotions, with each brotherhood fashioning multiple recitations of *Paters* and *Aves* particular to itself and varied, in

---

[61] "... sera più devotione perche li varii obiecti o de femene o pianti o altri strepiti multa fano variare li sentimenti." BBA Osp, ms. 10, cap. 9.

[62] J. Henderson, *Piety and Charity in Late Medieval Florence*, (Oxford: 1994), p. 160. In contemporary Venice, confraternities provided much of the grandeur for funerals of prominent public officials. Doge Leonardo Loredan's 1521 cortège included 119 *scuole*, Cardinal Corner's of 1525 had 111, and funeral processions for the French (1521) and Papal (1514) ambassadors had 96 and 64 respectively: R. Mackenney, *Tradesmen and Traders: The World of the Guilds in Venice and Europe*, (London: 1987), p. 140.

[63] Bursellis, *Cronaca gestorum, RIS* vol. 23, Pt. II, p. 103 [l. 37–9]. L. Frati, *La vita privata in Bologna dal secolo XIII al XVII*, (Bologna: 1928), p. 51.

some cases, according to members' condition or gender.[64] Yet the flagellants' collective or communal rites also focused on the dead as a group, limiting observance to frequent recitations of Offices of the Dead and monthly or annual requiem masses. Changes appearing in statute books from the mid-Quattrocento stand out not simply because they increased the practical services offered to dying members, but because they turned confraternal recognition of individual deaths from a private into a collective act. They can be seen as examples of the idea of "dying well" which spread generally in Europe from the later Trecento, stimulated by a growing preoccupation with mortality and assisted by numerous devotional guides patterned after the anonymous *Ars moriendi*. This treatise circulated widely in manuscript and print editions, with at least two published in Bologna in the 1470s.[65] The *ars moriendi* was not a purely private exercise, but a process of questioning, catechizing, and comforting the dying man in a circle of spiritual kin. Once the soul departed, these kin carried the art to its earthly conclusion by ensuring proper funerary and requiem observances. With its existing system of visitors, prayers, and requiems, the confraternal community was a natural locus around which this art could develop. Certainly flagellant brotherhoods began surrounding death with an increasing number of spiritual observances from the early Cinquecento. On the night death struck, SS. Sebastiano e Rocco posted a guard of four brothers reciting the penitential psalms and the vespers requiem. Many companies followed the example of Eliseo Mamelini's brothers and dressed the body in the robes which the defunto had worn in worship, procession, and flagellation.[66] On the evening of

[64] Examples of the wide variety of private devotions required of members to mark the death of a brother or sister: S. Ambrogio (1456) required 100 Paters and Aves or 5 recitations of the 7 penitential psalms; S. Francesco (1494) required 7 Paters and Aves; S. Geronimo (1433) 10 daily recitations of the penitential psalms for 15 days or, for illiterates, 150 Paters and Aves; S. Maria Maddalena (1515) a daily Pater and Ave for 3 months; S. Rocco (ca. 1511–23) 12 Paters and Aves. Buon Gesù had literates recite the Office of the Dead and illiterates the Pater and Ave. S. Bernardino (1451) had women say 100 Paters and Aves, and men say 50; SSmo. Crocifisso del Cestello (1538; 1570) had women say 5 Paters and Aves daily for a month; males said nothing.

[65] The editions of the *Ars moriendi* printed in Bologna were issued in 1475 and 1478. A. Tenenti, *Il senso della morte e l'amore della vita nel Rinascimento*, (Torino: 1957), pp. 80–102; p. 106 n. 67.

[66] Patrician companies like Buon Gesù, SS. Sebastiano e Rocco, and S. Croce dressed the defunto's body in confraternal robes as a matter of course; artisanal companies like S. Bartolomeo di Reno did so only if the robe had been paid for in advance: ASB PIE, Compagnia di S. Bartololmeo di Reno, ms. 1, c. 13r. Women in consororities subordinate to a flagellant confraternity shared in the company's merit through burial in its robes, even though they had not flagellated or worn the robes in procession: ASB Dem, Compagnia di S. Maria della Pietà, busta 10/7696, filza 3, cap. 8.

interment or at the next feast day, brothers assembled at the oratory and recited an Office of the Dead. Here they also gave alms for the requiem mass. Mid-Quattrocento Ordinarios simply arranged for a mass to be said at a time and place of their own convenience; by the early Cinquecento, more statutes specified that it be sung in the mendicant church associated with the company's hired priest, or, in the case of SS. Sebastiano e Rocco, ordered that the mass be conducted by the priest in the confraternal chapel and be preceded by all the brothers reciting the penitential psalms for an hour. All of these multiplying collective observances were in addition to both the prescribed series of private memorial devotions conducted by fratelli in their homes, and the annual requiem services for all the dead brothers.[67] Bolognese confraternities did not follow their Venetian counterparts in appointing professional visitors and mourners to carry out obligations to the dead and dying in return for regular alms or housing in confraternal properties. Rather, by the early Cinquecento, participation became a test of obedience, and some companies severely censured members who failed to fulfill their obligations to the dead.[68]

Participation could clearly become a problem in the case of those individuals who, like Eliseo Mamelini, joined more than one brotherhood. The practice seems to violate frequent statute prohibitions against "serving two masters," and raises questions about how seriously brothers took the meaning and obligations of confraternal membership. We can certainly interpret multiple memberships as indications of either spiritual indifference or anxiety, or as a purely practical means of expanding professional and political networks. Yet these spiritual and practical dimensions are united and deepened when seen through the complementary values of community and charity and in the context of developments in Bologna in the late fifteenth and early sixteenth centuries.

In a gospel passage familiar to all confratelli, Christ gives a lesson in charity and salvation (Matthew 25: 31–46). He warns that when judging humanity at the end of time, he will separate the sheep from the goats, admitting the former to eternal life and damning the latter to

[67] Most confraternities held a requiem service on the feast of All Saints, with such individual observances as the day following the Company saint's day (S. Bernardino: 1454), the first Sunday in Lent (Buon Gesù: 1521), or the first Monday of every month (S. Francesco: 1494).

[68] S. Francesco ordered all members to attend the monthly mass for the dead, but prescribed no penalties for violators. Buon Gesù punished those who avoided funeral processions by relegating them to the novices' bench for a month and requiring them to kiss the feet of other fratelli at every festival through this period. On Venice: Pullan, *Rich and Poor in Renaissance Venice*, pp. 76–8.

eternal punishment. Judgment will be based on charity: giving food and drink to the hungry and thirsty, clothing the naked, visiting prisoners and the sick, and sheltering strangers. Extending such charity to anyone extends it to Christ; refusing charity to anyone is a refusal of Christ, a refusal he will reciprocate. With the addition of burying the dead, the seven works of corporal charity moved to the center of Catholic theology and communal spirituality; as John Bossy notes, "the state of charity, meaning social integration, was the principal end of the Christian life, and any people that claimed to be Christian must embody it somehow, at some time, in this world."[69]

Confraternal charity extended in two directions: inward as spiritual and physical assistance to fellow brothers and sisters, and outward as assistance to the needy. The two were sometimes distinguished as *caritas* and *misericordia*, respectively, but both were equally parts of a whole spiritual life.[70] Inwardly directed charity strengthened individual bonds of brotherhood and hence the communal strength of the confraternity; no brother need fear hunger or the pauper's grave. Out of this communal strength arose charity to the community and strangers, by which the brothers expressed thanks and service to Christ in the spirit of his promise, "Whenever you did it to the least of these, you did it to me." "Caritas" and "misericordia" always worked reciprocally in the confraternities, and distinguished them from the guilds, which typically assisted only their own members. At the same time, some confraternities cultivated one or the other. Flagellant confraternities had traditionally concentrated their efforts within the brotherhood, making only token gestures of charity to the broader civic community in the form of periodic distribution of alms or bread. Praising confraternities dedicated themselves to the poor of Christ living in and passing through Bologna, and from the early Trecento established ospedali, or hostels, each of which met a variety of needs. This focus on "caritas" or "misericordia," respectively, reflected different conceptions of the meaning of brotherhood which are underlined in the injunctions against "serving two masters." The rule appears only in statutes of the close-knit and secretive flagellant brotherhoods, and applies to members who might wish to join another such group. Consistent with their image of themselves as a brotherhood of Christ's disciples, the flagellants aimed for a much more intense and exclusive form of

---

[69] Bossy, *Christianity in the West*, p. 57.
[70] *Caritas* was the love between equals while *misericordia* was help offered to the disadvantaged. Mackenney, *Tradesmen and Traders*, p. 6. See also: "Charité," *Dictionnaire de Spiritualitè*, vol. II (Paris: 1953), pp. 507–661; and "Miséricorde (Oevres de)," *Dictionnaire de Spiritualitè*, vol. LXVIII–LXIX (Paris: 1979), pp. 1328–49.

community than their praising counterparts. Flagellant brotherhoods did not object to members joining one or more of the more loosely structured and less-demanding praising confraternities, nor did the praising confraternities themselves rule against joining more than one group of this type.[71] Hence community and charity were complementary, and individuals could easily merge "caritas" and "misericordia" without violating confraternal statutes by joining one flagellant brotherhood, and more than one praising brotherhood.

Changes in Bolognese ospedali from the later fifteenth century encouraged those who looked on multiple membership as having both spiritual and practical benefits. Through this period the praising confraternities began redirecting their efforts from undifferentiated charity to the poor towards specializing instead in particular actions. We will look at this development in greater detail later, but a brief review will set this discussion of multiple confraternal memberships in context. The pattern began when four confraternities amalgamated in 1450 to form S. Maria degli Angeli, taking over an all-but-abandoned Benedictine hostel and transforming it into a civic foundling home on the model of Florence's recently opened S. Maria degli Innocenti; as costs mounted, more confraternities merged into the growing institution. At the end of this period, S. Maria del Baraccano transformed its hostel into a girls' orphanage in 1527, and S. Bartolomeo di Reno balanced this by turning its hostel into a boys' orphanage a few years later. Many changes occurred in between. In the spreading wake of the "*mal francese*," S. Maria dei Guarini began sheltering and treating only syphilitics. Meanwhile, a new charitable company arose to deal with the problem of *poveri vergognosi*, the shameful poor; the Compagnia di S. Maria del Morte established a separate *Scuola dei Confortatori* to comfort prisoners awaiting execution, and the *Opera dei Poveri Prigionieri* to give food, drink, and spiritual assistance to those in prison for debt or awaiting trial; and the Compagnia di S. Maria della Vita expanded its infirmary for ailing Bolognese. As these companies turned towards specializing in particular social problems, the confraternities of S. Francesco and S. Maria dei Servi expanded their hostels in order better to continue the traditional role of sheltering the thousands of pilgrims who streamed through Bologna on their way through the Apennine passes to Rome.

Communal governments encouraged this specialization through concessions on gate and mill taxes, grants for capital expansion, periodic alms for operating expenses, and legislation encouraging or re-

---

[71] Alberigo, "Contributi alla storia delle confraternite dei disciplinati," pp. 170–1.

quiring Bolognese guilds to support the new institutions of social welfare. Perhaps more significantly, politically dominant groups both under the Bentivoglio signory and under the papal regimes installed by Julius II in 1506 and again in 1512 realized that one means of consolidating a shaky hold on political power lay in gaining control of the institutions which sheltered Bologna's orphans, cared for its poor, and healed its sick.[72] In the specialization of confraternal ospedali, spiritual purposes combined with *raison d'état*. Giovanni II Bentivoglio's interest in confraternities grew noticeably during his effort to cement power after the Malvezzi conspiracy of 1488: already a member of the confraternity overseeing the family shrine of S. Maria del Baraccano, he enrolled himself, his legitimate and illegitimate sons, and large numbers of his supporters, in S. Maria degli Angeli in 1494, and S. Maria dei Centurati in 1495. The post-Bentivoglio oligarchs moved more carefully, gradually increasing their membership in the praising confraternities which sponsored ospedali and initiating constitutional changes which left these institutions in the care of a separate self-perpetuating Board of Governors whose patrician members served life terms. Many leading patricians enrolled themselves and their supporters in more than one confraternity and served as Governors of more than one ospedale.

This brings us back to Eliseo Mamelini. The Bolognese notary belonged to a reputable if not patrician family, and had married into a family better than his own.[73] He had held some minor positions in the communal government and guild administration, but was not closely identified with any faction.[74] Ready to trim his sails to the prevailing wind, he is more characteristic of Bolognese attitudes than those patri-

---

[72] Marvin Becker notes a similar drive to expand and control confraternal social assistance among Florentine patricians after the 1378 *Ciompi* revolt: M. Becker, "Aspects of Lay Piety in Early Renaissance Florence," in C. Trinkaus and H. Oberman (eds.), *The Pursuit of Holiness in Late Medieval and Renaissance Religion*, (Leiden: 1974), p. 189.

[73] Mamelini was prominent enough to marry Tadia, the daughter of Lodovico de Dolpho, in 1503, and receive from him a dowry of 1,600 lire *de bolognini* and the promise that Tadia would inherit half of his considerable estate. Lodovico Dolpho was also a notary and served in 1503 as Procurator of Bologna; the family was included in a list of 100 leading families compiled by Bentivoglio partisan Fileno della Tuate: Montanari (ed.), "Memoriale di ser Eliseo Mamelini," pp. 11–12; BBU Ms 437.

[74] Mamelini became a notary in 1486 and served as one of four *gonfalonieri del popolo* for the Quarter of San Procolo in 1505 and 1515; consul of the Notaries Guild for the second semester of 1519 and again in 1521 when consuls first received payment of 50 lire; and notary of the Guild in second semester of 1524: Montanari (ed.), "Memoriale di ser Eliseo Mamelini," pp. 12, 34, 40, 43.

cians whose convictions led them into revolution and exile. His legal skills and membership in Bologna's most prominent guild ensured that Mamelini could not avoid political involvement, however carefully he might wish to separate it from the potentially damaging taint of factionalism. With this we have enough for a functional analysis of Mamelini's membership in many confraternities: obliging and astute, he contributed to a process by which his superiors could solidify their power and dispense patronage. Lorenzo de'Medici and Giovanni II Bentivoglio had modelled this cunning detached approach long before with multiple memberships which allowed them to keep a finger on the political pulse of potentially disruptive groups.[75]

Adequate in itself, this analysis fails to deal with the confraternities as spiritual communities or with the importance of charity in contemporary piety. Recent studies of late-sixteenth century French flagellant confraternities have shown that pragmatic politics and intensely devout piety need not be seen as opposite or competing categories.[76] Quite apart from his political life, the confraternities organized Mamelini's devotional life; they were not chosen at random, but with a deliberate eye to fulfilling specific spiritual duties. The single flagellant group, the Compagnia di S. Croce, provided the closest structure of regular worship, spiritual kinship, and caritas. The numerous charitable confraternities channelled Mamelini's exercise of misericordia, not in any random way, but in fulfillment of all seven acts of corporal charity. Through S. Maria del Baraccano he clothed, fed, and dowered orphan girls; through S. Maria degli Angeli he cared for abandoned infants; through S. Maria della Morte he comforted prisoner's souls and buried their bodies; through S. Maria della Vita he assisted the sick; and through the Monte di Pietà he assisted the poor and widowed.[77] Parti-

---

[75] Giovanni II Bentivoglio joined at least three groups (S. Maria del Baraccano, S. Maria della Pietà, S. Maria dei Centurati). Lorenzo de'Medici joined six (Compagnia de'Magi, San Paolo, S. Domenico, Gesù Pellegrino, S. Maria delle Croce al Tempio, S. Agnese); of these, S. Agnese was Lorenzo's "neigborhood" confraternity, in which he frequently held office: Weissman, *Ritual Brotherhood*, pp. 169–70. In Venice, Antonio Tron, an unsuccessful candidate for the dogeship in 1523, was a member of six confraternities: Mackenney, *Tradesmen and Traders*, p. 139.

[76] R.R. Harding, "The Mobilization of Confraternities Against the Reformation in France," *Sixteenth Century Journal* vol. 16 (1980): 85–107. A.E. Barnes, "Religious Anxiety and Devotional Change in Sixteenth Century French Penitential Confraternities," *Sixteenth Century Journal*, vol. 19 (1988): 389–405. A.E. Barnes, *The Social Dimension of Piety: Associative Life and Devotional Change in the Penitent Confraternities of Marseille (1499–1792)* (Matwah, NJ: 1994).

[77] Mamelini and his wife Tadia joined "la Compagnia del Monte dela Pietà" in 1508, paying annual dues of 13 soldi. Montanari (ed.), "Memoriale di ser Eliseo Mamelini," p. 19.

cularly after Bologna's confraternities specialized their activities in the later fifteenth and early sixteenth centuries, multiple memberships could ensure that the prosperous and devout layman would perform all the canonical works of charity necessary in order to be counted among the sheep rather than among the goats at the Last Judgment. Political necessity required only that many be chosen; religious necessity required that each choice be deliberate. Hence far from being a sign of spiritual indifference, multiple memberships among the highborn are signs of a devotion alive to the common view that damnation awaited those who had the means to perform the works of corporal charity but failed.[78] As such, they fit in with the *ars moriendi* quite as well as with the *ars politica*. Each confraternity had its means of comforting the dying and remembering the dead. Confratelli gathering at the deathbed graphically reminded the dying man that he had done what Christ required; more to the point, their annual prayers and requiems reminded Christ himself of the brother's charity.

If all the confraternities participated in the funeral procession, the dead man's family and neighbors would also see a clear and comforting demonstration of his pious charity – a demonstration as helpful to the *onore* of the house as to the salvation of its *patrone*'s soul.[79] More likely, as with the case of Eliseo Mamelini, the dying man would appoint specific roles to individual confraternities within the extended ceremonies and among the competing professional and personal networks of his life. As his closest spiritual kin, the brothers of S. Croce won the right to dress Mamelini's body in their robes; as the most prestigious of all Bologna's approximately eighty confraternities, the Compagnia di S. Maria della Morte led his funeral procession. The Notaries' Guild, the Dominicans, Lateran Canons, and parish priests took over other functions. Much as civic processions put the religious and political hierarchy on a moving stage, so the funeral procession was a religious and political biography, a story told by marching ranks of confratelli, guildsmen, and clerics, and understood by all who watched. Looking at multiple memberships in this way through the focus of a single individual and in the twin contexts of civic politics and confraternal com-

---

[78] In his 1560 revision of an earlier catechism used in Schools of Christian Doctrine, the Theatine Giovanni Paolo Montorfano noted that for those lacking the means, it was enough to do the corporal works of charity "in desire"; those with sufficient means who failed to do them committed a grave sin, as proven by Christ's threat of damnation in Matthew 25:41–6. P.F. Grendler, "The Schools of Christian Doctrine in Sixteenth-Century Italy," *Church History* vol. 53 (1984): 327–9.

[79] S. Strocchia, "Death Rites and the Ritual Family in Renaissance Florence," M. Tetel *et al.* (eds.), *Life and Death in Fifteenth Century Florence* (Durham: 1988), pp. 120–5. S. Strocchia, *Death and Ritual in Renaissance Florence*. (Baltimore: 1993).

munity and charity allows us a deeper understanding of the intertwined spiritual and political concerns of those who joined more than one confraternity. The greatest, and to date unresolved, difficulty lies in determining how many Eliseo Mamelinis there were, and how common the practice was beyond the patriciate. Since those whose multiple memberships are best known are civic leaders, it is tempting to see the phenomenon in the limited functional terms of political patronage and control. Matriculation lists survive for less than a quarter of the roughly eighty confraternities active in fifteenth- and early sixteenth-century Bologna, and not all extant lists overlap. *Riccordi* may provide a key, as in Mamelini's case, but they too give only a spotty sample and as John Henderson has found in Florence, most diarists were curiously taciturn in reporting their confraternal memberships.[80]

Changing confraternal rituals, fluctuating membership retention statistics, and the practice and meanings of multiple memberships each lend their own color to our picture of confraternal death and dying. The complex image which they together present should remind us to be cautious when making firm distinctions between laudesi and disciplinati confraternities, or when emphasizing the practical or sociological functions membership may fulfill. We can assemble institutional differences into a picture of distinct strands within popular piety, only to find our neat categories blurred by those fratelli who found spiritual benefits in diversity. We can itemize the insurance and burial benefits which brotherhoods afforded their members, only to find that these were seldom drawn on. We can coordinate member's age with confraternal type, only to find that there may be a stronger pull between member's type and confraternal age. Ronald Weissman has suggested that flagellant confraternities were largely liminal groups for young patricians, and praising confraternities were primarily burial societies for artisans of modest means. While Bolognese confraternities did not record members' ages, their recruitment and retention appear to have had less to do with the life cycle of individual members than with the life cycle and institutional culture of the brotherhood itself.[81] Here too, political pragmatism and spiritual concern could find a happy union in individuals who joined both flagellant and praising in their search for community and charity.

[80] J. Henderson, "Le confraternite religiose nella Firenze del tardo Medioevo: patroni spirituali e anche politici?" *Ricerche Storiche* vol. 15 (1985), p. 79. Alberigo notes that multiple memberships were common in different parts of Italy: Alberigo, "Contributi alla storia delle confraternite," pp. 170–1.

[81] Weissman, *Ritual Brotherhood*, pp. 75–6.

The example of Eliseo Mamelini reminds us that confraternal statutes are only a beginning to understanding confraternal death and dying, or confraternal devotional life generally. Confraternal statutes set up *desideratae* which might find only partial translation into reality: apart from those inevitable communities whose observance was lax, not all members used the full range of services offered by their brotherhood. Some left before death, others received similar services from their guild, family, or other confraternities. Like all who kept an eye on eternity, Eliseo Mamelini fashioned a dense network of overlapping spiritual ties with mendicant orders, an individual confessor, and lay brotherhoods. He joined a cluster of confraternities whose social services he did not need, in order better to practice his daily worship, fulfill his political duties, and secure his eternal future. Artisans, small merchants, and all those lacking Mamelini's family sepulcher, high profession, political offices, or social connections would have more restricted networks, but would still have to mediate between these. Confraternal membership gave them cooperative access to the spiritual resources that Mamelini enjoyed by virtue of his personal wealth and status: a confessor, indulgences, an honorable funeral, and interment in mendicant robes. Beyond this, family, guild, and parish all laid their claims. Regardless of class, confratelli were never just confratelli. Not all who joined a brotherhood remained until death, or needed its extensive services. What they drew from the brotherhood depended largely on the strength of other strands in their kin, occupational, and parochial networks, and must often have resulted in very individual compounds. This is the negotiation noted at the beginning of the chapter. The very fact that it was possible should guard us against making rash statements about lay piety based on studies of parochial, guild, or confraternal life in isolation, or from assuming that common people were passive receptors of a ready-made spirituality handed down to them from above.

While they did not exhaust lay spirituality, confraternities were nonetheless the chief organized expression of that spirituality, and hence the chief agencies which allowed the layman to fashion a more individual liturgical life. In the life of the Renaissance Italian layman they offered the practical benefits of the parish, and the spiritual rules and community of the monastery. On one hand they provided communal worship, sacraments, and mutual assistance in sickness and death; all these were services later provided by the parish. On the other hand, they ordered the layman's devotional life by statutes which paralleled strict mendicant rules without requiring vows of poverty, chastity, and obedience. We cannot know how diligently confraternal statutes were followed, but it would be foolish to assume that the rule was always practiced as written. By the same token, given the individual's need to satisfy the demands of kin, fellow guildsmen, parish neighbors, and possibly more than one confraternity, we should not assume that departures from the rule signify laxness or indifference. Whatever the character of an individual's mediation of these competing demands, there is an underlying unity and that is the notion that mendicant spirituality was in some way normative. The involvement of confratelli and friars in Eliseo Mamelini's death and burial confirms the continuity of confraternal and mendicant spirituality. This continuity is symbolized in the transfer of his body from confraternal to mendicant robes for burial; the first are a foreshadowing, the latter a culmination, but to Bolognese confratelli the two formed a whole.

3

THE MECHANICS OF MEMBERSHIP

Questions regarding the source and significance of confraternal piety would be virtually meaningless if the spiritual companies were marginal groups attracting a handful of members. In fact, the Bolognese confraternities, like their counterparts across Europe, attracted from ten to twenty percent of the adult population through the fifteenth and sixteenth centuries.[1] At the beginning of this period, they drew men and women from a broad cross-section of Bolognese society; towards the end social and gender distinctions restricted access and led to new forms of confraternal association.

Statute provisions and membership statistics demonstrate again the self-regulating congregational nature of the spiritual companies, and underscore how they could function as lay alternatives to both the local parish and the monastery. We look first at the ceremonies surrounding the novitiate and profession to full membership, setting these against statistics showing how many novices of one company subsequently became professing members. The question of which confraternity an individual might approach is set in the context of the social geography of groups and the social standing of their members. Statistics on confraternal size, growth, and attendance indicate how many Bolognese claimed confraternal membership and how diligently they attended to the duties of membership. The processes and statistics of expulsions allow us to assess collective reaction to the less diligent, while statistics for members remaining until death indicate individual reaction to the collectivity. The mechanics of membership discussed in this chapter clarify the distinction which emerged in the previous chapter's discussion of confraternal spirituality generally and confraternal

---

[1] J. Bossy, *Christianity in the West*, (New York: 1985), p. 58. The Bolognese estimate is based on Tables 3.4 and 3.5, by which we can conservatively estimate approximately 5,000 confratelli by the early Cinquecento; a small proportion of these would be made up of multiple memberships.

treatment of death and dying: praising laudesi confraternities which had arisen in the Trecento tended to be inclusive groups which focused on and drew from the urban community, while penitential battuti and stretta groups which emerged out of the Quattrocento Observant reforms focused their attention more exclusively on the lay brotherhood itself. This chapter further explores the paradox of the fifteenth-century devotional reforms by considering their effect on women's participation in confraternities. Women had always participated in the laudesi confraternities because they were recognized as indispensable members of the local neighborhood with a role to play in the neighborhood's public worship and charitable service. Under the Observant reforms, battuti and stretta groups worked to create holy brotherhoods which transcended the neighborhoods and excluded all those who could tempt the brothers from the path of virtue. Where laudesi had recognized wives, daughters, sisters, and mothers, the battuti and stretta saw only the Temptress who would corrupt the pure brotherhood. The penitential devotional reforms pushed women out of most of the Compagnie Spirituali by the later fifteenth century. Yet as we have already seen, those same reforms also pushed artisanal men to the margins when patricians began to recognize the advantages of expropriating the reputation of Compagnie Spirituali as exponents of the civic religion and agents of civic welfare. We will see that women's reintegration into the confraternities in the mid-sixteenth century is set in the context of this politicization of the confraternities, and that as a result their membership and activities are on very different terms from what they had been in the laudesi confraternities of the Trecento.

I. NOVITIATE AND PROFESSION

The model of the mendicant rules emerges clearly in membership provisions that confraternities drew up and demonstrates their desire to provide the worship environment, devotional exercises, and spiritual benefits of the clerical vocation to those who remained in lay life. Like a religious order, the confraternity prepared its members for death in part by spiritual exercises which accustomed them to the rhythms of holiness in life, and in part by ensuring that only those predisposed to these rhythms could join the brotherhood. As it developed, the novitiate gave both the applicant and the full members opportunity to judge their mutual compatibility in devotions and character.

The Congregatio Devotorum civitatis bononie of 1261 had included a novitiate among its earliest statutes, stipulating that those who wished to join were to give their name, family name, and parish to the appointed official, who passed it on to the rector. For two months the novice followed the rule of the confraternity, including flagellation. If he observed the rule well, the rector initiated him into the brotherhood by investing him in the flagellant's robe during a chapter meeting; the novice provided his own robe for the ceremony. Existing members had no definite role in nominating, screening, or approving applicants for the Congregatio Devotorum, indicating that the secrecy and closed membership which later characterized flagellant confraternities had not yet been adopted. Rather, the Congregatio took all those of "*onesta vita*," who presented themselves. Even its definition of the honest life was generously inclusive, banning only usurers, those who took – or wished to take – concubines, and those who frequented taverns or disreputable places without good reason; visiting taverns in the company of fellow merchants in order to buy and sell was quite acceptable.[2] With this "open door" policy, the novitiate of the Congregatio Devotorum was less a means of selecting than of educating entrants to the confraternity. Trecento laudesi confraternities followed this openness and often dispensed with the novitiate altogether. Neither the 1317 statutes of the laudesi meeting in S. Francesco, nor the 1329 statutes for a company meeting in S. Procolo, specify procedures for accepting new members; applicants were put to a vote of the confraternal officials, and written into the matriculation list after they had acquired the appropriate cape.[3] Quattrocento laudesi groups such as the Compagnia di S. Bernardino of 1454 required only that applicants be innocent of any real or suspected heresy, that they give up any illicit or prohibited activity ("*l'arte prohibita*"), and that they confess to a priest within eight days of being added to the matriculation list.[4]

The openness of laudesi confraternities grew out of their view that the confraternity was to be a vehicle for mutual assistance in life and death, and an aid to greater public devotion by all in the neighborhood, including women; both S. Francesco and S. Bernardino accepted female members, as did most other laudesi confraternities until the later fifteenth and early sixteenth centuries. Membership was refused only to those who were too young, or those who habitually practiced very public sins. These would be common knowledge in the

---

[2] These regulations are discussed in Chapters 4 and 20 of the Statutes, which are reprinted in Angelozzi, *Confraternite laicali*, pp. 87, 90.

[3] Both sets of statutes have been published: Mesini, "S. Maria delle Laudi," pp. 366–72. Fanti, *San Procolo*, pp. 186–7.

[4] ASB Dem, Compagnia di S. Bernardino, busta 8/7639 filza 1, Section 1, Chapters i, ii, iii. Other statutes lacking a definite novitiate include: S. Maria della Pietà (1503); S. Rocco (ca. 1511–23).

neighborhood, and so there was no need for a trial period to test the moral and spiritual *conditione* of applicants to the confraternity.

Flagellant battuti and stretta groups operated with considerably more restrictive admission and membership requirements, for they viewed the confraternity as an apostolate of the virtuous. Members were chosen by God through the vehicle of the communal vote, and the novitiate demonstrated their virtues while showing whether they were fit for the devotions of any particular group. On a spiritual level, the battuti and stretta were fearful of admitting a wolf to the sheepfold of their brotherhood. On a practical level as well, they met more often and in closer groups than the large laudesi companies, making it important to determine mutual compatibility before admitting applicants to administrative and liturgical responsibilities.[5] The minimum age for applicants was almost uniformly eighteen, and apart from S. Girolamo, there do not appear to have been any children's companies through the fifteenth and early sixteenth centuries.

An applicant's first step towards membership in a flagellant confraternity was to find a member who was willing to nominate him.[6] Some confraternities allowed applicants to approach one of the officials directly, but more often an existing member had to submit the applicant's name to the officials. Similarly, some companies encouraged all members to seek out potential recruits, while others left this in the hands of the Padre Spirituale or the Master of Novices. The nomination might be announced to the entire company or simply left with the officials, but in either case it initiated an investigation taking eight days to two weeks. Most companies left it up to the members to conduct whatever investigation they might think best, but at least one

---

[5]   Two stretta companies almost a century apart repeated their concerns about wolves in the sheepfold, but dispensed with the novitiate nonetheless, relying instead on a single investigation and vote. S. Francesco (1443) BBA B983, cap. 17–18; S. Maria degli Angeli (1522): BBA Gozz #7, cap. 9, c. 14r. The Dominican Compagnia di S. Croce was restrictive without a novitiate. Applicants came to the Inquisitor, who enrolled or rejected them without reference to the brotherhood. The 1460 statutes are reprinted in Paolini, "Le origini della 'Societas Crucis'," p. 227.

[6]   The picture that follows is a composite based on the statutes of the following companies (organized chronologically): S. Girolamo di Miramonte (1425): ASB Dem busta 2/6719 filza 2, cap. 9. S. Geronimo (1433): BBA Gozz 206 #5, cap. 22. S. Maria della Vita stretta (1454): in Angelozzi, *Confraternite Laicali*, pp. 118–41, cap. 10–11. S. Ambrogio (1456): ASB Dem busta 3/6625 filza 2, cap. 11. SSmo. Crocifisso del Cestello (1514): BBA Gozz 206 #1, cap. 23–24. S. Maria Maddalena (1515): ASB PIE filza 1, cap. 7–8. Buon Gesù stretta (1520): ASB Dem busta 9/7631 filza 1, cap. 1. S. Maria del Baraccano stretta (1521): BBA Gozz 213, cap. 12–13. SS. Sebastiano e Rocco (1525): ASB Dem busta 16/6620 filza 1, cap. 16. SSmo. Crocifisso del Cestello stretta (1538) BBA Gozz #2, cap. 9.

assigned deputies to prepare a full report.[7] While his public life and morals were being examined by the fratelli, the applicant confessed his inner life to the confraternity's Padre Spirituale. If both brotherly and priestly investigations showed promising results, the applicant was invited to come to the company oratory during a regular Sunday worship service. In some cases he could attend the private service so as to assure himself that he wished to join in the confraternity's worship. After the service he was ushered into an anteroom and the fratelli, officials, and Padre Spirituale discussed his fitness for the brotherhood's life and worship. The nomination was put to a vote and if over two-thirds of the brothers approved, the applicant became a novice. His nominator or the Master of Novices ushered him back into the oratory to be received with the kiss of peace by the officials and all of the fratelli. He was now part of the spiritual body, a union given Christological significance by the Compagnia di S. Girolamo di Miramonte when it had the chief official wash the feet of the newly accepted novice surrounded by other members kneeling and reciting laude or "cose ecclesiatice."[8]

The confraternity began educating its novice immediately. Subject now to the vow of silence regarding all he knew about the company, the novice was allowed to read the confraternity's statutes for the first time. In the stretta company of S. Maria della Vita, a Master of Novices gave training in church doctrines and confraternal devotions. Other companies left this to the novice's nominator. In either case, nothing was assumed about the novice's knowledge of the Christian faith beyond the ability to recite from memory the Pater Noster and the Ave Maria. In Sunday afternoon sessions much like those of the later Companies of Christian Doctrine, the novice learned the Apostles' Creed, the Ten Commandments, the seven deadly sins, the seven works of corporal and spiritual mercy, the seven sacraments, and the seven cardinal virtues.[9] His master then led him through the company's particular rites, chiefly the Little Office of the Virgin, and the Office of Discipline. Other fratelli constantly watched the novice, observing how well he absorbed doctrine and put it into practice. Some companies allowed and others required that the novice practice flagellation; all required attendance at weekly services in the confraternal oratory, and confession and communion as frequently as full members. The novice participated in the devotional, but not the administrative life of

---

[7] ASB Dem, Compagnia di Buon Gesù, busta 9/7631 filza 1, cap. 1.
[8] ASB Dem, Compagnia di S. Girolamo di Miramonte, busta 2/6719, filza 2, cap. 9.
[9] Angelozzi, Confraternite laicali, cap. 7, pp. 124–5; ASB Dem, Compagnia di SS. Sebastiano e Rocco, busta 16/6620 filza 1, cap. 7.

the confraternity. Admitted to worship, he sat at the rear of the oratory and was required to leave when the fratelli discussed company business and voted, or when they confessed their statute violations to each other in the ceremony of the *Colpe* or the *Scuse*. No novice could hold administrative office.

In the mid-fifteenth century the average novitiate lasted six months; by the early sixteenth century it had stretched to a year with no appreciable increase in the "curriculum." The extended novitiate may simply have been a device for sorting the negligent from the dedicated. After the stated term, the dedicated once again approached the chief officials directly or through their master or nominator and asked for admission as full, professing members. Members once again had up to two weeks to consider the application. During this period the novice again visited the Padre Spirituale for confession. After worship on the appointed day, he was sent out to pray while the others discussed his service in the oratory, his morals outside of it, and in general whether he had lived what one confraternity described as a "Lenten life" ("*vita quadragesimale*").[10] If at least two-thirds of the members found him acceptable, he was inducted at the next meeting of the confraternity. This gave the novice time to acquire the confraternal robes and raise any dues he might be expected to pay.

Induction ceremonies differed significantly between individual confraternities, but all indicate the importance of becoming an active member of a restricted community. Profession into the stretta company of S. Maria della Vita occurred during Mass. Before the Magnificat, the Sacristan gave lighted candles to all the fratelli. The stretta Ordinario then presented the novice in his flagellant's robe to the Rector of the larga Company. Kneeling, all sang "Veni Creator Spiritus" and "Emitte Spiritum" before reciting the prayer "Deus qui corda fidelium." The Ordinario then returned to his place and all sang the Magnificat. After the office, as two brothers sang laudi, the novice gave the kiss of peace to the Ordinario and, kneeling, to the brothers who came to him one by one. The Ordinario then admonished him on the member's duties and his name was added to the matriculation list. That done, the Ordinario went to the Rector and Massaro of the larga Company to tell them of the perseverence of the novice and assure them that his induction was according to the statutes of the whole Company.[11]

Set in the context of the Mass, this mid-Quattrocento ceremony

---

[10] This was the goal of the stretta of S. Maria del Baraccano: BBA Gozz 213, cap. 12.
[11] Angelozzi, *Confraternite laicali*, cap. 11, pp. 127–8.

drew heavily on the mendicant example to reinforce the identity of the confraternity as a lay apostolate. By contrast, ceremonies prepared in the early Cinquecento for the Compagnia di S. Maria Maddalena drew on the example of the humanist oration and university graduation. Following a feast day celebration, or on a more convenient day, the novice came to the oratory with his white flagellant's cape and a pound of white wax for the service. All professing members assembled in the *arcibanco*, the raised section of the oratory where the officials usually sat. After the office the Master presented his kneeling Novice to the Ordinario, who asked, "What do you wish?" "The Grace of God, the Peace of this Company, and union with those devout brothers to be accepted among you as the least of your number." The Ordinario responded with an eloquent oration on holy obedience, reviewing all that the statutes required of members. The novice promised "with good and true intention" to observe them freely in all points for the love of God. The statutes themselves were then read to the still-kneeling novice. Following the reading, the novice received a lighted candle while other members sang "Veni Creator Spiritus." After the song the fratelli and Ordinario clothed the novice in the white cape of membership and crowned him with laurel (*"le ponga la capa bianca indosso, la ghirlanda di lauro in capo"*). Hand in hand all fratelli sang the "Te Deum Laudamus" before the Master raised his pupil to his feet and put him in the place of honor (*"lo ponga a sedere sopra tutti"*). If able, the newly inducted fratello then presented gifts to his confratelli.[12]

The subtle contrast between the two ceremonies illustrates two views of the novitiate and professing membership. It is not simply the better literary and oratorical style of the Maddalena ceremony. The brother of S. Maria della Vita entered an apostolate in which he continued the personal spiritual development begun in the novitiate. His counterpart in the Maddalena was admitted into a circle of initiates at the conclusion of his trial period. The physical separation of Maddalena's full members above the novice, their stepping down to offer the kiss of peace, the hooding and crowning of the "graduate," and his elevation by his mentor, followed by gifts to his new colleagues – all these were the rites of graduation, of completion rather than commencement. The difference between the two company ceremonies suggests a progressive secularizing of confraternal religious ritual and a *nobilitazione* of traditional pious rituals now considered embarrassingly uncultivated. Yet many companies held strongly to their own tradi-

---

[12] ASB PIE, Compagnia di S. Maria Maddalena, ms. 1, cap. 10, 11, 34.

tions. While a novice in S. Maria Maddalena was receiving his laurel crown, his counterpart in the Compagnia Buon Gesù flagellated before the assembled brothers. And while no one could apply as a novice to the Maddalena without giving proof of his own *qualità* and that of his father and mother, few companies could match the social standing of S. Maria della Vita. As with the flagellation liturgies discussed in the previous chapter, there was a plurality of devotional styles and models in Renaissance Bolognese confraternities, with no easy connection to social status. Both Buon Gesù and S. Maria della Vita were established companies drawing on older models and their own traditions, while the Maddalena confratelli had started gathering informally in 1502 before erecting their confraternity in 1512; their statutes were adapted from the now-lost first statutes of the contemporary patrician Compagnia di SS. Sebastiano e Rocco. Their concern with qualità and the aping of high-born ways spoke more of social climbing than aristocratic confidence.[13]

The induction ceremonies which confraternities devised and laid out in their statutes reveal what the brothers hoped the novitiate and profession to full membership would mean for applicants. Other membership records show that these statute prescriptions were more than just pious intentions. While capitular votes of approval were often simply formalities, many novices did not automatically pass on to profession. Using records of the Compagnia di SS. Girolamo ed Anna from 1472 to 1550, we can see that the ratio of inductees to novices is surprisingly low throughout the period, with a definite decline in the brotherhood's total membership appearing by the second decade of the sixteenth century. SS. Girolamo ed Anna originated as the elder half (the "*Maggiori*") of the split which in 1444 divided the Compagnia di S. Girolamo.[14]

The membership data is given in Figures 3.1 and 3.2. Bar graph 3.1 gives the total number of novices who joined every year, and the number of these who went on to profession. Although the minimum novitiate was one year, some waited longer before professing. Line graph 3.2

---

[13] The matriculation list contained in a 1522 licence from the suffragen bishop registers 21 men, "omnibus Civibus Bon." largely of the artisanal class: ASB PIE, Compagnia di S. Maria Maddalena, busta 3, filza 2.

[14] ASB Dem, Compagnia di S. Girolamo di Miramonte, busta 5/6722, filza 1. The membership record begins December 30, 1471; I have followed it to December 19, 1557. All the material given in Figs. 3.1, 3.2, 3.3, and in the text is drawn from this source. Although deposited with the records of S. Girolamo di Miramonte (the "*Minori*"), a number of the novices are noted as having come from the Compagnia dei Giovani or dei Putti, and comparison with S. Girolamo's matriculation list allows us to establish that it records entrants into SS. Girolamo ed Anna.

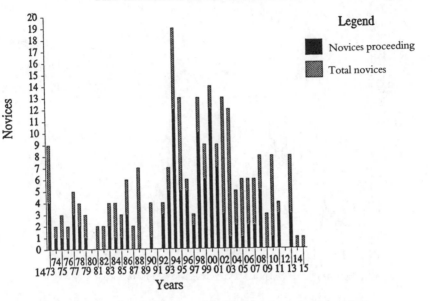

Fig. 3.1a.   Novices proceeding to profession (by year of novitiate):
SS. Girolamo ed Anna, 1473–1515
Source: ASB Dem, Compagnia di S. Girolamo di Miramonte, busta
5/6722, filza 1.

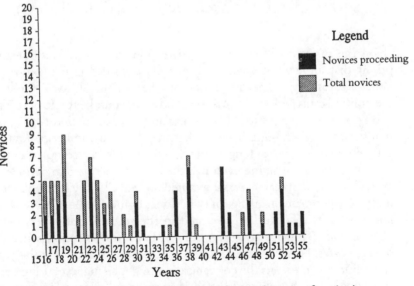

Fig. 3.1b.   Novices proceeding to profession (by year of noviate):
SS. Girolamo ed Anna, 1516–55
Source: ASB Dem, Compagnia di S. Girolamo di Miramonte, busta
5/6722, filza 1.

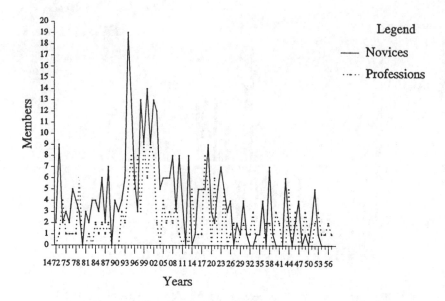

Fig. 3.2.   Novices and professing members added per year: SS. Girolamo
ed Anna, 1472–1555
Source: ASB Dem, Compagnia di S. Girolamo di Moramonte, busta
5/6722, filza 1.

charts the annual totals of both novitiates and inductions. It is not surprising that some novices would decide not to profess in the company.
What is surprising is that such a high number would fall away. Only in
the political crisis period of 1492–1501 did a large number of novices join
and a good percentage profess. The percentage for the period 1530–55 is
significantly higher, but is based on less than half the number of novices
gathered in over twice as long a time. On the whole, the company could
seldom count on retaining even half the novices recruited in periods of
average growth. In many years it retained none at all. Novices frequently
joined the company in groups of two, three, or four; some of these were
kin groups (with relationships noted in the record), but others were
likely friends. This clustering was not due to any pre-ordained schedule
of entry dates. Novices came into the brotherhood throughout the year
and while in some years the concentration might be highest during Lent
and Advent, in others it would be entirely random.[15] Vote tallies for pro-

[15]   The three novices of 1481 entered in June, July, and August; the three of 1491 in
July, August, and December; the nine of 1501 in April, May, June, August, and
October; the four of 1511 in December.

spective novices or professing members seldom recorded more than one or two of the black "nay" beans. But while the vote itself may have been a formality, the high dropout rate among novices shows that few saw promotion to professing membership as an automatic procedure. Almost anyone was welcome to try the company and its devotional exercises. Those who were unimpressed or incompatible with the confraternity slipped away of their own accord before the end of their novitiate. Many of those who failed to complete the novitiate were related to professing members and in most cases had been nominated by their kin. The fact that they never became full brothers indicates that kinship did not override basic membership qualifications in what was still a voluntary community of believers.

II. SOCIAL GEOGRAPHY AND SOCIAL STANDING

Before a Bolognese man or woman attempted the confraternal novitiate, he or she had first to decide which spiritual company to approach. The high dropout rate among novices suggests that many simply experimented, possibly by becoming novices in several companies in turn before seeking full membership in a single one. Their decision undoubtedly rested in part on the attraction of a group's devotional life and exercises, and the compatibility a novice felt with the group's members. It also rested on less overtly religious considerations such as location and social composition. With regard to the former, Bolognese laudesi confraternities of the Quattrocento retained their traditional neighborhood character, while battuti and stretta companies recruited from a broader geographical base. As regards social composition, Bolognese Compagnie Spirituali of the early Quattrocento professed the spiritual equality of all members and generally took in broad sections of guildsmen. Yet government "*del popolo e delli arti*" was largely a convenient myth even then, and the guilds' fading significance through the later fifteenth and sixteenth centuries was reflected by a progressive social stratification within and between the Bolognese confraternities.

Most Trecento laudesi companies had developed on specifically territorial lines, establishing themselves in existing churches and drawing members from a particular quarter of the city. This heightened awareness of geography continued with laudesi companies of the fifteenth and sixteenth centuries, which often noted a new member's parish when writing his or her name into the matriculation list. These lists show that most laudesi companies continued drawing the majority of their members from a few parishes near to the confraternal church, chapel or ospedale. Of seventy men recruited into S. Maria dei Guarini from 1356 to 1382, thirty-two are identified by parish; all but one of these came from the Porta Piera quarter and its suburbs. Little changed among the 627 men recruited from 1428 to 1525; while a few members came from the Ravennate and Procola quarters, the overwhelming majority lived in Porta Piera.[16] Figure 3.3a shows a similar concentration; most male and female members of S. Bernardino recruited from the mid-fifteenth until the end of the sixteenth century came from seven parishes in the Porta Stiera quarter, with a few drawn from three parishes in neighboring Porta Procola. Between half and three-quarters of members were listed according to parish, and seventy-five to eighty percent of these came from the immediate locality. The same was true of the brothers and sisters of the Compagnia di S. Francesco who met, as did S. Bernardino, in the conventual church of S. Francesco.[17] The pattern was the same for a S. Maria del Baraccano matriculation list commencing in the latter half of the fifteenth century and concluding in 1518. Most male and female members are listed by parish, and the majority of these come from five parishes within the Porta Ravennate quarter and one in Porta Procola. In short, Bolognese attracted to the devotions and charitable activities of laudesi and ospedali confraternities looked first and perhaps only to the group meeting in their immediate neighborhood. This further suggests that there were relatively few people who joined five or six confraternities like the notary Eliseo Mamelini discussed in the previous chapter.

It is less clear where battuti and stretta confratelli came from because these confraternities seldom recorded such information. We can imply from this silence that penitential confraternities were largely indifferent to geography, and that they possibly drew members from across the city; this was certainly the case in Florence.[18] Practical reasons point to this conclusion as well, since initially most of these groups had met in the Porta Procola quarter, where a low population made it easy to find space. Flagellant confraternities diffused more widely through the city in the mid-fifteenth century both on their own and in the form of stretta groups established within laudesi and ospedale confraternities; the latter usually continued meeting in facilities provided by their parent company. Since they were composed largely of members drawn from the laudesi parent, stretta groups began with a more strictly local membership than the older flagellant confraternities, and likely

[16] Fanti, "S. Maria dei Guarini," pp. 358; 368.
[17] M. Fanti, *La chiesa e la compagnia dei poveri* (Bologna: 1977), p. 20.
[18] Weissman, *Ritual Brotherhood*, pp. 44–5; 72–4.

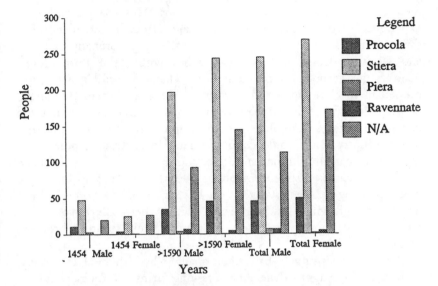

Fig. 3.3a. Geographic distribution of membership: Compagnia di
S. Bernardino
Source: ASB Dem, Compagnia di S. Bernardino, busta 8/7639, filza 1.

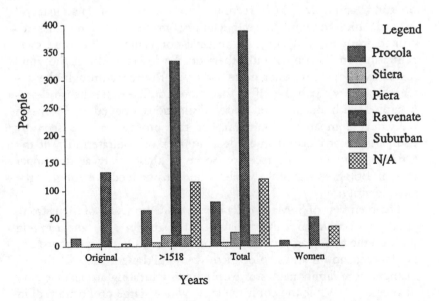

Fig. 3.3b. Geographic distribution of membership: Compagnia di
S. Maria del Baraccano
Source: ASB Osp, Compagnia di S. Maria del Baraccano, ms. 3.

retained this character for many generations. This was certainly the experience of the stretta of S. Maria della Carità. Most of its fifty-three members simply crossed over from the larga company in 1518, and all were from neighboring parishes within the Porta Stiera quarter; the company retained its local character until it was suppressed in the late eighteenth century.[19] Generally, then, Bolognese desiring the stricter devotional exercises of a penitential confraternity had more options than their laudesi counterparts. By the early sixteenth century, most could choose either a local stretta group or an established battuti confraternity meeting in Porta Procola. Many newer companies also automatically adopted the flagellant model when drawing up their statutes. Yet by this time, too, some Bolognese were growing less concerned with where they would be meeting, and more concerned with who their spiritual brothers would be.

Compagnie Spirituali had traditionally allied themselves closely with the Compagnie delle Arti, drawing many of their members from the artisanal guilds and experiencing their strongest growth and greatest activity at times when the guilds controlled Bologna's civil administration. Unlike Florence, Venice, and Rome, Bologna had no confraternities made up of the members of a single occupation or guild, and few which recruited on the basis of "nationality." Instead, until the mid-fifteenth century, its spiritual companies recruited from the full range of artisanal companies, with some concentrating on the upper and others on the lower ranks of the guild hierarchy. Popolo egalitarianism faded in Bologna through the fifteenth century, with the effect that more confraternities became preoccupied with qualità, and social distinctions opened up between individual companies. Something of this process can be seen by comparing matriculation lists for a number of confraternities of the Quattrocento and Cinquecento. Some of these were at the upper end of Bolognese society, while others maintained a strongly artisanal identity.

The members of S. Maria della Morte made no secret of their strong guild connections in a matriculation list begun in 1393 and running through the first quarter of the fifteenth century. Of 394 members, 235 noted occupations and 219 of these were guildsmen; most of the remainder bore family names or patronymics indicating artisanal activity or ancestry.[20] While the company drew widely, large proportions of its

---

[19] This was one of the few stretta companies to make note of its members' parish: M. Fanti et al., Santa Maria della Carità in Bologna: storia e arte, (Bologna: 1981), p. 39.
[20] Fanti, "S. Maria della Morte," pp. 42–3.

artisan members were from the major guilds and from guilds represented in the communal *Collegio dei Massari*. Strong guild representation reflected the high status enjoyed by the guilds in this, the last gasp of artisanal political strength before the oligarchy took power through the Sedici Riformatori. S. Maria della Morte progressively shed this *popolo* character through the next century. Two matriculation lists covering the late fifteenth- and sixteeth-century membership of the Compagnia di S. Maria del Baraccano show a similar metamorphosis. The first, dating from the later fifteenth century, began with 159 members, 70 of whom (44.02%) were guildsmen drawn from a relatively broad range of companies. Of the 563 members joining through 1518, only 151 (26.83%) claimed artisanal status. Proportionately more of these were from the upper guilds, with many of the lower guilds disappearing altogether.[21] The second list, spanning 1518 to ca. 1560 has 656 members, 89 of whom (13.71%) are guildsmen; almost all belong to Bologna's chief guild, that of the Notaries.[22] Decreasing guild membership and the narrowing focus on upper guildsmen demonstrate an ennobling process which is confirmed by a second index of social status, the member's name. Of the 159 members commencing the first list, 88 identified themselves by family names (55.34%), and 60 by patronymics; among members joining through 1518, those with family names rose to 63.71%. Almost all of those on the second list commencing in 1518 went by family names, with many drawn from the leading families of the city. S. Maria del Baraccano's experience was not isolated. The companies of S. Maria dei Guarini and S. Bartolomeo di Reno underwent similar transformations in the early to mid-sixteenth century, and a parallel process was at work in contemporary Florence and Rome. While confraternities had always been more class conscious than their egalitarian spiritual rhetoric suggested, deliberate exclusion of lower class and artisanal elements did not begin until the later fifteenth and early sixteenth century. Most new and some older companies started testing the *qualità* of their members, and as a result recruited

[21] Of the 722 members listed, 30.06% noted their guild affiliations. The two largest groups were the upper-rank notaries and drapers, with 30 each (13.5%); no other guild had over 5% of the total membership. ASB Osp, Compagnia di S. Maria del Baraccano, ms. 3.

[22] Of the 273 members written into the list in 1518, 56 (20.51%) note guild membership; 30 (53.57%) are notaries. Of the 89 guildsmen noted through the life of the list, 54 (60.67%) are notaries. ASB Osp, Compagnia di S. Maria del Baraccano, ms. 3.

fewer artisans and more upper guildsmen and patricians than the old neighborhood laudesi groups had.[23]

This ennobling of both new and established confraternities restricted the ordinary Bolognese layman in his search for a brotherhood, but he was not without options. Some confraternities, such as S. Bernardino and S. Maria della Carità began with a strongly mixed, artisanal membership and retained this character through the period under study. Judging by matriculation lists spanning the fifteenth and sixteenth centuries, relatively few of their members came from the upper guilds and most identified themselves by patronymics.[24] But groups like this were becoming a minority. As if to compensate for the marginalization of artisans within what had been popolo confraternities, Bishop Gabriele Paleotti heavily promoted parochial Compagnie del SSmo. Sacramento from 1566. These soon became artisanal enclaves largely shunned by patricians. While patterned after the Compagnie Spirituali, these were essentially parochial clubs under the priest's authority. The fact remains that by the mid-Cinquecento the common layman looking for a spiritual company had relatively fewer autonomous lay confraternities open to him than a century earlier, while his patrician counterpart had relatively more groups ready to welcome him.

III. SIZE, GROWTH, AND ATTENDANCE

Whatever the social or professional reasons for choosing one company or another, after induction the novice was inscribed in the confraternity's matriculation list as a full member of the spiritual community. Various membership records allow us to assess the size of these communities, how rapidly they grew or declined, and how seriously members treated their obligations.

Bolognese confraternities were free of the external constraints on

---

[23] Other companies becoming more exclusive in this period include S. Maria della Morte and S. Maria della Vita, Buon Gesù, S. Maria degli Angeli, and S. Maria del Baraccano. Companies more exclusive from the start include S. Maria della Pietà (1503), SS. Sebastiano e Rocco (1504), and SSmo. Crocifisso del Cestello (1514). The SSmo. Crocifisso *Libro della Morte*, commencing 1538, gives a good, albeit partial, picture. Of 147 members, 128 are listed by family name (87.19%); only 48 include occupation (32.65%), and of these 36 (75%) are notaries: BBA Gozz 206 #2, cc. 34v–36v.

[24] Of S. Bernardino's initial contingent of 82 men, 20 noted their artisanal status and none was of the higher guilds; of 337 recruited into the 1590s, 77 were artisans and the bulk of these (49) came from the lower guilds: ASB Dem, Compagnia di S. Bernardino, busta 8/7639, filza 1. Of 299 men joining S. Maria della Carità from 1399 to 1538, at least 124 are clearly artisans, drawn from 25 guilds and led by the middle-rank *calzolari*: Fanti, "S. Maria della Carità," p. 35.

membership found in Venice and Florence. In Venice, the Council of Ten had supervised confraternities since 1312, limiting the number and size of new foundations, scrutinizing lists of applicants for membership, and requiring the great Scuole Grande to add members when the public good dictated.[25] Considered agents of the state, their size and activities were closely regulated. Contemporary Florentine governments also dictated confraternal size and activities because wealthy charitable companies were considered convenient sources of forced loans, while secretive penitential groups were seen as potentially subversive. Civil administrations of the Trecento passed regulations giving themselves supervisory powers over confraternal property, while their Quattrocento successors brought in statutes preventing guild members from crossing over to confraternities, and dissolving confraternities not sanctioned by the commune. And if, "as was frequently the case, these decrees contained rather more bark than bite," they nonetheless inhibited free confraternal growth through much of the fifteenth century. Suppressive or repressive legislation issued from communal authorities in 1419, 1426, 1444, 1455, 1458, and 1466.[26] The situation worsened at the end of the century. "Almost every political revolution or change in government between 1494 and the beginning of the reign of Cosimo I [1537] was accompanied by a decree closing the confraternities of Florence, based on the precedents of the previous century." Beyond suppression by nervous governments, the Florentine confraternities were closed during plagues in 1522–23, 1524, 1527–28, and during the siege of 1530. The net result was that between 1521 and 1540 the confraternities were more frequently in a state of suspension than of legitimate operation. While some confraternities met sporadically, most saw their members and assets wither away until the politically inspired revival of confraternal life under Cosimo I.[27]

Although its political life was anything but placid in the fifteenth and sixteenth centuries, Bologna's various civil authorities never suppressed or otherwise regulated the confraternities. Brotherhoods were free to set their own membership policies, accepting, rejecting, or expelling whomever they wished. Estimating how many Bolognese claimed confraternal membership at any one time is difficult, since there is no single census of the confraternities. While many matriculation lists survive, most are running records which do not begin

[25] Pullan, *Rich and Poor in Renaissance Venice*, pp. 44; 90; 112–14; Mackenney, *Traders and Tradesmen*, p. 48.

[26] Hatfield, "The Compagnia de' Magi," p. 110. Henderson, "Confraternite religiose nella Firenze del tardo Medioevo," pp. 80–9.

[27] Weissman, *Ritual Brotherhood*, pp. 173, 178, 198–9.

noting the induction date for new members until the mid- to later sixteenth century. On the other hand, it is relatively easy to determine how many members a particular confraternity had in the year it began a new matriculation list. Other membership and legal records allow us to reconstruct attendance patterns for some of the smaller confraternities. And once again, the comparative data highlight distinctions between neighborhood-based, inclusive laudesi and ospedale confraternities, and the more exclusive penitential battuti and stretta companies.

Like their Trecento predecessors, Quattrocento laudesi and ospedali confraternities were generally far larger than the battuti. Table 3.1 gives statistics for those laudesi and ospedali confraternities starting matriculation lists during the fifteenth and early sixteenth century. Three of the smallest companies on the chart, S. Bernardino, S. Maria della Carità, and S. Maria della Pietà, were new groups when their matriculation list was drawn up. More established laudesi and ospedali confraternities typically gathered upwards of 250 members, with S. Francesco clearly the biggest in the city at 3,381. With the exception of S. Francesco, the Bolognese laudesi confraternities were significantly smaller than the Venetian Scuole Grandi, the smallest of which counted over 500 members. The high proportion of women in some groups is notable but deceptive for, as will be seen later in this chapter, women were gradually being eased out of most of the laudesi confraternities.

With one exception, none of the battuti or stretta companies could count as many as one hundred members and, as Table 3.2 shows, many counted far fewer than that. The exception, S. Rocco, was a new company which had begun as a group of worshippers meeting informally for a type of laudesi worship and had adopted the conventional battuti model when drawing up statutes. Most groups gathered from twenty to fifty members. While battuti or stretta statutes did not stipulate maximum membership, the closer spiritual community fostered in these groups would have been lost had numbers grown beyond a few dozen. As noted earlier, this spiritual community was modelled on that of Christ and his disciples, an imitation which some groups emphasized through the pious fiction of claiming that their origins and first statutes were the work of twelve men. Both SSmo. Crocifisso del Cestello and S. Maria degli Angeli had more than the twelve members they credited with erecting their brotherhoods. While they considered themselves disciples or apostles of Christ, they drew their dignity as much from contemporary society as from Christian tradition and boasted of members drawn from "noble and notably cultivated people," or the

Table 3.1. *Membership in the laudesi and ospedale confraternities*

Comapany	Date	Men	Women	Total	Source
S. Bartolomeo di Reno	1471	393	26	419	ASB PIE #1
S. Bernardino	1454	82	48	130	ASB Dem 8/7639.1
S. Francesco	1466	145	146	291	BBA Osp #73
S. Francesco	1494	1,976	1,405	3,381	ASB Cod Min #61
S. Maria Angeli	1479	302	–	302	BBA Gozz 203 #5
S. Maria Baraccano	1518	273	33	306	ASB Osp #3b
S. Maria Carità	1399	31	52	83	ASB Dem 4/7673.1
S, Maria Guarini*	1428	128	120+	248+	ASB Dem 6/6477
S. Maria Pietà	1550	?	71	71+	ASB Dem 7/7693.3
S. Maria dei Servi	1530	76	–	76	ASB Osp 3/188
S. Maria Vita	1520	283	–	283	BBA Osp #12

Note: * this list is alphabetical, but lacks pages for T, U/V, and Z in the women's section.

Table 3.2. *Membership in battuti confraternities*

Company	Year	#	Source
S. Ambrogio	1543	23	ASB Dem 3/6625
Buon Gesù (Stretta)	1565	28	ASB Dem 3/7625 #9
Collegio Laicale	1481	49	ASB Dem 1/6640 #10
Crocesegnati	1495	41	ASB Dem 3/6669 g
Crocifisso/Cestello	1514	13+	*
S. Domenico	1485	25	ASB Dem 3/6669 f
S. Domenico	1495	28	ASB Dem 3/6669 g
S. Giovanni decollato	1546	39	**
S. Girolamo	1436	24	ASB Dem 1/6718 #5a
SS. Girolamo & Anna	1439	26	ASB Dem 1/6716 #3
SS. Girolamo & Anna	1444	27	***
SS. Girolamo & Anna	1465	30	ASB Dem 2/6719 #24
S. Maria Angeli	1442	12+	****
S. Maria Pietà	1503	12+	BBA Gozz 206–7
S. Maria Maddalena	1522	22	ASB PIE #3
S. Maria della Vita	1463	51/90	BBA Osp #10
S. Rocco	1509	136	ASB Dem 6/6589 #2

Note: * M. Porco, *Il Santuario e la Confraternita del SS. Crocifisso del Cestello di Bologna,* (Bologna: 1961), p. 61
** G. Roversi, "La Compagnia e l'oratorio dei Fiorentini in Bologna," in *S. Giovanni Battista dei Celestine in Bologna.* (Bologna: 1970), p. 113.
*** A. Macchiavelli, *Origine ... della veneranda compagnia ... Santi Girlamo ed Anna,* (Bologna: 1754), p. 20.
**** A.M. Orsi, *Racconto istorico dell'origine, e fondazione della Veneranda confraternita di S. Maria degli Angioli di Bologna,* (Bologna: 1690), p. 17.

"most beautiful flower of the citizenry." Members such as these brought the Renaissance confraternity far more honor than a collection of fishermen and carpenters would have.[28]

However small or large, symbolic or real, the number of its members, no confraternity remained static. Year by year novices joined and professi died; both size and attendance fluctuated constantly and radically. Confraternal statutes often required that attendance records be kept, if only to keep track of those who failed to give the stipulated monthly or weekly donation. Laudesi confraternities usually required only monthly attendance at their large, public services. Given their size, consistent record keeping would have beyond the will or ability of officials serving only three- or six-month terms. Since flagellant confraternities were far more familiar and administratively manageable, it is surprising that only one set of battuti attendance records survives.[29] These records cover the years 1442–1460 in the life of the Collegio Laicale di Messer Gesù Cristo, a well-established but not particularly wealthy confraternity meeting in the Porta Procola quarter.

The Collegio Laicale's month-by-month attendance record allows us to chart the changing size of the confraternity and determine how long some members remained with it. Figure 3.4 shows the annual range recorded in the *Libro delle Scuse*. Membership moves constantly, changing by only one or two in some years, but by as much as nine or ten in others; over the course of the years the Collegio Laicale gathers as few as eighteen and as many as thirty-nine members. Such continual change may give the impression that the company was more a turnstile of religious malcontents than a stable worship group of devout laymen. But it should be remembered that this source was primarily a dues register; members away from Bologna for extended periods were exempt from payment and were left off the list until their return. The number of members affected is small, but occurs frequently enough to affect the month-by-month record.[30]

[28] A. Orsi, *Racconto istorico dell'origine, e fondazione della veneranda confraternita di S. Maria degli Angioli di Bologna*, (Bologna: 1690), pp. 17–19.

[29] A less consistent set of financial/membership records survives for the Company of S. Domenico: ASB Dem busta 1/6415 filza 2. Statutes written ca. 1433 for the Company of S. Girolamo di Miramonte require the rectors to record attendance at each meeting, and to note the excuses of absentees (together with many other types of record); the records either were never begun, or were lost. BBA Gozz 206 #5, cap. 35.

[30] Some examples: Antonio di Rubini and Biaxio Calcolaro are 1442 members missing from 1445 and returned in 1450. Andrea dai Cortelin is present in 1445, absent 1450, returned 1453. Antonio Calzolaro is present 1450, absent 1453, returned 1454. These could also be expelled members who subsequently rejoined the confraternity.

Even when absences are temporary, the Collegio Laicale's size varies widely from year to year. Yet there was considerable stability underlying this change. The bar graph, Fig. 3.5, tracks membership at five intervals in the eighteen years covered by the Libro delle Scuse and at a seventh point twenty-one years later.[31] The various strata in the stack bar graphs show when members were recruited. Although not as complete as a month-to-month breakdown, the bar graphs reveal that there was considerable continuity through the flux seen in Fig. 3.4, with three members remaining with the company for almost forty years, three for almost thirty, and three for over twenty. Of the thirty-four members of 1460, almost 40% had been in the confraternity for at least ten years, while just over half of these mature members had been with the company for eighteen years or more. Given that the Collegio Laicale had been considerably smaller in 1442, this means that almost 30% of the "original" members were still active in 1460.

The Collegio Laicale statistics reveal a pattern in confraternal membership. New records or renewed vigor in maintaining existing lists was usually part of the "turning over a new leaf" marking confraternal reform. The reformers attended more faithfully to the duties of membership, compared not only to those who had gone before, but also to those who followed. Hence the endurance of the 1442 members, parties to a minor reform, is not surprising. As for later recruits, Fig. 3.5 shows that roughly one-quarter to one-half the new members joining in each five-year interval drop away by the next interval. They may have died, quit, or been expelled; most often their names are simply crossed through without further explanation. This gives us a pattern with three elements: first, a core of dedicated members; second, a continuing but small-scale movement brought on by on-going recruitment, resignation, and death; and third, a periodic renewal when a large influx of new members regenerates the membership. James Banker's review of the succession of confraternities in San Sepolcro suggests that much the same pattern was at work there.[32]

Most confraternities grew in spurts, with more novices joining in groups than singly. The line graph, 3.6 shows the influx of males into the larga Company of S. Maria dei Servi from 1536 to 1569, and of females into the Company of S. Maria della Pietà from 1547 to 1583. The Servi had 76 members in 1530, adding 161 by 1569, an average of

---

[31] This last comparison is made possible by a matriculation list included with a plenary indulgence issued to the company on June 1, 1481. ASB Dem, Collegio Laicale di Messer Ges Cristo, busta 1/6640, filza 10.

[32] J. Banker, *Death in the Community: Memorialization and Confraternities in an Italian Commune in the Late Middle Ages* (Athens, GA: 1988).

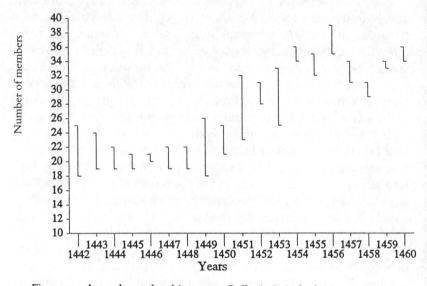

Fig. 3.4.   Annual membership range: Collegio Laicale di Messer Gesù
Cristo, 1442–60
Source: ASB Dem, Collegio Laicale di Messer Gseù Cristo, busta 1/6640,
filza 10.

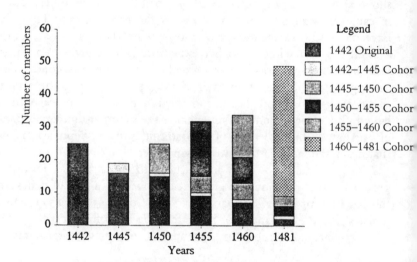

Fig. 3.5.   Membership continuity in Collegio Laicale di Messer Gesù
Cristo, 1442–81
Source: ASB Dem, Collegio Laicale di Messer Gesù Cristo, busta 1/6640,
filza 10.

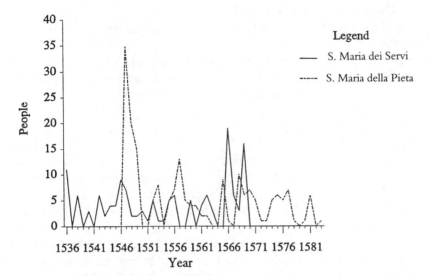

Fig. 3.6.   New memberships in two confraternities, 1536–83
Source: ASB Osp, Compagnia di S. Maria dei Servi, ms. 3/188.
ASB Dem, Compagnia di S. Maria della Pietà, busta 7/7693, filza 3a.

just over four members per year. The graph shows steady recruitment
through the entire period, with peaks roughly ten years apart: 1536–
38; 1546–47; 1555–59; and 1566–69. The number of women of the
Pietà grew rapidly for twenty-three months from their origin in November 1547 to August 1549, and then took in no new members until
August 1552. From this time until June 1583, they gathered 135
members, an average again of just over four per year. And again peaks
in 1556–58, 1568–70, and 1574–75 punctuate the steady rise. Shorter
lists for the contemporary stretta companies of S. Bartolomeo di Reno
and S. Maria della Carità echo both the average annual growth and the
fluctuating pattern of recruitment.[33] The more detailed list of S. Maria
della Pietà shows that members typically joined in groups of three or
four or more; this was the pattern seen above with the Compagnia di
SS. Girolamo ed Anna.[34] Most Bolognese confraternities shared such
erratic growth patterns. Groups of friends or kin who had joined at the
same time and age gave the brotherhood generational stability through
the annual fluctuations caused by individuals "passing through" the
confraternity.

[33] The S. Bartolomeo di Reno stretta recruited 85 members from 1502 to 1515 (6/
year), while the S. Maria della Carità stretta added 48 between 1546 and 1566 (4.8/
year). ASB PIE, Compagnia di S. Bartolomeo di Reno, ms. 1; BBA Gozz 210 #6.
[34] So, for example, six joined in April 1556; ten in January 1557, four in February
1569, and four in November 1575.

The normal waxing and waning of a confraternity was accentuated as members attended or missed the group's worship services. Turning again to the Collegio Laicale's records, Table 3.3 gives members' attendance in three sample years of the period 1442–60. The samples are typical of the other years in the picture they give of worship and attendance patterns. Members gathered for worship at least once but more often up to twice a week during the average month. There is no consistent pattern to the years; December was often marked by extra services due to Advent and the Company's major feast day on December 26. Lent was comparatively quiet and the summer months relatively busy. On a monthly basis, attendance was usually highest at the first meeting, traditionally the time when members confessed and communicated. Attendance varied widely from week to week but, considering the final column in the chart, very few members failed to attend at least one meeting in a month. At the same time, very few meetings were attended by all members together. Serving officers attended most faithfully. At the end of their terms however, they too reverted to the more irregular attendance of their fratelli.

The members of the Compagnia di SS. Girolamo ed Anna attended their worship meetings with similar inconsistency. In the case of this company, what survives is not an attendance record, but totals from the votes accepting applicants for the novitiate or full membership. In a strong year like 1498, three meetings in March attracted 31, 52, and 47 members; two in April drew 43 and 29; one in November brought 31. Attendance settled down somewhat after a recruiting boom in the 1490s, but still ranged broadly through the year. Four votes in 1505 drew from 34 to 52 members; six votes in 1513 attracted 20 to 29 members, five votes in 1526 gathered 23 to 44 members.[35]

These statistics confirm that however often confraternal statutes enjoined attendance at all ordinary and extraordinary meetings, individual confratelli were irregular if not unfaithful members. This was the situation in Florence and likely elsewhere throughout Italy.[36] On the

[35] ASB Dem, Compagnia di S. Girolamo di Miramonte, busta 5/6722 filza 1. See n. 14 above for reasons why this is likely the "Libro" of the Compagnia of SS Girolamo ed Anna.

[36] In a study of the Bolognese company of S. Maria della Carità, Mario Fanti assumes 50% of members regularly attend meetings, but gives no reason for the rule-of-thumb estimate: "S. Maria della Carità," pp. 39; 54. John Henderson's analysis of attendance by members of the Florentine company of S. Girolamo covers ten-year intervals from 1435 to 1465 and shows that between 19 and 39% of fratelli came regularly to confraternal worship. Company size ranged from 65 to 163 through these decades, but was most often above 100: Piety and Charity, pp. 141–2. Compared to the statistics for Bologna and Florence generally, the Company of S. Paolo highlighted in Ronald Weissman's study seems to have had an unusually low participation rate: Ritual Brotherhood, pp. 159–61.

Table 3.3. *Attendance in the Collegio Laicale di Messer Gesù Cristo,*
1444–1455

Year	Month	Total	No. of meetings									Abs
			1	2	3	4	5	6	7	8	9	
1444	Jan	20	18	19	20	18	18	18				0
	Feb	20	16	18	19	19	16	17				1
	Mar	20	17	17	18	17	17	17				1
	Apr	20	18	20	18	18						0
	May	21	18	17	18	18	16					1
	June	22	21	18	20	18	20	15	19	17		1
	July	21	19	21	18	18	18					0
	Aug	21	19	17	17	19	20	21	18	18		1
	Sept	20	18	16	15	15	15	16	12			2
	Oct	19	17	16	16	17						1
	Nov	20	19	13	14	17	15	16	17	15		0
	Dec	19	15	13	14	15	15	3	15			2
1450	Jan	25	23	20	22	21	9	19	20	20		2
	Feb	25	21	21	21	19	21	17				4
	Mar	25	23	22	22	21	22	20				2
	Apr	22	22	22	22	22	21					0
	May	23	19	22	20	21	21	21	16	19		1
	June	23	20	21	19	20	20	21	21	21		1
	July	22	22	18	16	17	19					0
	Aug	22	20	16	15	18	16	17	19	20	19	0
	Aug cont.								19	18	18	
	Sept	22	20	17	19	20	20	20	16	20		1
	Oct	21	19	19	19	19	20					0
	Nov	21	19	17	16	18	17	16	17			0
	Dec	22	21	21	20	19	20	21	19	20	20	0
	Dec cont.										19	
1455	Jan	35	30	30	30	28	30	28				0
	Feb	35	27	29	29	27	27					3
	Mar	35	31	30	30	31	28	26				3
	Apr	34	31	29	32	32	32					1
	May	34	33	33	34	34	30	34	34	33	29	0
	June	32	31	27	32	28	27	27	28			0
	July	32	32	28	26	25	25					0
	Aug	32	30	27	28	23	27	28				0
	Sept	31	26	26	27	28	27	22				0
	Oct	32	26	25	28	27	24	28				0
	Nov	33	31	30	27	27	31	29	32			1
	Dec	34	30	29	30	28	28	28	29	27		1

Note: Total = number of names listed in a month's record
Abs = number of members absent for the entire month
Source: ASB Dem, Collegio Laicale di Messer Gesù Cristo, busta 8/6647, filza 4.

whole, occasional absences are less surprising than the generally consistent attendance of most members. Members who missed confraternal worship services regularly without good reason were guilty of negligence, a serious but common enough failing. If they missed the sacraments as well their fratelli became more concerned, both for the erring individual and for the whole brotherhood. Was there a wolf in the sheepfold?

IV. EXPULSION

It was one thing to cry wolf in the brotherhood, quite another to remove the offender. Confraternal statutes described the behavior warranting expulsion, but included sufficient safeguards to discourage false accusations and encourage repentance both before and after expulsion. Members wanted to keep their brotherhood pure, but they also wanted to bolster spiritual backsliders and redirect moral wanderers who were kin by oath and possibly blood. The chief faults warranting expulsion were immorality, negligence, and disobedience to officials or the statutes. While some companies relied on votes to remove members, more left it explicitly or implicitly in the hands of their officials.

The Congregatio Devotorum civitatis bononie of 1261 wrote no provisions for expulsion into its earliest statutes, even though well over half of the chapters were dedicated to disciplining the followers of a movement into members of a respectable spiritual company. Erring members paid for their infractions with *Pater Nosters* and *Ave Marias*. The 1329 Statutes for the Compagnia del Corpo di S. Procolo gave officials general authority to reprimand members, but did not specify expulsion. By the fifteenth century, only the large laudesi confraternities such as S. Francesco and S. Bernardino lacked expulsion procedures, reflecting again their identity as open neighborhood devotional and charitable groups rather than closed brotherhoods of the virtuous.

By contrast, flagellant groups became ever more selective about whom they recruited and retained, the battuti because of their own longstanding practice, and the stretta out of a desire to assert their stricter rules *vis-à-vis* all existing confraternities. The chief difference in statutes was the stretta tendency to devise ever more explicit lists of the vices warranting expulsion; the difference in practice is impossible to determine. Where battuti statutes had traditionally outlawed the heretic, the usurer, the sodomite, and the adulterer, the stretta relished in cataloging all the vices of Renaissance Bologna and adding a few disreputable occupations as well. In 1454, S. Maria della Vita turned its back on gamblers, blasphemers, tavern owners, practitioners of illicit arts and keepers of *cattiva*, or nasty, company. In 1520, the stretta of Buon Gesù added public ruffians, graft takers, those who beat their parents or otherwise showed disrespect, actors, singers, magicians, practicing Jews, murderers and public combatants, thieves, assassins, "and others of bad reputation." Judging by 1564 additions to these statutes, fratelli were not above using violence; the new sections described penalties for fighting in a number of different categories, according to weapons, victims, and such. Anyone using a knife and drawing blood was to be chased out of the Oratory, followed as far as the door by the other fratelli, crying, "Out with the disturber of the peace of the men of Buon Gesù, and never again be admitted into our holy and peaceful company!"[37]

But the sheep seldom chased the wolf out the door quite so dramatically, particularly since negligence and disobedience were more common causes for expulsion than homicide. Attendance records helped officials keep track of whether members were coming for regular worship, and if they were receiving the sacraments as often as required. Although the confraternity was a voluntary society, participation in its religious ceremonies was compulsory. In most companies a member could miss occasional weekly services with permission of the Padre Ordinario, the confraternity's lay head. Some allowed a brother to miss occasional sacraments with permission of the Padre Spirituale, the confraternity's hired priest or friar, provided he gave good reasons for his absence.

Discipline of the negligent and disobedient was handled by the Padre Ordinario. A few confraternities authorized the Padre Spirituale to remove on his own authority those who missed confession or communion, but most required him to report delinquents to the Padre Ordinario. This initiated a series of visits based on the Pauline command to admonish erring brothers. In the stretta of S. Maria della Vita and the Compagnia del SSmo. Crocifisso di Cestello, two brothers would first visit the delinquent to determine why he stayed away and to encourage him to return. If they failed, the Padre Ordinario and one or two members carried out the next visit, followed on the third occasion by the Padre Spirituale. The Compagnia di S. Ambrogio reversed this order, having the Padre Spirituale commence and the Padre Ordinario conclude the visits, while the Compagnia di S. Maria del Baraccano had its Ordinario do all three visits. Whatever the order and its implicit hierarchy, a discontented or delinquent member had opportunity to vent his displeasure to whomever he felt most comfortable dealing with.[38]

---

[37] ASB Dem, Compagnia di Buon Gesù, busta 9/7631, filza 1, cc. 25v–27r.

[38] ASB Dem, Compagnia di S. Ambrogio, busta 3/6625, filza 2, cap. 7. For S. Maria del Baraccano: BBA Gozz 213, cap. 15. For SSmo Crocifisso del Cestello: BBA Gozz 203, #1b, cap. 29. For S. Maria della Vita: Angelozzi, *Confraternite laicali*, pp. 131–32.

Cases of open disobedience were less straightforward, for they pitted dissatisfied members against officials who, but for the grace of a short-term office, were fraternal equals and possibly social inferiors. For all his power, the Padre Ordinario served only three, four, or possibly six months before returning to his previous status and the possibility of reprisal. It is not surprising, then, that so many statute revisions are obsessed with disobedience. Judging by the offenses the revisions mean to uproot, administrative meetings could descend into shouting matches, with members exchanging threats and insults before a cowed Ordinario. This came about in part because those companies which left disciplinary responsibility to the Ordinario alone expected him to reprove the guilty member in the oratory itself before fellow members who knew the offense, the offender, and the official. All the officials, and possibly all the members voted to expel the unrepentant offender. In deference to his judgment, a subsequently repentant offender could not rejoin the confraternity until the Padre Ordinario's term of office was over.[39] Some companies tried diverting pressure from the Padre Ordinario by appointing disciplinary committees. In the early sixteenth century, the Compagnia di SS. Girolamo ed Anna began appointing annual commissions of ten members to examine, correct, and expel fratelli.[40] The alternative was to impose conditions which would effectively see disobedient members expel themselves. In 1519 the brothers of S. Maria della Morte suspended seven negligent members from the oratory for a year, but required that they continue to make monthly confession to the Padre Spirituale. If they missed three months, they would be automatically expelled from the confraternity without a further vote of the membership. The procedure was so effective that the brothers repeated it with an erring brother the following year.[41]

Given these conditions, expulsions were clearly not the work of a weak-willed or unsupported Ordinario, particularly since the procedure could be long while terms of office were short. As a result, many expulsions occured in clusters as the work of strong administrations seeking either reform or stronger control of the confraternity. Once again, laudesi confraternities showed less concern than battuti, seldom

---

[39] Some appear only as a crossed or rubbed-out name in the matriculation list, followed perhaps by the note "expelled as a rebel" ("*scancelo per ribelo*") or "cancelled for their poor bearing" ("*cancellati per soi mal portamenti*"). These two comments are drawn from the S. Maria degli Angeli list commencing in 1479 (BBA Gozz 203 #5).

[40] ASB Dem, Compagnia di SS. Girolamo ed Anna, busta 5/6722, filza 1.

[41] ASB Osp, Compagnia di S. Maria della Morte, busta 9/815, cc. 35r–37r.

expelling members at all, and never in large numbers.[42] The battuti were far more vigilant. The precise record keepers of SS. Girolamo ed Anna noted the dates when the brothers expelled erring or negligent members. Of 106 members recruited at the height of the 1440s dispute between the children's and adult branches of the confraternity, four resigned and twenty-five were expelled, most in groups of two to six.[43] These confratelli continued their periodic house cleaning in the next century. Of the sixty-seven professi gathered in the rapid-growth period of 1492–1501, seventeen, or 25%, were expelled in the years following. The percentage declines only slightly when the period is extended through the low-growth years to 1555; the company expelled twenty-nine of the 151 members it had accepted, a 20% loss.[44] Other companies were even more rigorous; the stretta of S. Maria della Carità expelled none of their original 1518 cohort of fifty-three, but 31% of the 146 members subsequently recruited to 1570.[45] The situation was by no means unique to Bologna. John Henderson estimates one Florentine confraternity expelled 16% of its members annually, most of them relatively recent recruits, and most dropped for negligence.[46]

Most confraternities willingly welcomed back in mercy those whom they had expelled in judgment. If the former member renounced his immoral behavior and sought pardon from the officials and members, a vote would be held to determine if he could return to the sheepfold. Some companies gave back the seniority he had lost, while a few required him to return to the status of a novice. Members not infrequently returned. Of the six expelled from SS. Girolamo ed Anna on Christmas Day 1508, three returned: Vincenzo Morbiolo in 1509, Rainaldo Bianchini in 1512, and Piero Maria Talcante in 1513. Of the 29 members the confraternity expelled from 1492 to 1555, at least

---

[42] Assuming that those in charge of matriculation lists obeyed the statutes and crossed expelled members off the list, the ospedale company of S. Maria degli Angeli expelled only 15 of 466 members recruited from 1479 through the early sixteenth centuries. The ospedale company of S. Maria del Baraccano expelled only 18 of 722 members on an undated list of the later fifteenth and early sixteenth century. Meanwhile, the stretta of S. Maria della Carità pruned 46 of 146 members recruited from 1518 to 1546.

[43] ASB Codici Miniati, ms 65, cc. 1r–7v. Expulsions by date: 1441, June 5 (1); 1442, Mar. 18 (2); Oct. 14 (3); Oct. 28 (3); 1444, Jan. 22 (1); Jan. 26 (5); Oct. 28 (1); Nov. 29 (3); 1462, Apr. 19(6).

[44] Four were expelled December 31, 1505; six on Christmas Day, 1508; and four again on June 14, 1517. ASB Dem, S. Girolamo di Miramonte, busta 5/6722, filza 1.

[45] Forty-six out of 146 members, or an average of 31.51%: BBA Gozz 210 #6.

[46] Henderson notes that most of the Florentine expellees had been members for less than five years, and that periods of rapid growth led to high expulsion rates. *Piety and Charity*, p. 137.

seven were readmitted. The contemporary Compagnia di S. Bartolomeo di Reno had a roughly similar rate of readmission.[47]

V. RETENTION

The confraternity was not a social institution operating only in the
present, but a spiritual brotherhood transcending time. The dead were
simply members who had passed one hurdle in the soul's ascent to
heaven. They were assisted in their ascent by the prayers of the living,
who would themselves be assisted after death by the prayers of future
members. The membership record most truly reflecting this spiritual
function was the Book of the Dead, a list of deceased fratelli which helped
the living play their commemorative role in the *ars moriendi*. Wealthy
members could make large bequests ensuring both a monument in the
oratory and a requiem mass said or sung by the company priest on the anniversary of their death. But with the *Libro delle Morti*, members of all
social conditions were sure that at least once annually the living members
would remember all their deceased spiritual kin by name in a special
requiem mass and feast. This encouraged moderately wealthy individuals
like the notary Eliseo Mamelini to keep up membership in more than one
confraternity. Whether one joined a single confraternity or many, the
post mortem spiritual benefits were available only if a member maintained his or her membership until death. Those who quit, drifted away,
or failed to pay their dues were not written into the Libro delle Morti, and
would not be mentioned in the requiem mass. While many confraternal
statutes required the company to maintain a Libro delle Morti separate
from the running matriculation list of professed members, most company
secretaries simply annotated the existing matriculation lists, using either
the symbol "+," or a phrase such as "*mortus est.*"[48] Since the record

[47] SS. Girolamo ed Anna expelled from 20–25% of members between 1492 and
1551, and saw just over 24% of the expellees return. In S. Bartolomeo di Reno, of
393 men joining in a reform of 1471, 25 (6.36%) were subsequently expelled and
10 (40%) of these later returned. Roughly half of the 253 members recruited into
the mid-sixteenth century suffered expulsion (125 of 253), with 17.6% (22) later returning. No one among the original core of 26 women or the 20 subsequently recruited was expelled: ASB PIE, Compagnia di S. Bartolomeo di Reno, ms. 1.
[48] There are at least three separate Books of the Dead in Bolognese confraternal archives. The manuscripts are not always designated as *Libri delle Morti* by either the
company or modern archivists but, judging by internal evidence and comparison
with other matriculation lists for the companies in question, the following are
likely Books of the Dead: ASB Dem, Compagnia di S. Ambrogio, busta 5/6627 (a
list commencing 1488). For SSmo. Crocifisso del Cestello: BBA Gozz 206, #2 (a
list commencing 1538). For S. Maria della Pietà: BBA Gozz 206 #8 (undated list
commencing early sixteenth century).

keepers marked only those members in good standing when they died, we can use the lists to determine what percentage of members remained with their confraternities until death.

Table 3.4 gives figures and percentages drawn from surviving Bolognese matriculation lists of the fifteenth and sixteenth-centuries. The number of members who died in good standing, broken down into male and female where applicable, is divided into two groups: first, the founding or reforming group; second, all subsequent recruits. Three of the lists are the work of founders, the rest were begun by groups of reformers giving the company a symbolic "fresh start." These figures confirm what was noted earlier with regard to long service by the 1442 reformers in the Collegio Laicale di Messer Gesù Cristo. Founders and reformers had the greatest stake in the company, and the greatest interest in seeing it prosper. They had broken from a more lax parent company. They had drawn up the statutes to which later members merely assented. They had reasserted the spiritual purpose of a confraternity in a new set of devotional exercises and duties reinforcing the bond of living members with the dead. It is not surprising that such a high percentage remained loyal to the company until their death.

Subsequent generations in the matriculation list had a less intense emotional commitment to the confraternity, so it is not surprising that a smaller percentage remained loyal until death. The rates confirm and are confirmed by the patterns of generational recruitment and loyalty already seen in the Collegio Laicale. In many cases they are also consistent with the percentage of expellees from the two companies of S. Girolamo and SS. Girolamo ed Anna. Finally, they match the retention rate that can be calculated by comparing the Compagnia di S. Ambrogio's Libro delle Morti with a 1543 matriculation list.[49] Thirteen of the twenty-three members noted on the matriculation list are also noted in the Libro, a very typical 56.52%.

These retention rates substantiate the argument made in the previous chapter that an individual's decision to keep up membership may have more to do with the life cycle of the confraternity than with the psychological and biological pressures arising out of his own life cycle. Growth, decline, and renewal affected all Bolognese confraternities at different times, depending on the circumstances in which the group came together, the purposes it served, how it related to clerics, or whether a religious revival was underway in society. As a confraternity matured through these circumstances and stages, its character altered and its attraction to new and existing, young and

---

[49] ASB Dem, Compagnia di S. Ambrogio, busta 3/6625, filza 2.

Table 3.4. *Retention rates in fifteenth- and sixteenth-century confraternities*

Company and source	Original	%	Total	%	Difference	%	Period
S. Bartolomeo di Reno (ASB PIE #1)	372 of 393 Male	94.66	481 of 646	74.46	109 of 253	43.08	1471–mid XVI
	14 of 26 Female	53.85	19 of 46	41.3	5 of 20	25	
S. Bernardino (ASB Dem 8/7639 #1)	53 of 82 Male	64.63	271 of 419	64.68	218 of 337	64.69	1454–late XVI
	18 of 48 Female	37.5	143 of 489	29.24	125 of 441	28.34	
S. Francesco (BBA Osp #73)	107 of 145 Male	73.79	268 of 602	44.52	161 of 457	35.23	1466–94
	98 of 146 Female	67.12	147 of 591	24.87	49 of 445	11.01	
S. Francesco (ASB Cod Min #61)	Male		1,691 of 1,976	85.58			1494–mid XVI
	Female		176 of 1,405	12.53			
S.Maria degli Angeli (BBA Gozz 203 #5)	132 of 302 Male	43.71	168 of 466	36.05	36 of 164	21.95	1479–?
S. Maria del Baraccano (ASB Osp #3a)	159 of 159 Male	100	488 of 722	67.59	329 of 563	58.44	XV–XVI
	Female		29 of 90	32.22			
S. Maria del Baraccano (ASB Osp #3b)	249 of 273 Male	91.2	415 of 656	63.26	166 of 383	43.34	1518–mid XVI
	13 of 33 Female	39.4	27 of 76	35.53	14 of 43	32.56	
S. Maria della Carità (ASB Dem 4/7673 #1)	31 of 31 Male	100	272 of 300	90.67	241 of 269	89.59	1399–mid XVI
	50 of 52 Female	96	142 of 219	64.84	92 of 167	55	
S. Maria della Carità (BBA Gozz 210 #6)	53 of 53 Male	100	133 of 199	66.83	80 of 146	54.79	1518–late XVI
S. Maria dei Guarini (ASB Dem 6/6477)	116 of 128 Male	90.6	248 of 627	39.5	132 of 499	26.45	1428–early XVI
	10 of 120 Female	8.3	27 of 239	11.3	17 of 119	14.28	
S. Maria dei Guarini/Larga (ASB Cod Min #60)	Male		223 of 336	66.37			1526–late XVI
S. Maria dei Guarini/Stretta (ASB Osp 1/870 #2)	Male		180 of 258	69.77			1526–?
S. Maria della Pietà (ASB Dem 7/7693 #3a)	61 of 71 Female	85.91	142 of 286	49.65	81 of 215	37.67	1547–late XVI

S. Maria dei Servi (ASB Osp 3/188)	74 of 76 Male	97.37	168 of 237	70.89	94 of 161	58.38	1530–69
S. Maria della Vita/Stretta (BBA Osp #10)	Male		35 of 90	38.89			1463–?
S. Maria della Vita/Larga (BBA Oso #12)	266 of 283 Male	93.99	708 of 1,369	51.72	442 of 1,086	40.7	1520–?
S. Rocco (ASB Dem 6/6589)	132 of 136 Male	97.06	311 of 544	57.17	179 of 408	44.09	1509–early XVII

old, members grew or declined. Ronald Weissman has argued that flagellant confraternities attracted late adolescents concerned with "the
crisis of personal integration into larger worlds," while praising confraternities gathered older heads of households concerned with insurance
against sickness and spiritual assistance after death.[50] This was no doubt
at least partially the case, given what we have seen of the different
ethos animating the different types of confraternity. At the same time,
Bolognese matriculation records never state the age of novices or inductees, so there is no way of testing the hypothesis. One general
problem with it, however, is that a confraternity could only mediate –
or even gain a reputation for helping mediate – an individual's passage
from childhood into adult society and from old age to death if it
enjoyed a high degree of stability or continuity as an institution. The
much-suppressed Florentine confraternities certainly enjoyed no such
continuity, and with obvious consequences; Weissman himself shows
that Florence's S. Paolo confraternity lost a third of its members in a
1458–64 suppression.[51] Bologna's Compagnie Spirituali enjoyed considerably more stability as institutions, and in most cases those who
joined could decide for themselves whether they would remain active
members or eventually drift away. This held for most of the people
who joined confraternities; some, however, were less free to choose
whether or for how long they prayed in the confraternal oratory and
remembered the confraternal dead.

VI. WOMEN

Mona Lucia Bolza and her spiritual sisters had a bone to pick with the
men of Bologna. Over a period of decades, women had been progressively shut out of worshipping in lay confraternities. Now, in 1547,
they made a stand. A group of perhaps thirty gathered at the shrine of
Santa Maria della Pietà on the eastern wall of the city before the men
of the shrine's confraternity met for evening prayers. With Mona Lucia
doing the talking, they demanded first of God, and then of the confraternity officials and men, permission to join in the gatherings under the
mantle of the Virgin Mary. The women wanted to congregate in the
shrine to the service, honor, and glory of God, and they wanted to be
subject to all that the confraternal statutes and oath required of the
men. The men received all of this in their hearts and, in a secret vote,
unanimously approved the women's demands. The women then asked

[50] Weissman, *Ritual Brotherhood*, pp. 75–6.
[51] Ibid., p. 118.

the men to give them a head and guide – so long as it was not one of their husbands. In prayer, and by the will of God, they elected and confirmed Mona Lucia as Prioress for the coming year.

This Authorized Version of the sisters' successful assault on a bastion of male privilege occurs in the prologue to the statutes drawn up for the women of S. Maria della Pietà in the following year.[52] The triumphal tone does not quite obscure the signs of advance planning evident in the ritualized assault, nor can it obscure the result which becomes clearer in the statutes themselves. The women did not join the men under the mantle of Mary, under the statutes and oath, or, for that matter, in the shrine. Their consorority was separated from, but administered by, the men's confraternity; their devotional exercises excluded the offices and flagellation characteristic of the men's devotion; and they were not given any reason to meet in the shrine's oratory. Even their statutes appear to have been written in part by the men.[53] Why then was the ritual confrontation staged, and why was the women's defeat portrayed as a victory? Why were the women not granted what they wished? Two views of women's proper religious role interacted in the confrontation: the first was the goal of an active apostolate of charity and public worship. This was most often found among artisanal praising confraternities which had originated in the Trecento, based themselves on neighborhood or quarter, practiced public worship and laude singing, and emphasized service to the community through charitable hostels. The second was the ideal of a contemplative discipleship of private prayer and devotion. This was more commonly found among the penitential confraternities which had originated in the Quattrocento and which gathered in smaller, exclusive groups to practice an Observant spirituality of mutual censure, frequent confession and communion, and flagellation. Women's removal from Bolognese confraternities was a consequence – likely unanticipated – of devotional reforms pursued through the later fifteenth and early sixteenth centuries by male artisans who wanted to remake their praising confraternities on the penitential model. They reentered the brotherhoods in the mid-sixteenth century thanks to calculated moves by patricians concerned less with religious expression than with maintaining

[52] ASB Dem, Compagnia di S. Maria della Pietà, busta 10/7696 filza 3.
[53] The statutes are written in two voices, with some provisions given as dictates from an unnamed higher authority to the sisters, and others as resolutions agreed upon by the sisters themselves. The consorority of SSmo. Crocifisso del Cestello received its 1549 statutes from its male sponsors, while the women of S. Maria della Carità had no statutes at all, in spite of the men's undertaking to write a set for them. ASB Dem, Compagnia del SSmo. Crocifisso del Cestello, busta 1/6378 filza 10. Fanti, *S. Maria della Carità*, p. 71, n. 39.

order and control in the city. The public, ritualized protest at S. Maria della Pietà in 1547 achieved the political purpose, but fixed patrician notions of the religious expression appropriate for women ensured that the sisters' aggressive demands could not be granted.

The circumstances and models shaping early confraternal development in Bologna determined women's early involvement in the spiritual companies. Born of public devotional movements, confraternities could not exclude from their worship the women who had sung and prayed in the processions. Governed on the model of artisanal guilds, they would not include in their councils a sex which played no administrative part in the guilds. The mendicant model was ambivalent. On one hand it advocated a life of piety expressed through public charity. On the other, it gave the example, from St. Clare onwards, of women whose desire to eumulate the friars was channelled into the strict boundaries of enclosure in Second Orders. Women joined the earliest praising confraternities and played an important part in the charitable work of their hostels, but were normally excluded from the penitential flagellant groups. The brothers explained this as necessary to avoid public scandal. It was hard enough explaining a nocturnal activity carried out in darkened rooms by semi-naked men.

Peter Damian had first advocated flagellation as a penitential exercise for laity of all social conditions in the eleventh century, and Franciscan preachers further popularized the practice from the thirteenth century. Italian women certainly flagellated from at least the eleventh century, but did so in private and risked incurring disapproval.[54] The sticking point then was not flagellation per se, but its collective practice in processions or confraternities. None of the chronicles documenting the 1260 movement of Disciplinati mentions women flagellating in streets or churches, and only one refers to women performing the exercise *"in cubiculis suis ... cum omni honestate."*[55] While the women of Ravenna were the first to win entry into a flagellant confraternity in

---

[54] In a letter to a female correspondent, Damian noted that both men and noble women eagerly embraced the practice of flagellation as a means of purgation and satisfaction for sins: cited in Scaramucci, "Considerazioni su statuti e matricole," p. 178 n. 65. Damian alluded to contemporary disapproval when mentioning a specific woman by carefully noting that she was the widow of an upstanding builder and was herself of some significant standing.

[55] Meersseman, *Ordo fraternitatis*, p. 498. Scaramucci, "Considerazioni su statuti e matricole," p. 141. An anonymous chronicler of events in the Florentine interdict of 1377 noted that women beat themselves in the confraternal processions, but this may refer to something distinctly less dramatic than public flagellation with knotted cords. R. Trexler, *The Spiritual Power: Republican Florence under Interdict*, (Leiden: 1974), pp. 131 n. 96; 132.

THE MECHANICS OF MEMBERSHIP

1265, it is doubtful that they were anything more than auxiliaries. This was certainly the case with women admitted into flagellant confraternities in contemporary Vicenza, Bergamo, Pisa, Udine, Modena, Cividale, and San Sepolcro.[56] As the wives and daughters of male members, they were of higher social standing than the women joining laudesi confraternities.

Women's exclusion from confraternal flagellation was based on more than just the shame of exposing their bodies or mixing male and female flagellants, since it continued through the period when those bearing the cords wore robes and hoods which obliterated their individual identity. More to the point, even the few "flagellant" consororities in thirteenth- and fourteenth-century Italy may not have practiced the exercise. Contemporaries referred to the women of the late-Trecento Company of S. Maria di Giosafat in the Sicilian town of Catania as "domne disciplinantes," but this appears to have been little more than a convention following the model of male confraternities from which women were excluded.[57] The consistency and completeness of the exclusion suggests that collective flagellation was seen as a distinctly male ritual, the characteristic expression of the generally more patriarchal mores of the battuti groups. Given these values, it is doubtful that women played more than an auxiliary role in any flagellant confraternities anywhere in Italy during this period.[58] Just as the flagellant confratello's collective devotions and charity were lay reflections of the mendicant rules, so the consorella's private devotions and limited activities reflected the strict enclosure of female religious.

As we saw in the discussion of confraternal devotional life, members of both praising and flagellant confraternities oriented their worship to death, dying, and salvation, accumulating through prayer, charity, and indulgences a fund of merit which would pass them to

[56] Meersseman, Ordo fraternitatis, pp. 500–1. Scaramucci, "Considerazione su statuti e matricole," p. 141. Banker, Death in the Community, pp. 146–9.

[57] None of the Sicilian flagellant confraternities followed the northern practice of admitting women to non-practicing membership. S. Maria di Giosafat sponsored a private oratory, as did two other female groups annexed to it in 1405 and 1436; administering these private chapels may have been the chief function of the consorority. Meersseman, Ordo fraternitatis, p. 502.

[58] In Italy generally, women received benefits by virtue of the principle of "one flesh," that is, as wives participating in the membership of their husbands. They had no role in statute composition or revision, no voice in chapter meetings, and no administrative duties. Angelozzi, Le confraternite laicali, p. 53. Sixteenth-century Spanish flagellant brotherhoods also enrolled small numbers of women, but allowed only men to flagellate publicly. W.A. Christian, Local Religion in Sixteenth-Century Spain (Princeton: 1981), p. 189.

heaven. Women contributed equally to the confraternal fund of merit with their worship, prayers, regular dues, and charitable works. Their charity was particularly evident in praising confraternities which operated hostels; fifteenth-century female members of S. Bartolomeo di Reno frequently clothed the poor clerics served by their hostel.[59] Moreover, through the fourteenth and early fifteenth centuries Bolognese women of artisan rank often outdid men in joining praising confraternities. Yet their involvement sharply declined from the latter half of the fifteenth century. To take one example: the Compagnia di S. Maria dei Guarini, an artisanal group centered in the southeastern quarter of Porta Piera, registered seventy men and seventy women in a matriculation list begun in 1356. By 1382 the female complement had risen to 181 and the male to 172. A 1428 revision showed at least 120 women and 128 men.[60] At this point the rough equality disappeared. The 1428 matriculation list extended to 1526, registering a total of 627 men and 239 women; women's recruitment had dropped to less than twenty-five percent, and was being gradually eliminated altogether. The men of S. Maria dei Guarini formed a penitential Stretta company in 1454, and neither the Larga nor the Stretta matriculations commencing in 1526 listed women as members. A similar process was underway in the Compagnia di S. Maria della Misericordia (also known as S. Maria della Carità), centered on the southwestern quarter of Porta Stiera. This was the group which had revived itself in the aftermath of the 1399 Bianchi devotional movement. The 1399 matriculation list showed fifty-two women and thirty-one men; over the life of the list into the 1530s, the proportions were reversed, with a total of 300 men to 219 women. The figures are deceptive. Most of the men went over to the Stretta group formed in 1518, and by the 1530s the Larga was on the verge of collapse. Table 3.4 and Figs. 3.7 a–c chart male and female recruitment for a number of Renaissance Bolognese confraternities, and show how with one exception the proportion of women declined through this period.

Recruitment was seriously dropping, but this was still only half the issue. How many of the women joining a confraternity drew on its fund of merit? Only those who were active members at the time of

---

[59] Female members made sheets for the hostel, and shirts and capes for its needy inmates. ASB PIE, Compagnia di S. Bartolomeo di Reno, ms. 1, cap. 8.

[60] The list is incomplete, with the men's list lacking the letters H, R, and Z, and the women's list lacking T, U/V, and Z. ASB Dem, Compagnia di S. Maria del Guarini, busta 6/6477. Fanti estimates 1428 membership at 150 men and 140 women: Fanti, "S. Maria dei Guarini," pp. 367–9.

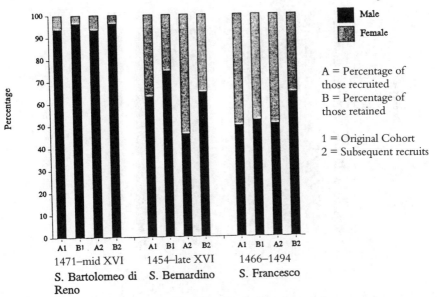

Fig. 3.7a.   Comparative percentages of male/female recruitment and
retention in Bolognese confraternities
Source: See Table 3.4 for archival sources.

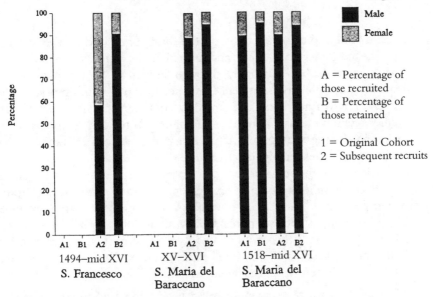

Fig. 3.7b.   Comparative percentages of male/female recruitment and
retention in Bolognese confraternities
Source: See Table 3.4 for archival sources.

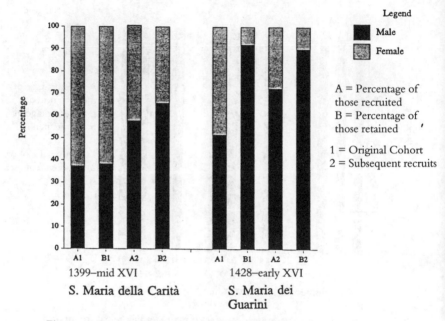

Fig. 3c.   Comparative percentages of male/female recruitment and
retention in Bolognese confraternities
Source: See Table 3.4 for archival sources.

death could, so to speak, draw on the fund. Their bodies were dressed
in the confraternity's robes and buried in its sepulcher, while their
souls were propelled quickly through Purgatory by the prayers, requiems, and plenary indulgences of their spiritual community. In the
event, few women lasted this far. Most confraternities had greater difficulty retaining female than male members. Of the 248 members participating in the Compagnia di S. Maria dei Guarini in 1428, ninety
percent of males remained active until death, but only eight percent of
females. Over the remainder of the matriculation list male participation
till death dropped to twenty-six percent, while women's rose to fourteen percent.[61] The female-dominated S. Maria della Carità group of
1399 retained ninety-six percent of women until death, but in subsequent generations this dropped to fifty-five percent. And while retention rates varied widely among confraternities, Table 3.4 shows that
those for women were usually about half of those for men.

[61]   Of the original 128 men, 116 (90.6%) are noted with a + in the matriculation list;
of the 120 women, 10 (8.3%) are noted. Of the subsequent 499 men, 132 (26.45%)
are noted; of the 119 women, 17 (14.28%) are noted. ASB Dem, Compagnia di S.
Maria dei Guarini, busta 6/6477.

Declining recruitment and retention rates for women were the consequence both of their exclusion from the administrative responsibilities of male membership, and of the growing predominance of the flagellant model in confraternal devotional reform. Ronald Weissman has shown that administrative responsibility was a condition for men continuing their membership in contemporary Florentine confraternities; without powers to exercise and duties to perform, members often lost interest and dropped away.[62] If women were accustomed to this kind of discrimination in artisanal society, they were less prepared for a redefinition of confraternal worship which would exclude them as a matter of principle. This is precisely what the Observant reforms accomplished from the mid-fifteenth century onwards. The clerics and male laymen who established Stretta sub-groups in laudesi confraternities emphasized the danger or *pericolosità* of Woman, an evil sex which led men away from devotion and into temptation. There was nothing particularly new in this revival of misogynistic and patriarchal themes in popular piety. Yet by making flagellation the characteristic mark of Stretta renewal, reformers excluded women from the most dynamic and fastest-growing segment of the confraternity.

In its fifteenth-century revival, flagellation was less an act of individual purification or expiation, than a demonstration of love and solidarity with Christ. It was one of many rituals of imitative piety which cast the brothers as disciples and their lay head as Christ, such as ascribing their origin to the actions of twelve men, having the Padre Ordinario wash the feet of all members – or a group of twelve – on the solemn feast of Holy Thursday festival, or limiting flagellation itself to groups of twelve. Squeamish or highborn members who wished to avoid potentially painful or demeaning exercises no doubt welcomed these numerical conventions, but they originated in the effort to underline the group's collective identity as friends, disciples, and imitators of the *Signore*. This sharing in the suffering of the Head and Groom of the Church gave collective discipline its strongly male meaning.[63] Bolognese battuti confraternities had been abandoning the exercise by the late Trecento, but Nicolò Albergati's enthusiasm for rituals of imitative piety ensured that it would be important for groups formed or reformed under his influence; hence the liturgy for S. Girolamo's "Office of Darkness" which Albergati clearly hoped other groups would adopt. As artisanal laudesi confraternities fell under the Observant influence, their Stretta groups also adopted the secrecy and mem-

---

[62] Weissman, *Ritual Brotherhood*, pp. 107–62.
[63] Alberigo, "Storia delle confraternite dei disciplinati," p. 181. Angelozzi, *Le confraternite laicali*, p. 62.

bership restrictions of the older battuti confraternities: all strangers, and particularly women, were excluded from the confraternal oratory.

Once a Stretta sub-group was erected within a praising confraternity, the Larga parent usually lost its devotional purpose and members. The Larga of S. Maria della Carità, which lost forty-two of its members to the Stretta in 1518, was extinct by 1542; the Stretta specifically prohibited creating another in its 1577 statutes.[64] S. Bartolomeo di Reno's Larga company waned so quickly after the Stretta emerged in 1502 that members joining a few decades later were unaware it had ever existed.[65] In S. Maria dei Guarini, the Larga group was reduced to a Board of Governors for the hostel. In none of these cases was any provision made for continuing the public worship once characteristic of the praising confraternities. As a result, Observant reforms shut women out of participating in either the devotional or the charitable activities of the confraternity.[66] Three groups continued admitting women. The patrician flagellants of S. Maria del Baraccano added small numbers of female relatives as auxiliary members in the form which more confraternities adopted in the mid-sixteenth century. The two praising confraternities meeting in the church of the Conventual Franciscans also resisted the tide. The Compagnia di S. Francesco was one of the early Trecento confraternities; based in the southeasterly quarter of Porta Stiera, it had spawned a Stretta company in 1443, but its Larga remained among the largest and healthiest in the city. The mid-Quattrocento Compagnia di S. Bernardino never split into Stretta and Larga groups or adopted flagellation, even though it was established to mark the memory of the Observant preacher Bernardino da Siena. Both of these confraternities saw the proportion of female members rise through the sixteenth century, evidence enough that women appreciated the opportunities for collective worship available through confraternities.

Ironically, women also appreciated the strict Observant life, or at least those parts of it open to them. Their enthusiasm can be seen in the number of recruits garnered by reformed convents, and in the en-

---

[64] Fanti, S. Maria della Carità, pp. 32; 39; 71.

[65] The late-sixteenth-century company historian Alessandro Stiatici, who had joined the stretta in the 1520s, was unaware of the prior existence of a larga company. A. Stiatici, Narratione, overo cronicha del principio e fundatione dell'Hospitale di Santo Bartolomeo di Reno ... (Bologna: 1590), pp. 20–2.

ormous popularity of two female spiritual leaders. In 1425, Bishop Albergati put the Augustinian nuns of S. Maria delle Virgini under a strict rule, and in seven years their numbers quadrupled from six to twenty-four, doubling again over the next four decades. Other mendicant orders imposed Observant rules on their Bolognese Second Order houses as well, notably the Cistercians (1429), the Camaldolese (1433) and the Franciscans (1436).[67] In 1432 the Franciscan tertiary Caterina di Vigri (1413–63) established a convent of Poor Clares in Ferrara in order to follow a strictly enclosed life. After relocating the convent to her birthplace of Bologna in 1456, she gained the patronage of the Bentivoglio and won such a reputation for sanctity that local followers founded a popular cult and pushed successfully for her beatification in 1524. All of the reformed convents won steadily increasing numbers of recruits. Some of this growth was undoubtedly a parental response to demographic and dowry pressures, but women's own participation in Observant values is confirmed by the wide lay following won in the early Cinquecento by Elena Duglio dall'Olio (1472–1520). Though married to a Bolognese notary, Elena followed and championed a life of chastity and contemplative devotion, and became a cult figure for men and women even before her death. Her followers emphasized her similarity to the Madonna, while Raphael was commissioned to depict her as an otherworldly St. Cecilia in the altarpiece for her chapel in the Lateran Canons' church of S. Giovanni in Monte.[68]

There is a further irony in the outworking of Observant reforms in Bolognese confraternities. In most cases lay artisanal women of the late fifteenth and early sixteenth centuries were being shut out of praising confraternities as their husbands, brothers, fathers, and sons decided to follow the Observant mendicant model in a segregated Stretta cell. Yet these artisanal men were themselves soon marginalized in their brotherhoods as Bologna's leading families moved systematically to take firmer control of the confraternities and their charitable institutions in the later fifteenth and early sixteenth centuries. As we will see in the final chapter, the patricians often ran foul of the artisans who had traditionally directed confraternal liturgical life and charitable administration. Many artisans initially welcomed high-born members whose deeper pockets would fund their faltering charitable institutions, and

---

[67] G. Zarri, "I monasteri femminili a Bologna tra il XII e il XVII secolo," *Atti e memorie della deputazione di storia patria per le province di Romagna*, n.s., vol. 24 (1973), pp. 138; 143; 159.

[68] G. Zarri, "L'altra Cecilia: Elena Duglio Dall'Olio (1472–1520)'" in S.B. Gajano and L. Sebastiani (eds.), *Culto dei santi, istituzioni, e classi notevoli in eta pre-industriale*, (L'Aquila: 1984), pp. 575–613.

few anticipated their own disenfranchisement. Yet all confraternal matriculation lists from the early sixteenth century onward show a growing number of prominent families, and decreasing artisanal membership in the Bolognese spiritual companies. A similar process was underway in Grand Ducal Florence.[69] Hence, while women were pushed out of artisanal confraternities as a result of patriarchal devotional reforms adopted in the fifteenth century, artisanal men were themselves marginalized within their confraternities by political developments of the following century which reinforced a hierarchical social order.

Given these developments, what was at work in Mona Lucia Bolza's appeal to the men of S. Maria della Pietà in 1547? The confraternity was impeccably upper class; all the legitimate males of the Bentivoglio family had joined it soon after it began in 1503.[70] The Bentivoglios' fall did little to hinder its ability to gather such leading families as the Gozzadini, the Bianchi, the Dolfi, and others. Mona Lucia's husband, Guaspar, was also a member. The prologue to the consoror17ity's 1548 statutes implies that Bolognese women strongly resented their marginalization in the confraternities, to the point perhaps where the oligarchy felt it advisable to contain the dissent. Yet while the dissenting women sought an active apostolate and full involvement in confraternal life, the only response Bologna's patricians seemed capable of offering was the contemplative devotional life of the Observants. The ritual assault by the stalking horse Mona Lucia symbolically put "women on top," while the statutes that followed firmly put women in place as the "enclosed" spiritual auxiliaries of the confraternity. Apart from coming to the chapel for monthly confession and quarterly communion, they sat at home repeating the *Paters* and *Aves* which made up their devotions. The statutes allowed for monthly meetings, but specifically prohibited the women from saying Divine Office, and are silent on what other duties they might perform or business they might transact. Unlike their sisters in Roman confraternities, the women did not join in confraternal processions, anniversary requiems, or feasts. One of their few public roles was dressing deceased sisters in the robes of the men's company and accompanying them to the con-

[69] Weissman, *Ritual Brotherhood*, pp. 197–201.

[70] Some children's discovery of a miracle-working leaden bas relief *pietà* in 1502 stimulated a popular cult which Bolognese patricians soon controlled by establishing a confraternity and shrine, whose main altarpiece was painted by the Bentivoglio court painter, Francesco Francia. Giovanni II, Annibale, Marcantonio, Galeazzo, Alessandro, and Ermes Bentivoglio were all among the first members. ASB Dem, Compagnia di S. Maria della Pietà, busta 7/7693, filza 4: 1, 1a. Guidicini, *Cose notabili*, III, (Bologna: 1868), p. 313.

fraternal sepulcher.[71] They were very tightly monitored, and enjoyed far less administrative or devotional autonomy than the Stretta group which had operated within S. Maria della Pietà since at least 1537.[72] The men's Ordinario and Prior supervised the women's annual election of a Prioress, and this woman was then put under the headship of a male Governor elected by the women but confirmed by a vote of the men's company. The Prioress was to be an honest and reputable married woman over twenty-five years old; she was assisted by two female counsellors who had no specific duties. All financial affairs and relations with the men's confraternity were handled by the Governor, who presented annual audits to his companions; after 1600 he was appointed directly by the men's company.[73] The recurring theme in the women's statutes was obedience: in the company, in the church, and in the body politic. Obedience to the Prioress and Governor was likened to the obedience due from Lords to the Emperor, from the French to their King, from ecclesiastics to the Pope. "Without obedience, our republic of Bologna would be full of atrocities and assassinations."[74] As, indeed, it usually was.

Husbands and fathers are conspicuously absent from this list of those to whom obedience is due. The authorities are all political rather than domestic. The women themselves underlined this distinction by requesting that their consorority's Governor not be the husband of one of the members. Even more conspicuously absent when we turn to this group's matriculation list are traceable kinship ties between the women's and men's groups. All women are identified by a male relation, but only fourteen percent of these men belong to the Compagnia di S. Maria della Pietà; of seventy-one women joining the consorority, only twelve are clearly related to a

---

[71] ASB Dem, Compagnia di S. Maria della Pietà, busta 10/7696, filza 3, cap. 3, 6, 8. Both the Roman Confraternity del Gonfalone and SS Sacramento di S. Maria sopra Minerva gave more scope to female members: A. Esposito, "Le 'confraternite' del Gonfalone (secoli XIV–XV)," Ricerche per la storia religiosa di Roma vol. 5 (1984), p. 130. G. Barbiero, Le confraternite del SSmo. Sacramento prima del 1539, (Treviso: 1944), p. 283.

[72] The original statutes make no mention of discipline, but a revised set issued in 1534 or 1537 includes the exercise: BBA Gozz 206 #8, cap. 9.

[73] On election procedures: ASB Dem, Compagnia di S. Maria della Pietà, busta 10/7696, filza 3, cap. 2. Direct appointment of the male Governor was one of the few substantial changes in the 1600 revision of the women's statutes: ASB Dem, Compagnia di S. Maria della Pietà, busta 10/7696 filza 4. The Company of SSmo. Crocifisso del Cestello followed the Roman model more closely by appointing the women's Governor from the start. ASB Dem, Compagnia di SSmo. Crocifisso del Cestello, busta 1/6378 filza 10/3.

[74] ASB Dem, Compagnia di S. Maria della Pietà, busta 10/7696 filza 3, cap. 1.

member of the confraternity.[75] This was a significant drop from the percentages found in mixed confraternities of the previous century and from the strong family connections normally found in confraternities. Forty percent of women entering the newly founded Compagnia di S. Bernardino in 1454 had been related to a male member, as were thirty percent of women joining S. Bartolomeo di Reno in a reform of 1471.[76] In most contemporary Italian high-born confraternities only female relatives of members could join the brotherhood. The women of S. Maria della Pietà suffered no such limitation; perhaps their greatest freedom lay in accepting whomever they wished, with applicants subject to an examination and vote through which the sisters separated the spiritual wheat from the blaspheming, gossiping, and dishonest chaff. By contrast, their sisters in the Roman Compagnia del Gonfalone had to submit all applicants to the men's company for investigation and approval.[77] The gap between men's and women's groups of S. Maria della Pietà is too great to be accounted for by either oblique lines of kinship or documentary lapses. It appears instead that the Bolognese patricians who had established the consorority and written its statutes were moving deliberately to broaden and reinforce obedience to the post-Bentivoglio hierarchy by casting the net of confraternal clientage over a broader social field.[78]

The patriciate's actions were consistent with the measures by which they had been extending control over artisanal men's confraternities. They can also be seen as an effort to control women whose religious zeal might lead them either to the numerous Protestant conventicles operating in Bologna, or to other independent action. It was a contemporary commonplace that women's weakness

---

[75] Twelve of the seventy-one women joining from 1547 to 1550 were related to ten men of the male group. Of the ten men, six do not remain active in S. Maria della Pietà until death; the two men who have both a wife and a daughter in the women's group do remain until death. ASB Dem, Compagnia di S. Maria della Pietà, busta 10/696 filza 3, cap. 1; BBA Gozz 206 #8.

[76] The exact percentages are 38.23% of S. Bernardino women and 30.76% of S. Bartolomeo di Reno women. Reversing the question, 15.85% of S. Bernardino men and 2.03% of S. Bartolomeo men were related to female members. ASB Dem, Compagnia di S. Bernardino, busta 8/7639, filza 1. ASB PIE, Compagnia di S. Bartolomeo di Reno, ms. 1.

[77] Esposito, "Le 'confraternite' del Gonfalone," p. 129.

[78] A remarkably similar case of men opening their confraternity to women during a time when authority was under threat occurred in Florence in 1377. With the city under an interdict, the only organized religious service open to the laity was through the confraternities, and the men of S. Zanobio were besieged with appeals from women seeking entry to the company and its spiritual benefits; they and many others complied with the request. Trexler, Spiritual Power, p. 131.

made them vulnerable to Protestant contagion, and as an international university centre, Bologna had more than its share of "*luterani*." Under Cardinal Giovanni Morone, Papal Governor since 1544, the city had avoided the worst of the decade's intensified prosecution of Protestantism.[79] Yet this tacit toleration could not be sustained past Morone's departure in 1547. From March to September of that year, delegates to the Council of Trent had relocated to Bologna in order to avoid the plague and Protestants threatening Trent. They immediately stopped the activities of two popular evangelical preachers, and stepped up investigations against local heretics. Over the next two years more friars and laymen were prosecuted, a local abbot was accused of distributing summaries of the *Beneficio di Cristo*, and eight prominent citizens were sent to the Inquisitorial prison in Rome. The city's local Inquisitorial tribunal was shaken up in 1550 to demonstrate both Rome's displeasure with Bologna's earlier mild approach, and its determination to institutionalize the new hard-line approach.[80] The turning point had been 1547, and Mona Lucia's protest occurred in November of that year.

Excessive devotion and independent action was as much a concern as heresy, particularly if it threatened conventional gender roles. Elsewhere in Italy, activist Catholic laywomen like the Franciscan tertiary Angela Merici (1474–1540) had raised suspicions among clerical conservatives and reservations among lay peers. Like the *beguines* of northern Europe, Merici's Ursulines had initially taken private or simple vows, worn simple clothing, and lived in non-cloistered informal communities, so as to avoid the limitations of female monasticism and dedicate themselves more fully to charitable works. In 1546, Paul III put them into a separate habit and under the rule of St. Augustine. The Barnabites had established a similar loosely structured group for laywomen in 1535, but were pressured into enclosing it by 1557. In its last sessions, the Council of Trent confirmed that all female religious had to be strictly enclosed, including those women who had previously taken only

---

[79] M. Firpo and D. Marcatto, *Il processo inquisitoriale del Cardinal Giovanni Morone. Edizione critica*, vol. IV: *Il processo difensivo bolognese. La sentenza* (Rome: 1987). The only executions for crimes which might be related to heresy occurred in 1545; three men were executed in May for attempting to break down the door of the Madonna di San Luca shrine, and three others in July for stealing and desecrating a Host. "Descrizione di tutti i Giustiziati in Bologna dal 1540 per tutto il 1714," AAB Aula 2a-C-VII-3, (May 30, 1545, July 8, 1545).

[80] The eight imprisoned citizens were released in the amnesty following the death of Paul III in November, 1549. A. Battistella, *I S. Ufficio e la riforma religiosa a Bologna*, (Bologna: 1905), pp. 26–8.

simple or private vows.[81] The Bolognese Senate sympathized with the conservatives on this score. It had already appealed to Rome in the early 1540s for help in expanding existing nunneries, and in creating new ones to handle the increasing number of women taking vows.[82] Creating new consororities was a natural extension of this concern from clerical to lay life, and the emphasis on political obedience in statutes of S. Maria della Pietà bears out the continuity. Bologna's patricians drew their power from Rome, and so could not stray far from the conservative Roman model. Since inability to control women's religious dissent or independence would have discredited the patricians in the eyes of their papal masters, there was far more at stake in the Mona Lucia Bolza episode than met the eye.

The oligarchs' strategy of containing dissent to confirm authority was effective. As seen in Fig. 3.4, the Pietà consorority grew quickly, numbering seventy-one in twenty-three months. Of these, sixty-one, or eighty-six percent, remained members until death, a degree of retention exceeded only by the women who formed a majority in S. Maria della Carità after its reform in 1399. Other patrician confraternities soon followed the Pietà example. A 1549 episcopal licence allowing the Compagnia del SSmo. Crocifisso del Cestello to add a women's section noted that the practice was being carried out by other confraternities. In 1552 the Compagnia di S. Croce followed suit, and by 1569 the high-born of Buon Gesù had also established a consorority. The move to sexual segregation was confirmed by the episcopal visits of the late sixteenth century; visitors sanctioned separate women's groups, while expressly forbidding the confraternity of S. Bernardino from continuing to admit women on equal terms with men.[83]

Over the long term, the new consororities saw a slackening of adherents and the erosion of their "enclosure." Among the two or three gen-

---

[81] In 1572, Carlo Borromeo "won" monastic status and strict enclosure for the Ursulines. The Ursulines had been resisting enclosure, as Borromeo's action came after the Fifth Decree on Regulars in Session 25 of the Council of Trent imposed strict enclosure on all female religious, and after Pius V's edict *Circa Pastoralis* of 1566 reinforced the Tridentine decree. R.P. Liebowitz, "Virgins in the Service of Christ: The Dispute over an Active Apostolate for Women during the Catholic Reformation," in R. Ruether and E. McLaughlin (eds.), *Women of Spirit: Female Leadership in the Jewish and Christian Traditions,* (New York: 1974), pp. 135–8.

[82] Gabriella Zarri sees this as a politically motivated appeal by an oligarchy in the process of consolidating its authority. Zarri, "Monasteri femminili," pp. 143–4.

[83] ASB Dem, Compagnia del SSmo. Crocifisso, busta 20/6397, c. 33r. ASB Dem, Compagnia di S. Croce, busta 3/6669, filze ii, iii. For Buon Gesù: BBA Gozz 203, #8. In the Episcopal Visit of 1593, the Company of S. Bernardino was expressly forbidden from continuing to include female members: ASB Dem, Compagnia di S. Bernardino, busta 8/7639 filza 2.

erations following the founders of S. Maria della Pietà, only thirty-eight percent of members remained active until death. With only the titular office of prioress open to them, women did not have significantly increased opportunities for administrative or liturgical responsibility and so eventually returned to the membership pattern characteristic before the mid-Quattrocento, dropping away as fast as or faster than their male counterparts. Nevertheless, greater numbers of women gathered in consororities and parish confraternities, and greater numbers of nuns entered convents; the latter made up 5.4% of the urban population by 1570, and 7.4% by 1631.[84] These increases can be credited to the demographic and economic pressures of the later sixteenth century, which had the additional effect of easing the new consororities' devotional enclosure and reintroducing the public charitable work characteristic of the earlier era. This charitable emphasis was strongest in the new parochial confraternities and consororities dominated by those of artisanal rank, but it also affected the high born, whose takeover of confraternal charitable institutions had left them with greatly enlarged social responsibilities. At one end of the social scale the artisanal women of S. Maria della Carità distributed bread to widows and poor confratelli; at the other, the patrician women of S. Maria del Baraccano served as Governesses overseeing the confraternal girls' home.[85] In both cases, this ostensibly public role was limited to work compatible with women's private identity as caretakers of domestic material welfare, and guardians of religious and moral values. Obedience and order were paramount concerns by the late 1540s. Ronald Weissman has noted that while fifteenth-century confraternities emphasized devotional community, their sixteenth-century successors emphasized obedience.[86] Bolognese artisanal women of the Quattrocento, who were accustomed to public worship and charity, were disenfranchised when the men of their confraternities created new devotional communities around exclusive patriarchal religious exercises. Yet they could be accommodated under the rule of obedience which spread in the Cinquecento. This is the opportunity that Mona Lucia Bolza's demonstration opened up. The origins, composition, and statutes of the S. Maria della Pietà confraternity and consorority demonstrate a subtle but consistent distinction between family

---

[84] The actual numbers in 1570 were 2,198 nuns in an urban population of 61,742. G. Zarri, "Monasteri femminili," p. 144.

[85] Three governesses were drawn monthly from the body of Baraccano consorelle to supervise the entry and deportment of orphaned and "vulnerable" girls. They were assisted by three confratelli and their own chaplain: ASB PIE, Compagnia di S. Maria del Baraccano, busta 561, c.93r; busta 563, c.7r. Fanti, S. Maria della Carità, pp. 50; 71 n.39.

[86] Weissman, Ritual Brotherhood, p. 219.

patriarchy and social hierarchy, with the emphasis in obedience on the latter rather than the former. This adds a new dimension to Joan Kelly's argument that women's segregation into a private, domestic sphere must be seen as men's reaction to the erosion of their own political power.[87] The papal reconquest of Bologna had reduced the oligarchy from real to merely deputed power, and led it to base this power at least in part on its ability to control various groups within the city, such as women. Thanks to the oligarchs' preoccupation with consolidating their authority, mid-sixteenth-century artisan women regained some of the latitude for confraternal participation that they had earlier lost. Yet this participation was limited to the private and domestic spheres which patrician men found familiar. A lay equivalent of strict enclosure initially limited women's prayers, praise, and service to their private homes. When the *consorelle* were finally let out of doors and allowed to exercise a more active charitable apostolate, it was on the terms which defined their domestic role and reinforced the oligarchy's own expanding control over social services.

VII. SUMMARY

By the middle of the sixteenth century Bologna's confraternities gathered possibly 20% of the adults in a city of 55,000. With respect to membership, confraternities operated as self-regulating congregations, offering laymen a freedom to choose and discipline their fellows which they did not find in the local parish church. Most members attended the worship services faithfully if not as frequently as their statutes dictated; on the whole, attendance rose and fell with the confraternity's own liturgical calendar. The confraternal congregation used its power to expel members for indifference or disobedience, but the pull of the group's worship was still strong enough to convince a good proportion of these "*cancellati*" to reform and return. The greater members' stake in the company, whether as reformers or officials, the higher the likelihood they would remain members until death. In all the mechanics of membership there were distinctions rooted in the inclusive, communal ethos of the praising confraternities and the exclusive, Observant ethos of the penitential companies and Stretta sub-confraternities. These distinctions had their greatest impact on the rights and terms of women's membership, which were further complicated by issues of class and politics. For both men and women, membership statistics reveal a re-

[87] J. Kelly, "Did Women Have a Renaissance?" *Women, History, and Theory* (Chicago: 1984), pp. 41–7.

curring tripartite pattern: first, the core of dedicated members; second, a continuing, small-scale movement brought on by recruitment, expulsion, resignation, and death; and third, a periodic renewing of the confraternity when a large influx of professing novices regenerates the membership. Each group followed its own cycle, but the general pattern can be traced through the devotional reforms of the fifteenth century and the political changes of the sixteenth.

4

COMMUNAL IDENTITY, ADMINISTRATION, AND FINANCES

Quattrocento Bolognese confraternities functioned as lay religious congregations whose members worked jointly to the goal of discipleship and salvation. Vowing neither poverty nor chastity, but valuing obedience and good order, they devised measures to preserve internal peace, and created administrations to oversee the ongoing communal life of the company. As some grew wealthier through multiplying legacies and investments, their administrations became less representative and more bureaucratic. By the early sixteenth century, confraternal statutes replaced pastoral injunctions with political models, and by the middle of the century some confraternal administrations put service to the patriciate ahead of service to the poor.

I. COMMUNITY

"The Holy Spirit speaks by the mouth of the prophet, saying 'Depart from evil and do good'" (Psalm 34: 14). So began numerous sets of confraternal statutes in Bologna and elsewhere. Departing from evil and doing good were "the two parts of justice," individually fruitless but joined together as the conditions of salvation. As seen in the previous chapter, most confraternities offered quite specific lists of the evil activities which members were to spurn. Doing good was more complex. It embraced worship, charity, and the catch-all phrase, "good life and reputation" (*"bona vita e fama"*). Neither avoiding evil nor doing good could be carried out in full individually. Mutual guidance, support, and admonition disciplined a moral life animated by love of God and neighbors. In joining a confraternity, members swore to give and receive this discipline.

Mutual peace was secured in statute, if not always in practice, by bans on taking one's confratelli to court, and procedures mediating internal disputes. The apostle Paul had set the tone when rebuking first-century Corinthian Christians for bringing their mutual disputes before Caesar's judges for settlement. More particularly, civic peace-making had been a central concern of the thirteenth-century confraternities and remained a primary practical and spiritual value thereafter. The 1261 Congregatio Devotorum civitatis bononie had simply banned all litigation between members, leaving disputes to the judgment of confraternal rectors and guardiani without room for appeal.[1] Absolute bans inspired ingenious circumvention, most commonly by having the case brought forward by a third party.[2] By the later Quattrocento some companies recognized that only internal mediation could divert public litigation. In the early sixteenth century, the Compagnia di Buon Gesù required that members bring any disputes with fellow members to the company's chief lay authority, who turned the case over to the company priest for reconciliation. If he proved unsuccessful, two or three fratelli took the case in hand. Court action was the third resort, but if it dragged on beyond a month the litigants were symbolically demoted for the duration by losing their Oratory keys and the right to hold office. The case concluded, they did not regain these privileges of full membership until they had spent fifteen days in the novices' benches. A fratello proceeding against a non-member first sought advice of his confratelli. If they advised against action and he brought suit nonetheless, he was stripped of keys and office, and expelled from the oratory for the duration of the case; on returning he spent a month with the novices before restoration to full membership.[3] The contemporary statutes of S. Maria Maddalena set out a ritual by which quarrelling members made peace in the Oratory. The initiator of the dispute asked pardon of the other in the Oratory following the Office and in the Padre Ordinario's presence. Then both asked each other's pardon, shook hands and kissed. Kneeling in the middle of the Oratory, the first offender said a Te Deum and the second a Magnificat; the latter then asked pardon of the Padre Ordinario and fratelli. Those rejecting this ritual reconciliation were fined and, if still obstinate, expelled.[4]

Procedures followed in other companies varied the details while echoing the basic meaning of the Buon Gesù and S. Maria Maddalena

[1] Angelozzi, Confraternite laicali, p. 87.
[2] The "interposita persona" mentionned by S. Maria del Baraccano in its 1521 statutes: BBA Gozz 213, cap. 19.
[3] ASB Dem, Compagnia di Buon Gesù, busta 9/7631, filza I, cap. 26.
[4] ASB PIE, Compagnia di S. Maria Maddalena, ms. I, cap. 29.

statutes.[5] Members readily explained differences as the results of human passions or the devil's mischief. Like disputes within craft guilds, arbitration procedures kept internal differences out of public courts. But where the guild claimed jurisdiction only over well-defined professional or occupational issues, the confraternity recognized no such limits; the fratello's whole life and social relations lay within its sphere. Lawsuits or disagreements violated the group's inner fraternity and undermined its public example of peacemaking; reconciling fratelli had to make their peace not only with each other, but with the confraternity as a whole. Two fifteenth-century developments underscore this determination to vent tensions within the brotherhood before they grew into open splits: ritual ceremonies of public confession and mutual admonition, and the creation of stretta flagellant cells within existing confraternities. The former accommodated individual violations of communal statutes, while the latter preserved confraternal unity in face of a faction's potentially schismatic discontent with devotional practices.

The rituals of public confession and mutual admonition were deliberately patterned as lay equivalents of sacramental confession and penance. In the latter, a brother confessed to the company's priest, naming his sins against God; in the former, he confessed to the company's chief lay officer, naming his sins against company statutes. Both the cleric and the lay officer had the power of symbolically restoring broken relations; the Padre Spirituale restored the penitent to the body of the Church, while the Padre Ordinario restored the fratello to the body of the brotherhood.[6] The confraternal practice of *dire colpe*, or admitting one's lapses, was fashioned into a ritual by being performed at specific times, in specific places, and according to formulas. The periodic sessions during which monks and friars confessed their sins to each other provided the obvious model. Most companies prescribed monthly sessions in continuity with monthly sacramental confession. But while the latter took place in private with the company priest at a mutually convenient time, the former was a public ceremony which commonly followed collective recitation of

---

5   See, for example, the 1514 statutes of the Compagnia del SSmo. Crocifisso del Cestello (BBA Gozz 206 #1, cap. 9), or the 1548 statutes of the women's Compagnia di S. Maria della Pietà (ASB Dem, busta 10/7696, filza 3, cap. 4). Among Stretta groups, undated late-Quattrocento statutes for S. Maria degli Angeli (BBA Gozz 203 #7, cap. 13, c. 9) and 1521 statutes for S. Maria del Baraccano (BBA Gozz 213, cap. 19) lay out similar procedures.

6   Bossy, "The Social History of Confession in the Age of the Reformation," *Transactions of the Royal Historical Society*, Series 5, vol. 25 (1975), p. 24. J. Henderson, "Confraternities and the Church in Late Medieval Florence," p. 74.

the Little Office of Our Lady on a Sunday morning. In stretta groups the monthly session opened with reading of the statutes to which fratelli had sworn obedience when first inducted into the confraternity.[7] Members then came individually to a tall bench placed in the middle of the oratory facing the Padre Ordinario's chair. The bench had arms of some sort, for fratelli were instructed while kneeling at the bench to put themselves over it as though on a cross ("*ponersi suso prostrato in croce*") Here they admitted their negligence or lack of decorum in worship, their violations of company secrecy, their insubordination to its officials, or their failure to visit the home of a deceased fratello; in short, anything breaking the recently read statutes.[8] Facing the Padre Ordinario, the fratello asked for correction and pardon. Like a priest, the Ordinario briefly lectured the penitent before handing down a penalty. Prayers and fasts were outside of his sphere, but he could draw on acts which temporarily humiliated or expelled the offender: kissing the ground, standing outside the oratory, kneeling, or even flagellation. The offender then asked pardon of his brothers and the Padre Ordinario allowed him to rise and return to his place. The sins, ceremony, and penalties were all public; they could not lie hidden in a guilty conscience. This was the chief distinction from sacramental confession, though it was less a difference of intent than of efficiency. Fratelli did not mount the *banco delle colpe* voluntarily; they were driven there by the orders of the lay officials and the accusations of their spiritual brothers. One company noted, "Always consider yourself as seen by a man of authority ("*huomo dauctorità*"), or by God, from whom nothing is hidden."[9] Fratelli were urged to be solicitous of each other's welfare, reproving each other privately and giving reports to the company officials or

---

7 What follows is a composite based on the statues of the following confraternities: (a) S. Ambrogio (1456), ASB Dem, busta 3/6625 filza 2, cap. 9; (b) SSmo. Crocifisso del Cestello (1514), BBA Gozz 206 #1, cap. 16. Stretta groups: (a) S. Domenico (1443), cap. 18: in Meersseman, *Ordo Fraternitatis*, pp. 669–89; (b) S. Francesco (1443) BBA B983, cap. 25; (c) S. Maria della Vita, (1454), cap. 13, in Angelozzi, *Confraternite laicali*, pp. 118–41; (d) S. Maria dei Guarini (1454), BBA Gozz 210 #11, cap. 14; (e) S. Maria degli Angeli, (ca. 1479), BBA Gozz 203 #7, cap. 8 (c.7v); (f) Buon Gesù, (1520), ASB Dem, busta 9/7631, filza 1, cap. 32; (g) S. Maria del Baraccano, (1521), BBA Gozz 213 #1, cap. 14.

8 In spite of the parallel ceremonies, members were frequently reminded of the distinctions between sacramental and confraternal confession, and warned against mentioning confraternal violations in sacramental confession or vice versa: e.g., 1443 statutes for S. Francesco (BBA B983, cap. 33) and 1521 statutes for S. Maria del Baraccano (BBA Gozz 213 #1, cap. 21).

9 This was in the 1433 statutes for the Compagnia di S. Girolamo (BBA Gozz 206 #5, cap. 11).

priest when one of the brothers persisted in breaking company statutes or God's law.[10] Further, in confraternal as in sacramental confession, the fratello was as likely to accuse others as himself. This
explains why statute provisions against yelling and arguing in the
oratory are so common, why novices were hustled out before the
ritual began, and why fratelli were pledged to secrecy on the pro-
ceedings. A ritual of mutual admonition could quickly descend into
mutual recrimination and spill out into public where, as SSmo.
Crocifisso del Cestello pointed out, "the error of one can stain the
many."[11]

Provisions against *tumulto* in the oratory notwithstanding, regular
public confession more likely involved uncontentious errors in a
close-knit brotherhood where authority rotated regularly among
members. Yet it grew up as a protective mechanism, a means of
maintaining the fifteenth-century devotional reforms and the communities of their adherents by expelling the negligent and obstrep-
erous. Officials had always had the authority to discipline members.
Yet public rituals modelled so closely on sacramental confession had
not been practiced in the thirteenth-century confraternities, and
were unknown in the large laudesi and ospedali confraternities of
the fifteenth century. Mutual admonition presupposed an exclusivity
and stronger sense of common mission than existed in those groups.
Battuti and stretta groups based their far livelier sense of communal
identity and purpose on the example of the earliest disciples of St.
Francis, and on the inspiration these first mendicants themselves
found in Christ's followers. "Love each other with the love which
Christ has and which he commanded the disciples to bear to one
another," commanded SSmo Crocifisso del Cestello, and in this
communal spirit the brothers of Buon Gesù put the confraternal
symbol of the Holy Name on the doors of their houses, while all
inductees into S. Girolamo received a woodcut of St. Jerome to
hang in their homes.[12] Confraternal robes deliberately symbolized

---

[10] In 1521 the Compagnia di Buon Gesù turned reporting into a formal act. Once annually the fratelli came privately to the company priest who went over the officials
and membership with them, asking what they knew of each one. This done, he
called all the delinquents to the Oratory on a separate day for correction and
penance. Those refusing to come had their cases discussed nonetheless, after which
the brothers were forbidden to tell the delinquents what had been discussed or determined: ASB Dem, Compagnia di Buon Gesù, busta 9/7631, filza 1, cap. 21, 25.

[11] BBA Gozz 206 #1, cap. 8.

[12] BBA Gozz 206 #1, cap. 10. ASB Dem, Compagnia di Buon Gesù, busta 9/7631,
filza 1, cap. 31. ASB Dem, Compagnia di S. Girolamo in Miramonte, busta 1/
6718, filza 3a, inventories of January and June, 1463.

this community through the way they overlay the clothing and faces of individual members with the uniform, all-concealing dress of the whole. This closer spiritual community was a development on and implicit criticism of existing laudesi and ospedali confraternities, not unlike the contemporary division between Observants and Conventuals in a number of mendicant and monastic orders. In the long term, Bolognese confraternities were no more successful than their mendicant mentors in reconciling tensions between these two poles and in subsequently accommodating devotional diversity within one administrative framework.

Quattrocento and Cinquecento devotional reforms could come in one of two ways. Either the entire company was completely renewed, or a group of brothers established a distinct offshoot like a Stretta company. Renewal embracing a whole company included not only new statutes and records, new robes, and possibly new worship practices, but also a new name. S. Maria della Carità became S. Maria della Misericordia, in imitation of the Bianchi cry of 1399. S. Maria della Mezzaratta became the Compagnia di Buon Gesù, in honour of the devotion to the Holy Name so central to the work of St. Bernardino da Siena whom company tradition identified as its reformer from "*fragilità e tepidita humana.*" Stretta companies were more delicate creations, deliberately intended to accommodate dissent while preserving the larger community. Nicolò Albergati had promoted this as a means of promoting confraternal reform without schismatic disruptions, but the device of devotional sub-groups within confraternities was neither new to the period nor unique to Bologna. A devotional cell apparently grew up within the Bolognese Company of S. Francesco in 1329, and similar arrangements were not unknown in fifteenth-century Florentine and Roman confraternities. At the same time, in no other Italian city were these divisions so common and so widely accepted.[13]

For all its implicit rejection of the confraternal status quo, Stretta reform remained a differentiation within an unbroken community, justified by St. Paul's metaphor of many functions in one spiritual body.[14] Different rules, different functions, and multiple memberships show how communal integrity was maintained in spite of potential tension. Each Stretta group wrote its own statutes describing its relation to the

---

[13] Weissman, *Ritual Brotherhood*, p. 58. Esposito, "Le 'confraternite' del Gonfalone," p. 129. Black, *Italian Confraternities*, pp. 88–9. Similar divisions also existed within Trecento Florentine confraternities: Trexler, *The Spiritual Power*, p. 129.

[14] BBA Osp, ms. 10, cap. 18 (S. Maria della Vita).

Larga and its stricter devotional practices.[15] Fratelli of the Stretta elected their own officers and, although the Larga did not appoint an overseer, both Stretta members and officials pledged obedience to the Rector and officials of the Larga. Obedience was phrased conditionally, hinting at possible tension in the relation: "in all lawful and honest things that work to the honour of God and profit of the neighbor, and in respect to the good administration of the ospedale and good example to all the earth in all those things which work together for charity."[16] Given that Albergati had set up the Stretta of S. Maria del Baraccano in 1439 precisely because the existing Company had more of an eye to its own profit than that of God or neighbor, and was causing scandal by its negligence, this conditional pledge was more than simply a polite formula; the stretta was the conscience of the whole confraternity. Its members were automatically members of the Larga, accepted by the Larga rector when they professed, and buried in his presence when they died. They swore to uphold the "old statutes" ("*statuti vecchi*") governing the Larga and its ospedale. And while they were free of office-bearing responsibilities in the ospedale, they could participate in the company meetings governing its affairs. At the same time, fratelli of the Larga could not freely participate in the Stretta's worship, and Stretta meetings were obscured from the view of the Larga by the cloak of secrecy indiscriminately hiding its affairs.[17] Not all members appreciated this asymmetrical approach, even though at least one company noted that Stretta secrecy was necessary to preserve

---

[15] Many stretta constitutions are similar to a set of statutes drawn up under Albergati's supervision for S. Girolamo in 1425 and envisioned by him as the model rule for all Bolognese confraternities (see chapter Two, n. 25). The stretta of S. Francesco credit Albergati directly with inspiring and approving their 1443 statutes (BBA B983 cc. 79–79v). A "model" stretta rule is adopted by S. Maria della Vita and S. Maria dei Guarini in 1454; S. Maria del Baraccano's stretta group first writes out a substantially similar rule in 1521, while claiming that it has abided by these statutes ever since its creation by Albergati in 1436; no earlier copy is extant and, unlike the 1425 S. Girolamo rule, Albergati's approval is not appended.

[16] "... in tute le cose licite e honeste che vegnano in onore de Dio e utile al proximo e in honor del bon governo del ospedale e bono exempio de tuta la terra in tute quelle cose che se conveneno per caritate." This is drawn from the 1454 statutes for the Stretta of S. Maria dei Guarini (BBA Gozz 210 11, cap. 15). Similar conditional formulas can be found in statutes of 1454 for the stretta of S. Maria della Vita, (BBA Osp, ms. 10, cap. 18), and those of 1521 for S. Maria del Baraccano (BBA Gozz 213, #10, cap. 9).

[17] This secrecy is required by S. Francesco in 1443 (BBA B983, cap. 23), S. Maria degli Angeli in 1479 (BBA Gozz 203, #7b, cap. 23, c, 146r) and 1522 (BBA Gozz 203 #7, cap. 7–8, cc. 148v–149r), and S. Maria del Baraccano in 1521 (BBA Gozz 213, #1, cap. 9).

good relations with the Larga.[18] Tensions were inevitable. Giorgio Guidotti considered the Stretta a necessary check on the Larga of S. Maria della Morte when he made a large legacy to the latter in 1441 contingent on it giving the former an annual subsidy and the right to worship unhindered in the confraternal quarters. Guidotti's safeguards suggest that many members of the Larga wanted to suppress or eject the Stretta, which had been established only five years before, for he further stipulated that if this ever happened, the Stretta could claim the entire legacy. On the other side, Ugo Ruggieri da Reggio was a member of S. Maria degli Angeli in the 1470s when some brothers renounced the work of the confraternity's foundling home and established a Stretta cell to develop their own devotions. Some twenty years later when he was writing the statutes of the Compagnia di Spirito Santo, Ruggieri specifically prohibited any division of the new confraternity into Larga and Stretta companies.[19] We have seen above that in some companies these divisions precipitated the domination of devotional life by the Stretta and the metamorphosis of the Larga into a purely administrative Board of Managers for the confraternity's charitable institution, to the detriment of those – particularly women – who wanted to keep alive the earlier tradition of praise through public psalm singing and charity.

Christopher Black speculates that creating Stretta cells could have simply been Bologna's way of addressing the fact that not all members of a confraternity wanted to flagellate. The Venetian *Scuole* formally distinguished between flagellant and non-flagellant members, and Bologna's Stretta–Larga division had much the same result.[20] Yet at issue here were not simply different worship practices, but different forms of community. The laudesi model was an ecumenical but comparatively passive sharing in the merits of the mendicant orders. The battuti and Stretta model focused on actively following the mendicant rule while living a lay life: it was exclusive, secret, and demanding.

---

[18] The 1521 statutes of S. Maria del Baraccano further enjoin members not to murmur against the members of the "Grande" (i.e., Larga), for all are equally brothers. BBA Gozz 213 #1, cap. 9. In fact company records show that the two groups had troubled relations for centuries, with the stretta attempting to separate in 1656 and 1720–22: "Ragioni del Corporale della Compagnia Grande, o sia Larga di S. Maria del Baraccano," BBA Gozz 209 #1.

[19] ASB Osp, Compagnia di S. Maria della Morte, busta 1/77 (1441). The matriculation list for S. Maria degli Angeli commencing in 1479 includes "Ugo da Rezo, Stampatore" BBA Gozz 203, #5 (letter V). In the statutes of the Compagnia di Spirito Santo he identifies himself as "Ugo già d'Antonio de Ruggeri da Rezzo, stampatore": BBA B3180, cap. 20.

[20] Black, *Italian Confraternities*, pp. 88–9.

Yet as the multiple memberships of the notary Eliseo Mamelini demonstrate, these two views coexisted without necessarily competing. The small group of flagellants was a fratello's closest community of mutually supporting and admonishing brothers; members could not join more than one such close community on the principle that no one can serve two masters.[21] Larga, ospedale, or laudesi groups put the fratello in a broader community of Christians benefiting from fellowship with the friars, and in turn benefiting others by collectively exercising charity. Through dues and alms to their various charitable confraternities, fratelli sheltered pilgrims, fed the hungry, helped the poor and orphans, ministered to the sick and imprisoned; in short, they fulfilled the seven works of charity. Multiple memberships do not indicate that confraternal membership was treated lightly, nor do they point to a vague spiritual anxiety. Distinct groups gave communal form to different elements of an individual's life and worship, and allowed laymen (and to a lesser extent laywomen) to determine their devotional exercises and spiritual kin through deliberately constructed networks.

In spite of occasional tensions, Stretta autonomy under Larga authority offered a model for accommodating tensions and diversity within individual confraternities. As confratelli became accustomed to the model, they extended it from devotional into functional and gender distinctions, particularly in companies that were undergoing *nobilitazione* and were taking on expanding roles in civic charity and the civic cult. The Compagnia di S. Maria della Morte offers a particularly clear example. From its origin in 1336, S. Maria della Morte's members had offered spiritual comfort and burial to prisoners sentenced to execution, had served the city's sick and dying with a large infirmary, and had given spiritual and corporal charity to convicts in Bologna's three jails. All of these charitable functions took place on an ad hoc basis under the general administration of the confraternity itself. S. Maria della Morte was among the first Bolognese confraternities to generate a Stretta company in 1436 and, despite Giorgio Guidotti's fears, the brothers' satisfaction with the arrangement is evident in the restructuring of the confraternity's charitable work with prisoners in the next

---

[21] Expressed this way by the stretta of SS Sebastian e Rocco, who go on to the more traditional formulation of not attending two oratories. Private oratories were the symbol of flagellant companies' exclusive community. Apart from a local tradition of opening the oratories one day in the year, no fratello could visit another company's oratory without permission of his own and the other group's chief lay officer. If frequent injunctions against the practice are any indication, this rule was frequently ignored. ASB Dem, Compagnia di SS. Sebastiano e Rocco, busta 16/6620 filza 1, cap. 17.

century. Both spiritual aid to the condemned and physical aid to the imprisoned appear to have gone into decline in the late fifteenth and early sixteenth centuries, due to the lack of formal administration, to the greater attention needed by the confraternity's infirmary, and to the political turmoil of the period. One of the brothers almost single-handedly undertook regeneration of the work with those imprisoned for debt and civil crimes. From the time he became a Sindic responsible for this work in 1504, Cristoforo Angelelli worked to recover and expand the charity's financial resources, and to establish it on something firmer than the distracted attention of frequently changing hospital administrators, and the memories of earlier participants in the work. Angelelli followed the Stretta blueprint in establishing the *Opera dei Poveri Prigionieri*. In 1523 he secured separate quarters for the charitable work and a set of statutes which defined its internal administration and its relations with the larger confraternity of S. Maria della Morte. Fifteen years later the work with prisoners awaiting execution was similarly overhauled with the appointment of six Masters to the *Scuola dei Confortatori*. The Scuola had separate administrative records, rooms in the Ospedale della Morte and, from 1556, statutes which gave it control over its own finances and recruitment.[22] As with the S. Maria della Morte Stretta company, membership in the Larga (the Compagnia dell'Ospedale) was a prerequisite for membership in the sub-group, but any member of the Larga who wished to join one of the sub-groups had to win its trust and approval. Each group had its own lay head, and the *Massaro* of the Ospedale, the *Priore* of the Stretta, the *Principe* of the Scuola dei Confortatori, and the *Prefetto* of the Poveri Prigionieri took their places under the over-arching presidency of the Rector of the Compagnia di S. Maria della Morte, with their relative precedence decided by the antiquity of their sub-group. Each group had an abbreviated administration sufficient for its particular needs, with as little duplication as possible. Hence the Stretta had a priest to carry out its larger liturgical and sacramental functions, and a Master of Novices to instruct its newly recruited members, but no separate notary or financial officer. The Opera dei Poveri Prigionieri had prison wardens and a notary, but no priest or Master of Novices. The Scuola dei Confortatori had a beadle, a secretary, and a book-keeper, but no separate priest or notary. Once annually, the officers of the Compagnia dell'Ospedale reviewed the finances and administration of

[22] N. Terpstra, "Confraternal Prison Welfare and Political Consolidation in Sixteenth-Century Bologna," *Journal of Modern History* vol. 66 (1994), 217–48. N. Terpstra, "Piety and Punishment: The Lay *Conforteria* and Civic Justice in Sixteenth-Century Bologna," *Sixteenth Century Studies*, vol. 22 (1991), pp. 679–94.

the sub-groups. They retained the power to overturn any of the decisions made by the sub-groups.

Since sub-groups' autonomy was limited to the details of their devotional or charitable function, it is perhaps not surprising that groups based on gender alone enjoyed almost no self-direction. Like the Stretta, the consororities that emerged in the mid-sixteenth century under confraternal sponsorship received their own rule, and members were considered sufficiently part of the larger spiritual brotherhood to be buried as the males were, wrapped in company robes and carried in procession to the grave. However, unlike the Stretta, they had virtually no supervision of their own affairs. As seen in the previous chapter, the sisters of S. Maria della Pietà elected a Prioress, but their choice was subject to review by the male company, which further reinforced its authority by appointing a male Guardian to review and supervise consorority finances and administration.[23] The sisters of SSmo. Crocifisso del Cestello did not even elect a Prioress. Neither confraternity was unfamiliar with the Stretta model since the more devout males of both companies had already established stretta groups for their collective worship. Yet they drew nothing more from their own experience than the simple possibility of creating a subordinate company. Under male supervision, the consororities could not become active and mutually disciplining spiritual communities on the Stretta model, but remained largely auxiliaries of their sponsoring confraternity. Moreover the *pericolosità* of women ensured that their sub-group would always be held more at arm's length than any male sub-group. The decline of laudesi worship reduced women's worship to an essentially private series of devotions carried out in the home. The sisters gathered together only occasionally for mass in their companies' public chapels.[24] Their spiritual community therefore remained far less developed than that of the stretta groups, and without a distinct charitable function, their autonomy and group identity was also less developed.

II. ADMINISTRATION

However strong or weak a community's spiritual sense of solidarity, communal life needed an administrative framework. The earliest confraternities adopted forms used in artisanal guilds; these were perpetuated well into the fifteenth century by Larga and ospedale confraternities. Fifteenth-century observant reformers initi-

[23] ASB Dem, Compagnia di S. Maria della Pietà, busta 10/7696, filza 3, cap. 2.
[24] ASB Dem, Compagnia di S. Maria della Pietà, busta 10/7696, filza 3, cap. 2, 3.

ally simplified and democratized confraternal administration. Yet the endemic Renaissance political tension between representative and autocratic forms of government affected all confraternities in the frequent changes to voting procedures and in an increasing reliance on self-perpetuating councils supervising growing confraternal wealth.

The Congregatio devotorum civitatis bononie of 1261 put good order uppermost when it devoted the first chapter of its statutes to naming the new company's officers. A Rector led the group, assisted by a financial officer, the Massaro, and advised by twelve counsellors, or Guardiani. Assuming, perhaps, that contemporary guild practice would simply carry over to the new confraternity, little was said about the functions of these different officials. Confusion and disagreements immediately followed and additional chapters clarifying appointment and duties were soon added to the statutes. Only the Rector was elected by the fratelli; the Guardiani chose both the Massaro and their own replacements. Rector and Massaro served for one year, the Guardiani for six months. Only company members could serve in any post. Due perhaps to financial irregularities, the Massaro's annual report, tendered upon completion of his term, was soon augmented with monthly accounts submitted to his fellow officers and to the membership at large. While the Rector was the supreme authority, the Guardiani carried out much of the daily administration and care for the sick and dead. This administrative model seems to have been adopted by most thirteenth- and fourteenth-century Bolognese laudesi confraternities, with the single change of reducing the number of Guardiani from twelve to six.[25] Ospedali companies occasionally added a notary to the ruling council.

The council of Guardiani was clearly the true power in these confraternities, and could easily become a self-perpetuating oligarchy. Across Italy fifteenth-century reforms tended to reduce this concentration of unelected power. Some new confraternities dispensed with the council altogether, while others made it an elected body. All new companies increased the authority of the chief lay officer, variously called the Rector, Prior, or, most commonly, the Padre Ordinario. The Padre Ordinario directed worship services in the confraternal oratory, appointing celebrants, setting the liturgy, and enforcing obedience to confraternal statutes. He also served as chairman in the

[25] Congregatio Devotorum: Angelozzi, *Confraternite laicali*, pp. 86–7, 91–4. S. Francesco (1317): Mesini, "S. Maria delle Laudi," p. 367. S. Procolo (1329): Fanti, *San Procolo*, p. 186. S. Maria della Carità (1399): ASB Dem busta 4/7673, filza I, c3v.

regular administrative meetings of the membership, and oversaw company duties to the sick and dead.[26] The increased power was offset by a shorter term of office; most companies limited their Ordinarios to three-month terms. Yet apart from the company priest, the Ordinario had no real challengers to his authority. Small councils of advisors had replaced the Guardiani. In early fifteenth-century statutes these were called the *Sollecituri* and were either chosen by the new Ordinario or elected when he was. They functioned as his executive assistants in finance (replacing the Massaro) and worship. In mid-century the Compagnia di S. Ambrogio rationalized this three-member council by teaming the "apprentice" and past Ordinarios with the one currently serving; it also restored the office of Massaro.[27] This ensured that all officials were elected and that the chief lay officer was familiar with his duties before taking them on. Most new companies of the early sixteenth century adopted this revised system.[28]

---

[26] The administrative sessions were often called the *parlamento*, where routine company business was handled by voting; this description of the parlamento is based on the statutes of: (a) S. Francesco, stretta, 1443 (BBA B983, cap. 19, c.69r); (b) S. Ambrogio, 1456 (ASB Codici Miniati, ms. 67, cap. 21); (c) S. Maria della Mezzaratta del Monte, 1484 (BBA Gozz 203 #8, c.158r–v); (d) S. Maria della Pietà, 1503 (BBA Gozz 206 #7, cap. 6, 10); (e) S. Rocco, ca. 1511–23 (ASB Dem, busta 6/6589, filza 2, c.vi); (f) S. Maria degli Angeli, stretta, 1522 (BBA Gozz 203 #7, cap. 8, c. 148v–149r); (g) S. Maria dei Servi (ASB Osp, ms. 2/307, cap. 10, c.111r); (h) SS. Sebastiano e Rocco, 1525 (ASB Dem, busta 16/6620, filza 10, cap. 9). Persuading members to attend the parlamento was always difficult, and from the early sixteenth century most companies began specifying a quorum for votes: Buon Gesù in 1521 required 50% + 1 (ASB Dem, busta 9/7631, filza 1, cap. 23); S. Maria della Pietà in 1503 required two-thirds (BBA Gozz 206 #7, cap. 10), as did S. Maria Maddalena in 1515 (ASB PIE ms. 1, cap. 1), and S. Maria del Baraccano in 1521 (BBA Gozz 213 #1, cap. 20).

[27] See the statutes for the companies of: (a) S. Girolamo di Miramonte (1425), ASB Dem, busta 2/6719, filza 2, cap. 8; (b) S. Girolamo (1433), BBA Gozz 206 #5, cap. 24, 27; (c) S. Bernardino (1454) ASB Dem, busta 8/7639, filza 1, cap. 8; (d) S. Maria dei Guarini/stretta (1454), BBA Gozz 210, #11, cap. 5; (e) S. Maria della Vita/stretta (1454), BBA Osp ms. 10, cap. 5; (f) S. Ambrogio (1456), ASB Codici Miniati, ms. 67, cap. 1.

[28] See the statutes for: (a) SSmo. Crocifisso del Cestello (1514), BBA Gozz 206 #1, cap. 11, 28; (b) S. Maria Maddalena (1515), ASB PIE, ms. 1, cap. 1, 2; (c) S. Maria del Baraccano (1521), BBA Gozz 213 #1, cap. 6; (d) Buon Gesù (1521), ASB Dem, 9/7631, filza 1, cap. 16, 28; (e) SS. Sebastiano e Rocco (1525), ASB Dem, busta 16/6620, filza 1, cap. 3, 4, 6. In its 1523 statutes, S. Maria dei Servi appointed the person with the second highest vote tally as the Companion Prior, ASB Osp, ms. 2/307, cap. 3.

Like his lay counterparts, the Padre Spirituale also went from appointment to election in the fifteenth century.[29] Many Trecento confraternities had no Padre Spirituale as such; from 1261, lay officials simply appointed priests to see that necessary services were carried out. They normally chose a mendicant friar, with company statutes sometimes prescribing the Order. Some fifteenth-century laudesi and ospedali companies continued leaving the choice with their lay officials. Battuti and Stretta companies expected far more from their Padre Spirituale, and so drew their members into the process of appointing him. The Padre Spirituale was at the centre of the confraternal community, both because of his sacramental and educational duties, and because he was seen as a neutral party who could mediate internal disputes. While elected by the membership, the Padre Spirituale had considerable powers in admitting and expelling members and supervising the election of officials. Moreover, while most Quattrocento companies moved to electing their Padre Spirituale and including him in the administrative council, few specified his term of office.[30] More importantly, few specified whether ultimate authority rested with the Padre Spirituale or with the Padre Ordinario. Most companies contented themselves with vaguely recommending that the counsel of the priest be sought in all important affairs, on the assumption that he had the best interests of the brothers' souls in mind.[31] All

[29] What follows is a composite based on the statutes of: (a) S. Girolamo Miramonte (1425), ASB Dem, busta 2/6719, filza 2, cap. 7; (b) S. Geronimo (1433), BBA Gozz 206 #5, cap. 1, 24; (c) S. Ambrogio (1456), ASB Codici Miniati, ms. 67, cap. 1, 16, 17; (d) S. Bartolomeo di Reno (1471), ASB PIE, ms. 1, cap. 12; (e) S. Maria della Mezzaratta del Monte (1483), BBA Gozz 203 #7, c. 153v; (f) S. Maria della Pietà (1503), BBA Gozz 206 #7, cap. 1; (g) S. Rocco, (ca. 1511–23), ASB Dem, busta 6/6589, filza 2, cap. 12; (h) S. Maria Maddalena (1515), ASB PIE, ms. 1, cap. 16; (i) SS. Sebastiano e Rocco (1525), ASB Dem, busta 16/6620, filza 1, cap. 2. Stretta groups: (a) S. Francesco (1443), BBA B983, cap. 11; (b) S. Maria della Vita (1454), BBA Osp, ms. 10, cap. 2; (c) S. Maria degli Angeli (ca. 1479), BBA Gozz 203 #7, cap. 21 (cc. vi–xvi); (d) S. Maria della Carità (1518), BBA Gozz 210 #6, cap. 2; (e) Buon Gesù, (1521), ASB Dem, busta 9/7631, filza 1, cap. 19; (f) S. Maria del Baraccano (1521), BBA Gozz 213 #1, cap. 2.

[30] S. Bartolomeo di Reno (1471) entrusted the Massaro with appointing a priest to perform specified religious functions. Those moving to election of the Padre Spirituale: S. Girolamo (1425, 1433); S. Francesco/stretta (1443); S. Maria della Vita (1454); S. Ambrogio (1456); S. Maria degli Angeli/stretta (ca. 1479); S. Maria della Pietà (1503); S. Maria Maddalena (1515); S. Maria del Baraccano stretta (1521); S. Maria della Carità (1577).

[31] Of companies with control over the appointment, only S. Ambrogio (1456) specifically submitted the priest to the Ordinario's authority, and only the Stretta of S. Maria degli Angeli (ca. 1479) and those of Buon Gesù (1521) specifically gave ultimate authority to the priest. The Dominican confraternities of S. Domenico and S. Croce gave ultimate authority to the supervising friar and the Inquisitor, respectively. Other confraternities left the question of relative powers vague.

confraternities wanted a priest of "good morals and reputation" ("*bona vita e fama*"), but some also specified that he be well educated, so as to lead with wisdom and teach by more than example.[32] Leaving ultimate authority vague may have been the most flexible option in Quattrocento lay confraternities but it was quickly abandoned in Cinquecento parish confraternities, where disputes clarified and increased the greater power of the priest relative to lay officials. Problems with over-zealous priests may have already arisen in the early sixteenth century, for this is when some statues begin specifically restricting the Padre Spirituale's term of office to one year. This is also when the Compagnia di S. Maria della Morte went a step further and began alternating the appointment between Franciscans and Dominicans.[33]

The administrative model emerging in most new companies of the fifteenth century assumed that the confraternity was an autonomous group with simple affairs. As responsibilities and assets multiplied over the following decades, new officials and new problems came in their wake. A *Depositario* might take over some of the Massaro's more mundane money-collecting duties, leaving the latter as the company's chief financial officer. A *Priore* would assume the religious duties fifteenth-century confratelli assigned to the Ordinario, while this latter official became once again a figurehead Rector or *Presidente*. One or two appointed or elected Sacristans looked after the details of worship in the oratory, buying candles, lighting lamps, checking attendance and observance, and keeping the oratory clean. As confraternal charity grew and became institutionalized through the early sixteenth century, the number of paid employees followed suit. The *ospedali* had traditionally employed jack-of-all-trades *guardiani* and kept doctors and notaries on retainer to handle occasional medical emergencies and to keep track of their investments. By 1555, the Ospedale di S. Maria della Vita had fourteen paid staff, most of them full-time employees and some hired with their spouses and children as "*famegli.*"[34] Similarly, when new Cinquecento companies assumed supervision of religious shrines, they too hired full-time caretakers of the company's

---

[32] S. Maria della Carità (1518) wanted a friar "*de scientia copioso*"; S. Girolamo di Miramonte (1425) one "*disientia salutare*"; and S. Rocco (ca. 1511–23) looked for one who was "*docto e experto.*" Others specifying learned friars: S. Maria della Vita (1454); S. Maria del Baraccano (1521). Of these, all but S. Maria della Carità and S. Rocco had significant numbers of high-born members.

[33] The practice began in 1504: "Nota de Reverendi Padri Spirituali dell'Oratorio della Compagnia, ora Arciconfraternità di Sa. Ma. della Morte," ASB Osp, Compagnia di S. Maria della Morte, busta 29/632 filza 5.

[34] ASB Osp, Compagnia di S. Maria della Morte, ms. 21/250a., cc. 13r–21r.

COMMUNAL IDENTITY, ADMINISTRATION, AND FINANCES 149

public site and private chapel. Sometimes confraternity members took on supervision of these employees in weekly rotation; S. Maria della Vita elected two members weekly to visit the Ospedale twice daily as *Visitatori de Poveri*. Yet the scale of some operations outgrew members' will and ability to supervise them on this essentially ad hoc basis, and councils of Sindics or Consuls gradually returned to oversee large expenditures, audit Massaros' and Depositarios' accounts, and supervise confraternal charities, shrines, properties, and investments. The self-perpetuating members of these councils often sat for life terms and gradually assumed powers formerly exercised by elected officials and supervised by confratelli voting in chapter meetings.[35] Administrative changes of the Quattrocento had usually followed the mendicant model by turning the Ordinario into a lay abbot over a lay brotherhood whose communal life centered on worship. The expanding bureaucracies of Cinquecento confraternities more often cited political models as the inspiration and example of good order and obedience for brotherhoods which were in the process of adopting a more public civic religious role as dispensers of charity and guardians of local shrines.[36]

As confraternal administration became more complex, problems with fraudulent elections led many groups to alter voting procedures. Fratelli had traditionally voted in public sessions where they individually went forward and either wrote the name of their nominee on a piece of paper left on the altar, or whispered it into the ear of the

[35] Confraternities cited more complex company business and the difficulty of meeting quorums as reasons for shifting authority from the confraternal assembly to the unelected council. Some examples of administration by sindics: (a) S. Ambrogio (1456) had four sindics elected to life terms: ASB Codici Miniati, ms. 67, cap. 23; (b) S. Maria della Mezzaratta del Monte (1483) elected four *consuli* to one-year terms: BBA Gozz 203 #7, c. 155r; (c) S. Maria della Pietà (1503) elected four *consuli* to one-year terms: BBA Gozz 206 #7, cap. 5; (d) S. Maria della Carità (1518) had four life-term *consiglieri*: BBA Gozz 210 #6, cap. 19; (e) S. Maria dei Servi (1523) elected seven life-term *"sinizi"*: ASB Osp. ms. 2/307, cc. 10r–v; (f) SSmo. Crocifisso del Cestello added three sindics serving six-month terms in 1538 statutes (BBA Gozz 206 #2, cap. 4), but replaced these with five elected, life-term *conservatori di beni* in a 1583 revision, and with two *conservatori di mobili e apparati* in 1589. A.M. Porcù, *Il santuario e la confraternita del SSmo Crocifisso del Cestello in Bologna* (Bologna: 1961), p. 70.

[36] Even the otherwise "pietistic" 1521 statutes of the company of Buon Gesù parallel the Ordinario's power and authority to that of a gentleman or prince (ASB Dem, busta 9/7631, filza 1, cap. 16, 24). Statutes which drew on political motifs tended to come out of largely patrician companies: S. Maria del Baraccano stretta in 1521 (BBA Gozz 213 #1, cap. 6); S. Maria della Pietà consorority in 1548 (ASB Dem, busta 10/7696, filza 3, Prologue and cap. 1); S. Maria dei Servi larga in 1523 (ASB Osp, ms. 2/307, cc. 4–4v).

Padre Spirituale. The system operated on a trust which was too easily abused, and from the mid-fifteenth century, Bolognese confraternities turned increasingly to various forms of sortition whereby names were pulled out of a closely guarded bag. Simply filling the bag with the names of all members risked including those who were neither fit nor able (terms inviting a wide variety of interpretations), so a nominating committee either picked the most fit, or ranked all the members into a series of lists.[37] Many companies restored the terms of office for the Ordinario and Massaro to the earlier standard of a year, and included a *vacazione* equal to or longer than the term of office itself to prevent retiring officials from being nominated or extracted for the same office they had just served.

Frequent administrative reforms suggest that accountability was a major problem. Financial accountability was the greatest concern. Confraternities commonly audited an outgoing financial officer's accounts and charged him for any discrepancies; at least two new confraternities of the early sixteenth century began requiring officials to post a bond.[38] But other issues of accountability emerge from minute books and frequent revisions to company statutes. Age and length of membership became a condition of office in Buon Gesù, S. Maria della Pietà, and S. Maria dei Servi. Absentee officials became a problem for S. Maria Maddalena. Holding two offices and disregarding company statutes were cited by SS. Crocifisso del Cestello.[39] And all companies had problems with members missing chapter meetings or being unwilling to serve in the office for which they had been nominated or drawn. Progressive ennobling of membership and the subsequent concentration of power and authority in a small and usually unelected elite

---

[37] Minute books for SS. Girolamo ed Anna show considerable experimentation with voting procedures during its period of rapid growth in the 1490s. In November 1498, 75% voted for extraction; six months later the same proportion voted to return to ballot voting. Eighteen months later this procedure was judged "troublesome" and replaced with voting by black and white beans. "Libro della Compagnia," (11/1/1498; 5/1/1499; 12/5, 12, 19/1501): ASB Dem, Compagnia di SS. Girolamo ed Anna, busta 5/6722, filza 1. See also: A.A. Machiavelli, *Origine, Fondazione, e Progressi della Veneranda Compagnia ... de Gloriosi Santi Girolamo ed Anna,* (Bologna: 1754), p. 22. SS. Sebastiano e Rocco started with written ballots, tried voice votes, and ended up with names of all members put in a bag from which four were drawn. These four chose four others, and all eight then went into a separate bag from which the name of the Ordinario was drawn. ASB Dem, Compagnia di SS. Sebastiano e Rocco, busta 16/6620, filza 1, cap. 20.

[38] The Company of S. Maria della Pietà (1503), and that of S. Maria Maddalena (1515), preceded by S. Maria degli Angeli in 1479 (BBA Gozz. 203 #7, c.5v).

[39] ASB Osp, Compagnia di S. Maria dei Servi, ms. 2/307, cap. 3, 5, 7, 9. ASB PIE, Compagnia di S. Maria Maddalena, ms. 1, cap. 4. For Compagnia del SSmo. Crocifisso del Cestello: BBA Gozz 206 #2, cap. 7; BBA Gozz 206 #1b, cap. 6, 10.

may have led remaining members to avoid office rather than play the powerless courtier; alternately, the unelected elite may have been filling a vacuum caused by members' indifference to office. By the mid-sixteenth century, confraternal administration had come full circle, with most of the real power vested in a small, self-perpetuating Board just as it had been with the Congregatio devotorum civitatis bononie of 1261. Yet the context was radically different. Where Due-cento fratelli were establishing a new form of lay corporate worship, their Cinquecento counterparts were establishing new forms of political and social domination in Bologna. The balance of this chapter expands on this process in relation to growing confraternal wealth and property.

III. INCOME, PROPERTY, AND OBLIGATIONS

By examining confraternal finances, we can see how companies raised and spent the money required for worship; how they grew more wealthy through legacies and donations; and how these gifts and the investments made with them both reflected and required greater involvement of the confraternal with the civic community. These three dimensions appear in virtually all confraternities, and the increasingly complex financial obligations of wealthier confraternities forced members into creating more bureaucratic administrations capable of handling the business of worship and charity.

Confraternal income came from three sources. Dues paid by members at matriculation and on a regular basis thereafter provided a regular income intended to cover worship expenses. Donations augmented this income. These came as offerings in the offering boxes which each company placed in churches or carried door to door, as alms received for performing masses, or as larger legacies given by members and non-members alike. Investments in land, loans, and the funded public debt, or *Monte*, provided the third source of income. Some companies drew income from all three sources, others from only one or two. As some companies' charitable activities were drawn into the civic bureacratic apparatus, they could count on communal subsidies or income from designated fines or taxes; these will be discussed further in the next chapter.[40]

Confraternal expenses were similarly divided in three directions. Worship could not be conducted without oil for the lamps, candles for the altars, and alms for the priests; periodic outlays for decorating,

[40] G. Mira, "Aspetti economic-finanziari," pp. 237–8.

improving, or expanding the oratory added to these expenses. Charity and testators' wills required regular outlays for feeding the poor, tending the sick, assisting pilgrims, and dowering orphan girls. Notaries and book-keepers required their fees, and investment properties required maintenance and improvement. No company could avoid paying any of these expenses.

We can track income and expenses through different types of financial records. Account books are the most helpful guides to determining changing yearly breakdowns of income and expenses, but are the rarest of surviving records. Companies also required officers regularly to compile inventories of the *"beni mobili et immobili,"* fixed and moveable assets found in the oratory, in the sacristy, and, in the case of real estate, in the streets and suburbs of Bologna. While less helpful than account books, relatively more inventories survive in the Bolognese archives; at the same time, wide variations between consecutive inventories done for a single company suggest that some officers fulfilled the task more diligently than others.[41] Most inventories occupy a few sheets, but the most impressive is the Company of S. Maria della Vita's *Liber Memoriale* of 1516, an extensive and beautifully written record of the company's many real-estate holdings. Legal records relating to confraternal legacies and investments are a third, more common, group of financial statements. Notaries recorded every will, every purchase and sale, every lease and lawsuit involving the company. Since these records never lost their utility, they are the most frequently surviving financial record in confraternal archives.

Surviving Bolognese account books include the Compagnia di S. Domenico's *Vacchetta della Spesa*, covering 1453–1483; the Compagnia di S. Ambrogio's records for 1539 to 1549; and a 1505 record of income and expenses for the Compagnia di SS. Sebastiano e Rocco.[42] With distinct functions, degrees of autonomy and social composition,

---

[41] Surviving fifteenth- and sixteenth-century inventories and their dates: (a) Compagnia di S. Ambrogio, (1480; 1490), ASB Dem busta 5/6627, c. 2–2v; (b) Compagnia di S. Domenico, (1477; 1484; 1486), ASB Dem, busta 1/6415, filza 2, n.p.; (c) Compagnia di S. Girolamo in Miramonte, (Jan. 1463; July 1463; n.d.), ASB Dem, busta 1/6718, filza 3a; (d) Compagnia di S. Maria della Carità, (1563), ASB Dem, busta 8/7677, filza 3a; (e) Compagnia di S. Maria dei Servi, (1453; 1479), ASB Osp ms. 4/188; (f) Compagnia di S. Maria della Vita, (1516), ASB Osp, ms. 12/11; (g) Compagnia di S. Rocco, (1540), ASB Dem busta 5/6588, filza 1, cc. 132v–133; (h) Compagnia di SS Sebastiano e Rocco, (n.d.), ASB Dem busta 14/6618, filza 6. The significant variations occur between the first and second inventories for S. Girolamo in Miramonte in 1463.

[42] All three records are in the ASB Fondo Demaniale: Compagnia di S. Domenico: 1/6415 #2. Compagnia di S. Ambrogio: 5/6627, c 5–16r. Compagnia di SS. Sebastiano e Rocco: 1/6605 #9.

they illustrate the range of confraternities operating in Renaissance Bologna. They demonstrate roughly similar patterns in their expenses, but differ significantly in their sources of income. S. Domenico drew its income solely from members' dues; S. Ambrogio from a combination of donations and investments; and SS. Sebastiano e Rocco from investments alone. Summaries of the companies' accounts are given in Tables 4.1, 4.2, and 4.3.

The Compagnia di S. Domenico (Table 4.1) was a flagellant confraternity established by Fra Manfredo da Vercelli in 1418. Its artisanal and high-born members acted as lay auxiliaries to the order, whose Prior wrote their statutes and supervised their activities. The company underwent a devotional revival in 1443, and as noted in Chapter Two the brothers attempted unsuccessfully to assert their autonomy in a dispute with the Dominican Prior and Inquisitor which ran through the 1480s and early 1490s.[43] The Compagnia di S. Domenico observed two major festivals annually: the August festival of the patron saint whose tomb was in the Dominican church, and a December festival honoring dead members.

Voluntary dues were collected before each festival, presumably to ensure that expenses would not exceed income.[44] Of the twenty-one festivals for which income and expense figures are available, small deficits occurred only six times. Costs were generally elastic and the sums involved were quite small. Fratelli regularly allotted two *soldi* for poor relief, paid the priest varying sums between one and one and one-half *lire*, and spent the balance on candles and decorations. While income and expenses are noted only for the two annual festivals, these were not the limit of group worship. Inventories for 1477, 1484, and 1488 list numerous altarcloths, candlesticks, chalices, and liturgical books used in worship, including some items reserved for Holy Thursday.[45] The group had no property. While the *Vacchetta delle Spese* from which the information in Table 4.1 is drawn may be incomplete, it nonetheless portrays a restricted worship and communal life consistent with its close supervision by the mendicant friars.

The Compagnia di S. Ambrogio was the first "ethnic" company in Bologna; it was founded by artisans of Milanese descent in 1456. Milan had repeatedly threatened Bologna through the early fifteenth century,

---

[43] ASB Dem, Compagnia di S. Domenico, busta 1/6415, filza 5, item 1; busta 7/6421, filza 3. See also Meersseman, *Ordo fraternitatis*, pp. 611–16.

[44] Dues ranged from 6d to 1s 6d in the 1450s, gradually rising to 2s or more in the 1460s and 1470s (see Table 4.1); some members paid in kind (candles in 1473 and 1474) and others did not pay at all.

[45] ASB Dem, Compagnia di S. Domenico, busta 1/6415, filza 2.

Table 4.1. *S. Domenico income and expenses (1451–79)*

	Festa S. Domenico (Aug.)			Festa delle Morti (Dec.)		
Year	Members present	Income	Expense	Members present	Income	Expense
1451	15	1.4.2		24	3.6.00	3.3.6
1452						
1453	34	3.00.06		23	2.10.00	
1454	32	3.02.02	1.09.02			2.14.00
1455	26	3.09.00		33	3.19.00	
1456	25	1.18.00		25	2.04.06	1.09.10
1457				27	2.10.03	2.02.10
1458	14	1.11.00				
1459						
1460	27	2.11.00	0.15.00	25	1.14.00	4.18.06
1461	15	1.09.00	1.15.08	19	1.18.10	1.18.04
1462	20	1.18.00	1.16.00	32	2.12.00	2.09.00
1463	18	1.14.06		19	1.16.00	2.04.00
1464	12	1.04.06	1.01.06	11	1.04.06	1.02.08
1465	20	2.09.06	1.13.03	18	1.13.06	1.13.00
1466	16	1.09.00	1.10.00	19	1.14.06	1.14.00
1467						
1468	15	1.10.06				
1469						
1470						
1471	20	2.02.06				
1472						
1473	14	1.16.06		15	2.09.00	
1474				13	2.04.06	1.06.06
1475				19	1.15.08	
1476	16	2.02.06		14	1.13.00	
1477				24	2.00.04	3.19.00
1478	23	1.18.06	2.09.00			
1479	15	1.19.10	1.16.00			

Source: ASB Dem, Compagnia di S. Domenico, busta 1/6415, filza 2.
Notes:
1. Neither the celebratory festival of S. Domenico nor the commemorative festival for the Dead Fratelli was celebrated on a fixed day of the month.
2. Entries are given in Bolognese lire.soldi.denari (1=20=240). Through this period the Florentine florin was worth 35–40 Bolognese soldi. (See: P. Spufford, *Handbook of Medieval Exchange*, London: 1986, pp. 72–80.)

so this company's very origins demonstrated confraternal peacemaking of a deliberately public and political kind. By the 1540s it had lost its ethnic character, and followed the conventions of local autonomous, artisan-dominated confraternities.[46] S. Ambrogio's accounts (Table 4.2)

[46] ASB Dem, Compagnia di S. Ambrogio, busta 3/6625, filza 2, c. 2r. Fanti, *San Procolo*, p. 144.

Table 4.2. *S. Ambrogio income and expenses (1539–49)*

Year	Income	Expense	Balance
1539	39.05.00	29.15.00	9.10.00
1540–41	63.06.00	77.09.00	[14.03.00]
1542	39.18.00	34.10.02	5.07.10
1543	59.09.06	29.04.10	30.04.08
1544	78.11.10	65.15.04	12.16.06
1545	70.02.02	51.00.01	19.02.01
1546	51.10.00	54.07.06	[2.17.06]
1547	63.19.06	62.12.04	1.07.02
1548	52.01.10	61.07.00	[9.05.02]
1549	43.11.00	43.11.00	----

Source: ASB Dem, Compagnia di S. Ambrogio, ms 5/6627, cc. 5r–16v.
Note: All figures are given in Bolognese lire.soldi.denari (1=20=240).

are more typical than S. Domenico's of the financial variations which lay-directed companies experienced. High turnover of officials and frequent difficulties in collecting rents led to unequal fiscal years.[47] The sudden rise in income in 1543–44 was due in part to new rents and in part to fines levied against Massaro Mathio Vaccharello to recover money he had defrauded the company of in preceeding years.[48] Two-thirds of the inflated expenses of 1544 went into repairs of investment property. Moving beyond these yearly totals into the accounts themselves, the most consistent ongoing expenses were those for worship: oil, candles, masses, and annual alms of eighteen lire to the friars of the nearby Carmelite monastery of S. Maria delle Grazie for the religious services they conducted in the Company oratory. The brothers regularly allotted small sums to prepare the oratory for special festivals, and distribute Christmas alms to the poor. Larger sums went periodically to repair or improve company property. Even with these latter expenses, well over three-quarters of confraternal expenses were dedicated to worship.[49] Inventories of 1480 and 1490 note the missals, chalices, altarcloths, and candlesticks used in worship, and the five urban properties from which the company derived the bulk of its income. In most years, rents accounted for over three-quarters of the company's

[47] For example, the 1542 financial year went from March to February; 1543 from February to January; 1548 from April to March; 1549 from March to January.
[48] ASB Dem, Compagnia di S. Ambrogio, busta 5/6627, cc. 10r–10v; busta 1/6623, p. 170.
[49] During the period 1539–44 when many of the repairs were carried out, expenses unrelated to worship were almost 30% of total expenses (i.e., 69.5.6 lire out of 236.14.2). In the more "typical" year 1549, they were just over 8% (3.6.0 lire out of 43.11.0). ASB Dem, Compagnia di S. Ambrogio, busta 5/6627, cc. 4r–10v, 11v–12v, 15v–16r.

income and sufficed in themselves to cover the costs associated with worship.[50] In spite of Mathio Vaccharello's fraud, the alternating surpluses and deficits, and the suspiciously perfect balance achieved in the last budget recorded, S. Ambrogio had arranged its finances quite well. There was little need for the alms raised from members and through its offering boxes.

The Compagnia di SS. Sebastiano e Rocco originated in 1504 around the shrine of these two saints in the church of S. Leonardo on Stra San Vitale. Crowds had been gathering at the shrine to pray and sing laudi but, like S. Ambrogio, this confraternity's origins were as much political as devotional. In the waning years of the Bentivoglio signory, when tensions with Julius II were growing, *Legato a latere* Andrea Vaghi gave a licence allowing SS. Sebastiano e Rocco permission to build an oratory and bell-tower, to conduct religious services without licence from any other religious superior, and to hire and fire a priest at will. Five months before the Bentivoglio fled, Cardinal Legate Galeotto Frangioni made a public visit to the confraternity's altar, and soon after their flight, the confraternity received the first of a series of indulgences and spiritual benefits which were to increase its profile and link it with Roman confraternities and the Curia. We have no early matriculation list, but company records indicate that Andrea Angelelli, together with Cornellio Bargellini, was instrumental in securing construction of the oratory from 1516 to 1521, and in winning exemptions from taxes on building materials during that time. Both were of patrician families which had opposed the Bentivoglio before 1506, and been rewarded with political office afterwards.[51] The suspicion that this company represented a civic-religious challenge to the Bentivoglio is supported by the fact that it was located in the Bentivoglio's own quarter and neighborhood. Angelelli and Bargellini were not the only patrician members of SS. Sebastiano e Rocco; its wealth and standing are illustrated by the 1505 balance sheet (Table 4.3) which shows that it was able to underwrite the cost of communal worship through returns on investments only one year after its founding. Its members spent more on one of their saint's days than S. Ambrogio spent in a year; at the same time they gave less in alms to their priest. One notable feature of this account is the amount spent on

---

[50] Rents as a proportion of total income in sample years: 1539: 30 lire (76.43%); 1542: 37 lire (92.73%); 1543: 48.9 lire (81.51%); 1549: 42.5 lire (97.01%). ASB Dem, Compagnia di S. Ambrogio, busta 5/6627, cc. 2r–v, 5r, 10r, 15v.

[51] ASB Dem, Compagnia di SS. Sebastiano e Rocco, busta 1/6605, filze 11, 13, 15, 24, 34, 35, 51. On Angelelli and Bargellini: G. Guidicini, *I Riformatori dello stato di Libertà della città di Bologna dal 1394 al 1797* vol. I, (Bologna: 1876), pp. 91, 137–8.

Table 4.3. *SS. Sebastiano e Rocco income and expenses (1505)*

A. Assets and Income (in lire)

credit on mill tax*	140.00
credit on gate tax*	107.00
credit on wine tax*	51.40
loan to Sig. Ghiradelli	60.00 [loan=2000 lire]
rents	90.00
TOTAL	448.40

B. Expenses (in lire)

Feast of S. Sebastian	50.00
Feast of S. Roche	40.00
Sung mass for Ghiradelli	25.00
Sung mass for Falanino	66.00
Worship materials	120.00
Priest's alms	13.10
Notary's salary	12.00
Book-keeper's salary	10.00
Guardiano's salary	20.00
Misc. worship expenses	25.00
maintenance and repairs	50.00
TOTAL	431.10

Source: ASB Dem, Compagnia di SS. Sebastiano e Rocco, busta 1/6605, filza 9.
* these were loans to the Commune which, from the late Trecento, were financed by revenues from specific taxes. G. Orlandelli, "Note di storia economica," p. 233.

masses generally and requiem masses in particular. As will be seen below, patrician companies grew wealthy in part because of their ability to attract the legacies of testators eager to ensure eternal rest by means of temporal generosity.

All three of these companies raised and spent very different amounts in quite different ways, with S. Ambrogio more typical than the rest in the scale and diversity of its income and expenses.[52] Their common identity as lay brotherhoods gathering for community and worship unites them, but significant financial and social distinctions and the influence of political considerations underline how much brotherhood functioned within the stratified, hierarchical social order and not – as friar preachers and Stretta idealists wished – in holy defiance of it. Differences in scale reflected the different roles taken on by the confraternal community and accepted and reinforced by the civic

---

[52] The breakdown of income and expense for the largely artisanal Compagnia di S. Maria della Carità in 1583 (budget of 294 lire). Income: rents (56.6%), dues (36.7%), offering box (6.8%). Expenses: friars' alms (50.3%), worship (34.8%), charity (14.9%). Fanti, "S. Maria della Carità," pp. 52–3.

community. While some confraternities remained essentially small worship groups, those dominated by the wealthy and high-born took on greater responsibilities in the spiritual, charitable, and cultic life of Bologna. They were assisted in this by donations and legacies from outside their membership.

Donations and legacies provide a significant point of contact between the confraternal and the civic community, because in most cases they were given by non-members. This was particularly the case with confraternities serving some civic religious function. Donors across Italy singled out confraternal hostels, hospitals, and orphanages when making up wills demonstrating their charity. The issue went beyond charity to trust, in particular the trust which confraternal communities inspired. Across Quattrocento Europe, increasing numbers of testators chose lay companies over clergy and even over family when funding anniversary requiem masses and charitable acts; they had more confidence that the confraternity would uphold their wishes and honor their memory.[53] In Bologna, this testamentary generosity benefited the larger confraternities operating ospedali or public shrines. Confratelli often pledged to include their brotherhood in their wills, but few seem to have honored the promise with any generosity. A list appended by the Compagnia di S. Francesco to its 1569 Statutes notes only two members and two relatives among forty-two donors in the period 1504–1569; of eleven major donors to the Compagnia di S. Bernardino from 1489–93, only three can be positively identified in the company's matriculation lists; of thirteen small and large donors to the Compagnia del SSmo. Crocifisso del Cestello from 1518 to 1574, none appears in matriculation lists.[54] The lack of fratelli in these records could indicate that many were too poor to leave legacies, yet of these only S. Bernardino was largely artisanal; SSmo. Crocifisso was dominated by wealthy notaries and patricians, while S. Francesco was the largest Compagnia Spirituale in the city. More probably, members' charity was implicit in the dues and duties of membership, and was sufficiently acknowledged in the annual Requiem honoring deceased fratelli. Like gifts to religious orders, special bequests reflected the desire of the wealthy to enjoy in death the spiritual communion they had

---

[53] Banker, *Death in the Community*, pp. 2–12. J. Chiffoleau, *La comptabilité de l'au-delà. Les hommes, la mort e la religion dans la région d'Avignon à la fin du moyen âge (vers 1320–vers 1480)*, (Rome: 1980), pp. 206–7; 282. P. Pavan, "La confraternite del Salvatore nella società romane del Tre-Quattrocento," *RSRR*, vol. 5 (1984), pp. 87–8. Henderson, *Piety and Charity*, pp. 155–95.

[54] ASB Dem, Compagnia di S. Francesco, busta 3/6454, filza 2; ASB Dem, Compagnia di S. Bernadino, buste 1/7632, 2/7633; ASB Dem, Compagnia del Crocifisso del Cestello, busta 20/6397.

avoided in life. We will look first at the various forms in which they were given and then at the obligations attending them. Benefactors often imposed conditions that turned the gift into a burden. If most gave ultimately to the glory of God and the relief of their souls, some were not above combining this with the comfort and continued prosperity of their families.

Donors gave in various ways and under different conditions. The most frequently recorded donations were sums given for celebratory masses in life, requiem masses at death, and commemorative masses in perpetuity.[55] Donors frequently gave goods or property in place of money, or stipulated temporal limits to the legacy. A short record of bequests to the Stretta of S. Maria della Morte between 1441 and 1541 demonstrates the range of possible gifts, including an investment in the communal salt tax, the *Monte del Sale*; the sum of one and one-half lire annually for thirty years; a yearly gift of cakes made from a specified amount of flour; parcels of land, and uncomplicated gifts of wax and money. Similarly, S. Francesco received liturgical vestments (complete with the donor's coat of arms), S. Maria della Vita received cattle, and other companies received altarpieces, candelabras, altars, or crucifixes.[56]

Whether money or goods, these gifts were generally uncomplicated transfers. Not all gifts were. Donors unwilling to reduce family capital frequently committed a sum, but left it in family control, with the heirs paying interest to the confraternity at a predetermined rate.[57] Confraternal records noted defaults so that, in the words of the Compagnia di S. Francesco, "one day, God willing, the soul of him to whom payment falls may be shaken and the redemption of the debt be

---

[55] In 1539, the Compagnia di S. Rocco's priest said individual masses (at an average rate of 1s. 2d) for fifteen men and nine women celebrating the August 15 festival of the Virgin Mary; ASB Dem, Compagnia di S. Rocco, busta 5/6588 filza 1, cc. 132v–134. By the mid-sixteenth century, donors were endowing annual masses on specified days while alive and stipulating that these be "rescheduled" as anniversary requiems after their deaths. See ASB Dem, Compagnia di S. Francesco, busta 3/6454, filza 2, (3/9/1554); (5/11/1564); (11/10/1566).

[56] ASB Dem, Compagnia di S. Francesco, busta 1/6452, (3/9/1554; 8/15/1563). ASB Osp, Compagnia di S. Maria della Morte, busta 7/132, filze 1–4, 6, 8–11; busta 15/113, cc. 2v–9r. ASB Osp, Compagnia di S. Maria della Vita, busta 12/11 (6/11/1519). ASB Dem, Compagnia del SSmo. Crocifisso del Cestello, busta 20/6397.

[57] ASB Dem, Compagnia di S. Franceso, busta 3/6454, filza 7, legacies of S. Bonacordi, (11/6/1520); A. dal Pradello (6/27/1525). ASB Osp, Compagnia di S. Maria della Morte, busta 15/113 cc. 4v, 8. Similar legacies required heirs to provide annual quantities of candles or wax: ASB Dem, Compagnia di SS. Sebastiano e Rocco, busta 15/6619a, (7/8/1527). BBA Malvezzi, Cart. 198 n.5, #10 (12/4/1531), #11 (4/25/1560).

made."[58] Usufruct clauses frequently allowed donors, their widows, and even second generations life use of the property before it reverted to the company; one generous donor gave three properties to the Compagnia di S. Maria della Vita in 1540 on condition that it collect all rents owing and pass them on to him and his widow after him.[59] In some cases, particularly with large legacies, the family heirs could not bring themselves to accept the donor's will, forcing the company to resort to long lawsuits or compromise settlements in order to gain the property granted it.[60] Knowing that confraternities would go to court in pursuit of a legacy led some donors to recruit them as unpaid watchdogs of their heirs' behavior, naming companies as eventual beneficiaries in the event that the first heirs did not fulfill specified moral, financial, or procreative duties.[61] In this way SS. Crocifisso del Cestello won in 1688 a legacy first promised it 167 years before, while in 1441 S. Maria della Morte gained property and two hundred lire first inherited by a rural rector who had not performed the masses required by the testator.[62] Unlike simple transfers of money, these conditional donations consumed confraternal energies in ever-multiplying administrative duties. Conditions could become so convoluted, and confraternities so self-interestedly vigilant, that some legators seem to have mocked the practice by devising ever more exaggerated conditions. Andrea Avoglio left his property to S. Maria della Morte in

---

[58] Noted with respect to defaults by the heirs of Sisto Bonacordi, who paid the 7% owing on his 1520 gift of one hundred lire only twice. ASB Dem, Compagnia di S. Francesco, busta 3/6454, filza 2, (6/11/1520).

[59] The company agreed, but did not note how long the arrangement lasted. ASB Osp, Compagnia di S. Maria della Vita, busta 12/11, (6/22/1540); (8/6/1540).

[60] The Compagnia di S. Francesco fought almost three years and paid recalcitrant heirs 200 lire before winning in 1560 a house willed it in 1504. ASB Dem, Compagnia di S. Francesco, busta 1/6452, (7/30/1504; 11/17/1557; 12/28/1558; 5/10/1560). Reluctant but more honest heirs might also negotiate cash equivalents in lieu of transferring property, as the della Croce family did when unwilling to part with the houses and shops granted by *pater* Bartolomeo to the Companies of S. Maria del Baraccano and S. Maria della Morte: ASB Osp, Compagnia di S. Maria della Morte, busta 1/77, (5/22/1455; 2/26/1458; 3/23/1458).

[61] If the heirs of Prof. Floriano Bianchi sold any part of the estate, it would revert in equal halves to the Monte di Pietà and the Company of S. Girolamo: ASB Dem, Compagnia di SS. Girolamo ed Anna, busta 1/6716 filza 1, c.10r (2/12/1538).

[62] Lazaro Sementi named SS. Crofisso del Cestello as *erede universale* in a will of 1/31/1521: ASB Dem, Compagnia di Crocifisso del Cestello, busta 20/6397. For S. Maria della Morte: ASB Osp, Compagnia di S. Maria della Morte, ms. 1/77 (7/26/1441). In a more convoluted 1542 will, Nicolò Aggochia named S. Maria della Vita heir with two other institutions should his family's male line ever fail; although Nicolò had four sons, the ever-vigilant company brought lawsuits to gain the property in 1645 and 1685. ASB Osp, Compagnia di S. Maria della Vita, busta 12/11, (10/10/1542).

1529, but only on condition that no one remained of his male heirs, female heirs, two sons of a friend, *their* legitimate and illegitimate sons, their daughters, or the poorest of the Avoglio family; even at that, the legacy would be shared with the Monte di Pietà and the S. Petronio building fund.[63]

The most common legacies stipulated anniversary requiem masses for the giver. Companies apparently made little effort to ensure any consistent relation between gift and obligation. Donors to the Compagnia di S. Francesco between 1504 and 1592 normally gave anywhere from five to fifteen lire for annual masses in perpetuity; at the same time some gave as much as forty, seventy or one hundred lire without any more elaborate masses being specified in the *Specchio per gl'Oblighi*, the record listing how and for whom masses were said.[64] This was not an inflationary spiral, for large and small amounts were intermixed through the period. Ledgers for the conventual Franciscan friars show two early sixteenth-century donors giving sixteen lire for 1,000 requiem masses.[65] Extreme variations are not unique to the friars and confratelli of S. Francesco, appearing as well in the records of S. Bernardino, SSmo. Crocifisso del Cestello, S. Girolamo, S. Maria della Vita, and others. Some donors certainly gave larger sums for greater numbers of, or more elaborate, masses, but the majority (e.g., over half of S. Francesco's benefactors) were content to fund a single *anniversario* in whatever amount the Spirit and the pocketbook moved.[66]

As the idea of faith active in charity took hold through the sixteenth century, more donors specified charitable acts that the company was to undertake in perpetuity on their behalf. Donors were less willing to

[63] ASB Osp, Compagnia di S. Maria della Morte, ms. 4/84, c. 74r. (5/15/1529).

[64] The most extreme comparison is the single annual mass required both by Carlo Giusti, 1504 donor of a house worth 1,500 lire, and by C. Gambalunga, 1505 donor of fifteen lire. Less extreme examples are juxtaposed through the record. The *Specchio per gl'Oblighi* noted the donor, the donation, and the company's obligations, carefully distinguishing where necessary between sung and said masses, and between masses performed by the company priest, or by one or more friars. ASB Dem, Compagnia di S. Francesco, busta 3/6454, filze 2, 7; busta 1/6452.

[65] BBA ms. B492, cc. 197r (1501); 209r (1508).

[66] None of these Companies kept records as precise as those of S. Francesco's *Specchio per gl'Oblighi*, and according to the records, none save S. Maria della Vita received quite as many gifts: ASB Dem, Compagnia di S. Bernadino, busta 1/7632 and busta 2/7633; ASB Dem, Compagnia del SSmo. Crocifisso del Cestello, busta 20/6397; ASB Dem, Compagnia di SS. Girolamo ed Anna, busta 1/6716B; ASB Osp, Compagnia di S. Maria della Vita, ms. 1. Twenty-two of the forty-two S. Francesco donors between 1504 and 1569 stipulated one mass only; many others stipulated two or three.

entrust their gift to the good will and good faith of any institution. They were more sensitive to the various needs of the Christian community, and more determined to decide which of those needs their earthly goods would meet. Charity could be directed at or away from company members specifically. In leaving his house to his brothers of S. Maria della Carità in 1492, fratello Antonio Montefiorini specified that it was to be rented to the poorest member of the company. Other donors charged companies with distributing all or part of the legacy to poor company members.[67] Suspicions that companies might not use their gifts altogether wisely or honestly led other donors to the opposite pole of stipulating that legacies would be forfeit if they benefited individual confratelli.[68]

Legators favored the larger established companies such as S. Maria della Vita, S. Maria della Morte, and S. Francesco when devising benefits for the poor generally. Confraternal ospedali had traditionally performed a number of charitable functions, but the Bolognese companies sought from the mid-Quattrocento to rationalize their operations by specializing on one charitable activity. Donors were often blithely indifferent to such efficiencies.[69] In extreme cases, companies administered legacies whose returns went not to themselves, but to a variety of other religious groups, including nunneries, monasteries, and confraternities.[70] Companies could seldom escape these obligations, for testators frequently prohibited alteration on pain of losing the legacy

[67] ASB Dem, Compagnia di S. Maria della Carità, busta 5/7674, filza 6. ASB Dem, Compagnia di S. Francesco, busta 3/6454, filza 7. ASB Osp, Compagnia di S. Maria della Morte, busta 7/132, filza 6. ASB Osp, Compagnia di S. Maria della Vita, ms. 1, (1/13/1544).

[68] So Bartolomeo Giovanetti prohibited members of the Company of S. Bartolomeo di Reno from occupying the house he gave in a 1540 legacy: ASB Dem, Compagnia di S. Bartolomeo di Reno, busta 2/7651, filza 13 (8/2/1540). In its 1523 statutes, S. Maria dei Servi stipulated that no members be tenants and no tenants be members: ASB Osp, Compagnia di S. Maria dei Servi, ms. 2/307, c. 17v.

[69] S. Maria del Baraccano's function of dowering infant girls was made the work of S. Maria della Morte: ASB Osp, busta 7/132 filza 10 (1541); busta 1/77, (3/15/1441; 5/22/1455; 8/23/1458). Assisting prisoners, the specialty of S. Maria della Morte, was made the work of S. Maria della Vita: ASB Osp, ms. 1 (2/12/1527; 1551).

[70] Two legators appointed S. Maria della Vita to oversee their generosity to the Poor Clares of Corpus Domini. Cristofaro Boncompagni (700 lire in 1544) and Francesca Bianca Parati (500 lire in 1553): ASB Osp, Compagnia di S. Maria della Vita, ms. 1, (4/30/1544; 7/25/1553). Later in the century, Cavaliere Ugolino Scappi gave 2,000 lire to the Compagnia di Poveri Vergognosi and required that it be invested in the Monte di Pietà with proceeds divided every five years among a specific group of companies: ASB Dem, Compagnia di S. Francesco, busta 3/6454, filza 7, (4/23/1584).

altogether. Bartolomeo Giovanetti required a daily mass in return for a house willed to the Compagnia di S. Bartholomeo di Reno in 1540. Even if rents did not cover the costs of the masses, selling the house would break the terms of the will and the legacy would revert to the Monte di Pietà and six other heirs; renting to company members would have the same consequences. For good measure, Giovanetti gave his wife life tenancy and ordered the confraternity to pay for her funeral and burial.[71] Once again, the energy needed for administering the bequests and dispensing their returns pushed the larger companies towards greater bureaucratization. John Henderson and James Banker note that multiplying legacies in the fourteenth and fifteenth centuries turned some worshipping communities in Florence and San Sepolcro into agencies, "dominated by the fulfillment of testamentary obligations," with professional singers and musicians taking over liturgical duties and unelected sindics taking over as company administrators.[72]

Florentine and San Sepolcran flagellant companies were alive to the temptations of wealth, and some sold all bequests of property and distributed the proceeds to the poor. Their Bolognese counterparts were apparently more confident of their own strength of will, yet enough difficulties arose that two companies took temporarily to voting on whether or not to accept individual gifts and legacies.[73] The larger and patrician-dominated companies accepted bequests in part because of the growing social and financial ambitions of their members. If most companies received only modest bequests, the larger, complicated gifts could usually be made to pay sufficient returns both to the company and, indirectly, to some of its leading members as well. This in turn increased the distinctions between Bolognese confraternities, with some becoming wealthy land-owing institutions and others remaining virtually landless. In the eighteen years from 1440, the patrician Compagnia di S. Maria della Morte received nine city houses, some shops, three farms, and was named in seven other wills; in the one hundred and eighty years from 1399, the artisanal S. Maria della Carità received

---

[71] ASB Dem, Compagnia di S. Bartolomeo di Reno, busta 2/7651, filza 13 (8/2/1540). Similar conditional legacies: ASB Osp, Compagnia di S. Maria della Vita, ms. 1, (4/30/1544; 7/25/1553); ASB Dem, Compagnia di S. Francesco, busta 3/6454, filza 2, c.36r; ASB Dem, Compagnia di S. Maria degli Angeli, busta 1/7718, filza 17; ASB Osp, Compagnia di S. Maria della Morte, busta 1/77, (3/15/1441; 7/26/1441; 6/15/1454; 11/19/1456; 3/6/1458).
[72] Henderson, Piety and Charity, pp. 193–4. Banker, Death in the Community, pp. 142–4.
[73] ASB Dem, Compagnia di S. Francesco, busta 3/6454, filza 2, (4/9/1553; 3/9/1554). A S. Maria del Baraccano benefactor names alternative recipients should the confraternity refuse the legacy and its attendant duties: ASB PIE, Compagnia di S. Maria del Baraccano, ms. 563, c. 8r (6/15/1558).

two houses and a few small legacies.[74] In tracing this difference, we can look first at the capital and financial investments made by different confraternities through the period, and then focus on the financial growth of a single company to illustrate how confraternal wealth could grow and how it compared to private holdings.

The chief capital investment was the confraternity's own quarters. Some groups found this home in existing parish or monastic churches, but an independent home was as much a condition of company longevity as an independent lay administration. Unlike contemporary Florence, where four out of five confraternities met in an existing church, two-thirds or more of Bolognese confraternities from the fifteenth through the first half of the sixteenth century met in their own oratories or ospedali.[75] Companies interested in safeguarding their independence set out immediately buying, adapting, and adorning properties for their communal needs.[76] The process of construction,

[74] ASB Osp, Compagnia di S. Maria della Morte, busta 1/77 (1440–58); ASB Dem, Compagnia di S. Maria della Carità, busta 5/7674, filza 1 (7/28/1492); filza 6 (2/17/1586).

[75] A provisional estimate for Bologna, based only on those companies which can be located definitely:

	1400	1450	1500	1550
Confrat. Oratory	7 (54%)	15 (71%)	24 (68%)	41 (71%)
Mendicant/Monastic	1 (8%)	4 (19%)	8 (22%)	11 (19%)
Parish/Canonical	5 (38%)	2 (10%)	3 (10%)	5 (10%)
Total	13	21	35	57

Adapting Henderson's findings for Florence:

	1340–60	1440–60
Confrat. Oratory	8 (26%)	20 (21%)
Mendicant/Monastic	16 (51%)	58 (59%)
Parish/Canonical	7 (23%)	19 (20%)
Total	31	97

J. Henderson, "Piety and Charity in Late-Medieval Florence: Lay Religious Confraternities from the middle of the Thirteenth Century to the Late Fifteenth Century," Ph.D. thesis (University of London, 1983), p. 39, n. 4.

[76] The ambitious confratelli of S. Girolamo spent 1,300 lire from the 1430s to 1470s buying ten houses and an abandoned nunnery for their own uses: ASB Dem, Compagnia di SS. Girolamo ed Anna, busta 1/6716A, (1/15/1459; 8/28/1459); busta 1/6716B, (11/21/1436; 1/4/1438; 11/9/1439; 11/15/1443). BBA Malvezzi Cart. 198 n. 5 #7(2); BBA Gozz 404–23, p. 21. Similarly, S. Maria del Baraccano bought nine properties along via San Stefano from the 1450s through the 1490s in order to expand its pilgrims' hostel and worship quarters. ASB PIE, Compagnia di S. Maria del Baraccano, ms. 561 (11/20/1459, 10/27/1460, 2/10/1473, 1/23/1478, 1/30/1483, 7/6/1486, 8/20/1491, 12/23/1500). Other companies focusing all their early efforts on building or expanding their own quarters: S. Bernardino (1451), S. Maria della Galiera (1479), SS. Sebastiano e Rocco (1504), SSmo. Crocifisso del Cestello (1512), S. Maria Maddalena (1514).

reconstruction, and furnishing continued through the later sixteenth century as Bolognese confraternities, competing among themselves for ever more elaborate quarters, spent large sums acquiring furniture, altarpieces, organs, and bell towers.[77]

Once the confraternity had established itself and began attracting legacies, it could begin acquiring land for rental purposes. Fifteenth-century confraternities focused on urban properties near the oratory or ospedale. By the early sixteenth century most groups had shifted to buying rural land. The process is most clearly seen in the case of large ospedali companies like S. Maria della Vita considered below, but affected companies of all sizes and stations.[78] By moving into the countryside, lay confraternities were imitating Bologna's patricians; more to the point, they were becoming one of the vehicles by which those patricians could make their rural investments. By the late fifteenth century, less than 20% of the population owned most of the Bolognese contado.[79] Whether inherited or bought, confraternities commonly rented their land on a short- or long-term lease, or sold it on life tenancies. Except for ospedale companies, most of the leases were short-term renewable *afitto* contracts rather than terminal *mezzadria* share-cropping arrangements. Ospedali made more use of the mezzadria in order to ensure a food supply for the institution in the face of severe, recurring famines through the first half of the sixteenth century.[80] Life tenancies were an occasional variation from the early sixteenth century by which the purchaser sought to provide income for a widow or a priest. The arrangement gave immediate funds to the confraternity

[77] Of 1,044.10 lire received from 1504 to 1569, the Compagnia di S. Francesco invested 219.10 lire in embellishing its oratory, and 400 lire in acquiring and improving a house granted in a 1504 legacy (and held back by heirs until 1560). Of a further 700 lire received by 1592, 300 lire went into the house and 200 went to an organ for the oratory. ASB Dem, Compagnia di S. Francesco, busta 3/6454, filze 2; 7.

[78] ASB Dem, Compagnia di S. Ambrogio. busta 1/6623 (1491); ASB Dem, Compagnia di S. Bernadino, busta 1/7632 filze 21, 23. ASB Dem, Compagnia di Collegio Laicale, busta 11/6650, (8/8/1467; 11/21/1484).

[79] Of Bolognese, 63% owned no land whatsoever, 19% owned small holdings, and the remaining 18% controlled the countryside: P. Jones in *The Cambridge Economic History of Modern Europe*, vol. I, (Cambridge: 1966), p. 416. See also: Benati *et al.*, *Storia di Bologna*, pp. 241–2. B Farolfi, *Strutture agrarie e crisi cittadina nel primo Cinquecento bolognese*, (Bologna: 1977), pp. 7–8; 48–50.

[80] Severe famines hit Bologna in 1504–5; 1524; 1527; 1530; 1539; 1558; 1561; and much of the 1590s. Farolfi, *Strutture agrarie*, p. 34. From the thirteenth century mezzadria contracts tend to be full farms rather than scattered fields; Bologna had revised its statutes governing the mezzadria contracts in 1454 to secure the laborer's portion and so increase food production: A. Palmieri, "I lavoratori del contado bolognese durante le signorie," *AMPR*, Series 3, vol. 28 (1910), pp. 46–54; 57–69.

while freeing it from the trouble of collecting rent. With a fixed price over an indefinite term the life tenancy was something of a gamble, but judging by the extant contracts of S. Maria della Vita, the gamble could benefit either party.[81]

Land was also the security for the loans which comprised confraternities' chief financial investment. Loans were usually conducted as a lease-back arrangement involving property; these were essentially emphyteutic leases. Owners "sold" their land to the confraternity, gaining the right of *francazione*, or redemption, after a specified period. The land was then rented back to the seller at a fixed rate, with the price of redemption fixed at no more than the original "sale" price. Most confraternities charged rents of five to six percent, with contract length usually between three and nine years. The lease-back arrangement seemed to benefit all sides: owners received capital without forfeiting their property, while the confraternity was guaranteed cooperative "tenants" and a predictable rate of return. While properties were frequently not redeemed within the specified period, the tenancy continued unaltered. S. Maria della Vita records note twenty-seven *locazioni emfiteotiche* in place at varying times in the first half of the sixteenth century, lasting from four to eighty-eight years before redemption. Most ranged in multiples of 100 lire up to 3,200 lire.[82] From the early sixteenth century these contracts covered rural land almost exclusively. Most of the borrowers were members of the Bolognese elite, who now dominated confraternal administration and who through emphyteutic leases could use confraternal funds to finance their own rural aquisitions.

The example of S. Maria della Vita can be sketched most clearly thanks to a Memorial Book produced for the confraternity in 1516,

---

[81] Terminal dates are available for seven life tenancies sold from 1522–52. Accompanying descriptions indicate most were bought to provide income to a third party. Short terms benefitted the confraternity, long terms the tenants. Page references are to ASB Osp, Compagnia di S. Maria della Vita, busta 12/11:

   c. 6 1522–35 400 lire (7.7%) investment
   c. 9 1522–35 850 lire (7.7%) investment
   c. 14 1531–64 300 lire (3.1%) priest
   c. 21 1550–64 300 lire (7.1%) priest
   c. 26 1534–65 370 lire (3.2%) widow
   c. 26 1530–82 650 lire (1.9%) widow
   c. 31 1552–78 3600 lire (3.8%)

[82] ASB Osp, Compagnia di S. Maria della Vita, busta 12/11, cc. 10; 10v; 12; 12v; 23; 31v; 32v; 33; 33v; 34; 35; 35v; 36; 36v; 38; 39. ASB Osp ms. 1, (4/2/1516 (Marescotti); 2/24/1540 (Nicoli); 1552 (Mangi)). Other companies involved include: ASB Dem, Compagnia di S. Francesco, busta 2/6453, filza 5 (1536 (Bolognini)); and ASB Osp, Compagnia di S. Maria della Morte, busta 15/113, c.5 (9/14/1533).

and updated periodically until late in the century. It listed all the properties and investments gathered by the company since its inception as the Congregatio Devotorum in 1261; the *Liber Memoriale* paints a picture of established wealth. S. Maria della Vita had its ospedale and two churches between two streets, via Clavature and via Pescharia, which ran east from the Piazza Maggiore. Both church and ospedale were built on the material and financial foundation of thirty-eight ground-level shops returning just over 900 lire together with rents in kind ranging from fish to candles.[83] These were complemented by sixty-four rural properties, many of them full farms, totaling almost three hundred hectares.[84] This made the confraternity one of the largest landholders in Bologna, with rural holdings equal to the top two percent of patrician families.[85] Seven of the properties were let on afitto contracts returning 224 lire annually, while the remaining fifty-seven were on mezzadria. Six emphyteutic leases in the city tied up 1,978 lire of company capital for an annual return of 128.6 lire, while nine rural ones returned 255 lire. Monte credits of 129.17 lire bore varying returns. Whatever the rise and fall of receipts in the collection box, by 1516 the Massaro of S. Maria della Vita could count on collecting at least 1,510 lire annually from these capital and financial investments alone.

Much of this wealth was necessary for, and had been generated by, the needs of the ospedale. Yet revenues were sufficiently far ahead of expenses that over the next four decades, large sums went into expanding the company's urban and rural holdings, into greater Monte deposits, and into ever greater emphyteutic leases to wealthy

[83] Rents in 1516 totalled 902 lire. The majority of shops housed fish sellers, but butchers, renderers and other merchants also rented from S. Maria della Vita. Most merchants leased shops for five- or ten-year terms, with rents ranging between ten and thirty lire. ASB Osp, Compagnia di S. Maria della Morte, ms. 12/11, cc 4–9v; busta 14/435 filze 15; 16. Most ospedali supported themselves by renting out shops. S. Maria Guarini had seven stalls in 1410, raising 52 lire: Fanti, "S. Maria dei Guarini," p. 366. S. Maria della Morte built its ospedale in 1427 and added shops facing Piazza Maggiore in 1437. Bursellis, *Cronaca gestorum*, pp. 76 (40–42); 82 (36). See also ASB Osp, Compagnia di S. Maria della Morte, busta 1/77 (6/22/1441; 7/26/1442).

[84] Land was measured in *tornature* (2,080.44 m² in Bologna) and *biolche* (2,836.48 m² in Modena). In 1516, the S. Maria della Vita rural properties totalled 919.5 tornature (1,912,964.5 m² or 191.3 hectares) and 306.4 biolche (869,381.12 m² or 86.91 hectares), for a total of 278.21 hectares. For land values: A. Martini, *Manuale di Metrologia* (Torino: 1883), p. 92.

[85] The 1502 *Descriptio bonorum comitatus*, a census of rural properties owned by Bolognese citizens, notes that of 783 families listed, only 17 (2.17%) owned more than 1,500 tornature; of 1,464 individuals listed, only 10 (0.69%) owned more than 1,500 tornature. Farolfi, *Strutture agrarie*, pp. 14; 18.

Bolognese families. From 1520 to 1554, the company invested over 40,000 lire in real estate, 11,700 to purchase nine more shops and expand the oratory, and the rest to increase its rural holdings by over 150 hectares.[86] Land was bought in many of the surrounding communes, with a focused efforts on Bagnarola, S. Giovanni in Basolim, and S. Giovanni and S. Giorgio in Persiceto.[87] Monte credits rose to over 3,300 lire. The number and amount of emphyteutic leases expanded quite steadily at the same time, reaching almost 13,000 lire by mid-century.[88] Land purchases could be as beneficial to patricians as the emphyteutic leases were. In 1553 the Company bought the property of two bankrupts, Alberto Sighicelli and Niccolo Villanova, for 13,878.3.8 lire, on condition that the proceeds be used to liquidate the pair's debts to fifteen high-born creditors, including members of Sighicelli's own family. This operation stretched confraternal resources to the point that the company was led to the rare recourse of letting some of its own land out on an emphyteutic lease in order to raise the capital without alienating the property.[89] Finally, in 1542, S. Maria della Vita expanded its rural presence further by unions with two ospedali in the Communes of Medicina and S. Antonio da Sabuin, both with significant

---

[86] Of thirty-three rural properties purchased, only twenty-four note the amount spent (totalling 22,660.10s.4d), while only twenty-five list the area of land acquired (327.5 tornature (68.13 hectares) and 276.5 biolche (78.29 hectares)).

[87] Concentrations in these communes:

S. Giovanni in Basolim	1,346.8+ lire (9 properties added to 12; prices lacking in 3). ASB Osp, ms. 12/11, cc.14v–15v;
Bagnarola	1,846.2.2 lire (2 properties added to 7). Ibid., c.20v;
S. Giovanni in Persiceto	(5 properties added to 10; no prices). Ibid., cc.16–17;
S. Giorgio in Persiceto	2,444.17.11 lire (10 properties acquired). ASB Osp ms. 1, cc.80–92v.

Bolognese patricians were focusing in particular on S. Giovanni in Persiceto: E. Arioti, "Proprietà collettiva e riparto periodico dei terreni in una comunità della pianura bolognese: S. Giovanni in Persiceto (secoli XVI–XVIII)," *Quaderni storici* 81, vol. 27/3 (1992), pp. 706–17.

[88] The total capital invested in francazioni contracts varied constantly as contracts were engaged and redeemed. Lire invested at ten-year intervals as per ASB Osp, Compagnia di S. Maria della Vita, ms. 12/11, cc. 10–39: 1499 (532); 1509 (2,432); 1519 (6,432); 1529 (6,284); 1539 (4,180); 1549 (12,818). On Monte credits: ms. 12/11, cc. 24v–25r, 35r.

[89] The property was used as security for the loans, and over the next four years all the creditors (including such patrician families as the Bianchi, Cospi, dall'Armi, Marescotti, Vitali, Pasolini, Sighicelli, Leoni, Pannolini, Serpa, Solimei) released their leins on the property. ASB Osp, Compagnia di S. Maria della Morte, ms 1, cc. 89v–92v. The company's 1555 francazione was an eight-year arrangement for 1,000 lire at 7%: ASB Osp, Compagnia di S. Maria della Vita, ms. 12/11, c.23.

landholdings.[90] While this financial activity absorbed considerable capital, institutional expansion was not entirely at the expense of charitable activity. Through this same period, fratelli added three infirmaries with a total of eighty-five beds to their ospedale.[91]

S. Maria della Vita was an exceptional confraternity. It had clearly moved beyond being a means by which a community of lay brothers worshipped and exercised charity, towards being a means by which the community of patricians extended Bologna's hold over the surrounding contado. In the space of four decades it tripled its landholdings, and dramatically increased the amounts lent out to wealthy Bolognese landowners.[92] S. Maria della Vita was perhaps the most aggressively expanding confraternity, but it was not unique. Through the same period the sindics of S. Maria della Morte's Opera dei Poveri Prigionieri negotiated numerous emphyteutic leases, some of which crossed the line into self-dealing. Sindic G.B. Buttrigari's negotiation of a 5,000 lire emphyteutic lease to the family of his daughter's second husband, Virgilio Panolini, in 1558 looks suspiciously like an element in marriage negotiations. When the family proved unable to redeem the property as stipulated in 1565, Buttrigari enlisted other kin to offer guarantees allowing the Panolini to retain the property. In 1571, Sindic Cesare Bianchetti sold some of his own property to the Poveri Prigionieri for 3,000 lire, and a year later his colleague Gaspare Grassi did the same for 4,000 lire. Over the next twelve years, Bianchetti's successor Vincenzo Campeggi accumulated debts and leases with the Poveri Prigionieri to the value of over 5,000 lire. In a number of these cases, the Poveri Prigionieri subsequently had difficulty collecting the rental or interest payments from the sindics' heirs. Moreover, as sindics devoted increasing amounts to financial dealings in service of self and kin, the amount left over for charitable assistance to poor prisoners declined. All of this passed the annual audits by officials of the Compagnia di S. Maria della Morte, but the situation clearly offended enough members

[90] The union with the Ospedale of Medicina brought in two urban houses and sixteen rural properties totalling 974 tornature (202.59 hectares), and the union with the Ospedale of S. Antonio da Sabuin brought in an urban house and fifteen rural properties totalling 86 tornature (17.89 hectares): ASB Osp, Compagnia di S. Maria della Vita, ms. 12/11, cc. 37–38; 41–42.

[91] Of the three infirmaries, one of twenty-five beds was for men, a second of twenty-six beds for women, and a third of eight beds for those with serious injuries ("camerini per feriti"); twenty-six beds were added in 1569. G. Forni, "Sette secoli di storia ospedaliera in Bologna," in Sette secoli di vita ospitaliera in Bologna, (Bologna: 1960), p. 18.

[92] The recorded land base expands from 278 to 645 hectares, but the Liber Memoriale omits dimensions for almost one-third of the properties purchased from 1516 to 1556.

that when the Poveri Prigionieri statutes were revised in 1595, strict rules against self-dealing were put in place.[93]

S. Maria della Vita and S. Maria della Morte exemplified to an extreme degree the forces fueling confraternal bureaucratization. The larger and more established spiritual companies were pulled by the amounts and obligations of legacies, properties, and investments, into devising administrations whose efficiency would match the growing complexity of confraternal finance. Yet such administrations too easily became self-serving and unrepresentative. Buying and administering rural property absorbed energies and funds which might otherwise have gone into expanding the work of the ospedale. Funds collected or given for the poor were too often diverted into self-dealing or into emphyteutic leases which reduced the confraternal community to a low-cost mortage fund for the patriciate. Archepiscopal visitors commonly complained of this when reviewing the spiritual and financial health of confraternities at the end of the Cinquecento; religious brotherhoods had become corporate institutions which were poor only in spirit. This was a departure from the congregational community envisioned in Quattrocento peace-keeping procedures and administrative reforms. The strength of that community attracted the attention of outside legators, and their generosity in turn attracted the attention of Bologna's patricians. The move from being a lay congregational community to being a sindic-ruled institution was a slow process already at work in the later Bentivoglio period. With the shift from despotic to oligarchic rule in Bologna, this development spread to a wider circle of confraternities. It is time now to examine that political process in greater detail.

[93] Terpstra, "Confraternal Prison Charity and Political Consolidation," 233–5.

5

CONFRATERNAL CHARITY AND THE CIVIC CULT IN THE LATE FIFTEENTH AND EARLY SIXTEENTH CENTURIES

We have seen that the Observant devotional reforms which created smaller, more closely knit confraternities devoted to penitential flagellation were broadly popular in the fifteenth century. They led to many new groups and the reform, through Stretta sub-groups, of many older ones. Though originating among patrician groups, it was a reform which was embraced eagerly by successive generations of artisanal confratelli, helped in part by the fact that it carried with it the rhetoric of spiritual equality. In practice, as women and later artisanal men found out, the rhetoric itself recast the notion of spiritual community. More intense Observant devotion was articulated in terms of male exclusivity and obedience to spiritual and temporal authorities. As it separated the *vita activa* from the *vita contemplativa*, it drove a wedge between a confraternity's inner devotional life and community, and its public charitable activity and cultic responsibilities. Administrations were initially democratized, but under the press of increasing charitable and devotional responsibilities they became more authoritarian; while Trecento authoritarianism had been necessary to hold together a loose community of lay brothers and sisters, its Cinquecento counterpart controlled a more strictly supervised brotherhood. Multiple memberships and human weakness always moderated the dichotomy in practice, but the stage was set for a change in confraternities' social role. Once it became possible to separate the internal devotional community from its public charitable or cultic expression, those public expressions became vulnerable to more intense politicization. As the Bentivoglio fought to retain power in the declining years of their signory, and the oligarchy fought to maintain local autonomy under the early years of papal rule, this more intense politicization of confraternities was inevitable. Politicization dovetailed with the emerging Catholic Reformation emphasis on public charity which in practice was often interpreted hierarchically as a form of *noblesse oblige*. While artisans were adopting as normative the

Observant reforms pioneered by patrician confraternities of the fifteenth century, patricians were moving on to a more deliberately elitist spirituality which reintegrated the active and the contemplative life through the vehicle of costly multiple memberships that conveniently brought together political and religious necessities. We need not see this as patrician Machiavellianism conveniently dovetailing with artisanal false consciousness; the truth of the matter is that in troubled sixteenth-century Italy, biblical injunctions to obedience struck a responsive chord. Like their Protestant counterparts in northern Europe, Catholic reformers saw obedience to political authorities as a form of obedience to God. If it was the responsibility of Christian citizens to follow, it was the responsibility of patricians and priests to lead.

The charitable institutions of the Trecento and the cultic ceremonies of the Quattrocento gave Bologna's patricians the tools with which to lead. This was more necessary and more complicated given the fact that patricians held only delegated authority, and had to keep a close eye on their papal overlords even as they kept a firm hand on their Bolognese underlings. We see as a result a consolidation of patrician control over confraternal charities, and an expansion of confraternities' public cultic role; both go hand in hand with the *nobilitazione* of confraternal membership, and both allowed a broader manipulation of "obedience." Both also brought the patricians into a necessary, if testy, alliance with the papacy as both sides realized that obedience in the city depended on cooperation in the government.

This chapter will first briefly sketch political developments from the mid-fifteenth through the mid-sixteenth century. It will then consider in turn the rationalization of confraternal charitable institutions and their consolidation in patrician hands, and the further expansion of the civic cult through largely patrician confraternities. Both were part of the drive to create *Bologna Perlustrata*, a religiously purified city which would enlighten the world.[1] This drive could only succeed if the actions of individual confraternities were coordinated by civic and ecclesiastical authorities; as the latter did so, the former progressively lost their independence and artisanal character.

I. FROM SIGNORIAL TO SENATORIAL OLIGARCHY

Sante Bentivoglio came to power in 1446 strengthened by the exhaustion of Bologna's factions and the lessons of Cosimo de'Medici. His

---

[1]   Taking the term from a guidebook to religious institutions, sites, and activities published in the seventeenth century: Carlo Antonio di Paolo Masini, *Bologna Perlustrata* (Bologna: 1650).

dynastic ambitions were limited by the realization that the Bentivoglio succession would go to Giovanni, the son born to Annibale as he lay in prison in Cremona. This did not eliminate the threat of factionalism at a time when a thousand prominent families were in exile and when even members of the Bentivoglio faction, chiefly Virgilio Malvezzi and his four brothers, feared that Sante would nonetheless make moves to seize power absolutely. Cooperative Legates, peninsular alliances, and a determination to rule indirectly as Cosimo did in Florence, prevented these threats from unseating Sante and brought unusual stability to Bologna. Cardinal Bessarion, Legate from 1450 to 1455, Luis Juan Mila from 1455 to 1458, and Angelo da Capranica from 1458 to 1467 were friends of Sante and advocates of the Bentivoglio faction in its dealings with the papacy and with other powers in Italy, chiefly Milan. While Sante had been raised in Florence, his closest political alliance was with Milan, where Francesco Sforza was determined to maintain influence over the unsteady states of Romagna by protection and influence rather than by conquest. The alliance was demonstrated publicly by Milanese military protection against the threat posed in 1455 by Jacopo Piccinino, son of the condottiere Nicolò Piccinino who had imprisoned Annibale, and by Sante's marriage to Francesco Sforza's illegitimate niece Ginevra. Sante was so eager for the latter alliance that he married Ginevra by proxy when she was only 10 or 12 years old, and waited two years before bringing her to Bologna in 1454.[2]

Bologna's autonomy had long been based on the sufferance of Milan or the Papacy or both, and this pattern continued when Giovanni II Bentivoglio succeeded Sante in 1463. Francesco Sforza eased the succession and, together with Legate Capranica, convinced Paul II to moderate his desire to change the system of government set up under the 1447 Concordat of Nicholas V. That Concordat had raised the position of the Sedici Riformatori to an executive body on par with the Legate, but required that its members be periodically elected. In practice, the Sedici became a self-perpetuating body whose members served life terms. Paul II proposed that the membership be raised from sixteen to twenty, with ten serving one year and ten the next in fixed rotation. This would have ended Bentivoglio primacy and reactivated the factions. At the urging of Sforza and Capranica, Paul II revised his plan by making the rotation semi-annual rather than biennial and, more significantly, by granting a twenty-first and permanent seat to the twenty-three year old Giovanni II Bentivoglio. The changes were ratified in January 1466 and remained in force until Giovanni was forced to flee before Julius II in November 1506. The Bolognese still called this council the "Sedici" or the "Reggimento."[3]

Paul II's changes increased Giovanni II Bentivoglio's power to the point where it became untenable. The external prop provided by Milan held firm through much of the period as Giovanni married Sante's widow Ginevra and became a *condottiere* for Milan. After Papal Legate Capranica's departure in 1467, the legatine office declined in significance; Capranica's close association with the Bentivoglio had made the very office suspect, and his successors chose to send their lieutenants rather than appear as Bentivoglio lap-dogs. Singled out even more than Sante as the *primus inter pares*, Giovanni succumbed to the ambitions of his office. He gradually dropped the consultation and consensus-building that had kept the Bentivoglio faction intact, and started searching for honors and privileges from outside powers which could grant the status of nobility and the promise of permanence to the family's rule. In 1473, Sixtus IV confirmed the right of his eldest son, the four-year old Annibale, to inherit the family's permanent seat in the Sedici. From the Holy Roman Emperors Frederick III and Maximilian I he gained the right to bear the imperial eagle, to create knights and doctors, and to mint coins; from 1494 Bologna's gold, silver, and copper coins bore the image and arms of the man who was Signore in all but name. Imperial and Spanish titles and Lombard fiefs added luster, while the expropriated properties of his enemies and the proceed of taxes on all contracts and on the profits of Jewish moneylenders added wealth. The wealth was channelled into construction of one of the most lavish palaces in Italy. It was also channelled into the effort to secure more honors for the family, and in particular into the ultimately futile effort to get a red hat for the second son, Antongaleazzo.[4]

Giovanni counted as a victory every peninsular treaty he was party to and every successful thwarting of papal efforts to influence the composition of the Sedici or the appointment of officials. Yet his power

---

[3] F. De Bosdari, "I primordi della Signoria di Giovanni II Bentivoglio a Bologna (1463–1477)," *Atti e memorie della Deputazione di storia patria per le province di Romagna* n.s. vol. 3 (1951–53), pp. 181–204. Ferri and Roversi, *Storia di Bologna*, pp. 183–94.

[4] F. Bocchi, "I Bentivoglio da cittadini a Signori," *Atti e memorie della Deputazione di storia patria per le province di Romagna* n.s. vol. 22 (1971), pp. 43–64. A. De Benedictis, "Quale 'Corte' per quale 'Signoria'? A Proposito di organizzazione e immagine del potere durante la preminenza di Giovanni II Bentivoglio," B. Basile (ed.), *Bentivolorum Magnificentia: Principe e cultura a Bologna nel Rinascimento* (Roma: 1984), pp. 13–34. W.E. Wallace, "The Bentivoglio Palace: Lost and Reconstructed," *Sixteenth Century Journal* vol. 10 (1979): 97–114.

was a mirage. Based entirely on the will of others, it could not survive when their wills changed. His unwillingness to share the spoils of office and determination instead to use them in the promotion of Bentivoglio magnificence alienated former supporters like Agamenone Marescotti and convinced them to support the conspiracy led by the four Malvezzi brothers in 1488. Though narrowly averted, the conspiracy chilled the Bentivoglio and led them as it had led Lorenzo de'Medici ten years before to bloody reprisals and more authoritarian rule. Those who were caught were hung from the battlements of the Podestà's Palace; those who escaped had their property confiscated. Giovanni II was guarded by armed men day and night.

The conspiracy demonstrated Giovanni's vulnerability within the city; the events of the years that followed demonstrated his vulnerability in the reshaping of peninsular politics. Desperate to avoid committing himself in the French invasion that cut across the alliances he had made with Milan and Florence, he had the misfortune to sit astride the passes which French troops took en route to Florence and Naples. His neutrality spared Bologna from harm, but demonstrated that his attempt to be treated as the Signore of a powerful city was empty bluster.[5] In the second French invasion of 1499 he sent troops too late to protect Milan, and for his trouble had then to pay a heavy price for French protection. The protector was Cesare Borgia, whose ambitions in Romagna were made clear by the conquest of Imola and Forlì in 1499, of Rimini and Pesaro in 1500, and of Faenza in 1501. In 1502, Louis XII and Alexander VI ordered Bologna to surrender to the pope's son and while publicly mounting a strong defense, Giovanni privately entered negotiations with Borgia. Well aware of Bentivoglio's vulnerability, Borgia inexplicably failed to attack. Within a year Alexander VI was dead and Cesare Borgia's power evaporated. Giovanni II soon faced a stronger threat in Julius II's determination to secure the entire Papal State under direct papal rule. Julius too was well aware of Giovanni's vulnerability, having heard from prominent exiles like the Malvezzi, Carlo Grati, Giovanni and Bernardino Gozzadini, and the Marescotti, once Bentivoglio's firmest allies but murdered and hounded out of the city as traitors in 1501. Julius moved from Rome in August 1506, taking Perugia in September and issuing an interdict against Bologna in October. Giovanni's two options of submission to the Papacy or flight to Milan underscored the fact that almost six decades of Bentivoglio rule had done nothing to alter the funda-

5   G. Picotti, "La neutralità Bolognese nella dicesa di Carlo VIII," *Atti e memorie della Deputazione di storia patria per le province di Romagna*, Ser. 4, vol. 9 (1919), pp. 165–249.

mental reality that Bologna's fate rested in the relationship between these two powers. He fled. Julius entered the city in the company of the exiled families and began remaking the city's constitution. Annibale and Ermes Bentivoglio attempted an invasion after Julius left the city in February 1507, but they were repulsed. The troops that defeated them returned to the city and began the sack which ended with the levelling of the family's palace; the large site remained vacant for two hundred years. A year later Giovanni Bentivoglio lay dying in Milan, his hopes for the family's return to power undimmed.[6]

Over the next decade Bologna's constitution was in almost constant flux as papal rule was established by Julius II in 1506, challenged by a Bentivoglio restoration in 1511, reestablished by Julius in 1512, and altered by Leo X in 1513. Through all these changes there was a common recognition that the oligarchic ruling council had to incorporate more than just 21 families and, in the case of the papal revisions, that control could not be focused on a single family. A week after arriving in Bologna, Julius II appointed a forty-member council drawing both on members of the old Sedici and on the prominent exiles. He pointedly refused to allow it go under the old names; these were the Forty Counsellors ("*Quaranta Consiglieri*"). Their subordination was clear when the pope left the city a few weeks later and entrusted full power to the Legate. All forty counsellors immediately resigned, and a commission of Cardinals appointed to mediate the dispute subsequently recommended that the power sharing between Legate and Sedici which had marked the 1447 Concordat be applied in relations between the Legate and the Quaranta. In the case of vacancies, the Quaranta would offer nominations from which the pope would make his appointment; Counsellors would serve life terms. Concerted action had preserved a form of local autonomy, but Julius' preference for absolute power emboldened his Legates Cardinal Antonio Ferreri and Cardinal Francesco Alidosi. Ferreri's excesses troubled even Julius, who stripped him of office and had him imprisoned in 1508, but Alidosi was scarcely less ruthless. A little more than a week after arriving in Bologna he challenged the Quaranta directly by jailing three of its members on false charges of having plotted a Bentivoglio restoration. They were executed the same day without trial and their Senate seats were filled the following day without consultation. Alberto Castelli, Innocenzo Ringhiera, and Sallustio Guidotti were not the only ones to suffer for suspected treason; three other Counsellors were deposed and

[6] R. Patrizi Sacchetti, "La caduta del Bentivoglio e il ritorno di Bologna al dominio della chiesa," *Atti e memorie della Deputazione di storia patria per le province di Romagna* n.s. vol. 2 (1950–51), pp. 109–56.

one renounced his seat.[7] Plots were indeed rife, and when Annibale Bentivoglio and his brothers returned in May 1511, they received a warm welcome. Like his grandfather and namesake, Annibale worked immediately to build bridges with some of his family's main rivals, chiefly the Malvezzi, the Marescotti, and the Gozzadini. But while assuring Julius II of his and the city's continuing loyalty, Annibale II dismissed the Quaranta and reconstituted the old "Sedici" Riformatori, raising it to 31 members who served biannually and taking for himself the family's permanent seat. Some traditional enemies retained their seats, but 22 former members of the Quaranta were dismissed.[8] The Bentivoglio restoration lasted little more than a year, supported by the French and collapsing when they retreated over the Alps after the Battle of Ravenna. By this time Bologna was under interdict and ringed by Spanish troops. Annibale and his brothers accepted defeat and left peacefully as their father had little more than five years before. Aging, sick, and enraged at the aid given by some members of the Quaranta to Annibale II, Julius dispensed with both Sedici and Quaranta and installed officials who would rule Bologna as directly as any other city in the Papal State. This could have been the end of any autonomy for the city had Julius not been succeeded by Giovanni de'Medici who, as Leo X, realized that if the leading families were not brought into papal rule, they would soon begin plotting against it. Leo also favored the Bentivoglio, inviting them to Rome to the alarm of their enemies in Bologna, and planning to reintegrate them into the local oligarchy. Annibale II's attempt to build consensus across the factions clearly counted for nothing as Bolognese families and ambassadors petitioned Leo to restore the Quaranta but to keep the Bentivoglio in exile. Leo's ambiguous answer came on June 22 with the resurrection of the Quaranta, now also known as the *Senato*. Thirty-nine appointments were made, with the last reserved for the Bentivoglio at such a time as Bologna was ready to readmit them. This would not be for some time. During the 1515 Congress of Bologna with Francis I and Leo X, the Senate sought pardons for all exiles save the Bentivoglio. Annibale himself lay low, renouncing his ambitions for the city and refraining from any attempt to regain it as long as Leo was pope. Leo's passing in December 1521 came as a signal; the following April Annibale appeared with 8,000 troops at the walls of the city. No one opened the city gates, and three days of assaults could not force them. His last attempt came five years later as the Papal State was disinte-

---

[7] Alidosi arrived on June 16, 1508 and had the three Senators executed on June 27. Guidicini, *I Riformatori*, I, pp. 85–7, 95–6.

[8] Ibid., pp. 108–12.

grating during the Sack of Rome. Once again however there was little support to be had within the city and Annibale was forced to retire, this time permanently, to Ferrara.[9]

The repudiation of Annibale indicates how well the Bolognese patricians understood the realignment of peninsular politics which had taken place since the French invasion of 1494. Full autonomy was out of the question, and signorial oligarchy brought most of its benefits to the ruling family alone while bringing potential instability to the rest of the ruling group. A broad-based oligarchy functioning with constitutionally guaranteed powers under the protection of a peninsular power offered the greatest freedom and security for the greatest number of patrician families. The constitution in this case was Nicholas V's Concordat of 1447, which Leo ratified in 1513. This is not to say that Senatorial oligarchy did not bring problems of its own. Leo had dismissed twelve of Annibale II's thirty-one Riformatori when appointing his Senate. Future appointments followed the precedent established by Julius, with the pope making his choice from among four nominees presented by the Senate. If he did not like the nominees offered, he could ask the Senate to prepare another list. The Senate wished to keep seats within families, but succeeding popes found it more advantageous to move these around to more loyal families or to more loyal branches within a single family. In the course of the sixteenth century seventy-two families held senatorial seats and there was considerable movement of the privilege from one branch of a family to another. Paolo Colliva has argued that the Senatorial oligarchy operated largely unchallenged from the late Bentivoglio years through the end of the *ancien régime*, but this minimizes the degree of instability for individuals within the oligarchy in the sixteenth century. From Leo X in 1513 through the end of Clement VIII's pontificate in 1605, thirteen popes made 248 appointments to the Senate.[10] Scarcely a year went by in which at least one Senate seat was not up for renewal. In 1590 Sixtus V overcame the determined opposition of the body and increased its membership to fifty; the patricians pointedly continued referring to themselves as *Signori Quaranta* and to their Senate as *Quadraginta Reformatores status libertatis civitatis Bononiae*. The insecurity of family tenure was the chief element of instability from the Senators' viewpoint, leading them to seek ways of individually and collectively

[9] Guidicini, *I Riformatori*, pp. 120–4. S. Verardi Venturi, "L'ordinamento bolognese dei secoli XVI–XVII," *L'Archiginnasio* vol. 74 (1979), pp. 321–38.

[10] BBA Gozz ms 395, pp. 322–5. P. Colliva, "Bologna dal XIV al XVIII secolo: 'governo misto' o signoria senatoria?", A. Berselli (ed.), *Storia della Emilia-Romagna*, vol. II, (Bologna: 1977), 13–32.

expanding their authority outside of the limits set by the constitution. Their search ranged over Bologna's social life and brought the Senators to intensify their involvement in two aspects of confraternal life: institutional charity, and the civic-religious cult.

II. FROM CONFRATERNAL *OSPEDALI* TO CIVIC POOR RELIEF

Michel Mollat has described the process by which the plethora of private, clerical, and confraternal ospedali which helped the poor of Europe's large cities and small towns were consolidated into larger institutions and specialized in their functions through the fourteenth and fifteenth centuries. The process of turning small ospedali which attempted to meet the needs of whoever showed up at the door into large institutions focused on the needs of the sick, the orphaned, the shameful poor, the dying, and the dowerless answered political needs as much as naked social realities. Laymen, clerics, and city councillors wanted charity dispensed with more equality, efficiency, economy, and discretion. Beyond this, the new institutions like Milan's Ospedale Maggiore, a cruciform building designed by Filarete, and Florence's Ospedale degli Innocenti, designed by Brunelleschi, could add greatly to the honor of the city and the magnificence of its architectural fabric. Mollat argues that the process moved in cycles which mirrored Europe's larger economic and demographic cycles, and was particularly evident in the early fourteenth century and the early sixteenth century.[11] Developments in Bologna largely correspond with Mollat's European pattern. The ospedali established in the early Trecento by laudesi spiritual companies could be seen as semi-official in that their sponsoring confraternities were organized according to the city quarters and drew widely from across the social spectrum. The subsequent rationalization of these ospedali in the later fifteenth and early sixteenth centuries answered local political realities while addressing the larger European economic and demographic realities as they struck Bologna. Serious plague devastated the city in 1527–28 and famines in 1558 and 1561 killed an estimated 10,000 in the city and 30,000 in the contado. Nonetheless, the city's population rose from approximately 50,000 at the beginning of the century to 62,000 in 1570 and 72,000 in 1587. An accelerating cycle of famines in 1588–89, 1590, and 1593–94 brought the population down to 59,000 by 1595; the catastrophic plagues of 1630 brought the population to its lowest point of 46,000.

[11] M. Mollat, *The Poor in the Middle Ages* (New Haven: 1986), pp. 251–300. See also Black, *Italian Confraternities*, pp. 130–67.

The decline of the city's economy through the later sixteenth and early seventeenth centuries compounded these social problems. Fifteenth-century wealth had been based on hemp, silk, wool, and the University; by the mid-sixteenth century, all but silk production were in decline.[12]

Communal and ecclesiastical officials encouraged the rationalization of confraternal ospedali through three intertwined processes: specialization, consolidation, and bureaucratization. Specialization entailed focusing charitable activities on exclusively defined groups such as orphans, the shameful poor, or those stricken with venereal disease. This entailed internalizing the ospedale's activities, that is, reorienting it from the earlier function of serving travelling pilgrims to new functions helping the needy of the city itself. Communal and ecclesiastical officials more directly facilitated the third process of consolidation, by which the smaller ospedali of city and contado were merged into larger institutions better able to cope with rising numbers of the poor and needy. The culminating process of bureaucratization saw self-perpetuating Boards of Sindics or Governors drawn from among the ranks of the Senatorial families take control of the ospedali and operate them largely independently of the devotional brotherhood which had founded and maintained them. Through these three processes, ospedali which had traditionally opened their doors to travellers, pilgrims, and strangers, now served few beyond the poor, sick, and needy of the city itself.

In this rationalization of confraternal ospedali, spiritual purposes combine with *raison d'état*. Confraternal ospedali became less autonomous and voluntarist, and more part of an organized communal response to communal poverty – a response entailing greater politicization. Giovanni II Bentivoglio enlisted the ospedali companies in his effort to cement power after the Malvezzi conspiracy of 1488, while the oligarchs of the post-Bentivoglio period pursued the same ends with more enduring success. Spiritual companies had always claimed status as the third pillar, together with the Armed and Artisanal companies, of Bolognese popolo society. They finally achieved this status when popolo society had all but disappeared, leaving only its words and symbols to be bandied in rhetoric. By the mid-sixteenth

---

[12] A. Bellettini, *La popolazione di Bologna dal secolo XV all'unificazione italiana* (Bologna: 1961), pp. 24–7. G. Calori, *Una iniziativa sociale nella Bologna del '500* (Bologna: 1972), pp. 62–4. Ferri and Roversi, *Storia di Bologna*, pp. 229–32. L. Gheza Fabbri, *L'organizzazione del lavoro in una economia urbana; Le Società d'Arti a Bologna nei secoli XVI e XVII* (Bologna: 1988), pp. 15–17. C. Pini, "Per la storia del distretto industriale serico di Bologna (secoli XVI–XIX)," *Quaderni storici* 73, vol. 25/1 (1990), pp. 93–124.

century, confraternal ospedali had become models and agencies for the social services of the centralizing state, and bearers of a myth of popolo culture which cloaked and preserved oligarchic power.

The movement to specialize, internalize, consolidate, and institutionalize confraternal ospedali develops progressively from the mid-fifteenth through the mid-sixteenth centuries. The progression can be traced through transformations within a few ospedali and the emergence of a community relief scheme in the 1550s and 1560s. Four ospedali are particularly important: S. Maria degli Angeli, S. Giobbe, S. Maria del Baraccano, and S. Bartolomeo di Reno; the community relief scheme is the Opera dei Mendicanti. All four confraternal ospedali serve initially as hostels for pilgrims, and all develop new specialized functions. More significantly, all lose their independent status and become instead elite-dominated semi-offical agencies of social welfare similar to the great Scuole of Venice.

The Ospedale company of S. Maria degli Angeli emerged in 1450 as a union of four confraternities brought together to resuscitate a monastic ospedale which had all but collapsed. Don Luca of Padua, Abbot of the Benedictines of S. Procolo who administered the pilgrims' hostel, orchestrated the union as part of a larger plan of reform incorporating the monastery itself. The ancient monastery and its thirteenth-century ospedale had been reduced through negligence, fraudulent abbots, and indifferent monks to a scandalous state by the early fifteenth century. Pope Eugenius IV's bull of 1436 uniting it to the Congregation of S. Giustina of Padua noted that its buildings were as desolate as its religious observances.[13] The Black Benedictines of S. Giustina brought new discipline to the monastery, but initially left the ospedale in the care of a lay rector. The rector was expected to provide both a living for himself and hospitality for strangers from the ospedale's land and investments. In the event, their appointee found it a losing proposition. A year after becoming Rector in 1444, notary Bartolomeo Castagnoli reported that revenues were lagging far behind expenses.[14] Abbot Don Luca declared him a creditor of the ospedale, authorized lawsuits against defaulting tenants, and began searching for alternatives.

---

[13] Fanti, *San Procolo*, p. 112. Eugenius IV was in Bologna from April 1436 to January 1438. Patron of the S. Giustina Congregation, he forced several Benedictine monasteries to join the Observant congregation, boosting its numbers to 16 by 1439. B. Collett, *Italian Benedictine Scholars and the Reformation: The Congregation of Santa Giustina of Padua*, (Oxford: 1985), p. 4.

[14] ASB Dem, Compagnia di S. Maria degli Angeli dell'Ospedale degli Innocenti, busta 1/7718 (10/7/1444; 11/5/1445); busta 4/7721, Libro 14, #2 c.3. See also: Fanti, *San Procolo*, p. 159.

That search brought him by 1450 to the idea of entrusting the ospedale to a lay confraternity, whose charitable will and pockets would be
deeper than those of an individual citizen. Deep pockets were certainly
needed, for in sketching the situation to his fellow monks, Don Luca
noted that their pilgrims' hostel was an ospedale in name only. Beds
were broken or missing and the very building itself was little more
than a ruin. Against this he drew a picture of the fine administration
given their ospedali by such Bolognese lay confraternities as S. Maria
della Vita and S. Maria del Baraccano, and noted that even the Cathedral canons had turned to erecting a lay confraternity when their Ospedale of S. Pietro had grown too burdensome.[15] The monks needed
little convincing, and gave approval to a scheme which had already
been drawn up by Don Luca in consultation with Bartolomeo Castagnoli and the rectors of the four confraternities concerned.

The S. Maria degli Angeli scheme contained many of the changes,
obligations, and safeguards which would become standard in ospedale
secularizations of the coming decades. The monastic pilgrims' hostel
became an orphanage under the name of the *Ospedale degli Esposti*;
within the city it was also variously known as the *"Innocenti,"* the *"Bastardini,"* or *"San Procolo."* Bartolomeo Castagnoli remained rector for
life, administering the ospedale property and investments and passing
on any excess funds to feed the orphans. The fratelli of S. Maria degli
Angeli agreed to rebuild and refurnish the buildings, and to conserve
and maintain the property and investments which would fall under
their care after Castagnoli's death. They also recognized the continuing
interest of the S. Procolo monastery in the ospedale by annually ren-
dering administrative accounts and a symbolic gift. Should the confraternity ever fall to fewer than ten members and be unable over five
years to raise its numbers, the ospedale and all its goods and properties
would revert to the monastery.[16]

Most of the partners to the union were well-established confraternities
from the Porta Procola quarter of Bologna. The companies of S. Eusta-
chio, S. Sisto, and S. Maria Maddalena had gathered fratelli for generations; S. Maria degli Angeli was a much newer company, originating in
the early Quattrocento and integrated by Nicolò Albergati into the
civic-religious cult. Albergati's favor and the Angeli's custom of having
children dressed as angels join the brothers' processions likely contrib-

---

[15] ASB Dem, Compagnia di S. Maria degli Angeli dell'Ospedale degli Innocenti,
busta 1/7718, filza 3 (9/2/1450).

[16] ASB Dem, Compagnia di S. Maria degli Angeli dell'Ospedale degli Innocenti,
busta 1/7718, filza 3 (9/2/1450; 10/12–13/1450). See also G. Guidicini, *Cose
notabile*, III, p. 15.

uted to the decision to use its name for the new consolidated confraternity. Don Luca's calculations as to the wealth and generosity of the new company's members were well founded. Although the earliest matriculation list for the federated company of S. Maria degli Angeli dates from 1479, it shows an established, if not entirely patrician, membership. Most of the 302 members of that year identified themselves by family names, and of the eighty-one who named occupations, half were notaries.[17]

Improving and expanding the Foundling Ospedale degli Esposti followed soon after the union. With Ospedale property still in Bartolomeo Castagnoli's control, the fratelli financed renovations by selling a house belonging to the Company of S. Sisto.[18] Properties adjoining the orphanage were purchased over the next decades, allowing expansion of facilities at the end of the century.[19] Yet greater expansion flowed from unions with other ospedali within and outside Bologna. These actions consolidated Bolognese attempts to deal with growing numbers of orphans, but by the end of the century had brought S. Maria degli Angeli more firmly into the Bentivoglio orbit. The first two unions had distinctly uneven success. Both S. Maria della Carità, an ospedale in the Porta Stiera quarter, and S. Maria di Piumazzo in the Bolognese contado, were joined to the Ospedale degli Esposti by episcopal fiat in 1456. The former had been operated by a group of Lateran Canons eager to be rid of it, while the latter was controlled by a curate who was reluctant to let it go. In the event, S. Maria della Carità was never entirely integrated into the Ospedale degli Esposti; for reasons that are unclear, it reverted to the rectorship of a Lateran Canon by 1463.[20] Despite guarantees of a pension equal to half his ospedale's income, S. Maria di Piumazzo's rector was not pried from his position until the power of Cardinal Legate Francesco Gonzaga was applied to the case in 1473.[21] Further setbacks came in 1479 when the brothers of S. Maria degli Angeli voted to pull out of the project and reestablish themselves as a separate confraternity, and when a group of those who stayed decided to distance themselves from the day-to-day operation of the foundling home by forming a Stretta company.

These unions and disunions undermined the work of the Ospedale

---

[17] For the matriculation list: BBA Gozz 203 #5. On the early history of the union: M. Fanti, "L'Ospedale di San Procolo o dei Bastardini tra Medioevo e Rinascimento," in Autori vari, *I Bastardini: Patrimonio e memoria di un ospedale bolognese* (Bologna: 1990), pp. 7–11.

[18] Guidicini, *Cose Notabili*, III, p. 114.

[19] Ibid., III, pp. 114–15.

[20] Fanti, *S. Maria della Carità*, pp. 20; 23 n. 35.

[21] ASB Dem, Compagnia di S. Maria degli Angeli dell'Ospedale degli Innocenti, busta 4/7721, Libro 14, #2; busta 5/7722 (1/16/1473).

degli Esposti, which was further hindered by the lack of clear public policy on the matter of dealing with Bologna's orphans. This situation changed in the 1490s as the needs of the orphans coincided with those of Giovanni II Bentivoglio. In 1494 the Comune directed the Esposti to take over responsibility for all orphans in the city. Until this time it had handled only an eighth of Bologna's foundlings; while there are few accurate statistics for this period, it admitted 51 from August 1475 to December 1478. From 1494 admissions rose to over 300 annually. The Esposti was soon desperately short of milk and food, causing the mortality rate to skyrocket.[22] In consolidating foundling care at the Esposti, communal and ecclesiastical authorities also sponsored a new spate of unions aimed at strengthening its financial base. In the spring of that year both the Compagnia delle Lombardi, the last remaining Compagnia delle Armi in Bologna, and the Ospedale of S. Pietro, sponsored by the canons of the Cathedral, joined the operation, bringing it new members and new revenue. Within two years, four more ospedali from the city and contado merged into the Ospedale degli Esposti, whose enlargment and maintenance were now becoming communal policy.[23] The initial union by the Lombardi arose less out of spontaneous pious devotion or charitable will than through the work of Giovanni II Bentivoglio and his supporters. Two years before, Bentivoglio and 47 of his followers had flooded the Lombardi, overcoming stiff opposition in order to win control of the group. The Lombardi history as an armed company, its traditional Milanese links, and its privileged place in the San Stefano basilica gave it popolo associations and status useful to a signore with dynastic ambitions; absorption into the Bentivoglio orbit eliminated its potential threat as a focus for opposition to a regime which was still reacting to the Malvezzi conspiracy four years before.[24]

---

[22]   Santini, *Bologna sulla fine del Quattrocento*, p. 142. Fanti, "L'Ospedale di S. Procolo," p. 17. P. Gavitt, *Charity and Children in Renaissance Florence: The Ospedale degli Innocenti, 1410–1536* (Ann Arbor: 1990), pp. 209, 217–18.

[23]   The rural Ospedali of Mongiorgio, Savigne, and Zappolino were added in 1495, and the ospedale of S. Bovo, located next to the basilica of S. Stefano, in 1497: BBA B36 #34, c. 103. In 1516 the Communal Reggimento added what proved to be the last merger for decades when it ordered the Ospedale of S. Maria della Viola into the union: BBA B36 #34 c. 104.

[24]   Of fifty-five members voting, twenty opposed the Bentivoglio influx. Adding insult to injury, the forty-seven new entrants did not pay the normal ten lire matriculation fee. Fanti, *San Procolo*, pp. 173–75. The 1488 revised statutes listed 40 patrician members, including many of the anti-Bentivoglio faction; in a 1502 reform, seventy-eight members of what was now a Bentivoglio company tightened entrance requirements and procedures; the statutes are reprinted in A. Gaudenzi, *Statuti delle società del popolo di Bologna*, vol. I: *Societa delle Armi*, Rome: 1889, pp. 377–92.

Giovanni II Bentivoglio now seized the opportunity to demonstrate his public-spirited charity by rescuing the Esposti foundling home with Lombardi wealth and episcopal collusion. The hard-pressed brothers of S. Maria degli Angeli greeted these machinations more eagerly than their counterparts of the Lombardi. Giovanni Bentivoglio had long since enrolled a number of his legitimate and illegitimate sons as members of the confraternity, and its administration already included supporters of the Signore.[25] Like Bentivoglio, the ecclesiastical participants to the union mixed equal parts of charity and cynicism in coming to the rescue of the Esposti. The orphanage of S. Pietro had long been more trouble than it was worth to the cathedral canons, and they gladly passed their obligations over to the Ospedale degli Esposti. They were less forthcoming with the properties belonging to their former orphanage, granting title only after the cash-strapped Esposti agreed to a substantial compensation payment.[26]

Out of these two mergers came a new institution refashioned to reflect changing political realities. Lest there be any doubt as to whence its help had come, it was renamed the Ospedale degli Esposti di SS. Pietro e Procolo, and its sponsoring confraternity was similarly redesignated the Compagnia di S. Maria degli Angeli de Lombardi. More than the names had changed. Union with the Lombardi included the provision that Lombards always form a majority on the administrative councils; union with S. Pietro added a cathedral canon to these same bodies. The Bentivoglio were now firmly entrenched in the ospedale, which emerged as a civic work on the model of Florence's pioneering orphanage, the Ospedale degli Innocenti. Other ospedali in the city and contado now passed orphans on to the Ospedale degli Esposti di SS. Pietro e Procolo, which found itself taking in over 300 of both sexes annually.[27] Like Florence's Innocenti, the foundling home was soon bursting at the seams. Having claimed the role of *pater*

[25] Anton Galeazzo, Alessandro, and Ermes Bentivolgio were all members of the confraternity, as was the illegitimate Ascanio: BBA Gozz 203 #5. ASB Dem, Compagnia di S. Maria degli Angeli dell'Ospedale degli Innocenti, busta 1/7718, filza 10a.

[26] ASB Dem, Compagnia di S. Maria degli Angeli dell'Ospedale degli Innocenti, busta 1/7718, filza 10b (4/19/1494); BBA B36 #34 cc.102r–3v; Guidicini, *Cose Notabili*, I, p. 185; III, p. 115.

[27] Rural ospedali feeding orphans into the Ospedale degli Esposti included those of Scaricalasino, Loiano, Livergnano, Pianoro, Vergnana, Reccardina, Castel San Pietro, Mongiorgio, and Vodrana. Santini, *Bologna sulla fine del Quattrocento*, p. 142. In most cases, rural ospedali merging into the Bolognese institution retained their local charitable function while surrendering assets, administration, and autonomy to the new parent company. G. Gentili, "Ospedali non più esistenti in Bologna," in *Sette secoli di vita ospitaliera in Bologna*, Bologna: 1960, p. 38.

patriae, Giovanni Bentivoglio now aspired to the additional status of *il magnifico* by giving the Ospedale a new architectural prominence. But Bentivoglio's aspirations to civic magnificence could often be rendered hollow by niggardliness. Perhaps too appropriately, the man who had built one of the finest Renaissance palaces for himself gave the orphanage little more than a facade, a portico designed in the Tuscan style and left unfinished in the Bolognese manner. Even then, the signore's contribution came more from his will than from his purse. Construction of the portico began in 1500, funded out of loans mortgaged against company properties, and carried on to 1511 when it halted with the upper storey still incomplete.[28] The expensive project gave little relief to the over-strained orphanage, and within a few years other Bolognese ospedali were again sheltering orphans.

Of dubious benefit financially, Bentivoglio domination was in any event short-lived. In 1505 Anton Galeazzo headed the Ospedale as Proconsul; a year later the family was in exile and its legacy was unravelling. The old families of the Compagnia dei Lombardi soon washed their hands of the Ospedale and reestablished themselves as an independent company in San Stefano.[29] Ospedali merged into the Esposti during the Bentivoglio period similarly tried regaining independence, although with less success. In most cases the problem lay with recalcitrant rectors reluctant to give up control of properties and investments. The Ospedale degli Esposti's control of the rural Ospedale of Zepolino was confirmed by the vicar general in 1511, but the Bolognese Ospedale of S. Bovo proved more resourceful, avoiding one episcopal confirmation in 1518 before finally submitting to another in 1540.[30]

Secession of the Lombardi, the ambiguous status of the merged ospedali, and the continuing flow of orphans set the stage for an administrative restructuring of the Foundling Ospedale degli Esposti di SS Pietro e Procolo. On the surface the constitutional changes of 1519 involved little more than granting greater stability by lengthening terms of office and increasing the powers of elected administrative of-

---

[28] On construction and reconstruction: Fanti, "L'Ospedale di San Procolo," p. 31. G. Monari, "Crescita e trasformazione di uno spazio ospedaliero," Autori vari, *I Bastardini: Patrimonio e memoria di un ospedale bolognese* (Bologna: 1990), pp. 139–46. Guidicini, *Cose Notabili*, III, p. 116.

[29] The Company began its new matriculation list in 1509, registering 168 people of thirty-eight families. Of these, twenty-one families dated from before and only three from during the period after the Bentivoglio takeover. The remaining fourteen were new families. Fanti, *San Procolo*, pp. 182–3.

[30] Zepolino confirmation came on May 10, 1511; S. Bovo confirmation came on April 15, 1518 and December 22, 1540: BBA B36 #34, c. 104r; Guidicini, *Cose Notabili*, III, p. 117.

ficials. Ten men elected by the confraternal *corporale* chose an additional fourteen companions, and these twenty-four became the new *congregazione* of Governors empowered with administering the orphanage. The canons of S. Pietro retained their representation, while the Stretta were also guaranteed a seat. One member of the Bolognese Reggimento would always serve as the Proconsul. Such safeguards preserved communal, ecclesiastical, and confraternal interests in the orphanage. The new constitution provided for regular election of administrative officials from out of the Governors, but weakened this by granting supreme powers to the appointed Proconsul.[31] This was the loose thread by which patrician power over the ospedale was soon tightened.

Five years following the constitutional revisions Proconsul Alessandro Pepoli persuaded the governors to appoint twelve of their number to the task of further refining the new constitution. The Pepoli had held signorial power over Bologna in the fourteenth century, and remained rivals of the Bentivoglio through the fifteenth; Alessandro had been among the Quaranta Consiglieri appointed by Julius II. Against the backdrop of famine, to which an orphanage was particularly vulnerable, and citing the difficulty of gathering all twenty-four governors for meetings, Pepoli won approval for a stronger administration with virtually absolute power. The eight members of the new Board of Sindics would have full authority over all legal matters, without needing to consult or win approval from the Governors. They were appointed to life terms, and replacements would be chosen not by the Governors, but by the Sindics themselves. The only membership qualification stated was Bolognese citizenship; Sindics need not be, and in many cases were not, members of the Compagnia di S. Maria delle Angeli dell'Ospedale degli Esposti.[32]

Creation of the Board of Sindics effectively completed the Ospedale's transformation into a civic institution. Token representation of cathedral canons and the Stretta company in the Congregation of Governors now meant little; the final annulment of the S. Procolo Benedictines' overlordship in the next century was little more than a formality.[33] By 1524, the Ospedale's confraternal overseers had been

[31] BBA B36 #34, cc.104r–105v.

[32] ASB Dem, Compagnia di S. Maria degli Angeli dell'Ospedale degli Innocenti, busta 1/7718, filza 14 (12/18/1524). Fanti, "L'Ospedale di San Procolo," p. 33.

[33] In time the stretta's right to choose its representative to the congregation was also limited; it presented two nominees and the congregation made the final appointment. Cessation of the Benedictine claim came with payment of 160 scudi by the Ospedale governors: Fanti, *San Procolo*, pp. 184–5.

marginalized, its civic identity had been underscored, and it had been taken over by oligarchic Sindics who treated their positions as family sinecures.[34] The takeover had been elegant and efficient, and if becoming a civic institution did not solve all of the Ospedale's problems, it nonetheless won it powerful political allies.[35]

Elegance and efficiency did not in the first instance characterize a similar takeover begun a year later at the Ospedale di S. Giobbe. This was one of the oldest laudesi ospedale in Bologna, established in 1317 as a pilgrims' hostel by the Company of S. Maria delle Laudi meeting in the Augustinian church of S. Giacomo. When syphilis struck Bologna in 1495–96, the confraternity, now called S. Maria dei Guarini, decided to move away from sheltering pilgrims and begin specializing in treating sufferers of venereal disease.[36] Renaming their Ospedale to indicate their specialization on "St. Job's disease," the brothers soon had difficulty raising money for their stigmatized patients. In 1520 the Bolognese Senate granted significant tax concessions and Ettore Vernazza, founder of the Oratory of Divine Love, organized a union with the Roman Ospedale di S. Giacomo degli Incurabili to allow the latter's indulgences to aid in S. Giobbe's almsgathering.[37] Continuing difficulties convinced the confraternity that an administrative change was in order. Alessandro Pepoli's actions at the Ospedale degli Esposti afforded a convenient example to S. Giobbe's rector Gaspare Fantuzzi, member of another of the leading senatorial families. In 1525, Fantuzzi convinced the confraternity to vest ultimate administrative power in a ten-member self-perpetuating Board of Sindics whose members served life terms; three of the Sindics were also members of the Board of Sindics of the Ospedale degli Esposti, and Alessandro Pepoli himself joined

---

[34] In 1543, Nestor de Raygusia succeeded his father Camillo as a Sindic. Two other Sindics replaced at this time, Silvio Guidotti and Carlo Poeti, had also been Governors of the S. Maria del Baraccano orphanage. ASB Dem, Compagnia di S. Maria degli Angeli dell'Ospedale degli Innocenti, busta 1/17718 filza 14 (9/20/1543); G. Giovanantonij, Historia della Miracolosa Imagine di Maria Vergine detta del Baraccano ..., (Bologna: 1674), p. 103.

[35] On his first visit to Bologna in 1537, Bernardino Ochino was persuaded by influential citizens to preach a series of sermons and recommend alms for the Ospedale dei Bastardini where, he noted, 300 infants had recently died. B. Nicolini, "Sui rapporti di Bernardino Ochino con le citta di Bologna e di Lucca," Studi Cinquecenteschi II: Aspetti della vita religiosa, politica e letteraria, Bologna: 1974, p. 41.

[36] P. Viziani, Dieci Libri della Historia della Sua Patria, (Bologna: 1601), pp. 433–4.

[37] ASB Osp, Compagnia d'Ospedale di S. Maria dei Guarini, busta 6/852, filza 2 (4/13/1520). The 1520 tax exemption covered twenty wagon-loads of grain, seventy-two loads of wood, and three and a half sacks of salt: ASB Dem, Compagnia di S. Maria dei Guarini, busta 1/6472, filza 6 (11/9/1520).

the confraternity of S. Maria dei Guarini so as to be eligible for office.[38] Although initially accepting the plan, the men of the Compagnia di S. Maria dei Guarini soon complained that they were being excluded from the infirmary's board while high-born non-members were being admitted. Attempting to reverse the constitutional change, the fratelli soon experienced the intractability of a determined oligarchy. The issue was complicated by a S. Maria dei Guarini's division, since 1454, into Larga and Stretta. The Larga had been in shaky health since the division, and collapsed after the Board of Sindics relieved it of its administrative *raison d'être*. The Sindics nonetheless argued that they had been appointed by the Larga and not the Stretta, and so had no obligations to the latter. The Larga's demise gave them a free hand which they exploited fully, refusing even to follow the precedent of the Ospedale degli Esposti and designate a token seat on the board for the Stretta. Angry at the theft of a charitable institution that their ancestors had founded two hundred years earlier, the Stretta artisans tried various avenues of protest before successfully bringing a suit to the episcopal court. The patricians initially refused to acknowledge the ruling, but finally tired of the artisans' relentless pursuit of their cause. In 1602 they offered the olive branch of an *ex officio* seat on the ospedale board, thereby winning peace without sacrificing control.[39]

The cases of the Ospedale degli Esposti and the Ospedale di S. Giobbe show how rationalization could ultimately take ospedali out of confraternal hands altogther. Lay confraternities which

---

[38] Fantuzzi had been a Bentivolio follower, imprisoned in 1513 and restored to favor in 1517. P.S. Dolfi, *Cronologia delle famiglie nobili di Bologna*, (Bologna: 1670), p. 302. Constitutional changes are noted in ASB Dem, Compagnia di S. Maria dei Guarini, busta 1/6472, filza 9. At least three men, Carlo Poeti, Francesco Dolfi, and Bartolomeo Montecalvi, served as sindics and/or governors of both the Ospedale degli Esposti and S. Giobbe; Alessandro Pepoli became a member of S. Maria dei Guarini: ASB Dem, Compagnia di S. Maria degli Angeli dell'Ospedale degli Innocenti, busta 1/7718, filza 14 (12/18/1524); ASB Codici Miniati, ms. 60. Poeti was also a governor of the Ospedale of S. Maria del Baraccano.

[39] When the sindics claimed they were responsible only to the defunct larga as the legitimate successor of the original fourteenth-century ospedale company of S. Maria delle Laudi, and not to the stretta, the latter responded by redating their documents to push their origin back to 1254. The oligarchs responded through the historian Ghirardacci, whose 1596 *Historia di Bologna* obligingly pushed the hostel's origin back to 1141. In spite of the agreement in 1602, verbal and historiographical sniping continued through the following century. Fanti, "Santa Maria dei Guarini," pp. 400–4.

turned pilgrims' hostels into specialized ospedali unwittingly initiated a process which ended in patrician control. By specializing
in areas of concern to the internal life of the early modern
commune, such ospedali became indispensable agencies of social
policy as it was emerging out of late medieval voluntarism. Communal and ecclesiastical officals might well assist a confraternal ospedale's work and clarify its communal role by merging similar
smaller institutions into one growing one, but this implicitly turned
voluntary charities into civic institutions. Individuals or groups
seeking to broaden their power in the city could do so by
winning control of these institutions. As seen above, jostling for
control of Bologna occupied most patrician groups in the city from
the 1490s through the 1520s. Where the Bentivoglio ultimately
failed, the Senatorial oligarchy succeeded.

The cases of S. Maria del Baraccano and S. Bartolomeo del Reno,
dating from the later 1520s, show a different side of the rationalization
process. Their transformation from pilgrims' hostels into orphanages
for older children was a result of deliberate state policy, framed by the
necessities of famine and plague. Like S. Maria degli Angeli, the Baraccano confraternity was already largely elite; like S. Maria dei Guarini,
S. Bartolomeo was largely artisanal. The result was a reprise of some of
the disputes which had marked the earlier rationalizations.

As already seen in Chapter One, the S. Maria del Baraccano shrine
and confraternity had a close relationship with the Bentivoglio family
from the time of Giovanni I's signory in 1401–2.[40] The shrine's symbolic associations and the confraternity's elite character made it by far
the most significant of all the ospedali under discussion here. Confratelli
first opened their ospedale in 1439, lodging pilgrims passing through
the city on their way to Rome.[41] Members soon turned the Baraccano
shrine into a pilgrimage destination in its own right, and gathered papal
indulgences and fratellanze from all the major religious houses of
Bologna to increase the Baraccano's spiritual treasury.[42] Bentivoglio

[40] When the confraternity renovated the shrine in 1472, it commissioned Bentivoglio
court painter Francesco da Cossa to repaint the frescoed image of the Madonna
and Child. Cossa included Giovanni I's brother, Bente, as a kneeling supplicant to
underscore the family's civic-religious piety and its connection to the shrine. *Arte e
Pietà: I patrimoni culturali delle opere pie,* (Bologna: 1980), pp. 146–7.

[41] Fanti (ed.), *Gli archivi,* p. 68.

[42] Fratellanze were granted in rapid succession by the Augustinian Hermits (1/16/
1452); Conventual Franciscans (6/9/1454); Celestines (6/6/1455); Observant Franciscans (1455); Canons Regular of S. Augustine (4/12/1456); Black Benedictines
(5/10/1456); Lateran Canons (7/6/1456); Servites (1/5/1469); and the Dominicans
(5/7/1476): ASB PIE, Compagnia di S. Maria del Baraccano, ms. 563, pp. 1–4.

patronage in the later Quattrocento underscored both its civic status and its close relation to the ruling family.[43] Bentivoglio partisans dominated the confraternity and both Giovanni II and at least one of his sons were members.[44] As with the Ospedale degli Esposti, Giovanni Bentivoglio's favor found architectural expression, although once again this took only the modest form of a portico built from 1491 to 1500 to unify a string of houses which the confraternity had been buying for decades.[45] When Ippolita Sforza arrived in 1492 to marry Giovanni's son Alessandro, the confraternity staged elaborate *sacre rappresentazioni* along the route of the wedding procession through Bologna, depicting the Coming of the Magi, the Passion of Christ, and the Court of Heaven. Connections between the shrine and the ruling elite were so clear that when wool workers rioted in 1493 seeking payment in cash rather than kind, and demanding a guild of their own, they marched not to the central square, but the shrine of S. Maria del Baraccano.[46]

Close associations with the ruling family could prove a liability when that family fell from power. Immediately after the fall of the Bentivoglio in 1506, the Baraccano shrine and confraternity experienced a decline in visitors and members, but Julius II's political astuteness ensured that this would not be permanent. As Francesco Guicciardini recognized, the pope's initial strategy in weaning Bologna from the Bentivoglio lay in appropriating the traditional symbols with which they had asserted their right to rule.[47] Hence the pope's statue placed above the main door of the S. Petronio basilica, traditional center of popolo spirituality and counterpart to the cathedral. And hence his use of the S. Maria del Baraccano shrine, master and pro-

---

[43] Signorial favor could be channelled directly or indirectly. After Alessio Orsi, Gonfaloniere di Giustizia overstepped his power by having two friars hung as thieves, his own punishment by Pope Innocent VIII in 1486 consisted of building the chapel of Madonna della Pace at the Church of S. Maria del Baraccano: C.A. Machiavelli, "Origine e progressi della sagra Scuola della Conforteria di Bologna: Tomo Primo: 1350–1713," BAA Aula 2a-C-VI-3, vol. 8, p. 8.

[44] An undated late fifteenth-century matriculation list notes both "Iohanes Bentivolus Secundus" and "Hanibal Filius." ASB Osp, Compagnia di S. Maria del Baraccano, ms. 3.

[45] All property purchases by the confraternity were aimed at increasing its campus in the southwest quadrant of the city, between the city wall and San Stefano street. ASB PIE, Compagnia di S. Maria del Baraccano, ms. 561, (11/20/1459; 10/27/1460; 2/10/1473; 3/30/1473; 1/23/1478; 1/30/1483; 7/6/1486; 8/20/1491; 12/23/1500). On the portico: Guidicini, *Cose Notabili*, v, p. 74.

[46] Both requests were granted and the new guild appeared that same year among artisanal companies in the Corpus Domini procession: Santini, *Bologna Sulla fine del Quattrocento*, p. 53. Ady, *Bentivoglio of Bologna*, p. 172.

[47] F. Guicciardini, *La storia d'Italia*, (Firenze: 1953), vol. II, p. 118.

tector of the Bentivoglio family. Shortly after the triumphal entry
which so disgusted Erasmus and led to his satirical "Julius Exclusus,"
Pope Julius headed for the S. Maria del Baraccano shrine, there to pay
honor at the shrine and so claim its blessing over his new government.
Julius' gamble had no guarantees; Bologna returned briefly to the Bentivoglio in 1511–12, when citizens melted the S. Petronio statue into
the "la giulia" cannon, and a new pro-Bentivoglio miracle was generated at the Baraccano shrine.[48] Yet the shrine's associations were so
compelling that Leo X paid a visit when in Bologna to sign the 1515
Concordat with France's Francis I, as did Clement VII during the
lavish imperial coronation of Charles V, held in Bologna in 1530.[49]
Whatever the rulers of the moment, control of the shrine and its confraternity was a means of legitimating power by drawing in a key locus
of Bologna's civic cult.

Control shifted easily from the Bentivoglio faction to the broader
patriciate after Annibale's failed return in 1512. With its papal impri-
mateur, the shrine attracted members of the city's most powerful families. A richly decorated matriculation list begun in 1518 indicates
how rapid, thorough, and self-conscious the Baraccano shrine and
confraternity's recovery was. Lest there be any doubt as to the status of
confratelli, the list noted their civic responsibilities. Among 273 male
members, four were members of the the Sedici, the former ruling
council under the Bentivoglio, and twenty-two were Senators of its
successor, the Quaranta. Other notables included the Papal Legate's
chaplain, Altobello Averoldo, and the diocesan Vicar, Agustin de
Zanite. In a rare addition there were thirty-three female members,
almost all from patrician families. Clearly this was a very powerful confraternity. Eager to increase their influence by appropriating yet more
symbols of the civic cult, these confratelli won from the Abbot of San

---

[48]   The miracle arose as Pope Julius' Spanish troops under Pietro Navaro bombarded
the city walls in the area of the Baraccano shrine during the seige of 1512. Earliest accounts noted simply that the wall held in spite of heavy bombardment, a
feat significantly notable that thanksgiving processions wound through the city
celebrating it (Chronicle of Antonio dalle Anelle, BBA B427 II, 2/1/1512). So
simple a miracle had little to recommend it to later generations, who proceeded
to embroider it. First, the bricks were said to have sprung back into place after
each dislodging by cannonballs, then with Pietro Viziani's 1596 Dieci libri della
Historia sua Patria (Bologna: 1602) the whole wall was said to have fallen down,
immediately reconstructing itself to the amazement of troops on both sides (pp.
500–1). An unflappable guardian dove entered the picture with Giovanantonij's
1674 Historia, (pp. 77f), to the extreme frustration of Spanish artillerymen and
sharpshooters.
[49]   Giovanantonij, Historia, pp. 90; 101–2.

Stefano in 1525 the highly prized right of assisting at the church's annual festival when the sepulcher of St. Petronio was opened for public devotion.[50]

Throughout these upheavals the confraternity's pilgrims' hostel had operated with few apparent changes and with little apparent impact on the confraternity itself. Much of this changed in 1527–28, years of terrible famine and plague in Bologna as elsewhere in Italy. The devastation emptied the roads of their pilgrims and Bolognese households of their parents. Thousands died and many orphaned children wandered the streets or were sent into orphanages. The situation in the Ospedale degli Esposti was worse than that outside; in 1528 it received permission from episcopal authorities to open up its own cemetery, dedicated solely to burying dead infants.[51] With its hostel empty and its city in chaos, the S. Maria del Baraccano confraternity began taking in orphan girls. This expedient soon turned into a permanent shift in the confraternity's charitable work.

No state regulation ordered the transformation into an orphanage, but the presence of over half the ruling Senate among the membership made distinctions between state and confraternal policy artificial at best; regulations ordering a similar transformation from hostel to boys' orphanage were issued to the artisanal Company of S. Bartolomeo di Reno at roughly the same time. More significantly, the Baraccano confraternity's voluntary entry into sheltering orphans allowed it to set the terms of its new charitable activity, while its high social status enabled it to undergird the work with ecclesiastical and civic favors. Whereas the Esposti took in all foundlings indiscriminately, S. Maria del Baraccano soon allowed entry only to those meeting strict conditions. The Baraccano orphanage admitted only girls in good health between ages ten and twelve, born in Bologna to Bolognese parents, with no experience of begging and no record of domestic service.[52] The patricians aimed to gather girls from the families of small artisans, saving them from begging and prostitution, and giving them education, a trade, and a dowry.[53] Sequestered from the city and their own

---

[50] ASB Osp, Compagnia di S. Maria del Baraccano, ms. 3. Giovanantonij, *Historia*, p. 104.

[51] AAB Miscellanee vecchie, cart. 647, fasc. 71, item D (6/20/1528).

[52] L. Ciammitti, "Fanciulle, monache, madre: Povertà femminile e previdenza in Bologna nei secoli XVI–XVIII," in *Arte e Pietà*, p. 467.

[53] Cinquecento Baraccano *donzelle* received 100 lire dowries, in line with contemporary standards for illegitimate daughters; notary Eliseo Mamelini gave dowries of 100 and 120 lire to illegitimate daughters marrying in 1519 and 1522 (a legitimate

relatives, the girls remained wards of the *conservatorio* for seven years before marrying or entering a nunnery.[54] The institution lifted direct responsibility of caring for orphaned or illegitimate relatives from worthy artisanal families, while encouraging these to dower or otherwise subsidize the *donzelle*; this was a fairly common request by contemporary orphanages, with which at least some Bolognese families complied.[55]

In spite of sheltering a relatively small number of well-connected orphan girls, the Baraccano conservatorio was soon richly endowed with ecclesiastical and communal favors. Clement VII was particularly generous during his Bolognese sojourn of 1530, granting exemption from all taxes, giving authority to levy forced contributions from monasteries and other *luoghi pii*, and ordering all notaries to recommend the work to those making up wills.[56] Later in the century the Bolognese Pope Gregory XIII endowed the conservatorio and its confraternity with indulgences to spur the flow of alms.[57] Civic guilds contributed money for dowries, and at least one, the Bakers' Guild, had to donate specified quantities of food annually as a condition of its Senatorial permit to make and sell white bread in the

daughter marrying in 1524 received 700 lire). The Baraccano dowry was released only upon proof of the groom's own private means, and on condition it be used to acquire accommodation, property, or furniture. It reverted to the widow or, if she predeceased her husband, to the Baraccano *conservatorio*. Ciammitti, "Fanciulle, monarche, madre," p. 485; Montanari (ed.), "Memoriale di ser Eliseo Mamelini," pp. 40; 45; 46.

[54] The governors preferred marital over monastic vows for the donzelle, and refused dowries to girls who left the conservatorio before their seven-year term of service was over. Ciammitti, "Fanciulle, monache, madre," p. 485.

[55] In 1553, Tommaso Passarotti agreed to pay 12 lire annually for his two sisters, Teresa and Milia, as long as they lived in the conservatorio; upon marriage, each would receive a 400 lire dowry left by their father Silvestro in his testament. In 1562, Matteo Mainardi left a 400 lire dowry to niece Lucia: ASB PIE, Compagnia di S. Maria del Baraccano, busta 561, p. 110 (9/24/1553); 563, p. 9 (7/28/1562).

[56] ASB PIE, Compagnia di S. Maria del Baraccano, ms. 563, p. 5 (4/16/1528); p. 6 (12/28/1529; 8/26/1530). BAA "Ricuperi beneficiari," fasc. 579. On his visit of January 28, 1530, Clement VII granted numerous indulgences, honors, and privileges, and created Baraccano Prior Conte Ottavio Rossi de Medici a "Cavaliero di Croce Rossa": Giovanantonij, *Historia*, pp. 101–3. In spite of Clement's order to the notaries, dowry bequests in Bolognese wills were neither numerous nor particularly generous: ASB PIE ms. 561, p. 71 (1/21/1535); p. 81 (6/9/1540); p. 103 (8/20/1551); p. 110 (9/24/1553); pp. 118–22 (3/7/1556); ASB PIE ms. 563, p. 9 (7/28/1562; 6/11/1565; 10/5/1565); p. 10 (8/19/1569); p. 12 (10/30/1576); p. 13 (4/26/1578).

[57] ASB PIE, Compagnia di S. Maria del Baraccano, ms. 563, p. 10 (3/22/1575); p. 12 (10/18/1576; 3/5/1577); p. 13 (8/24/1580).

city.[58] Due to its socially exclusive nature, mergers were less prominent in the conservatorio's early history than with the Ospedale degli Esposti; only one other girls' orphanage, that of S. Gregorio outside the city, joined with it in 1553.[59]

Administering the conservatorio required far greater attention than the former pilgrims' hostel had. The Larga company within the confraternity of S. Maria del Baraccano decided soon, and without objection from the Stretta, to turn administration over to a Board of Governors bearing powers similar to those of the sindics recently installed at the Esposti and S. Giobbe. The twelve Governors began their work in 1530, and included in their number Alessandro Pepoli of the Ospedale degli Esposti, and Carlo Poeti and Silvio Guidotti, both of Senatorial families and both sindics with the Esposti and S. Giobbe.[60] Such a concentration of offices by members of the urban elite underlined how seriously the new government took the civic role of the Bolognese ospedali. Given the social composition and status of S. Maria del Baraccano, confraternal membership by sindics could be taken as a given.[61] The only significant departure from what was emerging as a consistent model of Bolognese confraternal ospedale administration came in 1548 when the Governors appointed Governesses to supervise more directly the entry and deportment of the young girls. The three governesses were drawn monthly from the body of Baraccano sisters as enforcers of tightened regulations adopted to sift through the ever-increasing numbers of applicants. Each girl was now put to a secret vote of the

[58] This was a fine levied after the Bakers' Guild reneged on a 1536 agreement to supply the conservatorio with flour on a monthly basis. Their generosity on that occasion had won a Senate license to make and sell white bread, while their subsequent defaulting won a sentence to supply 20 *corbe* (15.72 hectolitres) of flour monthly to the Baraccano *putte* and 10 (7.86 hectolitres) to the orphan boys of S. Bartolomeo di Reno. The sentence was renewed in 1662 and 1665. ASB PIE, Compagnia di S. Maria del Baraccano, ms. 561, pp. 83–5 (3/5/1543); Giovanantonij, *Historia*, p. 111. In 1535, a number of guilds joined in giving 150 lire as dowry subsidies to three Bolognese orphanages, including S. Maria del Baraccano. ASB PIE, Compagnia di S. Maria del Baraccano, ms. 563, p. 6 (4/4/1535).

[59] The S. Maria del Baraccano conservatorio took over S. Gregorio in 1547, but did not formally unite with it until six years later. About one quarter of the fratelli opposed the merger with the less-prestigious S. Gregorio (36 pro/13 con). BBA Gozz 209 #1, c.39; Giovanantonij, *Historia*, p. 101.

[60] Giovanantonij, *Historia*, p. 103. L. Ciammitti, "Quanto costa essere normali. La dote nel conservatorio femminile di Santa Maria del Baraccano (1630–1680)," *Quaderni Storici* vol. 53 (1983), pp. 469–97.

[61] Of the twelve Governors and six *sopranumerarij* given in a 1553 notice, sixteen are listed in the 1518 matriculation list; nine of these remained members until death. ASB PIE, Compagnia di S. Maria del Baraccano, ms. 1 (Statutes); ms. 3 (Matriculation List).

governors before granted admission. By 1554 the conservatorio sheltered seventy-five girls.[62]

The Conservatorio of S. Maria del Baraccano was clearly a special case, distinct from the Esposti in both its social and sexual exclusivity. Not surprisingly, a complementary institution for young male orphans arose out of the same crises of 1527–28. Yet while the Orfanotrofio di S. Bartolomeo di Reno served a similar function, it was the work of a far less patrician confraternity. This social distinction introduced subtle differences into what otherwise became a traditionally paired relationship.

The S. Bartolomeo hostel was by far the smallest of all those under study here; a late sixteenth-century company historian claimed that before its metamorphosis into an orphanage, it had housed only four beds.[63] Located on the bank of the Reno canal, close to the late twelfth-century city walls, it first opened in the fourteenth century, and served clerical rather than lay pilgrims. While its early connection with the confraternity is vague, the lay company of S. Bartolomeo di Reno supervised it by the early fifteenth century.[64] A Guardiano and his wife lived in and supervised day-to-day operations of the hostel. Like S. Maria del Baraccano, the site had associations with a miracle-working image of the Virgin Mary, but the image had little of the significance or revenues of the Baraccano shrine.[65] The confraternity sub-

---

[62] The first *governatrici* were Francesca da Lignano, Giustina Gambarini, and Appolonia Sorani: ASB PIE, Compagnia di S. Maria del Baraccano, ms. 561, p. 93 (11/8/1548). They were "assisted" by three men, Andrea Bentivoglio, Giacomo Fava, and Francesco Maria Cospi, and were granted permission by the episcopal Vicar to elect their their own chaplain: Ibid., ms. 563, p. 7 (11/8/1548). Declining income and the opening of parallel conservatories over the following centuries led to a decline in the number of girls to 55 in 1674 and 40 in 1739. A. Giacomelli, "Conservazione e innovazione nell'assistenza bolognese del Settecento," in Autori Vari, *Forme e soggetti dell'intervento assistenziale in una città di antico regime* (Bologna: 1986), p. 208.

[63] A. Stiatici, *Narratione overo chronica del principio et fundatione et successo dell'Hospitale di Santo Bartolomeo*, Bologna: 1590, p. 8. ASB PIE, Compagnia di S. Bartolomeo di Reno, ms. 279 c.2r. (7/8/1407); c.3r. (3/20/1447; 8/9/1449); ASB Dem Compagnia di S. Bartolomeo di Reno, busta 2/7651, filza 4 (4/7/1449). Stiatici may have based his claim on the 1471 statutes, an illuminated manuscript with title page showing four beds in a room. ASB PIE Compagnia di S. Bartolomeo di Reno, ms. 1.

[64] The earliest definite reference to a "company of the ospedale" is in a 1403 instrument. ASB PIE, Compagnia di S. Bartolomeo di Reno, ms. 279 c.2r (6/20/1403).

[65] The earliest reliable documents regarding the confraternity's connection with the Madonna di Reno date from the early fifteenth century. In 1410 the company purchased the house which now contained the image, and in 1412 it won a license from Pope John XXIII to sponsor preaching in the new shrine. ASB PIE, Compagnia di S. Bartolomeo di Reno, busta 279 c.2v (8/14/1410); ASB Dem, Compagnia di S. Bartolomeo di Reno, busta 2/7651, filza 2 (4/7/1412).

sidized its charitable and devotional activities less through alms collection, which it farmed out to friars, than through rents on properties in the neighborhood acquired through the course of the fifteenth century. As late as 1471 the confraternity operated as a single body incorporating both men and women. Revised statutes and a matriculation list begun that year listed 393 male and 26 female members; the modest devotional exercises were typical of those of a larga or ospedale company. Reformers established a stretta company around 1502.[66] Complaints about poor attendance had already led members to reduce the quorums for company meetings in 1480; by the second decade of the sixteenth century the larga company was apparently extinct and women were no longer involved in the operation of the hostel.[67]

The confraternity's life was largely self-contained and devotionally focused when recurring plagues and famines hit Bologna in the 1520s and 1530s. Writing at the end of the century, company historian Alessandro Stiatici recalled how orphans were left to their own devices, half-naked, sleeping under porticos, reduced to skeletons by hunger, and crying for relief.[68] Whereas S. Maria del Baraccano had moved quickly of its own accord in offering shelter to some female orphans, help for males waited a few years until Filippo Guastavillani, Bologna's Gonfaloniere of Justice, ordered all male orphans gathered up and brought to the Ospedale di S. Bartolomeo di Reno. There they would be sheltered and fed through subsidies from the Communal Camera. Guastavillani also ordered all remaining female orphans brought to the Ospedale of S. Francesco, there to be cared for under similar arrangements.[69]

Guastavillani's orders were apparently issued without consulting the confraternity of S. Bartolomeo di Reno, for the group was soon in an uproar. The aged ospedale Guardiano quit as a deluge of orphan boys

---

[66] Women could not join in the monthly services, but recited their prayers at home. They were also responsible for making sheets, shirts, and capes for the ospedale. The folio containing the 1471 matriculation list includes an untitled list of 85 male members recruited from 1502 to 1515; this is likely the Stretta matriculation. ASB PIE, Compagnia di S. Bartolomeo di Reno, ms. 1, cap. 8; Postscript.

[67] Quorum reduction appears in an October 6, 1480 revision of the 1471 statutes. ASB PIE, Compagnia di S. Bartolomeo di Reno, ms. 1. The Larga fell away with hardly a trace, leading some modern authors, following sixteenth-century chronicler Stiatici, to assume that a Larga company didn't exist until administrative reforms of the 1540s. Fanti (ed.), Gli archivi, p. 64.

[68] Stiatici, Narratione, pp. 12–13.

[69] This short-lived provision showed the effects of restricted entry into the S. Maria del Baraccano and S. Gregorio conservatories. A complicating factor was the transformation in 1526 of the Conservatorio of S. Marta (established in 1505) into a convent. Fanti (ed.), Gli archivi, p. 62.

took the place of the normal handful of pilgrims and priests. Confraternal officials were suddenly forced to comb the city for alms when civic subsidies proved too meager to feed the orphans. The most pressing problem was space; with orphans arriving daily, the small hostel was soon overcrowded, forcing the company to turn its oratory into a makeshift dormitory, and forcing the fratelli to conduct their devotions as best they could in the public shrine. When younger members proposed building a dormitory and refectory, the older brothers revolted. Like most Stretta groups, they had established their devotional cell to avoid the administrative distractions of running a large charitable institution. Moreover, new construction would be an enormously expensive undertaking for their small and far from wealthy company. Yet younger members were in the majority, and launched into the work with energy and some patrician assistance. They tore down some of the confraternity's homes to make space, and sold other properties to raise funds for the expanded facilities. One property was sold to Cavaliere Ludovico Felicini, a member of the Quaranta, who paid half the 800 lire price in cash, and half in stone and other building supplies. This kept construction going until 1546, when the Quaranta itself gave a special subsidy to help finish the work. By this time Pope Paul III had also come to the aid of the new orphanage, granting it in 1543 the same exemption from all taxes and duties which had been won by S. Maria del Baraccano in 1530.[70]

The Pope's generosity was allied with, and likely stimulated by, a social change within the company of S. Bartolomeo di Reno. Patricians invited by company members to support the work by joining the confraternity were reluctant to commit themselves to its strict devotional exercises and artisanal membership. Seeking to accommodate them and so win the benefits of their patronage, the confraternity moved in the early 1540s to reestablish a Larga company, successfully attracting the socially superior members it knew were necessary for its financial survival.[71] Paul III's brief granting tax exemptions, indulgences, and other benefits was a formal recognition of the Larga company and its work.

[70] The Quaranta subsidy of 150 lire was a diversion of tax funds owed the Camera by the Ghisilieri family. ASB PIE, Compagnia di S. Bartolomeo di Reno, ms. 279, c. 19v (7/6/1543), c.21r (10/20/1546). Stiatici notes the particular assistance granted the ospedale by two members of the Quaranta with special responsibilities for civic financial matters, Cav. Marcantonio Marsilij and Conte Nicolò Ludovici. Stiatici, *Narratione*, pp. 16–17, 20–1.

[71] Because of heavy financial demands, the ospedale was sending its orphans out as alms collectors through the diocese of Bologna and further into Romagna. ASB PIE, Compagnia di S. Bartolomeo di Reno, ms. 279 c.23 (1/13/1550); Stiatici, *Narratione*, pp. 20–2.

From this point the status of the S. Bartolomeo orphanage steadily rose until it came to be considered the male companion institution to S. Maria del Baraccano. Even its image of the Madonna was promoted, gaining a new miracle, a new name, and new religious processions marking its civic importance. But from this point, too, it became a candidate for the administrative restructuring which patricians had adopted in or imposed on all the other Bolognese ospedali. A twelve-member Congregatione of Governors was soon installed as the ultimate authority over the ospedale, displacing the Stretta who were already experiencing the mixed blessings of patrician control. In their early enthusiasm for the project, the Stretta had allowed their rental properties to be incorporated into the expanded orphanage; hence they lost their major source of income and eventually went bankrupt. The patricians of the Larga gave little pity and no subsidy to the Stretta, who were saved only when a contested legacy was settled in their favor.[72]

Patrician sponsorship allowed further expansion of S. Bartolomeo's facilities. The orphanage gained an infirmary, an expanded dormitory, offices for its chaplain and administrators, and a school for its children. It gained the material goods of a rural ospedale through a 1552 merger, and the spiritual goods of a Roman *archiospedale* through a 1554 union.[73] The new Governors did not immediately restrict access to their orphanage as tightly as S. Maria del Baraccano. The term "orphan" could be used loosely, and often included children who had lost only their fathers; in Bologna as elsewhere in early modern Europe, a widow unable to care for all her children might try enrolling them in the local orfanotrofio.[74] The S. Bartolomeo governors only revised their open-door policy after plague swept the hospital twice in 1589, bringing to the point of death numerous orphans, officials, and a newly appointed Governor; when this man's wife and son passed away, the blame was fixed on the orphans, even though none had died of the plague. Using the pastoral imagery so common in confraternal texts, Stiatici compared an infected orphan "to a contagious sheep who infects the whole sheep-pen."[75] The Governors now drew on S. Maria

---

[72] ASB Dem, Compagnia di S. Bartolomeo di Reno, busta 2/7651, filze 13 (8/2/1540), 14 (3/8/1549). Stiatici, *Narratione*, pp. 21–5.

[73] ASB Dem, Compagnia di S. Bartolomeo di Reno, busta 2/7651, filza 15 (2/23/1554). Stiatici, *Narratione*, p. 26.

[74] Faustina Mangini, widow of Bartolomeo dalle Torre and mother of four, petitioned S. Bartolomeo to shelter "una delle mie Creatture di otto annj in circa per name Ercollo." The written request of October 5, 1569 was accepted. ASB PIE, Compagnia di S. Bartolomeo di Reno, busta 79, filza 16.

[75] Stiatici, *Narratione*, p. 27.

del Baraccano's example and restricted access to "worthy" boys between ages seven and twelve, born in Bologna of legitimately married Bolognese parents, with no record of domestic service or begging, and being of good health and morals.[76]

Through individual paths each of the four ospedali discussed above reached a similar position by the 1540s. Each was voluntarily or involuntarily rationalized, its charitable activities specialized to a single focus, its work internalized on the citizens of Bologna, its size increased by consolidation with other ospedali, and its administration taken over by a self-perpetuating patrician Board of Sindics or Governors. In short, each moved from being the voluntary charitable activity of a religious confraternity towards being an elite-dominated, semi-official institution of public social welfare, similar to the great Venetian Scuole. The process was pushed forward by the social distress and the political struggles of the 1490s through the 1520s, and by the new oligarchy's determination to extend its influence. Power rested in part on public displays of charity and magnificence, on providing for both the poor and the rich, on ensuring that poverty could be either solved or hidden away. Properly organized and properly controlled, the Bolognese ospedali could perform these functions.

Local politics were one force pushing ospedale rationalization. Yet beyond concerns of power lay shifting ideas as to the nature of charity itself, initiated by humanist movements and spurred by the cycles of famine and plague which wracked the sixteenth century. Specialization and internalization were early confraternal responses, but in Bologna as elsewhere, poverty soon grew beyond the resources of voluntary confraternities. In 1526 the Spanish humanist Jean Luis Vives published *De subventione pauperum*, proposing that civil governments move into the growing gap between social poverty and individual charity. Vives called for censuses to determine the extent of poverty; central lay-administered funds to feed the poor; civic-sponsored education and employment of all children to strike at the roots of poverty; hostels to house indigents; and prohibitions on begging to eliminate the image of poverty. *De subventione pauperum* was soon translated into many vernacular languages, and from 1527 civil governments across Europe were putting Vives'

---

[76] Full name and address were required, together with certificates of baptism for the father and son, a certificate of marriage, and a certificate proving that the father had died. These were presented to the *visitatore* when he came to the house to evaluate the petition. Only one child from the family would be taken in. ASB PIE, Compagnia di S. Bartolomeo di Reno, busta 79, filza 7.

ideas into action.[77] Each introduced variations and most made their provisions available for comparative scrutiny by publishing editions of local statutes regarding poor relief. Giovanni Domenico Tarsia prepared an Italian translation, *Il modo del sovvenire a poveri*, published in Venice in 1545, but by that time Vives' ideas would have been freely circulating among the Latin-educated elite.[78]

Vives expressed ideas which had already been taking practical shape in many Italian cities. Florence's Ospedale degli Innocenti, Milan's Scuole delle Quattro Marie, and Venice's great Scuole were all blurring the boundaries of private charity and state welfare in the Quattrocento, a process some historians see as the transvaluing of *caritas* into philanthropy.[79] The new approach

> implied a feeling for active but abstract benevolence or *humanitas* as a duty of the citizen, a civilized disgust for beggars, a hostility to many of the relationships which had hitherto been supposed especially to entail mutual charity, and a particular contempt for friars.[80]

Where the poor had once represented Christ, they now represented a problem and a threat. The rationalization of Bolognese confraternal ospedali from the mid-fifteenth century and their transformation into civic institutions in the early sixteenth developed into attempts to bring greater order, uniformity, and efficiency to the problem of poor relief by bringing it under closer supervision by the governing elite. The early growth of Stretta groups in the 1430s and 1440s had prepared the way for this development by separating religious devotion from ospedale administration. By 1450, Bologna's confraternal ospedali were turning from undifferentiated charitable works to servicing particular social and charitable needs. Specialization initially followed the traditional seven works of corporal charity, allowing the city to exercise charity more completely. Looking at the results on a civic scale, as contemporaries like the notary Eliseo Mamelini certainly did, Bolognese could count themselves among the charitable sheep rather than the selfish goats. The ospedali for foundlings, older male and female

[77] Following the first edition, presses in Paris (1530, 1532), Lyon (1532), Strasbourg (1533 – German), and Venice (1545 – Italian) published *De subventione pauperum*. C.G. Noreña, *Jean Luis Vives* (The Hague: 1970), pp. 96, 220–2, 302. For an English translation: A. Tobriner, *A Sixteenth Century Urban Report*, University of Chicago Social Services Monographs, Series 2, Number 6 (Chicago: 1971).

[78] Tarsia's translation was the earliest and only extant Italian translation of Vives' work before 1550: A.J. Schutte, *Printed Italian Vernacular Religious Books, 1465–1550: A Finding List* (Geneva: 1983), p. 376.

[79] Becker, "Aspects of Lay Piety," pp. 185–6.

[80] Bossy, *Christianity in the West*, p. 145. See also Black, *Italian Confraternities*, pp. 130–67.

orphans, and sufferers of venereal disease have been dealt with above. In addition there were S. Maria della Vita and S. Maria delle Morte for the poor infirm; S. Francesco and S. Biagio for pilgrims; the Monte della Pietà for poor artisans, the Opera dei Poveri Vergognosi for the respectable poor, and the Opera dei Poveri Prigionieri and Scuola dei Confortatori for prisoners and those condemned to death.[81] Other confraternities annually distributed alms to the needy of their immediate neighborhood.

In the early Cinquecento, practical and political necessities overwhelmed spiritual concerns. Only voluntary charity bore spiritual fruit, but even with specialization, voluntary confraternal ospedali could not address the growing social crisis of poverty. Proposals like those of Vives promised to solve both practical and political necessities in a single stroke, and working through existing ospedali would be an intermediate step towards the comprehensive system envisioned by the Spanish humanist. Hence by the 1520s, almost all of Bologna's confraternal ospedali owed their administration to the new oligarchy, with a number of examples of plural membership and overlapping officials indicating the importance of communication between the different institutions. Through progressive rationalization of these confraternal ospedali, the Bolognese elite provided the essentials of social welfare, devising an administrative model by which each ospedale functioned efficiently and all ospedali functioned in concert. While continuing confraternal involvement preserved the identification of charity with religious worship and alms-giving, communal subsidies underlined the fact that this was very much a civic work.[82]

---

[81] In the later sixteenth century the Vita and Morte ospedali had about 200 beds combined; the Esposti and S. Giobbe each had approximately 150; the pilgrims' hostels of S. Francesco, S. Giacomo, and S. Biagio approximately 50 each, and the five orphanages of S. Bartolomeo, S. Maria del Baraccano, S. Maria Maddalena, S. Marta, and S. Croce about 300 combined. Calori, *Opera Mendicanti*, p. 26. For the Conforteria: Terpstra, "Piety and Punishment," pp. 679–94. For the Poveri Prigionieri: Terpstra, "Confraternal Prison Charity and Political Consolidation," pp. 217–48.

[82] Subsidies could be either direct payments of alms, or exemptions from city taxes. They are noted in a series of manuscripts in the BBA containing extracts of decisions made by the ruling Reggimento; all references below are from this series. The Reggimento exempted the Ospedale of S. Maria della Morte from portions of the mill and gate taxes for ten-year renewable terms, transforming this into a perpetual exemption in 1496: B524 c.161 (10/3/1465); B525 c.150 (6/3/1475); B526 c.140 (11/21/1487); B527 c.37 (12/23/1496). The Ospedale of S. Maria della Vita received a similar perpetual exemption in 1507: B527 c.215 (11/5/1507). Christmas and Lenten alms were less predictable. The Ospedale degli Esposti received subsidies of 40 lire in 1483 (B526 c.50); 30 lire in 1486 (B526 c.112); 60 lire in 1492 (B526 c.224); 100 lire in 1498 (B527 c.50).

In the mid-sixteenth century, the Bolognese elite moved from working through and with confraternal ospedali to an approach more consistent with that proposed by Vives. This next step in the progressive rationalization of social assistance came with the *Opera dei Mendicanti*, a centralized and disciplined communal response to poverty. In plan it resembled Vives' model, while in execution it took on features which the patricians had developed in the course of their work with the confraternal ospedali.

The first plan, endorsed by the Papal Legate and Bolognese Senate, was published in 1548.[83] Working on the basis of the city's quarters, it envisioned "visitors" who went door to door establishing needs and alloting relief tickets, sending "foreigners" packing, soliciting alms for the relief program, and annually preparing a census of the poor. The relief tickets allowed the poor weekly rations of food, distributed by the mendicant church of their quarter. In time, a single great hostel would shelter those poor with no home of their own, and begging would be absolutely forbidden.[84] From 1550, the Communal government implemented its ambitious plan with revisions, additions, and improvisations which underlined contemporary efforts at separating the "legitimate" from the "illegitimate" poor.[85] Severe famines from 1558 through 1561 added sufficient urgency to the situation that by 1563 the full plan came into effect.[86] On April 18, 800 of Bologna's beggars – two-thirds of them women – marched in procession from the Cathedral courtyard to the monastery of S. Gregorio outside the S. Vitale gate, provided by the

---

[83] *Provisione elemosinaria per li poveri di qualunque sorte della città di Bologna*, (Bologna: 1548).

[84] G. Calori, *Una initiative sociale nella Bologna del '500: L'opera Mendicanti*, (Bologna: 1972), pp. 33–4. N. Terpstra, "Apprenticeship in Social Welfare: From Confraternal Charity to Municipal Poor Relief in early Modern Italy," *Sixteenth Century Journal* vol. 25 (1994), pp. 101–20.

[85] Within two years, the Legate and Senate published a revised plan, *Modo et ordine per li poveri mendicanti fatto nuovamente nella citta di Bologna* (Bologna: 1550). All poor were now required, but only the "illegitimate" were forced, to wear an identifying symbol representing charity. The time period defining foreigners – who were considered illegitimate – was expanded from one to three years, later rising to ten years during crises like the famine of 1591. Calori, *Opera Mendicanti*, pp. 36–8.

[86] Contemporary chronicler Pietro Viziani estimated that 10,000 Bolognese died; in spite of this possibly exaggerated number, the Bolognese population rose from approximately 55,000 in the mid-sixteenth century to 72,000 by the late 1580s. F. Giusberti, "Dalla pietà alla paura: note sulla povertà a Bologna nei secoli XVI–XVIII," in *Arte e pietà*, pp. 440–5.

Senate as the long-awaited beggars' hostel.[87] At this point, too, the Compagnia dei Poveri Mendicanti, first envisioned in the 1550 revised plan, came into operation; it gathered all the major donors to the work and, from 1574, gave them an expanded role in its administration. It was clearly modelled on a confraternity, complete with indulgences granted by Pope Paul IV. Statutes governing the Opera Mendicanti had initially called for a large council with representatives drawn from various sectors of society and serving for short terms, but with 1574 statute revisions, the new confraternal model prevailed and power was concentrated in a smaller inner council; significantly the Compagnia dei Poveri Mendicanti provided the avenue for this shift.[88]

The Opera Mendicanti was a culmination of the process that had transformed Bologna's confraternal ospedali since the mid-fifteenth century. It brought together not only all the elements of rationalization in a consolidated civic institution, but also the intertwined motives of local politics and humanist efficient charity. While not conceived of as a confraternity, it relied heavily on the practical and symbolic elements of the lay religious brotherhoods. For centuries artisanal confratelli had provided the funds and manpower fueling organized charity in Bologna; from the early Cinquecento, their ospedali gave patricians a training in useful and well-tested methods of administering social aid. This experience and the confraternal model emerged clearly in the shape eventually given to the Opera Mendicanti, lending it familiarity and legitimacy; Paul IV's brief authorizing erection of the Opera dei Mendicanti made the connection explicit by specifically ordering that the choice and election of officials be modelled on the example of the Ospedale degli Esposti, S. Maria del Baraccano, S. Giobbe, S. Bartolomeo di Reno, and the Opera dei Poveri Vergognosi. The confraternal model of overlapping board memberships and officials drawn from the senatorial elite was also followed. The Opera dei Mendicanti's chief financial officer was not an individual, but the Monte di Pietà, and a number of officials held or had held positions with other Bolognese confraternal charities. Ultimate authority, together with the

---

[87] A second hostel, allowing segregation of the sexes, did not come into operation until 1567. Figures for those assisted in the hostels: 1570 (1,123); 1581 (921); 1587 (1,001); 1591 (1,697); 1595 (1,044); 1597 (1,286). Calori, *Opera Mendicanti*, pp. 17; 26. Fanti (ed.), *Gli archivi*, p. 91.

[88] As a purely public institution, the administration could not be as restricted as that of a confraternal ospedale. Nevertheless, the initial administrative body of 68 was cut in half by 1573, and reduced to 21 in the next century. Calori notes, however, that the Opera Mendicanti retained more of an open, citizen character than many contemporary institutions: Calori, *Opera Mendicanti*, p. 41.

power unilaterally to change the statutes, lay with the Papal Legate, the Bishop, and the Senate.

III. DEVELOPING THE CIVIC CULT

Bologna's patricians drew on confraternal charitable traditions and institutions when framing an approach to poverty that answered political as well as social problems. Another avenue open to them as they sought to broaden their local authority under the wing of papal sovereignty lay in the ceremonies of the civic cult. Thanks to Nicolò Albergati's reforms of the 1420s through 1440s, lay confraternities had taken on a larger role as the custodians of religious shrines, the organizers of religious processions, and the teachers of religious truths. Little in the way of an organized civic cult had existed before Albergati, and much of what came through and after him was defined and maintained by confraternities. We have already seen above the enormous prestige which came to the Compagnia di S. Maria della Morte as a result of its custodianship over the shrine of the Madonna di San Luca, and to the Compagnia di S. Maria del Baraccano as a result of its association with the shrine of the same name. In the case of the latter, the connection was deliberately created and fostered by successive generations of Bentivoglio who drew the confraternity into their pageants and who lent the shrine and confraternity greater magnificence through architectural patronage. Rioting wool workers and conquering popes alike recognized the potent connections between the shrine and the aspiring Signorial family, and worked deliberately to tap and redirect that symbolism to their own purposes.

From the later fifteenth through the course of the sixteenth century, Bologna's civic-religious cult expanded as new images gave birth to new shrines superintended by new confraternities which staged new processions. An incredible florescence of miracle-working images testifies to the spiritual impetus of the Catholic Reform movement as it was sharpened in the social and political troubles of the turn of the century. The fact that confraternities took on the task of building the shrines and organizing public devotions testifies to the continuation of Albergati's drive to put the local cult in the hands of the local laity. But as with the charitable confraternities, the very success of these new confraternities ensured that they would gain a profile and influence which would attract the attentions of Bologna's patricians.

Common *topoi* mark the legends of the new Marian shrines established in the later fifteenth and early sixteenth century, and connect them to the existing shrines of the Madonna di San Luca and S. Maria del Baraccano. All arose out of the rediscovery of a long-neglected or possibly buried or damaged image of the Madonna. Marginalized people – usually old women or young children – made the discoveries in run-down or neglected areas of the city. People of the neighborhood then placed the image in a makeshift shrine where it began to perform miracles. A few weeks, months, or years later the image's reputation had expanded beyond the neighborhood and a confraternity was established to build a decent shrine and organize regular processions. Gabriella Zarri sees the *topoi* as a means of affirming both the *plebs sancta* and the *popolarità* of the Christian message and notes that this ethos remains even when confraternities and the ecclesiastical hierarchy move in to regulate the local cult and attempt to move it beyond the control of the *plebs* without sacrificing *popolarità*.[89] The pattern of these *topoi* reinforces Richard Trexler's argument that in the later middle ages possession of spiritually powerful images shifted in three ways: from the stable to the mobile (i.e., from monks to friars), from the sacerdotal to the charismatic (from clergy to the unordained holy man), and from the ecclesiastical to the tertiary or lay (from church to confraternity). These shifts established a new dynamic between the devotee, the image, and the patron of the image, with increasing emphasis on the patron's power and influence.[90] Through the sixteenth century the confraternities and their high-born members and officers emerged as the patrons of a host of new Marian images. They maintained the public shrines sheltering the images, organized public laudesi-style worship and feast-day processions to honor, display, and sometimes parade the images, and, once established, provided themselves with private oratories for their own purely confraternal devotions. But as in politics and charity, their success rested on cooperation with the papacy which alone could bestow the honors, privileges, and indulgences necessary to turn neighborhood shrines into *loci* of the civic-religious cult. We can see this process at work by looking more closely at five of the most significant new shrines: S. Maria Coronata, the Madonna del Piombo, the Madonna del Soccorso, the Crocifisso del Cestello, and the Madonna del Pioggia. Taken together, these five demonstrate the variety of circumstances in which images were recovered and patronage over them was extended.

The Bentivoglio were particularly eager to take shelter under the mantle of Mary, and so apart from S. Maria del Baraccano, two of the

---

[89] G. Zarri, "Istituzione ecclesiastiche e vita religiosa nell'età della Riforma e della Controriforma," in A. Borselli (ed.), *Storia della Emilia-Romagna*, II, (Bologna: 1977), pp. 246, 250–2.

[90] Trexler, "Florentine Religious Experience," pp. 30–1.

new shrines were located relatively close to the palace they were building near to the Augustinian church of San Giacomo Maggiore. At a point in the city wall where the small gate of Borgo San Giacomo had been sealed up in 1326, there was an old church which had been taken over by the Augustinians and turned into a hospice. The hospice had an image of the Virgin in it, and at some point in the middle of the fifteenth century this image began to attract devotees. Why they gathered to honor this particular image is unclear, but their numbers began to interfere with the running of the hospice. In November 1465, three years after Giovanni II succeeded Sante, the Augustinians ceded the site to a lay confraternity and the Sedici authorized construction of a church. The new shrine was dedicated to S. Maria del Baraccano del Borgo San Giacomo, underlining its connection both to the main Bentivoglio shrine of S. Maria del Baraccano, and to the neighborhood of Borgo San Giacomo which served as the Bentivoglio power base. We know little about the development of either the shrine or the confraternity through the later fifteenth century. It seems clear that the Bentivoglio played a large part however, for after the family's fall from power, the image and shrine were renamed S. Maria Coronata.[91]

The second shrine emerged as political tensions mounted in the wake of the French invasions, when new signs of the Virgin's favor to the city and its ruling family were needed. The "Madonna del Piombo" was unearthed in 1502 by children playing in debris lying near the eastern city wall in the Porta Ravennate quarter. The leaden bas-relief of Mary cradling the dead Christ was deposited in one of the nearby arches within the city wall where it quickly attracted a reputation for miracles. An early company history claimed that as its fame spread and the number of its devotees grew, a group of twelve pious and devout men purchased the image from the children and established the confraternity of S. Maria della Pietà to reorganize the makeshift shrine on a firmer footing.[92] The history is silent on the correspondence between the rapid development of the cult and confraternity and Alexander VI's contemporaneous demands that the Bentivoglio and Bologna submit to Cesare Borgia. As noted in an earlier chapter,

---

[91] The Augustinian cession and Sedici authorization were both given on November 25, 1465. Guidicini notes that the confraternity did not adopt formal statutes until 1499, though the earliest extant statutes come from 1566, with a revision "fatto per la conservazione della santa pace" in 1568: BBA Gozz 206, cc. 106r–120v; BBA Gozz 210, cc 81r–82v. See also Guidicini, *Cose Notabili* II, p. 235; III, p. 343. On public devotions in the seventeenth century: C. Masini, *Bologna Perlustrata*, p. 30.

[92] ASB Dem, Compagnia di S. Maria della Pietà, busta 7/7693, filza 4, item 1, 1a.

an early matriculation list for S. Maria della Pietà shows that the original confraternity had far more than twelve members, and that it included Giovanni II Bentivoglio among its largely high-born early brothers. Bentivoglio patronage was further underlined when the family's favored painter, Francesco Francia, painted the new shrine's altarpiece. Reading through the legend, it seems clear that Giovanni II was attempting to secure signs of the Virgin's patronage of his family, much as his ancestor Giovanni I had done with S. Maria del Baraccano a hundred years earlier. Confraternities were among the groups ordered at this time by the Sedici to visit the papal ambassador and confirm their loyalty to the regime and their unwillingness to allow its head to leave the city.[93] Bentivoglio's effort to capture the Madonna del Piombo's patronage proved unsuccessful, but the confraternity continued gathering patricians and prestige and, as seen in an earlier chapter, in 1547 it was the first spiritual company to organize a separate consorority.

The rest of the new shrines emerged after the final fall of the Bentivoglio. Only one was not centered on an image of the Virgin or on an image which had miraculously resurfaced after years of neglect. The Crocifisso del Cestello emerged as a shrine in 1514 when miracles began occurring at a large fresco painted on a bridge which skirted the garden wall at the rear of the Dominican monastery in the Porta Procola quarter. The image of the crucifixion had been painted by Jacopo Avanzi (d. 1416) in the early years of the fifteenth century, and had attracted no particular attention for over a century. In May 1514 it began to sweat from the middle upwards (*"fù veduta sudare dal mezzo in su"*). Crowds gathered and some began to claim healing. The area was one where murders and *"altri mali"* frequently occurred, but when one of the local cynics mocked the others and climbed up for a closer look he was immediately struck with fire; upon asking pardon he was *"liberato."* Within two months, a group of laymen drew up and notarized an account of events, and received permission from the Bishop to establish a confraternity and oratory. Over the next forty years the brothers widened the bridge, built and then enlarged a public church and confraternal oratory and, in 1549, followed S. Maria della Pietà's lead and added a consorority. The work was financed by the wealthier citizens of the neighborhood, who progressively worked their way

---

[93] The Madonna del Piombo was discovered June 12; Alexander's order came on September 17, and rejection which Giovanni II orchestrated among the guilds, the confraternities, and the members of the Sedici occurred on September 20. Antonio dalle Anelle, "Diario delle cose notabili successe in Bologna." BBA B427 II, (17, 19, 20 settembre).

into the confraternity itself. On a matriculation list begun in 1538, 128 of the 147 members identified themselves with family names and only 19 with patronymics; of the 48 giving occupation, 36 were notaries, 2 were doctors, and 10 were of the middle or lower guilds.[94]

The case of the "Madonna del Soccorso" introduces a different element into the *topos* of the "image rescued from obscurity." In 1517 Giovanni Alessandro Salani and Pietro dalla Barba, two common men, were digging at a point in the city wall at the northeast Borgo S. Pietro where an old gate had been walled up in 1327. In the course of their excavation, they uncovered an image of the Virgin. Salani and dalla Barba cleaned off the image and erected a small shrine against the city wall to house it, hoping perhaps that it would attract devotees and alms as other shrines had, and that they would be able to profit from their patronage. Trexler has noted that Renaissance supplicants were not abject and passive towards images of Mary and the saints but, aware that their own devotion was necessary to the image's power, would threaten, cajole, and perhaps even defile an inactive image to stir it into more lively intercession on their part.[95] Salani and dalla Barba were definitely of this mind, but their shared frustration over their Madonna's inactivity only pushed them further apart. Within a few years Salani replaced the excavated image with another one, hoping perhaps that the new image would demonstrate more power than the old one had. The only problem here was that he did this without consulting his colleague. An enraged dalla Barba came at night and secretly replaced the new image with one of his own, at which point Salani reciprocated with yet another. The dispute was only settled – and the *topos* restored – when a painter from the neighborhood, Filippo Altesani, intervened. He offered Salani and dalla Barba an old carving of the Virgin with Child, her arm raised in blessing, which he had discovered in a nearby house. Once again, the Virgin herself decided through which image she would act.[96] The men made their peace in 1523, but rather than wait passively for this new image to demonstrate its miraculous power, they immediately formed a confraternity to expand the

[94] ASB Dem, Compagnia del Crocifisso del Cestello, busta 1/6378, filza 10; busta 20/6397 A, pp. 1–5. 1538 matriculation: BBA Gozz 206 #2, cc. 34v–36v. See also A.M. Porcù, *Il Santuario e la Confraternita del SS. Crocifisso del Cestello in Bologna* (Bologna: 1961), pp. 9–22.

[95] Trexler, "Florentine Religious Experience," pp. 19–29.

[96] Trexler has argued that for Renaissance Italians "a practical identity existed between Mary and image." This part of the Madonna del Soccorso legend suggests instead that contemporaries did distinguish between image and saint, and assumes that the saint actively decided on her representation. See Trexler, "Florentine Religious Experience," p. 18.

shrine further. Their eye had been on the success of other confraternities all along, and now they went to the Compagnia dell'Ospedale di San Giobbe for their statutes, and to the Compagnia di Buon Gesù for their spiritual exercises. The real transformation of the shrine took place when a plague broke out in the neighborhood in 1527. The lay brothers intensified their religious services and, as the plague worsened, they lifted the image from its place and began carrying it in procession through the area. The plague subsided across the city and the image gained the name and reputation of the "Madonna del Soccorso." Cardinal Bishop Lorenzo Campeggi and the Senate immediately decided that each year on that same day (the second Sunday after Easter) the image would be brought in a procession across the city to the shrine of S. Rocco, the patron saint of those suffering from plague, against the western city wall in the Porta Stiera quarter. S. Rocco's church had further civic significance, as it was built at that point in the wall where the Pratello gate had once stood. The gate had been the escape route for the assassins of Annibale Bentivoglio in 1444, and was sealed up the following year. The shrine of the Madonna del Soccorso attracted such crowds that in 1581 the brothers of the Compagnia di S. Maria del Soccorso del Borgo S. Pietro were able to build a new and larger church under the sponsorship and with the funds of their Rector Conte Alessandro Bentivoglio. In 1612 the Madonna del Soccorso was crowned in a special ceremony on the steps of the civic basilica of S. Petronio.[97]

The last case here regards an image whose elevation from obscurity was more deliberate. The Marian image held by the Ospedale di S. Bartolomeo di Reno had its status raised soon after the Ospedale itself was turned into an orphanage in the 1520s, and its elevation was clearly part of the effort to reinforce the parallel with the Conservatorio di S. Maria del Baraccano. In 1410 the confraternity had purchased a house built against the thirteenth-century city wall, and with it gained possession of an image of the virgin which had been found there. The image came to be known as either the "Madonna del Serraglio" (after the name given to the gates in this ring of walls) or the "Madonna del Reno" (after the Canal which ran nearby), and had only a small following until a deliberate effort to expand the cult began in the early sixteenth century. In 1522 the Senate granted land and permission necessary to expand the oratory, and in 1553 Julius III offered plenary indulgences. At some point brothers began taking the image in an annual Ascension Day procession south through the center of the

---

[97] Calzoni, *Storia della chiesa parrochiale di Santa Maria in via Mascarella*, pp. 109–17. ASB Dem, Compagnia di S. Maria del Soccorso, busta 7/6340, filza 2.

city to the old church of S. Antonio just inside the S. Mamolo gate. During an extended drought in 1555, the brothers brought the image in procession to each of the "Quattro Crociati," four crosses reputedly dating to the fourth century which marked crossroads near the center of the city. The rains fell, and the Image was propelled into a larger role in the civic cult. Renamed the Madonna del Pioggia, it developed a new series of civic religious processions which included participation by guilds which depended on the water of the Reno canal for their livelihood. Among the chief of these new processions was that on the morning of the third Sunday of Lent when the confraternity bore the Madonna to one of the four crosses before moving to Piazza Maggiore where, from the head of the stairs of the civic basilica of San Petronio, she blessed the people in the square. The brothers of S. Maria del Soccorso then took up the image and brought it to their shrine where it stood before the high altar until the end of Lent when it returned home. This became a particularly mobile image, with annual processions taking it across the city to the shrines and oratories of S. Maria del Baraccano, the Ospedale di S. Biagio, and S. Maria de'Poveri. In 1604, it too was crowned by Cardinal Archbishop Alfonso Paleotti, ten months after he had crowned the Madonna di San Luca.[98]

These were only some of the leading shrines which emerged in the late fifteenth and early sixteenth centuries. Among others, the Madonna di Galliera sanctified the neighborhood immediately west of the Cathedral from 1478 when her image survived the demolition of a thirteenth-century church, produced other miracles, and became the centerpiece instead of a new church with an elaborately carved sandstone facade. S. Maria delle Febri arose in 1480 when workmen repairing the city wall between Porta S. Mamolo and Porta Castiglione came across an image of the Virgin which subsequently brought healing to those suffering from a fever epidemic in the city. S. Maria delle Rondini came about in 1502 when a host of birds gathered around an image of the Virgin hung in a tree near the Saragozza gate. From 1508, devotees of the Madonna del Asse claimed part of the wall of the Palazzo Communale. From 1520, S. Maria del Paradiso was sheltered in a church on Via Nuova in the Porta Stiera quarter. Each had its own confraternity and came, though these lay brothers' work, to gain a following and significance beyond its immediate neighborhood. The incredible florescence of new Marian shrines in the period was unprecedented, and their miracles contributed to the popular

[98] The Madonna del Pioggia was also popularly known as the Madonna di S. Bartolomeo. ASB PIE, Compagnia di S. Bartolomeo di Reno, ms. 279, cc. 2v, 12. Masini, *Bologna Perlustrata*, pp. 31–2.

conviction that whatever temporal political vicissitudes might befall, Bologna was a city dear to the Virgin Mary's heart (Fig. 5.1).[99]

But there was more to the multiplication of holy places in the city, and in particular to the logic by which certain shrines gained an important role in the civic religious cult. The shrines which had defined that cult into the early Quattrocento had been outside the city walls; Albergati's vigorous promotion of the Madonna di San Luca on the Guardia hill southwest of the city followed the precedent set by the Madonna del Monte on the Osservanza hill nearby. On this model, the sacred existed apart from the city and had to be sought out or brought in from time to time to signal the city's penitence and answer its crises. The Madonna dei Monte never moved, while the Madonna di San Luca came within the walls only as a last resort to alleviate dangers when other forms of supplication had failed. As Florentine lawmakers noted in 1435, "Sacred objects and those dedicated to God are normally respected and held in greater reverence if they are rarely seen [and so there ought to be concern to prevent devotion] toward the *tavola* of Our Lady of Impruneta from being diminished by her being brought to Florence too frequently."[100] The Madonna di San Luca remained – and remains – a key figure in the local cult, but from the later fifteenth century new shrines followed instead the model set by the S. Maria del Baraccano, and moved the locus of the sacred from outside to inside the city walls. Each quarter gained shrines at the city walls, and with the exception of the smallest, Porta Ravennate, each gained additional shrines within the neighborhoods of the quarter. There was a further complementarity to the new shrines. Some, like S. Maria Coronata, the Madonna del Piombo, and SS. Crocifisso del Cestello were fixed shrines in the manner of S. Maria del Baraccano which drew Bolognese out of their neighborhoods and quarters to religious loci held up as having the broadest civic significance. Others like the Madonna del Soccorso and the Madonna del Pioggia followed the model of the Madonna di San Luca which left its shrine and moved through the quarters of the city, symbolically drawing the city together during Lent and particularly Holy Week. These processional routes deliberately connected sites of profoundly religious and profoundly civic

---

[99] For S. Maria di Galliera: Bursellis, *Cronaca gestorum, RIS* vol. 23, Pt. II, p. 104 [1–8]; Fileno della Tuate, "Cronaca della città di Bologna," BBU ms. 437, II, 1478; Sebastiano Buonhomo, "Alcuni cose notabili di Bologna . . .," BBA B427 VIII (1478). For S. Maria delle Febri, Guidicini, *Cose notabili*, III, p. 315. For S. Maria delle Rondini: Fileno della Tuate, "Cronaca," (3/20/1500); Guidicini, *Cose notabili*, IV, p. 328. For S. Maria delle Asse: Guidicini, *Cose notabili*, I, p. 79. For S. Maria del Paradiso: Buonhomo, "Alcuni cose notabili," 1466; Guidicini, *Miscellanea*, p. 339.
[100] Cited in Trexler, "Florentine Religious Experience," p. 17.

G. Blaeu, "Bononia docet mater studiorum" (Amsterdam: 1663)

SHRINES

A. SSmo. Crocifisso del Cestello
B. Madonna del Asse
C. Madonna di Galliera
D. Madonna della Pioggia
E. Madonna del Piombo

F. Madonna del Soccorso
G. S. Maria del Baraccano
H. S. Maria Coronata
I. S. Maria delle Febri
J. S. Maria delle Rondini

K. S. Rocco

L. Civic Bascilica of San Petronio (on Piazza Maggiore)

CITY QUARTERS

1. Porta Ravennate   2. Porta Procola   3. Porta Stiera   4. Porta Piera

Fig. 5.1.   Confraternal shrines (G. Blaeu, "Bononia docet mater studiorum")

significance, like the Quattro Crociati, S. Petronio, or the Piazza Maggiore, the heart of the city where all four quarters met and where all civic-religious festivities had their climax with mass celebrated on the steps of San Petronio. In the case of each of these shrines lay confraternities took the initiative in organizing the devotional movement which had arisen through miracles associated with a Marian image; the civic government ordered processions, gave subsidies, and offered the land necessary to allow construction of an oratory around which a more permanent cult could develop; and the papacy offered the indulgences and spiritual benefits necessary to give the cult a firmer foundation once popular memory of the original miracles had faded. Those confraternities, like S. Maria del Soccorso and SS. Crocifisso del Cestello, whose initial complement was largely artisanal, soon underwent a *nobilitazione* in membership parallel to that already seen in the confraternal ospedali as they were drawn into a more comprehensive civic relief scheme. Nobilitazione was the prerequisite for development from purely local to truly civic significance, for patrician intercession was needed to secure spiritual benefits from the hierarchy, land concessions from the Senate, and the funds necessary to construct a suitable church and stage impressive processions.

Richard Trexler and Edward Muir have examined the relationship between control of civic cults and control of civic politics in Italian cities of the fifteenth and sixteenth centuries. In a study of four cities, Muir argues that control over religious symbolism and the use of it to achieve the "sacralization of urban spaces and institutions" was the key to broader civic control.[101] Those political elites, as in Florence and particularly Venice, which could appropriate the symbols could use them as a unifying focus for civic loyalties and so overcome neighborhood, kinship, and other social divisions. Others, as in Naples and Udine, which could not appropriate the symbols, paid for their failure by continuing social divisions which fractured their power and condemned them to subservience. One could argue that these arguments from social psychology are overshadowed by more elementary political facts: Venice and Florence were autonomous while Naples and Udine were not. Bologna provides an intermediate test case as a formerly autonomous city whose local political elite had seen the power of civic-religious symbols before losing sovereignty to an outside power. Certainly the development of the cults of both the Madonna di San Luca and S. Maria del Baraccano demonstrate a

[101] E. Muir, "The Virgin on the Streetcorner: The Place of the Sacred in Italian Cities," in S. Ozment (ed.), *Religion and Culture in the Renaissance and Reformation* (Kirksville: 1989), p. 37.

determined attempt to make clear the association between the Queen of Heaven and the rulers at the time. Both Julius II and Leo X ordered processions of the Madonna di San Luca to celebrate their "liberation" of Bologna, and both made formal visits to the shrine of S. Maria del Baraccano to ensure that its potent civic-religious symbolism would be associated with their rule and not with a potential Bentivoglio restoration.

Simple association was not enough, for civic saints and rituals could organize dissent as much as obedience; the key to control lay in ensuring that processions, rituals, saints, and shrines had a city-wide rather than a purely neighborhood focus, and that the public expressions of the cult emphasized hierarchy, deference, and obedience.[102] The case of Bologna enlarges Muir's thesis, for it shows that in the right political setting local elites could work cooperatively with outside overlords in using the civic-religious cult to secure peace on the streets and obedience in the populace. Moreover, in taking over the confraternities, the patricians captured not only time and space, but also the powerful Bolognese tradition of Spiritual Companies as third pillars of popolo society; this tradition itself had further articulation through the Trecento ethos of lay-directed charity, and the Quattrocento ethos of a lay-directed civic cult. Certainly the development of Bologna's confraternal charities and its civic-religious cults reflected the reciprocal realization noted earlier. Patricians knew that peninsular political realities ruled out autonomy, and local power and legitimacy could come only through cooperation with the papacy. Popes realized that sovereignty over the Papal State's richest city after Rome could only come through cooperation with local elites. Wariness, suspicion, and manipulation marked the relationship as much as cooperation, but it paid the expected rewards in the form of peaceful and secure possession for both sides until the end of the *ancien régime*.

Both the reorganization of charitable relief and the development of city-wide cults focused within the walls of Bologna added the force of religious patronage to the power already enjoyed by members of the senatorial elite, and so contributed significantly to cementing that power in relation both to the papacy above and to the populace below. Bologna's patricians achieved the type of control over sacred space and time which Muir argues was necessary for political and social control of the early modern Italian city. They could not have done so without first gaining control of confraternal charities and shrines. Yet some cautions should be raised lest this be seen as a deliberate policy fueled mainly by a cynical appraisal of the realities of urban power

---

[102] Muir, "Virgin on the Street Corner," p. 39.

politics. Bologna's patricians were participants in the world of religious charity and powerful images, not simply actors in a process which they did not believe but which they knew could bring them power. As Richard Trexler so forcefully reminds us, there is no disjunction between believing fervently in an image's power and yet attempting to capture or manipulate the patronage of and over that image.[103] We must resist the urge to project on early modern elites an essentially modern functionalism which distances them emotionally from the religious ceremonies and institutions through which they consolidate their power. They dominated, promoted, and expanded these charitable institutions and religious shrines because they knew that the construction of a holy city was a deliberate process, and they were convinced that such construction was a good in itself and in the eyes of God. Such construction could only be achieved through the spiritual tools dispensed by the papacy. The flow of indulgences, benefits, and graces to Bologna's ospedali and shrines underlines the cooperation between local and papal authorities in the drive for a holy city. The cooperation continued through the end of the *ancien régime*, and some of its consequences are seen in a guide to civic-religious ceremonies published by Carlo Antonio di Paolo Masini in 1650 and republished many times thereafter. *Bologna Perlustrata* catalogs the processions, the devotions, and the exercises practiced through the year in the churches, monasteries, shrines, and confraternities of the city. Masini does not distinguish confraternal from parochial, monastic, or mendicant activities, and in so doing demonstrates the gradual merging of confraternal and clerical elements within the civic cult that had taken place over the previous hundred years. The civic-religious calendar created through this process testified to the cooperation between civic and ecclesiastical authorities in their drive to create a sacred city. Working cooperatively with confraternal institutions and with new institutions organized on the confraternal model, these authorities devised better ways of feeding the hungry, sheltering orphans and strangers, healing the sick, caring for prisoners, and assisting the poor. They also added considerable depth to the local civic-religious cult. In the process, however, as the past few chapters have shown, they eased the men and women of artisanal ranks out of the Compagnie Spirituali and gradually turned the confraternities themselves into little more than bureacratic agencies that operated in that grey area where lay and clerical, local and papal, patrician and plebian all met.

[103] Trexler, "The Sacred Image," p. 16.

EPILOGUE

On a June morning in 1574, Bologna gathered to bring Christ in procession around the town. The annual Corpus Domini procession opened with children drawn from twenty of the city's Schools of Christian Doctrine, all dressed as angels or saints, as if to underscore their nature as "the purest of the pure."[1] These were followed by the twenty-six artisanal companies ranked in their usual order from the weavers to the notaries.[2] The spiritual companies followed, led by the confraternity of S. Maria della Vita. Confraternities associated with shrines and ospedali took pride of place, and the confraternity of S. Maria della Morte closed this section of the procession. The male orphans of the ospedali of S. Maria Maddalena, S. Giacomo, and S. Bartolomeo di Reno accompanied their confraternal sponsors. Laymen of both the artisanal and spiritual companies dressed in their characteristic robes, and all carried lit torches. Then came the regular and secular clergy, all carrying large candles. The vicar and suffragen bishops preceded the host, which the Cardinal Legate or Archbishop carried under the shelter of a baldachino supported by Senators. Magistrates of all the governing

---

[1] A 1568 census indicated 4,338 pupils in the Schools, broken down by Quarters: P. Stiera (1,279); P. Ravennate (1,483); P. Procolo (178); P. Piera (1,398): G. Lercaro, "La riforma catechistica post-tridentina a Bologna," *Ravennatensia*, vol. 2 (1971), p. 14. On the children's "purity", see: Rubin, *Corpus Christi*, pp. 250–1; and R. Trexler, "Ritual in Florence: adolescence and salvation in the Renaissance," in H. Oberman and C. Trinkaus (eds.), *The Pursuit of Holiness in Late Medieval and Renaissance Religion* (Leiden: 1974), pp. 245–6.

[2] This order established not only the relative status of the artisanal companies, but also the relative amounts the Reggimento taxed them to pay for ceremonial processions. Artisanal companies paid for the celebrations held when Gabriele Paleotti first entered Bologna after being appointed its bishop, the notaries being charged the highest sum (120 lire), and the cordwainers the lowest (4 lire). "Tasse delle Compagnie delle Arti della città di Bologna," BBU Ms. 356 #10.

councils followed the host, closing with the Senators accompanied by their officials and courtiers.[3]

Corpus Domini processions had spread across Europe since Urban VI instituted the festival in 1264, steadily gaining signficance through the centuries, and rising to particular prominence in the sixteenth century. As Protestants rejected transubstantiation in the Eucharist, the Tridentine Church gave ever more emphasis to a procession in which Christ himself played the leading role. Against the plethora of local cults, Corpus Domini recruited the entire community in an affirmation of the Church Universal. In the rhetoric of its advocates, it defined relations within that community while underlining the whole community's relation to God and his Church.

Until the later fifteenth century, Bologna's Corpus Domini celebrations had been relatively modest and closely identified with the clergy. The annual rogation procession of the Madonna di San Luca, which took place about three weeks earlier, overshadowed it thoroughly. Italian laity were late in joining the circuit of the Eucharist through their cities, with most becoming involved only in the fifteenth century. As late as 1470 in Bologna, the Corpus Domini procession included only the secular and regular clergy, culminating with members of the chapters of the basilica of S. Petronio and the cathedral of S. Pietro.[4] Some confraternal statutes mention Corpus Domini processions, but do not state clearly whether they were confraternal or broader civic events.[5] The procession grew more significant locally through the sixteenth century, and was particularly promoted by Gabriele Paleotti after he became bishop in 1566 (1566–97). Miri Rubin has argued that lay participation marked a "penetration of the secular and the civic-political into the eucharistic procession," which led civic officials to control and regulate, and civic elites to use the procession as a stage on which to re-express their power.[6] In Bologna the dynamic seems rather the reverse. The processional order of 1574 signals both Paleotti's efforts at changing the position of confraternities in the local cult, and the new hierarchy emerging within the body of Compagnie

---

[3]   Guidicini, Cose notabili, IV, pp.1 69–75. The order was similar to that followed in contemporary Venice: Muir, Civic Ritual, pp. 223–30.

[4]   Guidicini, Cose Notabili, IV, p. 169. Rubin, Corpus Christi, p. 258.

[5]   The 1492 Corpus Domini procession included sacre rappresentazioni from the Old and New Testaments staged by the Compagnia di S. Maria del Baraccano and other spiritual companies. A. d'Ancona, Origini del teatro italiano, I (Rome: 1966), p. 297. According to one contemporary chronicler, this was "la più bella festa che mai fusse veduta": Varignana [Cronaca B], RIS vol. 23, Pt. I, vol. iv, p. 526 (16–18); 529 (13–17).

[6]   Rubin, Corpus Christi, p. 259.

Spirituali as a result of progressive nobilitazione of devotional and ospedale companies.

The Corpus Domini processional order signaled two changes in the
relations between confraternities, piety, and politics. First was the prominence given the parochial Schools of Christian Doctrine. Their
young scholars were taught by members of the Compagnie del Santissimo Sacramento. In a synodal order issued the year he was appointed
bishop, Paleotti had ordered these confraternities established in every
parish; eight years later in 1574 there were at least forty-eight in the
city.[7] These were not independent lay confraternities, but parish auxiliary bodies, under the rectorship of the priest.[8]

As for the traditional spiritual companies, their place in the whole
procession was constant, but their order within that place carried
subtle hints that something had changed. Their usual place between
the artisanal companies and the clergy had traditionally symbolized
how artisanal membership and mendicant devotional exercises gave
them a foot in both camps. Their relative internal order had traditionally been based on historical precedence, the same principle
used when determining rank within companies. In the Corpus
Domini procession, position now became a mirror of the social and
ecclesiastical hierarchy. Companies were ranked according to the
qualità of their membership, itself now a reflection of the range and
importance of their charitable activities, their custodianship over
shrines, or their connection with Roman archconfraternities. As
leader of the Madonna di S. Luca procession and sponsor of numerous quasi-governmental charitable activities, the Compagnia di
S. Maria della Morte had risen to the peak of the social pyramid
and the place of honor among confraternities participating in the
procession. By traditional chronological reckoning, leadership should
have fallen to the rival company of S. Maria della Vita, while
newer Ospedale companies like S. Maria degli Angeli del Ospedale
degli Esposti and S. Bartolomeo di Reno should not have figured
as prominently as they did.[9] Aggregation to Roman archconfraternities also allowed some other newer patrician companies such as
SS. Sebastiano e Rocco and eventually SSmo. Crocifisso del Cestello

[7] P. Prodi, *Il Cardinale Gabriele Paleotti* II, (Roma: 1967), pp. 182–7; Guidicini, *Cose
     Notabili*, IV, pp.169–71.
[8] Prodi, *Gabriele Paleotti* II, pp. 188–9.
[9] Alessandro Stiatici unwittingly indicated the incompleteness of the shift when he
     based his erroneous claims for the great antiquity of the S. Bartolomeo di Reno
     company on the basis of its honored position at the rear of the confraternities' pro-
     cession. Stiatici, *Narratione*, p. 6.

to advance in the hierarchy. The archconfraternity was a relatively new institution, "empowered to aggregate or affiliate other confraternities of the same nature and to impart to them its privileges and indulgences."[10] Aggregation could only be done by those who had received explicit permission from the Holy See and for those who had received the written consent of the local bishop. Hence for the first time, status obtained in the local confraternal hierarchy was in the power of the Pope and the local bishop.[11] In the 1570s, Bolognese confraternities could only boast aggregation to Roman groups; from 1585 they were themselves being designated archconfraternities, a status conferred first to S. Maria della Vita by Sixtus V and eventually to at least four others.[12] Archconfraternities had traditionally been a means of creating ties of dependence between autonomous lay brotherhoods across the Italian peninsula and Roman parent bodies. This centralized hierarachy was now duplicated on the urban level as S. Maria della Vita became the parent over ten other Bolognese confraternities.[13] Each papal and archepiscopal honor affected a confraternity's social standing. As subtle as these changes might be, processional order was a sensitive point over which confraternities willingly went to law, precisely because they were public demonstrations of the relative power and prestige of each spiritual company within the group. The order

[10] F.P. Donnelly, "Archconfraternities," *The Catholic Encyclopedia*, I, (New York: 1913), p. 692. See also Black, *Italian Confraternities* , pp. 72–74.

[11] Some Bolognese aggregations: (a) SS. Sebastiano e Rocco to the Ospedale di S. Giovanni Lateran in Rome in 1533: ASB Dem, Compagnia di SS. Sebastiano e Rocco, busta 15/6619, filza A; (b) S. Bartolomeo di Reno to the Arciospedale di S. Maria della Visitazione in Rome in 1554: ASB Dem, Compagnia di S. Bartolomeo di Reno, busta 2/7651, filza 15; (c) SSmo. Crocifisso del Cestello to the Arciconfraternita del SS. Crocifisso in the Church of S. Marcello in Rome in 1580: ASB Dem, Compagnia del SSmo. Crocifisso del Cestello, busta 20/6397, c. 21.

[12] When conferring archconfraternal status on S. Maria della Vita, Sixtus V also fixed Bologna's confraternal processional order, using the order followed in the 1574 Corpus Domini procession: Anon., "Principio dell'Origine delle Compagnie in Bologna, e particolarmente dell'Archconfraternita di S. Maria della Vita," BBU Ms. 2022 #2, c. 34r–34v. Bolognese confraternities which eventually gained archconfraternal status include: S. Maria della Morte, Buon Gesù, SS. Sebastiano e Rocco, and S. Maria Maddalena.

[13] The ten subordinate confraternities were: S. Sigismondo, S. Andrea, S. Giacomo e Filippo, S. Maria Maddalena, S. Maria delle Neve, Spirito Santo, S. Maria degli Angeli, and three companies previously referred to as "sisters" of S. Maria della Vita: la Rissurezione, Capugrano, and S. Giacomo. On May 17, 1586, all the companies went in procession from the church of S. Maria della Vita (where they had pledged obedience to the Vita Rector) to the cathedral, where Paleotti gave his blessing. "Principio dell'Origine della Compagnie in Bologna, e particolarmente dell'Arciconfraternita di S. Maria della Vita," BBU ms. 2022, #2, cc. 34r–35r.

was fraught with tensions as groups jockeyed for positions closer to the Eucharist, which was the strategic center of the procession.[14] The Corpus Domini order showed that selective nobilitazione of ospedali companies had done more than change the inner workings of individual confraternities. Nobilitazione and the Tridentine push to parish confraternities under the priest's control worked together to bring the period of artisanal devotional confraternities to an end.

In her study of Roman confraternities, Anna Esposito asserts that in public religious festivals the curial and municipal poles of the Holy City experienced a rare unity. These "two souls of Rome" were usually distinct and opposed, but they could join under the *devozione municipale* of confraternal religious processions. Paolo Prodi used the same metaphor in his description of the papal monarchy as "one body and two souls," with the pope serving as both pastor and prince over the papal state.[15] Both intend the metaphor to underscore the reciprocation and merging of interests between temporal and spiritual government in the Papal State. Prodi further speaks of the secularization of the papal bureaucracy and the "ecclesiasticization" of the political classes to demonstrate the gradual merging of interests and even of families within the ruling group. The previous chapter demonstrated that this was indeed the case in Bologna as well, as the ennobled confraternities, the city government, and the regular and secular clergy cooperated in the construction of *Bologna Perlustrata*. But cooperation did not entail equality, and upper clergy remained uncomfortable with some of those symbols of Bologna's civic religion which seemed to put too much power in lay hands. Civic-religious processions like those of the Madonna di San Luca underlined confraternities' role as the spiritual pillar of popolo society and the guardians of its holy places. The processions included magistrates, guilds, and clergy, but symbolically put them all under the leadership of a confraternity. The meaning was so clear that Archbishop Paleotti felt compelled to engineer a counterbalance, limiting and controlling these confraternal rituals so as to position the church universal over the local cult, and underline ties of dependence to the local parish and the church hierarchy.[16]

---

[14] Rubin, *Corpus Christi*, pp. 265–71.

[15] A. Esposito, "Le 'confraternite' del Gonfalone," p. 104. P. Prodi, *The Papal Prince. One Body and Two Souls: The Papal Monarchy in early modern Europe*. trans. S. Haskins (Cambridge: 1987).

[16] A. Prosperi, "Parrocchie e confraternite tra cinquecento e seicento," in *Per una storia dell'Emilia-Romagna*, (Bologna: 1985), p. 170.

Gabriele Paleotti did not see confraternities themselves as a threat. On the contrary, he was an enthusiastic supporter of lay spirituality and religious brotherhoods throughout thirty-one years as bishop and, from 1582, archbishop; he was without question the most dedicated supporter to have occupied the episcopal throne since Nicolò Albergati. Paleotti was committed to the Tridentine reforms; he had been a legate to the Council, becoming a close friend and frequent correspondent of Carlo Borromeo. Like Nicolò Albergati one hundred and fifty years before, Paleotti was also a citizen of Bologna who was dedicated to devotional reform of the diocese and who saw in confraternities a proven and effective vehicle. He aimed to reduce the division between laymen and clergy by drawing the two together in the devotional and administrative life of the local church. He envisioned laymen working closely with priests in supervising and conducting each parish's social and educational work. To this end he issued his order establishing Compagnie del SS. Sacramento in every parish, making these spiritual companies the focus not only for eucharistic devotion, but also for teaching Christian doctrine to children and for assisting the priests in parish administration.[17] The experiment built on the confraternity's reputation as a lay organization, but violated the local model in critical ways. For one, Paleotti made all the new confraternities subject to a standard missal in 1574, and a single set of statutes issued in 1583. This followed the model which Carlo Borromeo was implementing in Milan, but reduced the traditional independence and self-direction of the lay Compagnie Spirituali.[18] For another, these statutes appointed the parish priests as perpetual rectors of the new groups, eliminating the confraternity's autonomy and undermining any authority they might have had over the priest. As elsewhere in Italy, the number of Compagnie del SS. Sacramento proliferated rapidly, but Paleotti's hopes for devotional revival and lay participation in the church were

---

[17] In 1535 Bishop Lorenzo Campeggi prohibited administering the Eucharist to anyone who did not know the Pater, Ave, and Credo. Lercaro, "Riforma catechistica," p. 12. G. Barbiero claims Bologna's first SS. Sacramento confraternity originated in 1483, but I have been unable to find any primary or secondary sources verifying this: G. Barbiero, Le confraternite del Santissimo Sacramento prima del 1539, (Treviso: 1949), p. 295. For Paleotti's program: Prodi, Gabrielle Paleotti, II, pp. 181–9, and: Prodi, "The Application of the Tridentine Decrees: The Organization of the Diocese of Bologna During the Episcopate of Cardinal Gabriele Paleotti," E. Cochrane (ed.), The Late Italian Renaissance: 1525–1630 (New York: 1970), pp. 226–43.

[18] G. Cherubino, Libro da compagnie spirituali (Bologna: Alessandro Benaci, 1574). A. Prosperi, "Parrochie e confraternite tra cinquecento e seicento," in Per una storia dell'Emilia-Romagna, (Bologna: 1985), pp. 167–70. Lercaro, "Riforma catechistica," p. 20.

not realized. Frequent disputes demonstrated the priests' power over the new companies and their membership and importance steadily declined.[19]

Paleotti's actions sum up the paradox of Catholic Reform in its impact on the confraternities. In the Duecento and Trecento they had claimed to be vital institutional elements of the urban society being built by guildsmen. That society would gather in Artisan's Companies to work, in Militia Companies to defend itself, and in Spiritual Companies to pray. In truth, the Spiritual Companies were more peripheral to the success or failure of popolo society than they imagined, and it was not until that society was effectively dead that the confraternities could play the social role that their rhetoric had prepared them for. The factional struggles and Observant devotional reforms of the early fifteenth century provided the political and religious context for the confraternities to take a larger role in defining and maintaining the civic-religious symbols of a city which wanted to assert an independence that it did not have. Their public role as the guardians of the cult was matched by inner devotional reforms, and the two together revitalized the confraternities and gave them a greater prominence in the city through the fifteenth and into the sixteenth century.

It was this very prominence which set in motion the forces that would fundamentally change the confraternities. The success and prospects of confraternal charitable institutions and of confraternal shrines attracted the participation of high-born and senatorial families. Some joined out of political expedience, and others out of a genuine concern for shaping Bologna as a sacred city; whatever their motivations, they squeezed the artisans out of positions of authority and in some cases out of the brotherhoods altogether. All of the extant matriculation lists for charitable and shrine confraternities demonstrate increasing numbers of members drawn from the upper guilds and from the Senatorial patriciate through the sixteenth century; notaries like Eliseo Mamelini begin predominating over cordwainers, carpenters, and the *sottoposti*. This concentration of secular power in turn enabled these confraternities to serve political roles such as the reincorporation of women into subordinate consororities after Mona Lucia Bolza's protest in 1547. More to the point, they allowed the confraternities better to fulfill their charitable or cultic roles, for high-born members brought with them greater funds, greater influence in civic and ecclesiastical forums and, in consequence, greater ability to organize lavish

---

[19] Weissman, *Ritual Brotherhood*, pp. 206; 214–25; 223. Fiorani, "L'esperienza religiosa," p. 173.

processions, build impressive oratories, orphanages, and ospedali, and accumulate powerful spiritual benefits. Confraternities gave such liturgical, festive, and architectural articulation to the civic cult, that the Senate could even afford to sacrifice San Petronio when the papacy demanded it. Pius IV's Bull of 1561 ordering construction of the Palazzo del'Archiginnasio to house the university specified a location which the Commune had designated for the east transept of the civic basilica. The Senate, the guilds, and even the university itself fought for almost two years to preserve the dream of Bologna's civic basilica as the largest church in Christendom, but given the pope's dream for St. Peter's in Rome, their cause was hopeless. What helped the Senators eventually to acquiesce was the fact that the expansion of the confraternal shrines, festivals, and processions had made San Petronio less of an epicentre of Bologna's civic-religious cult. Moreover, given the ennobling of the brotherhoods, this confraternal articulation of the cult was more definitely under *their* control. San Petronio did not lose significance, but it did sacrifice priority, for if there was nowhere for it to go architecturally, there was really nowhere for it go symbolically. The attention given it over the next few centuries was devoted to running debates about whether the facade ought to be built in the Gothic or the classic style; in the end, it was not built at all. By contrast, in 1605 Giovanni Ambrogio Magenta drew up the plans which transformed San Pietro, home of the archbishop's throne, into a masterpiece of Baroque architecture and a significant focus of an increasingly clerical civic cult.[20]

The movement by confraternities to the civic-religious center stage was made possible by the changes which Albergati had initiated out of the Observant ethos of the early fifteenth century. These changes created lay religious institutions which seemed custom-made to take on the spiritual mission as proponents of Catholic Reform in the sixteenth century. A reform movement which was at once more populist and more hierarchical could find few vehicles better suited for its ends than the transformed confraternities of the sixteenth century. Reformers like Paleotti and Borromeo aimed to increase lay participation in parish spiritual, educational, and charitable life, but discipline it with increased parochial and episcopal direction. There is no consensus on the nature of the movements shaping the Catholic Church in the sixteenth century, pictured alternately as an authori-

---

[20] Plans for completing the facade of San Petronio emerged periodically until 1933, when the municipality closed the final competition by voting to leave the basilica as it was. Miller, *Renaissance Bologna*, pp. 65–9. For the plans and debates from the sixteenth through the eighteenth centuries: R. Wittkower, *Gothic vs. Classic: Architectural Projects in Seventeenth-Century Italy* (New York: 1974), pp. 65–78.

tarian Counter-Reformation or a spiritual Catholic Reform, but it can be said that by increasing the power of now-resident bishops, the Council of Trent threatened both the independence and the lay character of confraternities.[21] But even regardless of the Council, bishops held authority which could have an enormous impact on confraternities; the example of Albergati had demonstrated that. What distinguishes Paleotti's from Albergati's reform is the former's determination to attempt greater control and greater uniformity. The parish confraternities with their ambitious educational programs, the priest-rectors, the standardized statutes, the more vigorous program of visitations to confraternal oratories, the inspection and approval of confraternal statutes, the promotion of aggregations to Roman archconfraternities and the designation of Bolognese archconfraternities all point to a great appreciation for the potential of lay confraternities, and a great determination to use them as vehicles for a spiritual reform of Bologna. The promotion of confraternities to the front rank as sponsors of charitable institutions, custodians of cultic sites, and teachers of Christian truths certainly represented the validation of all that the lay confraternities had been working to achieve since the Trecento. At the same time, the civic-religious goal first framed by autonomous artisans' lay brotherhoods of the thirteenth and fourteenth centuries was only achieved at the expense of their autonomy, their popular composition, and their genuinely lay character. The *popolo* ideal of compagnie spirituali as the spiritual pillar of Bolognese society was finally realized, but in a radically transvalued form. Here lies the paradox of confraternal participation in the civic-religious cult. Thanks to patricians the autonomous confraternities were no longer artisanal, and thanks to Paleotti the artisanal confraternities were now parochial.

---

[21] Confraternities were discussed in Session 22 (September 17, 1562). For some results: G.G. Meersseman and G.P. Pacini, "Le confraternite laicali in Italia dal Quattrocento al Seicento," *Problemi di storia della chiesa nei secoli XV/XVI*, (Naples: 1979), pp. 129–32.

BIBLIOGRAPHY

A. PRIMARY SOURCES

Abbreviations

AAB = Archivio Generale Arcivescovile di Bologna
ASB = Archivio di Stato di Bologna
ASB Dem = ASB Fondo Demaniale
ASB Osp = ASB Archivio degli Ospedali
ASB PIE = ASB Archivio dei Pii Istituti Educativi
BBA = Bologna: Biblioteca Comunale dell'Archiginnasio
BBA Gozz = BBA Fondo Gozzadini
BBA Malvezzi = BBA Fondo Malvezzi
BBA Osp = BBA Fondo Ospedale
BBU = Bologna: Biblioteca Universitaria

1. Collegio Laicale di Messer Gesù Cristo

ASB Dem
1/6640 Istrumenti e Scritture
6/6645 Misc. mandati
7/6646 Misc. varij libri e cose
8/6647 Libri di partiti
11/6650 Repertorio degl'Istrumenti e Scritture
BBA
Gozz 204 #2 cc. 1–92 [Sermons and Statutes]
BBU
Ms.1560 Caps XIII JJ–m: "Dell'origine e principio della veneranda Compagnia laicale detta di Messer Gesù Cristo"

2. Compagnia di S. Ambrogio

ASB Dem
1/6623 Storia (libro)

2/6624 Strumenti 1587–1790
3/6625 Scritti, memoriali, etc.
5/6627 Atti 1488–1794
Codici Miniati #67 Statuti [1456]
BBU
Ms. 1232 #6; #7
Ms.1791 Caps LXXVI #1

3. Compagnia di S. Bartolomeo di Reno
AAB
Ricuperi Beneficiari: fasc. 97
ASB Dem
1/7650 Repertorio delle scritture
/7651 Sommario delle scritture diverse
ASB PIE
1 Statuti e matricola [1471]
79 Miscellanea
279 Sommario Tomo I 1204–1728

4. Compagnia di S. Bernardino
ASB Dem
1/7632 Istrumenti e scritture 1430–1523
2/7633 Istrumenti e scritture 1524–1630
6/7637 Atti
7/7638 Breve d'indulgence
8/7639 Capitoli, regole, atti, memorie diverse

5. Compagnia del Buon Gesù [Mezzaratta del Monte]
ASB Dem
2/7624 Sommario delle scritture
3/7625 Istrumenti e scritture
9/7631 Libri delle visite, statuti antiche, regole, altri atti
ASB Codici Miniati #80 Officio [1493]
BBA
Gozz 203 #7 Statuti [1484]
Gozz 203 #8 Statuti [1490]
BBU
Ms. 2022 cc. 37–67 Statuti e Matricola [1490, 1520]

6. Compagnia della S. Croce anche detta dei Crocesegnati
ASB Dem
1/6667 Istrumenti e scritture
3/6669 Misc. istrumenti, scritture, memorie diverse

7. Compagnia del SSmo. Crocifisso del Cestello
ASB Dem
1/6378 Istrumenti e scritture 1456–1579
20/6397 Origine e stato della confraternita e sommario de processi
21/6398 Sommario degli istrumenti
BBA
Gozz 206 # 1 Statuti [1514]
Gozz 206 # 2 Matricola [1538]
BBU
Ms. 3689 Statuti e capitoli.

8. Compagnia di S. Domenico
ASB Dem
1/6415 Istrumenti e scritture 1418–1649
7/6421 Miscellanea
8/6422 Istruzioni per il voto publico, statuti antichi, regole, processione
BBA
Ms. B2219 "Origine e progressi dell'Ordine di Milizie di Gesù Cristo ... ora detta Compagnia di S. Domenico ..."

9. Compagnia di S. Francesco
AAB
Ricuperi Beneficiari fasc. 652
ASB Dem
1/6452 Sommario degli istrumenti
3/6454 Inventario, scritture, statuti e regole
ASB Osp
1/230 Sommario cronologico
6/922
8/220 Istrumenti
Codici Miniati #61 Statuti e Matricola [1494]
BBA
Ms. B983 Statuti [1443]
Osp. 73 Matricola e statuti della Compagnia delle Laudi 1329–1492

10. Compagnia di SS. Giacomo e Filippo del Ponte delle Lamme
BBU
Ms. 3689 V "Origine della Madonna del Ponte delle Lamme e sua Compagnia"

11. Compagnia dei SS. Girolamo ed Anna di Bagnomarino
ASB Dem
1/6716 Istrumenti con due sommari
2/6717 Miscellanea, documenti antichi

BBA
Gozz 404 #21 "Origine, Fondazione, e Progressi della Compagnia di SS. Girolamo ed Anna posta nella via di Bagnomarino"
Malvezzi Cart. 198 #5 Sommario 1427–1603

12. Compagnia di S. Girolamo in Miramonte

ASB Dem
1/6718 Libri di vari atti e memorie
2/6719 Istrumenti e scritture 1410–1599
5/6722 Libri, atti di congregazione
Codici Miniati #65 Matricola [xv]
BBA Gozz 206 #5 Statuti [1425]

13. Compagnia di S. Maria degli Agocchietti alias del Bottazzo

BBA
Gozz 203 #1 Statuti [1326]
Gozz 203 #2 Statuti [1354]
B1006 Capitoli [1536]
B2218 Statuti [1536–1538]

14. Compagnia di S. Maria degli Angeli detta degli Innocenti

AAB
Miscellanea vecchie 647 fasc. 71 D
ASB Dem
1/7718 Scritture diverse
4/7721 Bolle, breve, notizie diverse
5/7722 Inventario, statuti
6/7723 Atti a tutto 1711
8/7725 Ricordi diverse
BBA
Gozz 203 #5 Statuti e Matricola [1479]
Gozz 203 #7 Statuti [1479, xv–xvi, 1522]
Ms. B36 f.102 "Memorie concernenti origine e fondazione ..."

15. Compagnia di S. Maria degli Angeli nella via del Truffailmondo

ASB Dem
1/7697 Istrumenti e scritture
11/7707 Memorie diverse
13/7709 Sommario degl'istrumenti

16. Compagnia di S. Maria dell'Aurora

BBA

Gozz 404 #5 "Notizie in ristretto concernanti alla Ven. Confraternita di S. Maria detta dell'Aurora"

17. Compagnia di S. Maria del Baraccano

ASB PIE

1b Statuti [1553, 1446]

3 Matricola [1518]

561 Sommario degl'istromenti

563 Sommario per aggiunte

BBA

Gozz 209 #1

Gozz 213 cc. 1–26 Statuti [1521]

Osp 83 Miscellanea

18. Compagnia di S. Maria della Carità [Misericordia]

AAB

Ricuperi Beneficiari, fasc. 599

ASB Dem

4/7673 Catologo della compagnia

5/7674 Istrumenti e scritture 1529–1815

8/7677 Miscellanea

BBA

Gozz 210 #6 Matricola, capitoli, ordinamenti

19. Compagnia di S. Maria dei Guarini detta di S. Giobbe

AAB

Ricuperi Beneficiari, fasc. 673

ASB Dem

1/6472 Istrumenti e scritture

4/6475 Processi e atti

5/6476 Fasciola di miscellanea

6/6477 Miscellanea, atti e memorie

Osp 1/870 Miscellanea, nota di scritture, libri contabili

ASB Codici Miniati #60 Matricola [1428]

BBA

Gozz 210 #11 Statuti

Gozz 210 #12 Statuti

Ms. B3180 #1 Statuti [1524]

20. *Compagnia di S. Maria Maddalena*

ASB PIE
1 Statuti [1514]
2
3 Miscellanea
103 Sommario delle scritture

21. *Compagnia di S. Maria della Morte*

AAB
Aula 2a-c-vi-3 "Origine e progressi della sagra scuola della conforteria di Bologna"
Aula 2a-c-vi-4 "Pratica del Modo di Confortare li condennati a Morte"
Aula 2a-c-vi-8 "Descrizione di CXIV Maestri"
Aula 2a-c-vii-3 "Descrizione di tutte le giustiziati di Bologna dal 1540 per tutto il 1740"
Aula 2a-c-vii-19 "Le Prime ed Antiche legge della Sacra Scuola delli Conforti"
Aula 2a-c-viii-30 "Istruzioni per la Conforteria di Bologna del P.M. Cristoforo da Bologna dell'ordine de Frati Eremitanij di S. Agostino"
ASB Osp
1/77 Sommario degli istrumenti 1270–1599
4/84 Sommario degli testamenti xvi–xviii
7/132 Sommario dei documenti 1441–1796
8/826 Sommario dei strumenti e scritture
9/815 Libro dei partiti
15/113 Libro contenente varie memorie xiv–xviii
17/72 Libro di spese dell'Oratorio 1538–1615
19/2108 Libro Campione 1522–1595
21/250 Statuti con notizie di viaggi BVM Luca
25/842 Cerimoniale della Compagnia dell'Oratorio dell'Ospedale de S. Maria della Morte
29/632 Miscellanea 1436–1730
BBA
Ms. B502

22. *Compagnia di S. Maria della Pietà, detta del Piombo*

ASB Dem
7/7693 Statuti, processi, poetiche, etc.
10/7696 Strumenti
BBA
Gozz 206 #7 Statuti [xvi]
Gozz 206 #8 Statuti [1534–1537]

23. Compagnia di S. Maria dei Servi

ASB Osp
2/182 Repertorio cronologico 1244–1598
2/307 Statuti [1523]
3/188 Matricola [1530]
4/888 Inventario

24. Compagnia di S. Maria del Soccorso nel Borgo S. Pietro

ASB Dem
7/6340 Miscellanea
17/6350 Inventario delle scritture

25. Compagnia di S. Maria della Vita

ASB Osp
1 Sommario cronologico delle eredità
1/173 Libro della Congregazione 1473–1479
12/11 Registro dei Beni [1516]
14/435 Locazioni diverse e processi
19/463 Istrumenti e scritture 1504–1773
BBA Osp
10 Statuti e Matricola [1454, 1463]
12 Matricola [1520]
13 Statuti [1553]
BBU
Ms. 2022 #2 "Principio dell'origine delle Compagnie in Bologna e particolarmente dell'Arciconfraternitade di S. Maria della Vita"

26. Compagnià di. S. Pellegrino

ASB Dem
13/6537 Repertorio delle scritture

27. Compagnia di S. Rocco

ASB Dem
1/6584 Istrumenti e scritture 1504–1748
4/6587 Miscellanea: atti, istrumenti, scritture
5/6588 Libri, atti del congregazione
6/6589 Libro da compagnia, statuti e matricola

28. Compagnia di SS. Sebastiano e Rocco

ASB Dem
1/6605 Istrumenti e scritture 1456–1533
14/6618 Miscellanea
16/6620 Diverse libri, capitoli, statuti
BBA
Gozz 209 #6

29. Compagnia dello Spirito Santo

BBA Ms. B3180 #8

B. CONTEMPORARY CHRONICLES AND MANUSCRIPTS

Abbreviations:

RIS = *Rerum Italicarum Scriptores*, New Edition (edited by G. Carducci and V. Fiorini)

Alberti, L. *Chronichetta della Gloriosa Madonna di S. Luca del Monte della Guardia di Bologna, e de suoi miracoli dal suo principio infino all'anno MDLXXVII.* Venice: Domenico e Giovanni Battista Guerra, 1579.

dalle Anelle, A. "Diario delle cose notabili successe in Bologna." BBA B427 II, cc. 15–61.

Anon. "Fragmenti di storie Bolognesi diverse di diversi Anni." BBU Ms. 582 Tomo I, ii.

di Bolognini, H. "Cronica di Bologna di Hieronimo di Bolognini dall'Anno 1494 sino all'anno 1513." BBA B436.

Bonincini, G.B. "Cronica del Monastero e Chiesa di S. Francesco di Bologna." 5 vol. BBA Ms. B417.

Buonhomo, S. "Alcune cose notabili di Bologna cavate da una cronica manoscritta che si conserva appresso M. Sebastiano Buonhomo per me Valerio Buonhomo del mese d'April 1613." BBA B427 VIII, cc. 143–320.

Bursellis, H. *Cronaca gestorum ac factorum memorabilium civitatis Bononie ab urbe condita ad anno 1497.* Edited by A. Sorbelli, *RIS* vol. 23, Pt. II.

Cherubino, G. *Libro da compagnie spirituali.* Bologna: Alessandro Benacii, 1574.

Codibo, G. *Diario Bolognese (1471–1504).* Edited by A. Macchiavelli. Bologna: Nicola Zanichelli, 1915.

Diario Bolognese Ecclesiastico, e Civile per L'anno 1770. Bologna: Lelio dalla Volpe, n.d.

Ghirardacci, C. *Historia di Bologna.* Bologna: Giacomo Monti, 1657. Reprinted Bologna: Arnaldo Forni, 1973.

Grossi, G. "Memorie istoriche Bolognese del Terz'Ordine Secolare e Regolare di S. Francesco, detta della Penitenza." Biblioteca di S. Francesco di Bologna, Ms. 20.

Guicciardini, F. *La storia d'Italia.* 4 vols. Firenze: A. Salani, 1953.

Mamelini, E. "Cronaca e storia bolognese del primo Cinquecento nel memoriale di ser Eliseo Mamelini." Edited by V. Montanari. *Quaderni Culturali Bolognesi* 3 (1979): 3–70.

Moretti, G.M. "Raccolta di tutte le volte nelli quale la Divota e Miracolosa imagine della Beata Virgine dipinta di S. Luca è stata portata in Bologna, con la Relazione del Tempo, e causa di tanti delazioni, dal anno 1302 sino all'anno 1761." BBA Osp #61, #62.

Rampona [Cronaca A]. *Corpus Chronicorum Bononiensium.* Edited by A. Sorbelli. *RIS* vol. 23, Pt. i, vol. iv.

Stiatici, A. *Narratione, overo cronicha del principio, & fundatione, & successo dell'Hospitale di Santo Bartholomeo.* Bologna: Alessandro Benacii, 1590.

"Tasse delle Compagnie delle Arti della citta di Bologna." BBU Ms. 356 #10.

della Tuate, Fileno [Seccadenari], "Cronaca della citta di Bologna." 3 vols. BBU Ms. 437 i–iii.

Varignana [Cronaca B]. *Corpus Chronicorum Bononiensium.* Edited by A. Sorbelli. *RIS* vol. 23, Pt. i, vol. iv.

Viziani, P. *Dieci Libri della Historia della Sua Patria.* Bologna: Heredi di Gio. Rossi, 1602.

C. SECONDARY SOURCES

Abbreviations

AMPR = *Atti e Memorie della deputazione di storia patria per le province di Romagna.*
RSLR = *Rivista di storia e letteratura religiosa.*
RSRR = *Ricerche per la storia religiosa di Roma.*
Il movimento dei disciplinati = *Il movimento dei disciplinati nel settimo centenario dal suo inizio (Perugia: 1260).*
Risultati e prospettive = *Risultati e prospettive della ricerca sul movimento dei disciplinati.*

Ady, C.M. *The Bentivoglio of Bologna: A Study in Despotism.* Oxford: Oxford University Press, 1937.

Alberigo, G. "Caterina da Bologna dall'agiografia alla storia religiosa," *AMPR.* n.s. 15–16 (1963–65): 5–23.

"Contributi alla storia delle confraternite dei disciplinati e della spiritualità laicale nei secc. XV e XVI," in *Il movimento dei disciplinati,* pp. 156–252.

Angelozzi, G. *Le confraternite laicali: un'esperienza cristiana tra medioevo e età moderna.* Brescia: Editrice Queriniana, 1978.

Arioti, E. "Proprietà collettiva e riparto periodico dei terreni in una comunità della pianura bolognese: S. Giovani in Persiceto (secoli XVI–XVIII)," *Quaderni storici* 81 (1992): 706–71.

Banker, J. *Death in the Community: Memorialization and Confraternities in an Italian Commune in the Late Middle Ages.* Athens, GA: University of Georgia Press, 1988.

Barbacci, A. *L'Annunziata: vita, morte, e rinascità di un'antica chiesa francescana di Bologna.* Bologna: Nuova Abes Editrice, 1968.

Barbiero, G. *Le confraternite del Santissimo Sacramento prima del 1539.* Treviso: Vedelago, 1944.

Barnes, A.E. "Religious Anxiety and Devotional Change in Sixteenth Century French Penitential Confraternities," *Sixteenth Century Journal* 19 (1988): 389–405.

The Social Dimension of Piety: Associative Life and Devotional Change in the Penitent Confraternities of Marseille (1499–1792). Matwah, NJ: Paulist Press, 1994.

Barone, G. "Il movimento francescane e la nascità delle confraternite romane." *RSRR* 5 (1984): 71–80.

Battistella, Antonio. *Il S. Officio e la riforma religiosa in Bologna.* Bologna: Nicola Zanichelli, 1905.

Becker, M.B. "Aspects of Lay Piety in Early Renaissance Florence," in *The Pursuit of Holiness in Late Medieval and Renaissance Religion.* pp. 177–99. Edited by C. Trinkaus and H.O. Oberman. Leiden: E.J. Brill, 1974.

Bergonzoni, F. "Le Origini e i primi tre secoli di vita (secc. XIII–XV)," in *La Piazza Maggiore di Bologna: Storia, Arte, Costume.* pp. 17–37. Edited by G. Roversi. Bologna: Aniballi Edizioni, 1984.

Venti secoli di città: Noti di storia urbanistica Bolognese. Bologna: Capelli, 1980.

Berrigan, J.R. "Saint Catherine of Bologna: Franciscan Mystic," in *Women Writers of the Renaissance and Reformation.* pp. 81–95. Edited by K. Wilson. Athens: University of Georgia Press, 1987.

Black, C, *Italian Confraternities in the Sixteenth Century.* Cambridge: Cambridge University Press, 1989.

Bornstein, D. *The Bianchi of 1399: Popular Devotion in Late Medieval Italy.* Ithaca: Cornell University Press, 1993.

Bossy, J. *Christianity in the West: 1400–1700.* Oxford: Oxford University Press, 1985.

"The Social History of Confession in the Age of the Reformation," *Transactions of the Royal Historical Society* Series 5, 25 (1975): 21–38.

"The Counter Reformation and the People of Catholic Europe," *Past and Present* 47 (1970): 51–70.

Breventani, L. *Supplementa alle cose notabili di Bologna e alla miscellanea.* Bologna: A. Garagnani, 1908. Reprinted Bologna: Arnaldo Forni, n.d.

Busachi, V. "L'Ospedale della Morte," in *Sette secoli di vita ospedaliera in Bologna.* pp. 73–96. Bologna: Capelli, 1960.

Calori, G. *Una initiativa sociale nella Bologna del '500: L'Opera dei Mendicanti.* Bologna: Azzoguidi, 1972.

Calzoni, F. *Storia della chiesa parrochiale di Santa Maria in via Mascarella e dei luoghi più cospicui che si trovano nello di lei giurisdizione.* Bologna: Stamperia di San Tommaso d'Aquino, 1785.

Cavallaro, A. "Antoniazzo Romano e le confraternite del Quattrocento a Roma," *RSRR* 5 (1984): 336–66.

Chiffoleau, J. *La comptabilité de l'au-delà: les hommes, la mort et la religion dans la région d'Avignon à la fin du moyen âge (vers 1320–vers 1480)*. Rome: Ecole Français de Rome, 1980.

Christian, W.A. *Local Religion in Sixteenth Century Spain*. Princeton: Princeton University Press, 1981.

Ciammitti, L. "Quanto costa essere normali. La dote nel conservatorio femminile di Santa Maria del Baraccano (1630–1680)," *Quaderni storici* 53 (1983): 469–97.

"Fanciulle, monache, madri. Povertà femminile e previdenza in Bologna nei secoli XVI–XVIII," in *Arte e Pietà. I patrimoni culturali delle opere pie*. pp. 461–99. Bologna: Istituto per i beni culturali della regione Emilia-Romagna, 1980.

Clawson, M.A. "Early Modern Fraternalism and the Patriarchal Family," *Feminist Studies* 6 (1980): 369–91.

Collett, B. *Italian Benedictine Scholars and the Reformation: The Congregation of Santa Giustina of Padua*. Oxford: Oxford University Press, 1985.

De Bartholomaeis, V. *Le origini della poesia drammatica Italiana*. Torino: Società Editrice Internazionale, 1952.

De Benedictis, A. "Quale 'Corte' per quale 'Signoria'? A proposito di organizzazione e immagine del potere durante la preminenza di Giovanni II Bentivoglio," in *Bentivolorum Magnificentia: Principe e cultura a Bologna nel Rinascimento*. pp. 13–34. Edited by B. Basile. Roma: Bulzani, 1984.

De Bosdari, F. "Il primordio della signoria di Giovanni II Bentivoglio a Bologna (1463–1477)," *AMPR* n.s. 3 (1951–53): 181–204.

De Töth, P. *Il Beato Nicolò Albergati e i suoi tempi (1375–1444)*. 2 vols. Aquapendente (Roma): Lemuria, 1922; 1934.

La Decennale Eucaristica nella chiesa priorale e parrocchiale di Santa Maria Maddalena in Bologna. Bologna: Scuola Tipografica Salesina, 1915.

Di Matthia Spirito, S. "Assistenza e carità ai poveri in alcuni statuti di confraternite nei secoli XV–XVI." *RSRR* 5 (1984): 137–54.

Dolfi, P.S. *Cronologia delle famiglie nobili di Bologna*. Bologna: Gio Batt. Ferroni, 1670. Reprinted Bologna: Arnaldo Forni, 1973.

Esposito, A. "Le 'confraternite' del Gonfalone (secc XIV–XV)." *RSRR* 5 (1984): 91–136.

Fanti, Mario. "La confraternita di Santa Maria dei Guarini e l'ospedale di San Giobbe in Bologna," in *Il Credito Romagnolo fra storia, arte, e tradizione*, pp. 343–454. Edited by G. Maioli and G. Roversi. Bologna: Il Credito Romagnolo, 1985.

ed. *Gli archivi delle istituzioni di carità e assistenza attive in Bologna nel Medioevo e nell'Età moderna*. Bologna: Istituto per la storia di Bologna, 1984.

"La basilica di San Petronio nella storia religiosa e civile della città," in *La Basilica di San Petronio in Bologna*. vol. 1. pp. 9–40. Bologna: Cassa Di Risparmio, 1983.

San Procolo: Una parrocchia di Bologna dal medioevo all'età contemporanea. Bologna: Capelli Editore, 1983.

"La confraternita di Santa Maria della Morte e la conforteria dei condonnati in Bologna nei secoli XIV e XV," *Quaderni dei centro di ricerca di studio sul movimento dei disciplinati* 20 (1978): 3–101.

La chiesa e la compagnia dei Poveri in Bologna: un'istituzione di mutuo succorso nella società bolognese fra il cinquecento e il seicento. Bologna: Centro Editoriale Dehoniano, 1977.

"La Madonna di San Luca nella leggenda, nella storia, e nella tradizione bolognese," *Il Carrobbio* 3 (1977): 179–98.

"Gli inizi del movimento dei disciplinati a Bologna e la confraternita di Santa Maria della Vita," *Bolletino della deputazione di storia patria per l'Umbria* 66 (1969): 181–232.

Il restauro della chiesa dello Spirite Santo, gia Santa Maria dei Celestini. Bologna: n.p., 1965.

"Il fondo ospedali nella biblioteca comunale dell'Archiginnasio," *L'Archiginnasio* 58 (1963): 1–45.

Fanti, M., et al. *Santa Maria della Carità in Bologna: storia e arte.* Bologna: n.p., 1981.

Fanti, M. and Roversi, G. *Il santuario della Madonna del Soccorso nel Borgo di San Pietro in Bologna*, 2nd edn. Bologna: Parrochia della Beata Virgine del Soccorso, 1975.

Farolfi, B. *Strutture agrarie e crisi cittadina nel primo cinquecento bolognese.* Bologna: Patron, 1977.

Fasoli, G. "Le compagnie delle armi a Bologna," *L'Archiginnasio* 28 (1933): 158–83; 323–40.

"Le compagnie delle arti a Bologna fino al principio del secolo XV," *L'Archiginnasio* 30 (1935): 237–80 and 31 (1936): 56–80.

Ferri, A. and Roversi, G. eds, *Storia di Bologna.* Bologna: Edizioni ALFA, 1978.

Fiorani, L. "L'esperienza religiosa nelle confraternite romane tra Cinque e Seicento," *RSRR* 5 (1984): 155–96.

Firpo, M. and Marcatto, D. *Il processo inquisitoriale del Cardinal Giovanni Morone. Editzione critica, Vol. 4: Il processo difensivo bolognese. La sentenza.* Roma: Istituto storico italiano per l'età moderna e contemporanea, 1987.

Fornasini, D.G. *La chiesa priorale e parrochiale di S. Maria e S. Domenica detta della Mascarella in Bologna.* Bologna: La Grafica Emilia, 1943.

Forni, G.G. "Sette secoli di storia ospedaliera in Bologna," in *Sette secoli di vita ospitaliera in Bologna.* pp. 3–28. Bologna: Capelli, 1960.

Frati, L. *La vita privata in Bologna dal secolo XIII al XVII.* Bologna: Nicola Zanichelli, 1928.

Galpern, A.N. *The Religions of the People in Sixteenth Century Champagne.* Cambridge: Harvard University Press, 1976.

Gaudenzi, A. *Statuti delle societa del popolo di Bologna: Societa delle armi.* vol 1. Roma: Istituto Storico Italiano, 1889.

Gavitt, P. *Charity and Children in Renaissance Florence: The Ospedale degli Innocenti, 1410–1536.* Ann Arbor: University of Michigan Press, 1990.

Gentili, G. "Ospedali non più esistenti in Bologna," in *Sette secoli di vita ospitaliera in Bologna.* pp. 29–47. Bologna: Capelli, 1960.

238   BIBLIOGRAPHY

Gheza Fabbri, L. *L'organizzazione del lavoro in una economia urbana: Le Società d'Arti a Bologna nei secoli XVI e XVII*. Bologna: CLUEB, 1988.

Giacomelli, A. "Conservazione e innovazione nell'assistenza bolognese del Settecento," in Autori vari, *Forme e soggetti dell'intervento assistenziale in una città di antico regime*. pp. 163–265. Bologna: Istituto per la storia di Bologna, 1986.

Giovanantonij, G. *Historia della miracolosa imagine di Maria Vergine detta del Baraccano, e dell'origine e governo dell'opera pia delle zitelle, e de gli huomini della compagnia sotto la protettione di essa Beatissima Vergine*. Bologna: Giacomo Monti, 1674.

Giusberti, F. "Dalla pietà alla paura: note sulla povertà a Bologna nei secoli XVI–XVIII," in *Arte e Pietà: I patrimoni culturali delle opere pie*. pp. 438–55. Bologna: Istituto per i Beni Culturali della Regione Emilia-Romagna, 1980.

Gottarelli, E. *I viaggi della Madonna di San Luca*. Bologna: Tamari Editori, 1976.

Grendler, P.F. "The Schools of Christian Doctrine in Sixteenth Century Italy," *Church History* 53 (1984): 305–32.

Guidicini, G. *Cose notabili della città di Bologna*. 5 vols. Bologna: Giacomo Monti, 1868–73. Reprinted Bologna: Arnaldo Forni, 1982.

Miscellanea storico patria Bolognese. Bologna: Giacomo Monti, 1872. Reprinted Bologna: Arnaldo Forni, 1980.

Harding, R.R. "The Mobilization of Confraternities Against the Reformation in France," *Sixteenth Century Journal* 16 (1980): 85–107.

Hatfield, R. "The Compagnia de'Magi," *Journal of Warburg & Courtauld Institutes* 33 (1970): 107–62.

Hay, D. *The Church in Italy in the Fifteenth Century*. Cambridge: Cambridge University Press, 1977.

Henderson, J. *Piety and Charity in Late Medieval Florence*. Oxford: Oxford University Press, 1994.

"Religious Confraternities and Death in Early Renaissance Florence," in *Florence and Italy: Renaissance Studies in Honour of Nicolai Rubinstein*. pp. 383–94. Edited by P. Denley and C. Elam. London: Committee for Medieval Studies, Westfield College, University of London, 1988.

"Confraternities and the Church in Late Medieval Florence," *Studies in Church History* 23 (1986): 69–83.

"Le confraternite religiose nella Firenze del tardo medioevo: patroni spirituali e anche politici?" *Ricerche Storiche* 15 (1985): 77–94.

"Piety and Charity in Late-Medieval Florence: Lay Religious Confraternities from the middle of the Thirteenth Century to the Late Fifteenth Century," Ph.D. thesis, University of London: 1983.

"The Flagellant Movement and Flagellant confraternities in Central Italy, 1260–1400," *Studies in Church History* 15 (1978): 147–60.

Hilton, W. *The Scale of Perfection*. Translated by G. Stilwell. London: Burns, Oates, 1953.

Hinnebusch, W.A. *The History of the Dominican Order: Vol II: Intellectual and Cultural Life to 1500*. New York: Alba House, 1973.

Hyde, J.K. "Commune, University, and Society in Early Medieval Bologna," in *Universities in Politics: Case Studies from the Late Middle Ages and Early Modern Period*, pp. 17–46. Edited by J.W. Baldwin and R.A. Goldthwaite. Baltimore: Johns Hopkins University Press, 1972.

Jungmann, J.A. *The Mass: An Historical, Theological, and Pastoral Survey*. Translated by J. Fernandes. Collegeville, MN: Liturgical Press, 1976.

Karant-Nunn, S. "Continuity and Change: Some Effects of the Reformation on the Women of Zwickau," *Sixteenth Century Journal* 13 (1982): 17–42.

Klapisch-Zuber, C. *Women, Family, and Ritual in Renaissance Italy*. Translated by L.G. Cochrane. Chicago: University of Chicago Press, 1985.

Klauser, T. *A Short History of the Western Liturgy: An Account and Some Reflections*. 2nd edn. Translated by J. Halliburton. Oxford: Oxford University Press, 1979.

Kristeller, P.O. "Lay Religious Traditions and Florentine Platonism," In *Studies in Renaissance Thought and Letters*, pp. 99–122. Rome: Edizioni di Storia e Letteratura, 1956.

Lea, H.C. *A History of Auricular Confession and Indulgences in the Latin Church*. Philadelphia: Lea Brothers, 1896.

Lechner, J., and Eisenhofer, L. *The Liturgy of the Roman Rite*. Translated by A.J. and E.F. Peeler. Edinburgh: Nelson, 1961.

Lercaro, G. "La riforma catechistica post-tridentina a Bologna," *Ravennatensia* 2 (1971): 11–23.

Liebowitz, R.P. "Virgins in the Service of Christ: The Dispute over an Active Apostolate for Women during the Counter Reformation," in *Women of Spirit: Female Leadership in the Jewish and Christian Traditions*. pp. 131–53. Edited by R. Ruether and E. McLaughlin. New York: Simon and Schuster, 1974.

Lotz, W. "I primi simboli religiosi e del potere," in *La Piazza Maggiore di Bologna: storia, arte, costume*, pp. 123–42. Edited by G. Roversi. Bologna: Aniballi, 1984.

Machiavelli, A. *Origine, fondazione e progressi della veneranda compagnia laicale sotto l'invocazione de'gloriosi Santi Girolamo ed Anna posta nella via di Bagnomarino*. Bologna: il Sassi, 1754.

MacKenney, R. *Tradesmen and Traders: The World of the Guilds in Venice and Europe*. London: Croom Helm, 1987.

"Devotional Confraternities in Renaissance Venice," *Studies in Church History* 23 (1986): 85–96.

Maragi, M. *I cinquecento anni del monte di Bologna*. Bologna: Banca del Monte di Bologna e Ravenna, 1973.

Martines, L. *Power and Imagination: City States in Renaissance Italy*. New York: Knopf, 1979.

Martini, A. *Manuale di Metrologia ossia misure, pesi e monete*. Torino: Ermanno Loescher, 1883.

Masini, A. *Bologna Perlustrata*. Bologna: Carlo Zenero, 1650.

Meersseman, G.G. *Dossier de l'ordre du penitence au XIIIe siècle.* Fribourg: Editions Universitaires, 1982.

Ordo fraternitatis: confraternite e pietà dei laici nel mondo medioevo. 3 vols. Rome: Herder Editrici, 1977.

Meersseman, G.G. and Pacini, G.P. "Le confraternite laicali in Italia dal Quattrocento al Seicento," in *Problemi di storia della chiesa nei secoli XV–XVII.* pp. 109–36. Naples: Edizioni Dehoniane, 1979.

Melloni, G.B. *Atti o memorie degli uomini illustri in santità, nati o morti in Bologna.* Monumenta Italiae Ecclesiastica: Hagiografica #1. Rome: Multigraphica Editrice, 1971.

Meluzzi, L. *I vescovi e gli arcivescovi di Bologna.* Bologna: n.p., 1975–76.

Mesini, C. "La catechesi a Bologna e la prima compagnia della dottrina cristiana fondata dal B. Nicolò Albergati (1375–1444)," *Apollinaris* 54 (1981): 232–67.

"La compagnia di Santa Maria delle Laudi e di San Francesco di Bologna," *Archivum Francescanum Historicum* 52 (1959): 361–89.

Miller, N. *Renaissance Bologna.* New York: Peter Lang, 1989.

Mira, G. "Prima sondaggi su taluni aspetti economico – finanziari delle confraternite dei disciplinati." in *Risultati e prospettive*, pp. 229–65.

Monti, G.M. *Le confraternite medioevali dell'alta e media Italia.* 2 vols. Venice: La Nuova Italia, 1927.

Monticone, A. *et al.* "La storiographia confraternale e le confraternite romane: tavola rotonda." *RSRR* 5 (1984): 19–70.

Moorman, J. *A History of the Franciscan Order from its Origins to the year 1517.* Oxford: Oxford University Press, 1968.

Morghen, R. "Le confraternite di disciplinati e gli aspetti della religiosità laica nell'età moderna," In *Risultati e Prospettive*, pp. 317–27.

Il movimento dei disciplinati nel settimo centenario dal suo inizio (Perugia: 1260). [Convegno Internazionale: Perugia, 25–28 Sett., 1960]. Perugia: Deputazione di Storia Patria per l'Umbria, 1962.

Muir, E. "The Virgin on the Street Corner: The Place of the Sacred in Italian Cities," in *Religion and Culture in the Renaissance and Reformation.* pp. 25–40. Edited by S. Ozment. Kirksville, MO: Sixteenth Century Journal Publishers, 1989.

Civic Ritual in Renaissance Venice. Princeton: Princeton University Press, 1981.

Muzzi, S. *Del Santuario della Beata Virgine Della Pioggia e del Orfanotrofio di S. Bartolomeo di Reno.* Bologna: Tipographia Sassi, 1851.

Nicolini, B. "Sui rapporti di Bernardino Ochino con le città di Bologna e di Lucca," *Studi Cinquecenteschi II: Aspetti della vita religiosa, politica, e letteraria.* pp. 35–54. Bologna: Tamari, 1974.

Nicolini, U. "Nuove testimonianze su fra Raniero Fasani e i suoi disciplinati," *Quaderno del centro di documentazione sul movimento dei disciplinati* 2 (1965): 3–17.

Noreña, C. *Juan Luis Vives.* The Hague: Martinus Nijhoff, 1970.

Novelli, L. "Ms. 2005 della Biblioteca Universitaria di Bologna, 'Liber collecte imposite in clero Bonon.', con postille del Card. Nicolò Albergati," *Ravennatensia* 2 (1971): 101–62.

Origo, I. *The Merchant of Prato.* Harmondsworth: Penguin, 1963.

Orlandelli, G. "Note di storia economica sulla Signoria dei Bentivoglio," *AMPR* n.s. 3 (1951–53): 205–399.

Orsi, A. M. *Racconto istorico dell'origine, e fondazione della veneranda con fraternita di Santa Maria degli Angoli di Bologna.* Bologna: Girolamo Cochi, 1690.

Palmieri, A. "I lavoratori del contado bolognese durante le signorie," *AMPR* Series 3, 28 (1910): 18–78.

Paolini, L. "Le origini della 'Societas Crucis'," *RSLR* 15 (1979): 173–229.

L'eresia a Bologna fra XIII e XVI secolo. 2 vols. Rome: Istituto storico italiano per il Medio Evo, 1975.

Partner, P. *The Papal State under Martin V: The Administration and Government of the Temporal Power in the Early Fifteeth Century.* London: The British School at Rome, 1958.

Pastor, L. *The History of the Popes from the close of the Middle Ages.* 7th edn. London: Routledge & Kegan Paul, 1949.

Patrizi, S.R. "La caduta dei Bentivoglio e il ritorno di Bologna al dominio della chiesa." *AMPR* n.s. 2 (1950–51): 109–56.

Pavan, P. "La confraternite del Salvatore nella società romana del Tre-Quattrocento," *RSRR* 5 (1984): 81–91.

Petrocchi, M. "Una 'Devotio Moderna' nel Quattrocento Italiana." *Storia della spiritualità Italiana: vol. I: Il Duecento, Il Trecento, Il Quattrocento.* pp. 125–54. Roma: Edizioni di Storia e Letteratura, 1978.

Piana, C. *Il beato Marco da Bologna e il suo convento di San Paolo in Monte nel Quattrocento.* Bologna: Editrice "Nuova Abes," 1973.

Picasso, G. "L'Imitazione di Cristo nell'epoca della 'Devotio Moderna' e nella spiritualità monastica del sec. XV in Italia," *RSLR* 4 (1968): 10–32.

Pini, A.I. "Le ripartizioni territoriale urbane di Bologna medievale," *Quaderni Culturali Bolognesi* 1 (1977): 4–50.

I libri matricularum societatum Bononiensium. Bologna: Archivio di Stato di Bologna, 1967.

Pini, C. "Per la storia del distretto industriale serico di Bologna (secoli XVI–XIX)" *Quaderni Storici* 73 (1990): 93–124.

Porco, A.M. *Il santuario e la confraternita del SS Crocifisso del Cestello in Bologna.* Bologna: Arti Grafiche Tamari, 1961.

Post, R.R. *The Modern Devotion: Confrontation with Reformation and Humanism.* Leiden: E.J. Brill, 1968.

Prodi, P. *The Papal Prince, One Body and Two Souls: The Papal Monarchy in Early Modern Europe.* Translated by S. Haskins. Cambridge: Cambridge University Press, 1987.

"The Application of the Tridentine Decrees: The Organization of the Diocese of Bologna during the Episcopate of Cardinal Gabriele Paleotti," in *The Late Italian Renaissance, 1525–1630*, pp. 226–43. Edited by E. Cochrane. London: Macmillan, 1970.

Il Cardinale Gabriele Paleotti (1522–97). 2 vols. Roma: Edizioni di storia e letteratura, 1959; 1967.

Prosperi, A. "Parrocchie e confraternite tra cinquecente e seicento," In *Per una storia dell'Emilia-Romagna*, pp.161–252. Bologna: Istituto Gramsci, 1985.

" 'Dominus beneficiorum': il conferimento dei benefici ecclesiastici tra passi curiale eragione politiche negli stati Italiani tra '400, e '500," in *Strutture ecclesiastiche in Italia e in Germania prima della riforma*, pp. 51–86. Edited by P. Johanek and P. Prodi. Bologna: Il Mulino, 1984.

"Il sangue e l'anima. Ricerche sulle compagnie di giustizia in Italia," *Quaderni Storici* 51 (1982): 959–99.

"Intellettuali e Chiesa all'inizio dell'età moderna." in *Storia d'Italia.* Vol. IV: *Intellettuali e potere.* Torino: Einaudi, 1981.

Pugliese, O.Z., "The Good Works of the Florentine 'Buonomini di San Martino': An Example of Renaissance Pragmatism," in *Crossing the Boundaries: Christian Piety and the Arts in Italian Medieval and Renaissance Confraternities.* pp. 108–220. Edited by K. Eisenbichler. Kalamazoo: Medieval Institute Publications, 1991.

Pullan, B. *Rich and Poor in Renaissance Venice: The Social Institutions of a Catholic State.* Cambridge: Harvard University Press, 1971.

Ricci, G. *Bologna.* Roma: Gius Laterza, 1980.

"I primi statuti della compagnia bolognese dei Poveri Vergognosi," *L'Archiginnasio*, 74 (1979): 131–59.

"Povertà, vergogna e povertà vergognosa" *Società e Storia* 5 (1979): 305–37.

Rice, E.F. *Saint Jerome in the Renaissance.* Baltimore: Johns Hopkins University Press, 1986.

Risultati e Prospettive della ricerca sul movimento dei disciplinati. [Convegno internazionale di studio, Perugia, 5–7 dicembre, 1969]. Perugia: Centro di documentazione sul movimento dei disciplinati, 1972.

Rossi, S. "La Compagnia di San Luca nel Cinquecento e la sua evoluzione in Accademia," *RSRR* 5 (1984): 367–94.

Rotondo, A. "Per la storia dell'eresia a Bologna nel secolo XVI," *Rinascimento* 13 (1962): 107–54.

Roversi, G. "La compagnia e l'oratorio dei Fiorentini in Bologna," in *San Giovanni Battista dei Celestini in Bologna*, pp. 105–37. Bologna: Tamari editori, 1970.

"La compagnia e la Chiesa di Santa Maria degli Angli nella via di 'Truffailmondo'," *Strenna Storica Bolognese* 12 (1962): 267–98.

Rubin, M., *Corpus Christi: The Eucharist in Late Medieval Culture.* Cambridge: Cambridge University Press, 1992.

Rusconi, R. "Confraternite, compagnie e devotioni," *Storia d'Italia. Annali* 9 (1986): 469–506.

Santini, U. *Bologna sulla fine del Quattrocento.* Bologna: Nicola Zanichelli, 1901.

Scaramucci, L. "Considerazioni su statuti e matricole di confraternite di disciplinati," in *Risultati e Prospettive* pp. 134–94.

Scarisbrick, J.J. *The Reformation and the English People*. Oxford: Oxford University Press, 1984.

Schutte, A.J. *Printed Italian Vernacular Religious Books, 1465–1550: A Finding List*.
Geneva: Librarie Droz, 1983.

——— "Printing, Piety and the People in Italy: The First Thirty Years," *Archiv Für
Reformationsgeschichte* 71 (1980): 5–19.

Serra-Zanetti, A. *L'arte della stampa in Bologna nel primo ventennio del Cinquecento*.
Bologna: A spese del Comune, 1959.

Sorbelli, A. *I Bentivoglio: signori di Bologna*. Bologna: Capelli, 1969.

Spufford, P. *Handbook of Medieval Exchange*. London: Royal Historical Society,
1986.

Strocchia, S. *Death and Ritual in Renaissance Florence*. Baltimore: Johns Hopkins
University Press, 1993.

——— "Death Rites and the Ritual Family in Renaissance Florence," in *Life and
Death in Fifteenth Century Florence*. pp. 120–45. Edited by M. Tetel *et al*.
Durham: Duke University Press, 1988.

Tenenti, A. *Il senso della morte e l'amore della vita nel Rinascimento*. Turin: Giulio
Einaudi, 1957.

Terpstra, N., "Apprenticeship in Social Welfare: From Confraternal Charity to
Municipal Poor Relief in Early Modern Italy," *Sixteenth Century Journal* 25
(1994): 101–20

——— "Confraternal Prison Charity and Political Consolidation in Sixteenth-
Century Bologna," *Journal of Modern History*, 66 (1994): 217–48.

——— "Death and Dying in Renaissance Confraternities," in *Crossing the Boundaries:
Christian Piety and the Arts in Italian Medieval and Renaissance Confraternities*.
pp. 179–200. Edited by K. Eisenbichler. Kalamazoo: Medieval Institute
Publications, 1991.

——— "Piety and Punishment: The Lay *Conforteria* and Civic Justice in Sixteenth
Century Bologna," *Sixteenth Century Journal* 22 (1991): 679–94.

——— "Women in the Brotherhood: Gender, Class, and Politics in Renaissance Bolognese Confraternities," *Renaissance and Reformation* 24
(1990): 193–212.

——— "Renaissance Congregationalism: Organizing Lay Piety in Renaissance
Italy," *Fides et Historia* 20 (1988): 31–40.

Torre, A. "Politics Cloaked in Worship: State, Church and Local Power in
Piedmont, 1570–1770," *Past and Present* 134 (1992): 42–92.

Trexler, R.C. *Public Life in Renaissance Florence*. New York: Academic Press,
1980.

——— *The Spiritual Power: Republican Florence under the Interdict*. Leiden: E.J. Brill,
1974.

——— "Charity and the defense of Urban elites in Italian Communes," in *The Rich,
the Well-Born, and the Powerful; Elites and Upper Classes in History*, pp. 64–
109. Edited by F.C. Jaher. Urbana: University of Illinois Press, 1973.

"The Foundlings of Florence, 1395–1455," *History of Childhood Quarterly* 1 (1973): 259–284.

"Infanticide in Florence: New Sources and First Results," *History of Childhood Quarterly* 1 (1973): 98–116.

"Ritual Behaviour in Renaissance Florence: The Setting," *Medievalia et Humanistica* 4 (1973): 125–144.

"Florentine Religious Experience: The Sacred Image," *Studies in the Renaissance* 19 (1972): 7–41.

Turchini, A. "Per la storia religiosa del '400 italiano. Visite pastorali e questionari di visita nell'Italia centro-settentrionale," *RSLR* 13 (1977): 265–90.

Vallania, M.E. "Gli statuti e le matricole delle compagnie delle arti conservati alla sezione medioevale del Museo Civico di Bologna," *L'Archiginnasio* 63–65 (1968–70): 323–43.

Vandenbroucke, F. "New Milieux, New Problems: From the Twelfth to the Sixteenth Century," in *The Spirituality of the Middle Ages.* pp. 223–543. Edited by J. Leclercq and L. Cognet, London: Burns & Oates, 1968.

Vasina, A. "Pievi e parrocchie in Emilia-Romagna dal XIII al XV secolo," *Pievi e parrocchie in Italia nel basso medioevo (sec XIII–XV): Atti del VI convegno di storia della chiesa in Italia* (Firenze, 21-25 Sett., 1981). pp. 725–50. Roma: Herder Editrice, 1984.

Vecchi, G. "Le sacre rappresentazione della compagnia dei battuti in Bologna nel secolo XV," *AMPR* n.s. 4 (1951–53): 281–324.

Vittorio, G.A. *Origine, fondatione, e progressi della venerabile confraternita laicale di San Girolamo posta nella via della Savonella di Miramonte. Et della segregatione, et fondatione di quella de SS. Girolamo, et Anna nella via di Bagnomarino sotto la direttione del glorioso promotore beato Nicolò Albergati Cardinale di Santa Croce in Gierusalemme, e Vescovo di Bologna.* Bologna: Angelo Custode, 1698.

Wallace, W.E. "The Bentivoglio Palace: Lost and Reconstructed," *Sixteenth Century Journal* 10 (1979): 97–114.

Weissman, R. "Cults and Contexts: In Search of the Renaissance Confraternity," in *Crossing the Boundaries: Christian Piety and the Arts in Italian Medieval and Renaissance Confraternities.* pp. 201–20. Edited by K. Eisenbichler. Kalamazoo: Medieval Institute Publications, 1991.

"Brothers and Strangers: Confraternal Charity in Renaissance Florence," *Historical Reflections /Reflexions Historiques* 15 (1988): 27–45.

Ritual Brotherhood in Renaissance Florence. New York: Academic Press, 1982.

Wiesner, M. "Women's Defense of their Public Role," in *Women in the Middle Ages and the Renaissance: Literary and Historical Perspectives.* pp. 1–27. Edited by M.B. Rose. Syracuse: Syracuse University Press, 1986.

Wittkower, R. *Gothic vs. Classic: Architectural Projects in Seventeenth-Century Italy.* New York: G. Braziller, 1974.

Zanetti, V. *Celebrandosi il sacro natale del gloriosissimo lor fondatore S. Filippo Benizi nella domenica dopo la sua festa. Dalla venerabile Compagnia di S. Maria dei Servi in Strasteffano.* Bologna: Giacomo Monti, 1671.

Zardin, D. "Le confraternite in Italia settentrionale fra XV e XVIII secolo," *Società e Storia* 35 (1987): 81–137.

Zarri, G. "L'altra Cecilia: Elena Duglioli dall'Olio (1472–1520)," in *Culti dei Santi, istituzioni, e classi notavoli in età preindustriale*, pp. 575–613. Edited by S. Boesch Gajano and L. Sabastiani. L'Aquila: Japadre, 1984.

"Istituzioni ecclesiastiche e vita religiosa nell'età della Riforma e della contrariforma," In *Storia della Emilia-Romagna*, pp. 245–70. Edited by A. Berselli. Bologna: University Press, 1977.

"I monasteri femminili a Bologna tra il XIII e il XVII secolo," *AMPR* n.s. 24 (1973): 133–224.

INDEX